59 1071299 2

D1765937

Critical Issues in Psychotherapy

UNIVERSITY CAMPUS BARNSLEY
HELPDESK: 01226 644281
24HR RENEWALS: 01484 472045

Critical Issues in Psychotherapy

Translating
New
Ideas
Into
Practice

Brent D. Slife
Richard N. Williams • Sally H. Barlow
EDITORS

Sage Publications
International Educational and Professional Publisher
Thousand Oaks ■ London ■ New Delhi

Copyright © 2001 by Sage Publications, Inc.

All rights reserved. No part of this book may be reproduced or utilized in any form or by any means, electronic or mechanical, including photocopying, recording, or by any information storage and retrieval system, without permission in writing from the publisher.

For information:

Sage Publications, Inc.
2455 Teller Road
Thousand Oaks, California 91320
E-mail: order@sagepub.com

Sage Publications Ltd.
6 Bonhill Street
London EC2A 4PU
United Kingdom

Sage Publications India Pvt. Ltd.
M-32 Market
Greater Kailash I
New Delhi 110 048 India

UNIVERSITY
LIBRARY

1 7 APR 2013

HUDDERSFIELD

5910712992

Printed in the United States of America

Library of Congress Cataloging-in-Publication Data

Critical issues in psychotherapy: Translating new ideas into practice /
edited by Brent D. Slife, Richard N. Williams, and Sally H. Barlow.
    p.cm.
Includes bibliographical reference and index.
    ISBN 0-7619-2080-3 (cloth)
    ISBN 0-7619-2081-1 (pbk.)
    1. Psychotherapy. I. Slife, Brent D. II. Williams, Richard N. III.
Barlow, Sally H.
    RC480 .C756 2001
    616.89'14—dc21

                                    00-012405

01   02   03   04   05   10   9   8   7   6   5   4   3   2   1

Acquiring Editor: Nancy Hale
Editorial Assistant: Vonessa Vondera
Production Editor: Denise Santoyo
Typesetter/Designer: Denyse Dunn
Indexer: Christina Haley
Cover Designer: Michelle Lee

Contents

Acknowledgments

The editors express their appreciation to Clayne Pope, Dean of the College of Family Home and Social Sciences at Brigham Young University, for his moral and financial support of the conference that led to this volume.

BRENT D. SLIFE,

RICHARD N. WILLIAMS,

SALLY H. BARLOW

Introduction

Brent D. Slife
Brigham Young University

The hallmark of any science is investigation. Nothing should go uninvestigated, particularly if it bears directly on the phenomena being studied. Unfortunately, this hallmark is often taken to mean that science investigates only empirical questions. That is, science only deals with questions that can be conceptualized in terms of its methods (e.g., observable variables, operationalized factors). Questions that cannot be understood in these terms—questions that are not necessarily empirical—are frequently thought to be "unscientific" and outside the realm of science.

The contributors to this book do not share this narrow view of science. Although empirical issues are obviously important to any scientific discipline, there are many vital issues that cannot be investigated by empirical means alone. Particularly in the realm of psychotherapy, there are pivotal nonempirical questions—"critical issues," as the title of this book indicates—that have escaped careful consideration. The purpose of this book is to pursue such careful consideration. At the dawning of a new millennium, it seems appropriate that we investigate these issues in ways that help not only the frontline psychotherapist but also the therapist in training.

The Significance of the Nonempirical

Many scholars have noted over the years that it is the nonempirical, rather than the empirical, that lies at the heart of therapy's most pressing problems (Koch,

1959, 1992; Miller, 1992; Robinson, 1985; Rychlak, 1981, 1988; Sass, 1992; Slife & Gantt, 1999; Slife & Williams, 1995). For example, the heart of the controversy over prescription privileges is the mind-body issue. If the mind is merely a by-product or an aspect of the body—completely controlled by the neurological system of the brain—then psychopharmacology (or surgery) is the only real intervention. Traditional therapy models are merely stopgap approaches until the biological basis for all human behavior is fully established. From this perspective, the traditional discipline of psychotherapy itself is in peril. Its peril depends, however, on whether mind is *merely* brain, an issue that cannot be settled by purely empirical means alone (see Williams, this volume).

The problem is that very few therapists have been trained to deal with such critical issues. Most have been trained to be practitioners or scientist-practitioners; they can conduct either therapy or research (or some combination of the two). Their training does not assist them in recognizing, let alone investigating, the nonempirical issues that pervade and tacitly influence their therapy and research. This lack of training does not mean that these therapists avoid making decisions about nonempirical issues. It only means that these therapists cannot make explicit, *informed* decisions about such issues.

For example, the position taken (above) on the mind-body issue is not the only one that is available or justifiable. This position is a variant on "eliminative materialism," as it is sometimes labeled, and is, to say the least, controversial (Churchland, 1986; Fisher, 1997; Muse, 1997). Nevertheless, many therapists apparently hold this position on the prescription privilege issue, often without knowing they do. Does this "philosophical" and sometimes unrecognized position influence the everyday treatment decisions of these therapists? As we will show in this book, such positions are not just philosophical or professional; they influence the moment-by-moment decisions that affect the therapy session itself. For instance, eliminative materialists probably have little faith in traditional psychological interventions. They view such interventions as providing little genuine resolution of the fundamental causes of pathology, and thus use them grudgingly, if at all.

Of course, nonempirical issues are not just involved in disciplinary *problems*; they are also involved in disciplinary *opportunities*. Some of the greatest advances in science have occurred through the consideration of nonempirical issues. Einstein's work is probably the most famous example, questioning as he did the nonempirical assumptions of his discipline. To be sure, Einstein's "gedanken experiments"—his nonempirical inquiries—ultimately led to many testable, empirical questions, but they *began* with what could only be viewed as "philosophical" questions (e.g., What is the nature of time?).

In the same sense, the authors of this book welcome the many empirical investigations that may follow from or lead to this exploration of nonempirical issues. They do not, however, require that testable implications be the primary reason for their gedanken experiments. More important for this book is the significance of the issues for the field. That is, critical issues do not have to result in empirical hypotheses. An issue could have important disciplinary consequences, and thus significance, without necessarily leading to a program of scientific research.

Karl Popper's (1959) pivotal work in the philosophy of science illustrates this point. His work eventually influenced the important notion of *falsifiability*, which many in psychology consider to be crucial in distinguishing science from pseudoscience (e.g., Radner & Radner, 1982). Yet his examination of scientific method and the philosophy that underlies this method could hardly be considered empirical in nature. Indeed, he could not, in principle, use empirical methods to examine the fundamental character of empirical methods; this would be tautological. His inquiries were instead philosophical in nature, leading to no testable hypotheses per se. But these inquiries have great significance for science in general and the entire enterprise of statistical analysis (e.g., denying or falsifying the null hypothesis).

The upshot is that examining the nonempirical—the critical issues of a discipline—has the potential not only to resolve disciplinary problems but also to create disciplinary opportunities, opportunities for new understandings and new approaches. The contributors to this book do not consider themselves to be in the company of such thinkers as Einstein and Popper. Still, each has embarked on a similar quest: illuminating overlooked problems that cannot ultimately be decided by empirical criteria alone. Each trusts in the significance of investigating the "sacred cows" of the discipline as well as rethinking its familiar and seemingly settled elements.

The Context and Impetus for the Book

What are the sacred cows of the discipline, as well as its important settled and unsettled nonempirical elements? The editors of this volume created a list of such issues, much like any therapist's list of important issues in the field: empirically supported treatment, assessment, pharmacology, spirituality, culture, managed care, individualism, the scientist-practitioner model, determinism, eclecticism, postmodernism, multiculturalism, diagnosis, and feminism. We then asked a distinguished panel of contributors to address one or more of the overlooked, nonempirical elements of these topics and begin a conversation about them. Part of this conversation took place in a conference (held at Brigham Young University in 1999) that allowed this distinguished panel to discuss these issues with practicing psychotherapists.

None of the contributors was asked to tackle an overly broad or abstract issue, such as "What is the nature of therapy?" or "What is the nature of abnormality?" Nor was anyone asked to resolve a particular issue in a definitive fashion, assuming this were even possible. The main thrust of each chapter of this book, then, is to describe a relatively ignored problem and begin to find the language—in therapist's rather than philosopher's language—to raise our consciousness about it. Some authors attempt to solve the problems raised; others attempt to show new ways of dealing with these aspects of the therapy enterprise. In all the chapters, however, the emphasis is on illuminating pivotal nonempirical issues, so that the reader can join the conversation about them and ultimately deal with them more effectively in practice.

To reinforce this emphasis on practical conversation, the editors also asked practicing psychotherapists (who also attended the 1999 BYU conference) to comment on each of the chapters. These commentators were given relatively free rein, addressing such questions as, what did they think about the issues raised? Were the chapters helpful? Did they illuminate a previously overlooked perspective? How might they, the commentators, extend or elaborate the points made? Were there other implications of these ideas for practice? Unfortunately, space constraints limited these helpful contributions considerably. Still, they prompted the chapter authors to move away from their sometimes obscure language to talk directly to the commentator, and thus the practicing psychotherapist.

The Critical Issues of Psychotherapy

What are the nonempirical aspects of the issues addressed? Stanley Messer of Rutgers University begins the book by tackling important aspects of the issue of **empirically supported treatments.** He discusses some of the relevant philosophy of science considerations, showing how frequently the unacknowledged assumptions of science play a role in what seems to be "empirically supported." Is it possible that these nonempirical factors bias empirical "support" toward some therapies and away from others? Are there therapies that would never be empirically supported, given current methods, despite their effectiveness?

What about conventional approaches to **psychological assessment?** Is the potential of today's assessment instruments generally actualized in practice? How much does the usual sterile and mechanical style of assessment prevent the richness of clients from coming through? Is there another framework for assessment that provides more useful information, allows the humanness of the client to be communicated, and yet is scientific and valid? Constance Fischer of Duquesne University addresses these questions with numerous case examples. She describes some of the problems with the traditional approach to assessment and advocates an alternative that may overcome these problems.

One of the clear trends of psychotherapy is the movement toward biological conceptions. From the increasing popularity of prescription privileges to a heavier reliance on medications, there seems to be an increasing **biologization** of the discipline. Some professionals would consider this an unqualified good, whereas others are much more wary. In either case, Richard Williams of Brigham Young University explicates the nonempirical issues frequently overlooked. Have we overestimated what biological interventions can offer? Can such a biologization take away the meaning of our client's behaviors? Is there an alternative approach that allows us to value the body but not assume that it is all there is?

What about the other side of the ontological coin? What role should **spirituality** play in psychotherapy, if any? Traditionally, therapists have assumed that anything that smacked of religion was off limits, including spirituality. Moreover, spirituality was considered to be outside the domain of the sciences associated with psychotherapy. Increasingly, however, both assumptions are being challenged. As Sally Barlow and Allen Bergin of Brigham Young University show, it is difficult to deal with whole persons in therapy without encountering their spirituality. Bergin is also noted for his rigorous program of spiritual research, indicating how spiritual interventions can facilitate client care.

The therapeutic influence of **culture** has also been relatively ignored until recently. In the not too distant past, personality theorists assumed a type of universality that transcended culture—human nature was human nature, regardless of its context. Cultural issues were "add-ons"—incidental aspects of more basic personality structures. More recently, however, therapists such as Lisa Hoshmand of Lesley College have considered culture to be more than incidental. Indeed, Hoshmand shows that traditional theorists themselves were functioning within particular cultures when they formulated their explanations. Are conceptions of abnormality and treatment also bound to culture? What would a truly sophisticated approach to culture be like for a psychotherapist?

The bane of every therapist's existence is **managed care,** or so it would seem. Many therapists do their best to manage their associations with managed care and keep its influence to a minimum. Nevertheless, there is no denying the huge impact that this system has had on the psychotherapy enterprise, from the types of therapies now considered to be appropriate (e.g., short term) to the assessment instruments now being developed (e.g., the Outcome Questionnaire). What is behind the managed care regime? What impact is it having and why? Where is it going, and how will it affect client care? Don Polkinghorne of the University of Southern California attempts to address these questions.

Many psychotherapists take it for granted that people should be treated and assessed, if possible, as individuals. However, this assumption is not one that has been rigorously tested. Rather, it originates from certain cultural biases, including the North American notion of a "rugged individualist." How has this **individualism** affected the therapist's understanding of therapy? Is our standard focus on individual autonomy, self-esteem, and personal freedom a reflection of this bias? What alternatives are there, and what ramifications would these have for therapy? Frank Richardson and Timothy Zeddies of the University of Texas—Austin address these provocative issues.

Another sacred cow in the training of psychotherapists, especially in psychology, is **the scientist-practitioner model.** This model assumes that teaching the practice of psychotherapy (and how to consume research) is insufficient. Practitioners should also be taught to produce research; practitioners should be taught to be scientists. Ideally, the two roles—scientist and practitioner—are combined to produce a down-to-earth but rigorous therapist. Yet how effective is this model? How necessary are the two main facets of this model, and how effectively are they combined? Hendrika Vande Kemp of Fuller Theological Seminary addresses these questions through a dramatic portrayal of her own physical and emotional problems.

Joseph Rychlak of Loyola University of Chicago next shares his travails with the prevalent, but frequently unacknowledged, notion of **determinism.** As he defines it, theories of therapy are hard pressed to avoid this notion, because they describe "what's responsible for" a particular behavior or problem. What influence does this type of theorizing have on the therapist? Does it necessarily presume that clients are not responsible for themselves? Could the therapist assume that the client has a type of self-responsibility? Rychlak explores all these questions and outlines—through the treatment of a particular client—a self-deterministic style of therapy.

Another undeniable trend in the field is the popular movement toward **eclecticism.** What is behind this trend? Are traditional single theories failing to measure up to modern standards? Is eclecticism a type of miscellaneous category for homegrown (and thus relatively unevaluated) theories? Or are therapists bothered about the biases of traditional theories and thus wish to escape these theoretical "chains"? Brent Slife and Jeffrey Reber of Brigham Young University first analyze the many mansions and motives of eclectic psychotherapists. This analysis, however, leads them to question whether eclecticism will really satisfy most eclectic therapists. They propose an alternative that they believe better meets the needs of eclectics, and they illustrate it with a therapy case.

One of the most recent developments of the academy has finally made its way into the practice of psychotherapy—**postmodernism.** Barbara Held of Bowdoin College evaluates this development. She asks the important questions: What is this seemingly ineffable philosophy? and, How is it currently affecting psychotherapy? Is there anything really different and useful for the practicing therapist? Dr. Held surveys prominent postmodernists and finds their proposals wanting. She then turns to an alternative that seems to address the concerns of the postmodernists, but without postmodernism's dangerous side effects.

Multiculturalists can be congratulated for generally raising most therapists' awareness of the cultural identities of their clients. Greater stress than ever has been placed on properly dealing with ethnicity in the training and evaluation of competent therapists. Still, is there a "dark" side to this training? Is there a problematic framework that underlies some of the seemingly innocuous rhetoric of **multiculturalism?** Blaine Fowers of the University of Miami believes that there can be. Multiculturalism can too easily evolve into a penicious relativism, if psychotherapists are not careful. Is there some other way to value the cultural context of clients without falling into these conceptual and practical traps?

No book of critical issues could be complete without considering the problem of **diagnosis.** The *Diagnostic and Statistical Manual of Mental Disorders* (DSM; American Psychiatric Association, 1994)—in all its revisions—has been one of the most used and yet maligned elements of the therapeutic enterprise. The advent of managed care has given it even more prominence. Many of its supporters view it as a relatively value-free and objective (though imperfect) set of descriptors for the major disorders, much like the functional analysis that has worked so well for medicine. Robert Woolfolk of Princeton University reveals the controversies over such an analysis, even in medicine. He shows how this affiliation with medicine does not save diagnosis from its value-laden nature. What implications, then, do these values have for diagnosis and treatment?

Surely no modern social movement can claim greater visibility than **feminism.** For some time now, the theories that have underlain this movement have made their inimitable presence known in psychotherapy. Has this presence been good? Is feminism an all-or-none affair, or is there feminist "wheat" that can be separated from feminist "chaff"? What is the status of this movement at this juncture? Jeanne Marecek of Swarthmore College brings her considerable evaluative powers to bear on these questions. She presents a sympathetic picture of feminism, but also puts it in proper perspective.

Daniel Robinson of Georgetown University concludes the book. Though not a psychotherapist himself, there is no more astute observer of the nonempirical issues of the social sciences, including the intellectual and practical concerns of psychotherapists. Robinson first draws attention to some of the prominent themes of this panel of authors and commentators, and later adds his own incisive observations about an issue that undergirds all genuinely therapeutic efforts—the "good life."

References

American Psychiatric Association. (1994). *Diagnostic and statistical manual of mental disorders* (4th ed.). Washington, DC: Author.

Churchland, P. S. (1986). *Neurophilosophy: Toward a unified science of the mind-brain.* Cambridge: MIT Press.

Fisher, A. (1997). Modern manifestations of materialism: A legacy of the Enlightenment discourse. *Journal of Theoretical and Philosophical Psychology, 17,* 45-55.

Koch, S. (1959). *Psychology: A study of science* (Vols. 1-3). New York: McGraw-Hill.

Koch, S. (1992). Psychology's Bridgman vs. Bridgman's Bridgman: An essay in reconstruction. *Theory and Psychology, 2,* 261-290.

Miller, R. B. (Ed.). (1992). *The restoration of dialogue: Readings in the philosophy of clinical psychology.* Washington, DC: American Psychological Association.

Muse, M. (1997). The implicit dualism in eliminative materialism: What the Churchlands aren't telling you. *Journal of Theoretical and Philosophical Psychology, 17,* 56-66.

Polkinghorne, D. E. (1983). *Methodology for the human sciences.* Albany: State University of New York Press.

Popper, K. (1959). *The logic of scientific discovery.* New York: Basic Books.

Radner, D., & Radner, M. (1982). *Science & unreason.* Belmont, CA: Wadsworth.

Robinson, D. N. (1985). *Philosophy of psychology.* New York: Columbia University Press.

Rychlak, J. F. (1981). *Introduction to personality and psychotherapy: A theory-construction approach* (2nd ed.). Boston: Houghton Mifflin.

Rychlak, J. F. (1988). *The psychology of rigorous humanism* (2nd ed.). New York: New York University Press.

Sass, L. (1992). *Madness and modernism.* New York: Basic Books.

Slife, B. D., & Gantt, E. (1999). Methodological pluralism: A framework for psychotherapy research. *Journal of Clinical Psychology, 55* (12), 1-13.

Slife, B. D., & Williams, R. N. (1995). *What's behind the research? Discovering hidden assumptions in the behavioral sciences.* Thousand Oaks, CA: Sage.

Issue 1

Empirically Supported Treatments

Empirically Supported Treatments

What's a Nonbehaviorist to Do?

Stanley B. Messer
Rutgers University

A committee of the Division of Clinical Psychology of the American Psychological Association (Division 12 Task Force, 1995) recently published a report listing those therapies that it viewed as efficacious for various psychological disorders. First known as Empirically Validated Treatments, an inappropriately strong designation given the data on which they rest, they are now more modestly referred to as Empirically Supported Treatments, or ESTs. The major impetus for this task force was to provide balance to similar reports published by the American Psychiatric Association and the Agency for Health Care Policy and Research that gave primacy to biomedical treatments for the same mental disorders. The advent of medication for the treatment of psychiatric disorders, after all, has taken on the characteristics of a juggernaut that threatens to crush the practice of psychotherapy of every stripe. By issuing a list of approved treatments, the committee was recognizing the realpolitik of the current situation. In addition, insofar as clinical psychology regards itself as a scientific, data-based profession, the committee's efforts, on the face of it, are unexceptional, even praiseworthy. In such a charged political climate, showing that psychotherapy stands up to empirical scrutiny seems appropriate and wise (Nathan, 1998).

It gives one pause, however, to learn that the vast majority of studies that meet the criteria set forth by the task force are cognitive-behavioral in orientation, or what can be referred to as outcome-oriented therapies (Gold, 1995). To be specific, my calculation based on the task force figures is that of the 22 so-called "well-established" empirically supported treatments, 19 are behavioral, and of the 7 "probably efficacious" treatments, 6 are behavioral. In the later update on

ESTs (Division 12 Task Force, 1996), I found that of the 27 treatments added to these categories, 22 are behavioral. Almost totally absent are the psychodynamic, experiential, client-centered, family, and existential therapies. It is likely that therapies emphasizing process rather than behavioral outcomes will be put in jeopardy by the dissemination of these results. Not surprising, the advent of ESTs has ignited a substantial and controversial literature on their pros and cons with major journals in clinical psychology devoting special series to the debate (e.g., *Clinical Psychology: Science and Practice,* Fall 1996; *Journal of Consulting and Clinical Psychology,* February 1998; *Psychotherapy Research,* Summer 1998).

In this chapter, I examine the premises of ESTs and some of the political, conceptual, and methodological problems they present. I offer an alternative for the practitioner to the strict EST format, a way of blending the advantages of both process and outcome features in a nonbehavioral treatment. I use brief psychodynamic therapy (BPT) to illustrate such a blend, although other brief therapies are available as well. The chapter mentions how the visions of reality—romantic, ironic, tragic, and comic—are altered in brief treatments to highlight the trade-offs involved in effecting this compromise approach. I start by presenting one of my current clinical cases as a means of exploring some problems with EST ideology.

Case Illustration: The Man Who Wants More Joy in His Life

Jack is a 55-year-old white male who has been married for 23 years. There are grown, married children from both his and his wife's first marriages. He met a woman, Lisa, about 8 months ago; fell in love with her; and is considering leaving his wife, Ruth. His paramour, at 33, is 22 years younger than he is, has been married for one year, and is a fellow employee in a distant branch of the large corporation in which Jack is a middle manager. He has been feeling anxious and guilty about cheating on Ruth and is turning to me for "a process to help figure things out" and to arrive at a decision about whether to leave Ruth for Lisa.

On the one hand, Jack first reported that he had no major complaints about Ruth, who has been good to him. (This view changed, however, as he began to admit to himself several sources of dissatisfaction in his marriage.) He is also concerned about how their adult children, to whom he is close, would view his infidelity and the prospect of his leaving their mother or stepmother. On the other hand, he regards the quality of his relationship with Lisa as greater by several orders of magnitude and potential than what he currently shares with his wife. He finds that he communicates with Lisa on a deep level, that they share many interests, and that she is exciting to him. After explaining the conflict in detail, he questioned me carefully about whether I could approach his problem in an impartial way, to which I answered, after some reflection, that I thought I could. What this meant was that I would not prejudge the merits of one or the other side of his conflict but would help him clarify the psychological features and consequences of either choice. I should add that a minister, priest, rabbi, or therapist with a strongly held point of view regarding the moral dimension of his issues, such as the sanctity of marriage, may very well have answered the question differently. In the predominating psychotherapy tradition of secular individualism, my value stance placed primary emphasis on the client's freedom to choose (see Richardson and Zeddies, this volume).

In trying to understand what led Jack to engage in this affair, I inquired about important events in recent years and learned that he had had a mild heart attack 2 years earlier, at which point he began reassessing his life. The heart attack left him feeling that life is fragile and wanting more joy than he was experiencing. He never discussed these feelings with his wife and was not looking for another woman when Lisa came along, but the attraction just happened, he said. In a way, he wished it had not. He and his wife are like roommates now, and she, not knowing about Lisa, is concerned about his lack of sexual interest in her. He has been telling her that this is a function of the medication he is taking for his heart. Jack is unhappy about lying to Ruth and is considering telling her about his liaison with Lisa.

What the Case Illustrates About ESTs

The ESTs as presently constituted presume (a) a diagnosis (usually derived from the *Diagnostic and Statistical Manual of Mental Disorders* [*DSM*; American Psychiatric Association, 1994]), (b) use of a treatment manual, and (c) specified outcome measurements related to the diagnosis. Each of these serves a particular purpose within the EST outlook. Diagnosis allows a categorization and specification of the problem domain that can be reliably assessed; a manual permits administration of a standardized protocol so that it is known with some degree of precision what treatment was delivered; and outcome measurement gauges improvement, especially a decrease of symptoms and a return of the person to nonpathological functioning. I examine each of these three features in some detail.

Issues of Diagnosis and Formulation

How useful is the *DSM* for specifying Jack's problem? Does he have, perhaps, a Hypoactive Sexual Desire Disorder (*DSM*: 302.71). At first it appeared that he did, but as it turned out, this was only in relation to his wife, not his lover. There is nothing hypoactive about his sexual desire for Lisa. Should the hypoactive desire for his wife be the focus of an empirically supported treatment? That, however, is not what he is seeking.

An alternate focus of treatment could be the anxiety that Jack experiences. The anxiety, however, is subclinical, that is, it does not meet the criteria for any of the formal *DSM* anxiety-related disorders—such as Generalized Anxiety Disorder, Panic Attacks, or even Adjustment Disorder. Is lack of diagnosis among clients a rare phenomenon? Not at all. According to large epidemiological surveys, about 43% of those who visit a mental health specialist (Epidemiologic Catchment Area Program; Howard et al., 1996) and 35% of those who seek treatment (National Comorbidity Study; Kessler et al., 1994; Warner, personal communication) do not currently carry a *DSM* diagnosis.

Let us take a different tack for the moment, and imagine that Jack's anxiety was diagnosable. One could then apply one of the ESTs that have been shown to be effective in reducing anxiety, such as cognitive behavior therapy or stress inoculation training for coping with stressors. If the person is sufficiently distraught and the anxiety needs immediate attention, such procedures can be useful. Being able to call on an empirically supported technique that is known to alleviate such suffering may be regarded as a decided plus, especially for a man like Jack whose heart is presumably in a weakened state. (As an aside, one could make the case that such anxiety is a motivator for self-reflection and treatment, a signal that not all is well, and therefore that one should not be in a hurry to reduce it. The same would hold true for his strong guilt feelings.) If the anxiety was all that was attended to in this case, however, we would miss the point because it would not take account of Jack's central dilemma, namely, his ambivalence about whether to leave his wife for Lisa. How exactly could one formulate Jack's specific yet complex problem to allow us to call on a reliable diagnostic scheme and an associated manualized technique? The answer clearly is not forthcoming from either the *DSM* or current EST approach.

From a humanistic therapy perspective, and going back as far as Carl Rogers, diagnosis is considered overly mechanistic and medical in conception and as offering a dehumanized view of psychological problems (Faidley & Leitner, 1993). If a diagnosis is used at all by therapists in this tradition, it is never viewed as fixed. When it is necessary to use one for insurance or research purposes, it is decided on jointly by client and therapist (Bohart, O'Hara, & Leitner, 1998). In a similar vein, family and couple therapies were not set up to diagnose individual pathology. Drawing on systems theory, they posit that the problem resides *between* the two partners of a couple or *among* members of the family. Because of National Institute of Mental Health (NIMH) priorities, we have studies of the effects of family therapy on schizophrenia rather than of family process itself, which is the focus of this therapy (Lebow, personal communication).

Viewing diagnosis through the lens of Romanticism, an 18th-century movement stressing, among other features, the value of individual depth and experience, the search for such discrete categories leads to superficial solutions—those readily apparent, measurable, and capable of isolation (Schneider, 1998). Romanticism posits that the world is too interconnected to be readily carved at its presumed joints in *DSM* fashion. The human "life world," as Husserl called it, is holistic, complex, and multitextured. The anxiety of a particular individual such as Jack must be understood, then, in the context of his personality and lived experience. The emphasis in Romanticism on a person's individuality and uniqueness is diametrically opposed to a system that reduces a person to preset categories, however constituted. Better than a diagnosis would be a formulation of

Jack's situation that takes into account his unique attitudes, needs, defenses, and conflicts and the personal history that has shaped them. Surely the fact that Jack had a heart attack, which affected his sense of vulnerability, mortality, and general life outlook, is an important feature of the case.

Another limitation of *DSM* categorization is that there is a gap between the task force recommendations stemming from the research findings (e.g., "use interpersonal or cognitive therapy for depression") and the more nuanced nature of clinical problems to which the ESTs are to be applied (e.g., Garfield, 1996). The DSM categories are much more heterogeneous than is typically acknowledged in these studies. For example, it is well known that there are two quite different types of problems underlying depression (Blatt, 1995): (a) dependency, that is, "anaclitic" or interpersonal issues, based on fear of abandonment; and (b) self-critical thoughts and feelings, that is, "introjective" issues, based on negative self-evaluation and guilt. These subtypes of depression require different treatment approaches, whether in the psychoanalytic, cognitive, or interpersonal therapy spectra. In a randomized trial, some patients are matched to the correct intervention and some are not. This increases within-group variance and ends up revealing little about the efficacy of the treatment being studied (Goldfried & Wolfe, 1998; Persons, 1991; Raw, 1993). In a similar vein, Garfield (1998) has pointed to other variables in any one diagnosis that will influence the duration and outcome of therapy and that are not taken account of in the EST studies; for example, expectations about therapy, motivation, socioeconomic factors, and cultural and ethnic attributes.

Furthermore, almost all the ESTs studied are theoretically pure, whereas most practitioners identify themselves as eclectic or integrative in orientation (Jensen, Bergin, & Greaves, 1990; Norcross, Prochaska, & Gallagher, 1989), frequently assimilating techniques from other therapies in their favored approach (Messer, 1992; Stricker & Gold, 1996). There exists, therefore, a substantial gap between the ESTs as recommended and the eclectic and integrative work of most frontline clinicians. This is the problem of internal versus external validity where the randomized controlled trials (RCTs) of single-diagnosed, pure form therapies, on which ESTs are largely based, lead to good internal (or scientific) validity but poor external (or real-life) validity. That is, the effectiveness or applicability of the ESTs is questionable when applied to the dual- or triple-diagnosed patients treated with the eclectic or integrative therapies favored in daily practice.

Problems of Manualized Treatment

The Division 12 Task Force requirements for efficacy research on ESTs include use of a manual that specifies the content of the techniques and the process of implementing them. (See Sanderson & Woody, 1995, and Woody & Sanderson, 1998, for a list of available manuals.) Among the arguments for using manuals are that it is possible to know roughly how clients were treated, which enables replication of the procedures in a standardized way. It also allows one to check therapists' adherence to procedures. Moreover, because a manual provides a careful description of what is involved in conducting a particular therapy, it may be a good training device, and one which can be readily disseminated (Calhoun, Moras, Pilkonis, & Rehm, 1998; Shoham, 1996).

Insofar as psychotherapy manuals are what we used to call books, I have no problem with them. If they were merely books, however, they would be presenting general theoretical principles and techniques of practice at a fairly high level of abstraction and generality, not necessarily directed to any one specific disorder. For the most part, the manuals connected to ESTs are quite specific and do focus on a particular dysfunction, such as agoraphobia, obsessive-compulsive disorder, or panic attacks. Such manuals can function as straitjackets, constraining therapist responses too rigidly (Goldfried & Wolfe, 1998). In fact, there is research that has confirmed the negative effects of overly close adherence to a manual (e.g., Castonguay, Goldfried, Wiser, Raue, & Hayes, 1996; Henry, Strupp, Butler, Schacht, & Binder, 1993). This may occur because manuals pay more attention to techniques than to the process of how these are to be implemented, such as the interpersonal sensitivity and skillful timing of the therapist. Coming from an empirically oriented task force, the emphasis on technique is ironic in that empirical research has shown that techniques account for only 15% of the outcome variance of psychotherapy. Common factors, including alliance, account for about 30%; placebo effects, 15%; and client and external factors, 40% (Lambert, 1992). Whereas the implicit assumption of ESTs is that it is the techniques that cure the disorder, it appears much more likely to be the therapist who promotes change and healing, or some form of interaction among client, therapist, technique, and outside support. Psychotherapy is about treating persons, not syndromes, in the context of a human relationship, even if manualization makes it appear otherwise (Strupp & Anderson, 1997).

To my mind, the word "manual" conjures up a set of instructions that detail the steps one should take to repair one's bicycle or automobile, not to engage in a craft that requires artistry, flexibility, reflection, and imagination, as well as knowledge of scientific findings. Regarding flexibility, manuals give little space to advising therapists how to react to patients' varied responses or to surprises or crises that arise (Stricker, 1996). Even if they did, the system of payers and institutions will not support therapist creativity because of their fear of longer-term therapy. What is the manual-based therapist to do in such situations? In this regard, manual-based therapy limits external validity because it is not tailored to the vicissitudes of the individual patient, whose responses are often unpredictable. In other words, manuals tend to be procrustean (Fensterheim & Raw, 1996). To the extent that they are used very flexibly, as claimed by some EST proponents, their validity is compromised, and more of the active ingredients determining outcome shift to the therapist.

In the case of Jack, I do not know what kind of a manual, at least in its current, narrowly focused incarnation, would have served to help me offer a more scientifically based therapy. "As we move toward broader, less circumscribed problems of meaning, the more merely mechanical procedures fall away as having less and less to offer" (Smith, 1995, p. 39). It appears that more people are so afflicted and want and need more than the alleviation of a diagnosis-based disorder.

In spite of their constraints, manuals do not prevent the occurrence of large differences in therapeutic results obtained by individual therapists, who are the source of much therapy outcome variance. For example, Shapiro, Firth-Cozens, and Stiles (1989) found that despite use of the same manual, one therapist did better with cognitive-behavioral therapy (CBT) than other therapists. In a review of studies by Luborsky, McLellan, Diguer, Woody, and Seligman (1997), among three therapists who had more than one caseload and who took part in more than one study, two consistently had the best results and one consistently had the worst, although all three used the same manual. This confirms what Bohart et al. (1998) have stated, namely, "The therapist is a disciplined improvisational artist, not a manual-driven technician" (p. 145). It is interesting to note that managed care companies are moving to a system of evaluating therapists and referring cases to the successful ones, rather than requiring use of ESTs.

Stated more broadly, there is important therapist variance determining therapy outcome, which a manual may narrow but does not eliminate. One can achieve and measure technical adherence to a manual, but there still could be, and frequently are, large differences in interpersonal variables in the therapeutic relationship. It is these interpersonal variables rather than technical adherence to a manual that are most related to outcome (Henry, Schacht, & Strupp, 1986, 1990). As Henry (1998) has pointed out,

> The largest chunk of outcome variance not attributable to pre-existing patient characteristics involves individual therapist differences and the emergent interpersonal relationship between patient and therapist, regardless of technique or school of therapy. This is the main thrust of three decades of empirical psychotherapy research. (p. 128)

He goes on to argue that randomized clinical trials (RCTs) have outlived their usefulness and that we would be much better off studying common processes, alliance variables, and differences between more and less successful therapists, a point of view that I express.

Outcome Issues

EST outcomes are typically evaluated in terms of alleviation of the disorder that was chosen for study, be it bulimia, enuresis, marital discord, chronic headache, or depression. Also included may be measures of psychological adjustment, which gauge the extent to which patients come to feel and function better. I am not arguing that these are trivial goals to be taken lightly. At times, symptomatic relief and increased feelings of well-being are exactly what patients are looking for and are satisfied with when attained. Let us examine, however, what sorts of outcome psychoanalytic and humanistic therapists would view as desirable and contrast them to the medical thinking that characterizes the ESTs. In this way, I wish to highlight the difference between the typical EST and some process therapies. Psychoanalytic goals have been set out very aptly by McWilliams (1999), and I will draw on her schema in this discussion, following which I will apply these goals to the case of Jack.

Insight. At one time, insight was considered to be the result of accurate interpretations offered by the therapist and accepted by the patient. In the newer approaches to psychoanalytic therapy, a narrative that makes sense of the client's problems and background is coconstructed by therapist and patient. Clients very often want to understand what is happening to them, why they behave, think, and feel the way they do, both for the sake of increased knowledge and for the therapeutic benefit this may bring.

Agency. When people come to therapy, they often feel out of control, driven by forces they neither understand nor can tame, which compromises their subjective sense of agency. It is a goal of psychoanalytic and other process therapies to help restore this lost capacity to feel free to choose one's own destiny. In accordance with the centrality of this goal, psychoanalytic and humanistic therapists try to give patients maximal space to arrive at their own insights and conclusions. If suggestions are made, they are offered in a way that patients can refuse. At the end of such a process, patients should feel that they own and control their thoughts and behavior.

Identity. In the Middle Ages, the configuration of the self was rather modest; individuals were defined largely by their social rank, family ties, and religion. There is little evidence that people engaged in the kind of introspection and inner struggles that we currently view as normative (Messer & Warren, in press b). With the advent of modernity, the self took on new proportions: "Society stopped telling people who they were, and instead it was left up to the individual to construct his or her identity" (Baumeister, 1991, p. 95). This had the advantage for the individual of greater freedom of movement, thought, and self-expression, but also brought with it all the stresses and strains of having to establish one's place in the world, a task that falls particularly heavily on adolescents. Values, too, came to be regarded as an expression of one's inner self (Baumeister, 1991) rather than a reflection of external norms. Thus the modern self is disengaged, private, and inward turning. It is no wonder, then, that people come to therapists for "help in their efforts to experience and verbalize who they are, what they believe, how they feel, and what they want" (McWilliams, 1999, p. 18). These are not the kind of goals one finds in the ESTs.

Self-Esteem. People seeking the help of a therapist often have suffered a drop in self-esteem or it is chronically low. Following therapy, patients with low self-regard should have an improved sense of themselves.

Recognizing and Handling Feelings. Clients are often cut off from their true feelings and need help coming to recognize them. Why are they feeling the way they do about someone or something, or why are their feelings ambivalent? The consequence of increased affective self-awareness is the ability to handle feelings in less destructive ways and to be freer to choose among different possibilities for acting on them.

Ego Strength and Self-Cohesion. Ego strength and self-cohesion refer to the ability to cope with adversity without falling apart. This means that reality is not ignored or distorted but rather is taken into account. The person is not paralyzed by feelings such as guilt but, at the same time, does not impulsively respond to every fleeting impulse.

Love, Work, and Mature Dependency. At the end of a psychoanalytic or humanistic therapy, clients should be less afraid of love and intimacy, of speaking openly and honestly with their significant others, having exposed their deepest feelings and thoughts to the therapist. They should be more forgiving of themselves and others for what fate and endowment have conspired to bring about and be able to move forward with what is in their own control. At work, they should find their creative potential enhanced by feeling less conflicted and more spontaneous. There also should be a shift in the person from childlike dependency to mature give-and-take relationships.

Pleasure and Serenity. A person's very existence can be refreshed by a successful therapy. There can be genuine pleasure and contentment in place of the angst and despair or momentary highs that preceded them. Accepting that some things are not possible to have or achieve opens the way to enjoy that which is attainable.

The humanistic therapist, while endorsing many of these goals, might add to them self-actualization; enhanced spirituality; the ability to use one's imagination (Schneider, 1998); deeper experiencing; and recharting and pursuing a more satisfying, meaningful life (Bohart et al., 1998). I have dwelt on psychoanalytic and humanistic outcome criteria to demonstrate the very different premises on which they are based compared to the medical-like criteria that are being used by EST researchers, insurance companies, government, and managed care. Even if many of those who are cognitively or behaviorally oriented would say that they, too, work to shape, reinforce, and develop such goals, market forces are not interested in these values because there is no profit in them.

Starting with *insight* and *agency*, how are such psychoanalytic goals connected to Jack's therapy? What came to light was that Jack had had affairs twice before, once in each marriage, but over 20 years before. The circumstances in these two cases and the present one were similar, namely, a dimly perceived but unacknowledged feeling of neglect by his spouse. Achieving this insight was important to him in that he was able to acknowledge a point of vulnerability. He became more confident that he would be aware of, and be able to guard against, this vulnerability in any future relationship by being more communicative with his partner, whoever that turned out to be. That is, the increase in both insight and agency were significant outcomes for him.

Although *identity* is more frequently an issue for younger clients, it also applied to Jack in his need to examine and clarify his values and life goals as a middle-aged man who had suffered a heart attack. *Self-esteem* was not a particularly salient problem for Jack except insofar as his guilt feelings tended to lower it to some extent These feelings continued to bother him because of the pain he had inflicted on others by his actions. Note that one cannot easily determine what would be considered a satisfactory goal or outcome in this instance.

For Jack, as a person who tended to be very rational and problem-focused, *recognizing feelings* was an important area of improvement. He came to acknowledge and experience the extent to which he suppressed his anger at having to go along with his spouse to maintain their relationship. It remains to be seen how he will act on his feelings in the future. At times, therapy outcome must be gauged well after its completion.

There were no particular problems with *ego strength and self-cohesion* or in the *work* sphere. His *ability to love* was not impaired, but his capacity for expressing intimate feelings was enhanced through therapy. At the time of this writing, Jack was committed to being with Lisa and was awaiting her decision. He had arrived at a point in therapy where he could imagine accepting Lisa's decision, whatever it would be.

Empirical and Methodological Issues Regarding ESTs

I mention only a few of the many empirical and methodological issues that place the value of ESTs in perspective:

1. Listing behavioral treatments as ESTs typically says little about whether they are any more efficacious than psychodynamic, experiential, family, or other nonplacebo treatment since many of the EST comparisons were with psychological placebos or minimal treatments, not with bona fide process treatments.

2. That a therapy is considered efficacious should not lead one to conclude that the results are due to the specified theory of the EST or its unique procedures (Wampold, 1997). It may very well be that factors common to all therapies, such as the qualities of the therapeutic relationship, are what matter most.

3. The EST studies have been conducted mostly by investigators who have a behavioral orientation, and it is well known that the theoretical allegiance of the researcher is a strong predictor of the findings of studies claiming differences among classes of treatment (Stiles, Shapiro, & Elliot, 1986). In fact, in the most recent review of 29 studies of treatment comparisons (Luborsky et al., 1999), a combination of three measures of allegiance explained 69% of the variance in outcomes, which corresponds to a very hefty correlation of .85.

This correlation emerged despite the fact that differences in effectiveness between the therapies was rather small to begin with and not clinically significant.

   4. In the RCTs on which ESTs are based, there is no random assignment of therapists, so the results of such trials are confounded with therapist characteristics.

   5. Neither is there true randomization of patients in RCTs, which would require many trials to accomplish, not just the two called for by the EST criteria. If a person with whom you were playing poker or bridge won the first two hands, you would not conclude that he or she was the best player at the table. Before arriving at such a conclusion, many hands would have to be played to even out the effect of the kind of hands that people have been dealt. Because there are many ways in which patients or therapists in RCT comparison groups differ, we would need many clinical trials to control for the differences (D. Orlinsky, personal communication).

Process Versus Outcome Therapies

In the previous sections, I have referred to outcome versus process therapies (Gold, 1995). As is true of the ESTs, outcome therapies—which are largely cognitive and behavioral—traditionally have been oriented to modifying psychiatric disorders. The object is to accomplish this goal as directly and efficiently as possible. Process therapies (psychoanalytic, existential, systems, experiential, and client-centered) view such symptomatic change as occurring indirectly through the change in emergent themes, schemes, unconscious fantasies, and structures of subjectivity following a process of exploration and clarification. What needs to be understood and resolved in these therapies are intrapsychic states, interpersonal maladaptive patterns, or dysfunctional family processes. The role of the therapist is to encourage a process that leads clients to an awareness of their potential for self-direction rather than primarily directing them along preset lines in accordance with the dictates of a manual or specific technique. "The two major variables in this approach are therapist and client, not treatment and disorder" (Bohart et al., 1998, p. 146). Other features of process therapy are described as follows:

> Interventions are used to move the therapeutic interchange away from conventional conversation to deeper aspects and spheres of psychological life, without a precise destination or end point in mind. An intervention is judged to be helpful, or "correct" in so far as it affects the process of therapy by eliciting new material, by correcting an impasse or stalemate, or by enriching the patient's self-experience and awareness. (Gold, 1995, pp. 62-63)

   Clients in humanistic therapy often focus on future goals and personal development, using the therapy relationship to try out new skills (Bohart &

Tallman, 1996). The process is one of discovery and meaning making, allowing for "emergent new directions in each moment" (Bohart et. al., 1998). This is the romanticist sensibility that considers "the broader context of people's lived and intimate realities" (Schneider, 1998, p. 281).

What's a Nonbehaviorist to Do?

Based on the above arguments and analysis, my recommendation is that practitioners of the process therapies should be in no rush to hang up their spurs. There are many empirical, conceptual, and value-based reasons to continue practicing longer-term therapies of the psychoanalytic, humanistic, existential, and systems variety. One need not be guided by the current diagnostic system, by narrowly focused manuals, or by restricted outcome criteria. We should call on the ESTs, however, in situations where direct intervention is necessary or desired, as might be the case, for example, in panic disorder or obsessive-compulsive disorder, and where some degree of eclecticism or integration is called for. Pure cases of such disorders are relatively rare; hence the necessity for going beyond narrowly technical approaches, which may be what therapists of all stripes actually do in many instances. Once the complexity and interconnectedness of the different aspects of an individual's life are recognized, it becomes clearer that therapy cannot be practiced in too narrow or manualized a way. Of course, the more that therapy strays from an EST manual, the less relevant are the research studies establishing its validity.

Although continuing business as usual is a good alternative in theory, the reality facing most practitioners is that the number of therapy sessions available is limited—by insurance companies, managed care, clinics or hospitals, or patients' or therapists' time schedules. In such circumstances, or where it is specifically indicated, I recommend brief or time-limited therapy—but one that is guided by the same outlook and values as the process therapies to which I have been referring. Because a therapy is brief does not mean that it need be primarily symptom oriented, although it can and often does include symptom alleviation as one of its goals. As an example, I next describe a few of the major characteristics of time-limited dynamic psychotherapy and demonstrate how it combines features of both process and outcome therapies.

Brief Psychodynamic Therapy

Brief psychodynamic therapy (BPT), which typically ranges from 12 to 25 sessions, is based on the same theoretical principles as long-term psychoanalytic therapy. These include the continuity of normality and psychopathology, waking and dream life, childhood and adulthood. BPT draws on the concepts of psychosexual and psychosocial stages of development, unconscious processes, and hidden motivations—that is, their nontransparency. Regarding technique, it emphasizes clarification, interpretation, and confrontation of interpersonal patterns, defenses, and conflicts just as does long-term psychodynamic therapy. It includes exploration, the process of discovery, and meaning making. Two important features of BPT make it more akin to the outcome therapies, namely, goals and a focus, though one not based primarily on symptoms or diagnoses.

Clinical Focus. Employing a focus involves the formulation in the early sessions of a central clinical theme that serves to organize the therapist's observations and points the way to clinical interventions (Messer & Warren, in press a; Messer & Wolitzky, 1997). Such a formulation is based on the current situation, relevant history, and psychoanalytically based inference. The focus may be verbalized directly to patients as a form of working contract or to increase their motivation and interest in the therapy process. Some therapists do not state the central focus explicitly, but instead use it as a device to organize the ongoing flow of clinical information and to guide their interventions (Messer & Warren, 1995, in press a).

Although all psychodynamic treatment approaches rely on clinical formulations, in short-term therapy the central focus tends to be more circumscribed in scope, limiting the therapeutic inquiry so that clinical goals may be achieved within the time frame. In this regard, it is more akin to the outcome-oriented ESTs. In addition, the focus is generated more rapidly at the outset of treatment and is used more actively in brief psychotherapy than in open-ended treatment. There are now available formalized, reliable methods for constructing a formulation, which could become part of a more useful diagnostic strategy and guide for the process therapies than is the *DSM*. These include the Core Conflictual Relationship Theme (Luborsky, 1997), the Plan Formulation Method (Curtis & Silberschatz, 1997), and Interpersonal Case Formulation (Henry, 1997).

Goal Setting. The brevity of short-term psychotherapy, with the accompanying constraints on what can be accomplished, requires the setting of clinical priorities so that the time available is used most effectively. Thus goal setting is linked to the use of a central focus, as well as to the time limit and the centrality of termination. Goal setting reflects the therapist's acceptance of limitations on what can be accomplished and embodies an individualized approach to the aims of psychotherapy. It also provides the means for assessing therapy outcome in an individualized and dynamically informed fashion (Messer & Warren, in press a).

The concept of goal setting reflects the greater degree of problem-solving and symptom focus that is characteristic of time-limited treatments. Although sharing some features of the medical model found in the ESTs, including the emphasis on diagnosis (but in the form of individual-based clinical formulation) and symptom reduction, BPT adds a further dimension to treatment goals. This includes psychoanalytically informed ideas about emotional health and the aims of psychoanalytic treatment, which extend beyond, but include, the symptom focus. Such aims might include an increase of insight into, and at least partial resolution of, personal conflicts; getting in touch with one's feelings; an increased capacity for intimacy in relationships; and a lessening of anxiety and depression. Goals can be set with an individual patient in mind and directed at those problems that are of most immediate concern. BPT can also incorporate integrative elements that broaden its applicability to those who will not profit from a standard process therapy.

I have previously described the change required for therapists in going from long-term to short-term psychodynamic therapy in terms of the "visions of reality" they encompass (Messer, 2000; Messer & Warren, 1995). These visions refer to assumptions about the nature and content of human reality and have been used to describe different genres of literature as well as psychoanalytic, behavioral, and humanistic models of therapy (Messer & Winokur, 1986). BPT is seen as having more aspects of the comic and romantic, and fewer of the tragic and ironic, visions of reality than does long-term psychoanalytic therapy. For example, the therapist's heightened activity in BPT is more consonant with the comic and romantic visions' stress on problem solving and action, compared to the more contemplative and reflective stance of the therapist operating within ironic and tragic views. To the extent that specific goals and foci are set and aimed for in brief therapy, it tilts toward the comic view more than the romantic. It is more tragic in setting limits on what is possible by virtue of its brevity, focus, and goal setting. Thus, for practitioners whose major mode of practice is long-term therapy, an adjustment in viewpoint is required to conduct brief therapy, but not necessarily a radical one.

Although I have focused on brief therapy of the psychodynamic variety, there are comparable brief experiential and family therapies as well. From the viewpoint of a long-term therapist, brief therapy is an accommodation to the realities of the marketplace, but one that adopts the style and values of a process orientation with a flexible focus and goals. It also happens to be one of the few nonbehavioral therapies to earn recognition from the Division 12 Task Force as "probably efficacious" for the treatment of depression. More research on the outcomes of process therapies, especially those that are brief, is needed, as well as the funds from national agencies, currently lacking, to conduct them.

In conclusion, there should be room for the practice of process therapies—be they short or long term—alongside practice of the ESTs or in combination with them. It would be a travesty to foreclose the study, implementation, and teaching of therapies that respond to much of what human beings value and need to live their lives in a satisfactory manner. From a research perspective, there exists a large literature on the study of psychotherapy process that has been ignored by the Division 12 Task Force because of its strict outcome orientation and emphasis on showing cause and effect scientifically. This literature shows how therapist interventions relate to changes in patient progress *within* therapy along dimensions such as affective experiencing and insight that are the bread and butter of the experiential and psychodynamic therapies (e.g., Messer & Holland, 1998; Silberschatz & Curtis, 1993). There is also a substantial literature on the relation of process variables to *outcome* of therapy (Orlinsky, Grawe, & Parks, 1994). We should use such research to establish guidelines for *processes* of therapy that are effective, as a companion or alternative to those offered by EST proponents. We also need more qualitative, contextually sensitive research and more single-subject research, both quantitative and qualitative, on the process therapies. In these directions lies a fruitful partnership between practitioners and researchers, one that has considerable potential for influencing everyday practice.

References

American Psychiatric Association. (1994). *Diagnostic and statistical manual of mental disorders* (4th ed.). Washington, DC: Author.

Baumeister, R. F. (1991). *Meanings of life*. New York: Guilford.

Blatt, S. I. (1995). The destructiveness of perfectionism: Implications for the treatment of depression. *American Psychologist, 50*, 1003-1020.

Bohart, A. C., O'Hara, M., & Leitner, L. M. (1998). Empirically violated treatments: Disenfranchisement of humanistic and other psychotherapies. *Psychotherapy Research, 8*, 141-157.

Bohart, A. C., & Tallman, K. (1996). The active client: Therapy as self-help. *Journal of Humanistic Psychology, 36*, 7-30.

Calhoun, K. S., Moras, K., Pilkonis, P. A., & Rehm, L. P. (1998). Empirically supported treatments: Implications for training. *Journal of Consulting and Clinical Psychology, 66*, 151-162.

Castonguay, L. G., Goldfried, M. R., Wiser, S. L., Raue, P. J., & Hayes, A. M. (1996). Predicting the effect of cognitive therapy for depression: A study of unique and common factors. *Journal of Consulting and Clinical Psychology, 64*, 497-504.

Curtis, I. T., & Silberschatz, C. (1997). The Plan Formulation Method. In T. D. Eells (Ed.), *Handbook of psychotherapy case formulation*. New York: Guilford.

Division 12 Task Force. (1995). Training in and dissemination of empirically validated psychological treatments: Report and recommendations. *The Clinical Psychologist, 48*, 3-23.

Division 12 Task Force. (1996). An update on empirically validated therapies. *The Clinical Psychologist, 49*, 5-18.

Faidley, A. J., & Leitner, L. M. (1993). *Assessing experience in psychotherapy: Personal construct alternatives*. Westport, CT: Praeger Publishers.

Fensterheim, H., & Raw, S. D. (1996). Psychotherapy research is not psychotherapy practice. *Clinical Psychology: Science and Practice, 3*, 168-171.

Garfield, S. L. (1996). Some problems associated with "validated" forms of psychotherapy. *Clinical Psychology: Science and Practice, 3*, 218-229.

Garfield, S. L. (1998). Some comments on empirically supported treatments. *Journal of Consulting and Clinical Psychology, 66*, 121-125.

Gold, J. R. (1995). The place of process-oriented psychotherapies in an outcome-oriented psychology and society. *Applied and Preventive Psychology, 4*, 61-74.

Goldfried, M. R., & Wolfe, B. E. (1998). Toward a more clinically valid approach to therapy research. *Journal of Consulting and Clinical Psychology, 66*, 143-150.

Henry, W. P. (1997). Interpersonal case formulation: Describing and explaining interpersonal patterns using the structural analysis of social behavior. In T. D. Eells (Ed.), *Handbook of psychotherapy case formulation* (pp. 223-259). New York: Guilford.

Henry, W. P. (1998). Science, politics, and the politics of science: The use and misuse of empirically validated treatment research. *Psychotherapy Research, 8*, 126-140.

Henry, W. P., Schacht, T. E., & Strupp, H. H. (1986). Structural analysis of social behavior: Application to a study of interpersonal process in differential psychotherapeutic outcome. *Journal of Consulting and Clinical Psychology, 54*, 27-31.

Henry, W. P., Schacht, T. E., & Strupp, H. H. (1990). Patient and therapist introject, interpersonal process and differential psychotherapy outcome. *Journal of Consulting and Clinical Psychology, 58*, 768-774.

Henry, W. P., Strupp, H. H., Butler, S. F., Schacht, T. E., & Binder, J. L. (1993). Effects of training in time-limited dynamic psychotherapy: Changes in therapist behavior. *Journal of Consulting and Clinical Psychology, 61*, 434-440.

Howard, K. I., Cornille, T. A., Lyons, J. S., Vessey, J. T., Lueger, R. J., & Saunders, S. M. (1996). Patterns of mental health service utilization. *Archives of General Psychiatry, 53,* 696-703.

Jensen, J. P., Bergin, A. E., & Greaves, D. W. (1990). The meaning of eclecticism: New survey and analysis of components. *Professional Psychology: Research and Practice, 21,* 124-130.

Kessler, R. C., McGonagle, K. A., Zhao, S., Nelson, C. B., Hughes, M., Eshelman, S., Wittchen, H., & Kendler, K. S. (1994). Lifetime and 12-month prevalence of DSM-III-R psychiatric disorders in the United States. *Archives of General Psychiatry, 51,* 8-19.

Lambert, M. J. (1992). Psychotherapy outcome research: Implications for integrative and eclectic therapists. In J. C. Norcross & M. R. Goldfried (Eds.), *Handbook of psychotherapy integration* (pp. 9-129). New York: Basic Books.

Luborsky, L. (1997). The Core Conflictual Relationship Theme: A basic case formulation method. In T. D. Gells (Ed.), *Handbook of psychotherapy case formulation* (pp. 58-83). New York: Guilford.

Luborsky, L., Diguer, L., Seligman, D. A., Rosenthal, R., Krause, E. D., Johnson, S., Halperin, G., Bishop, M., Berman, J. S., & Schweitzer, E. (1999). The researcher's own therapy allegiances: A "wild card" in comparisons of treatment efficacy. *Clinical Psychology: Science and Practice, 6,* 9-106.

Luborsky, L., McLellan, A. T., Diguer, L., Woody, G., & Seligman, D. A. (1997). The psychotherapist matters: Comparison of outcomes across twenty-two therapists and seven patient samples. *Clinical Psychology: Science and Practice, 1,* 53-65.

McWilliams, N. (1999). *Psychoanalytic case formulation.* New York: Guilford.

Messer, S. B. (1992). A critical examination of belief structures in integrative and eclectic psychotherapy. In J. C. Norcross & M. R. Goldfried (Eds.), *Handbook of psychotherapy integration* (pp. 130-165). New York Basic Books.

Messer, S. B. (2000). Applying the visions of reality to a case of brief therapy. *Journal of Psychotherapy Integration, 10,* 55-70.

Messer, S. B., & Holland, S. J. (1998). Therapist interventions and patient progress in brief psychodynamic therapy: Single-case design. In R. F. Bornstein & J. M. Masling (Eds.), *Empirical studies of the therapeutic hour* (pp. 229- 257). Washington, DC: American Psychological Association.

Messer, S. B., & Warren, C. S. (1995). *Models of brief psychodynamic therapy: A comparative approach.* New York: Guilford.

Messer, S. B., & Warren, C. S. (in press a). Brief psychodynamic therapy. In R. J. Corsini (Ed.), *Handbook of innovative psychotherapies.* New York: John Wiley.

Messer, S. B., & Warren, C. S. (in press b). Understanding and treating the postmodern self. In J. C. Muran (Ed.), *Self-relations in the psychotherapy process.* New York: Guilford.

Messer, S. B., & Winokur, M. (1986). Eclecticism and the shifting visions of reality in three systems of psychotherapy. *International Journal of Eclectic Psychotherapy, 5,* 115-124.

Messer, S. B., & Wolitzky, D. L. (1997). The traditional psychoanalytic approach to case formulation. In T. D. Gells (Ed.), *Handbook of psychotherapy case formulation* (pp. 26-57). New York: Guilford.

Nathan, P. E. (1998). Practice guidelines: Not yet ideal. *American Psychologist, 53,* 290-299.

Norcross, I. C., Prochaska, J. O., & Gallagher, K. M. (1989). Clinical psychologists in the 1980s: Part 2: Theory, research, and practice. *The Clinical Psychologist, 42,* 45-53.

Orlinsky, D. E., Grawe, K., & Parks, B. P. (1994). Process and outcome in psychotherapy—nach einmal. In A. E. Bergin & S. L. Garfield (Eds.), *Handbook of psychotherapy and behavior change* (4th ed., pp. 270-376). New York: John Wiley.

Persons, J. B. (1991). Psychotherapy outcome studies do not accurately represent current models of psychotherapy: A proposed remedy. *American Psychologist, 46,* 99-106.

Raw, S. (1993). Does psychotherapy research teach us anything about psychotherapy? *The Behavior Therapist, 16,* 75-76.

Sanderson, W. C., & Woody, S. (1995). Manuals for empirically validated treatments. A project of the Division of Clinical Psychology, American Psychological Association, Task Force on Psychological Interventions. *The Clinical Psychologist, 48,* 7-11.

Schneider, K. J. (1998). Toward a science of the heart: Romanticism and the revival of psychology. *American Psychologist, 53,* 277-289.

Shapiro, D. A., Firth-Cozens, J., & Stiles, W. B. (1989). The question of therapists' differential effectiveness: A Sheffield Psychotherapy Project addendum. *British Journal of Psychiatry, 154,* 383-385.

Shoham, V. (1996, April). *The promise (?) of empirically validated psychotherapy integration.* Paper presented at the meeting of the Society for the Exploration of Psychotherapy Integration, Berkeley, CA.

Silberschatz, G., & Curtis, J. (1993). Measuring the therapist's impact on the patient's therapeutic progress. *Journal of Consulting and Clinical Psychology, 61,* 40-411.

Smith, E. W. L. (1995). A passionate, rational response to the "manualization" of psychotherapy. *Psychotherapy Bulletin, 30,* 36-40.

Stiles, W. B., Shapiro, D. A., & Elliot, R. (1986). Are all psychotherapies equivalent? *American Psychologist, 41,* 16-180.

Stricker, G. (1996, April). *Empirically validated treatment psychotherapy manuals and psychotherapy integration.* Paper presented at the meeting of the Society for the Exploration of Psychotherapy Integration, Berkeley, CA.

Stricker, G., & Gold, J. R. (1996). Psychotherapy integration: An assimilative psychodynamic approach. *Clinical Psychology: Science and Practice, 3,* 47-58.

Strupp, H. H., & Anderson, T. (1997). On the limitations of therapy manuals. *Clinical Psychology; Science and Practice, 4,* 7-82.

Wampold, B. E. (1997). Methodological problems in identifying efficacious therapies. *Psychotherapy Research, 7,* 21-43.

Woody, S. R., & Sanderson, W. C. E. (1998). Manuals for empirically supported treatments: 1998 update. *The Clinical Psychologist, 51,* 17-21.

Commentary

Empirically Supported Treatments: Some Thoughts on the Nonbehaviorists' Dilemma

Marian S. Bergin

L.C.S.W. psychotherapist in private practice, American Fork, Utah

As a practicing clinician of a cognitive psychodynamic bent, I appreciated Dr. Stanley Messer's dismay at learning "that the vast majority of studies that meet the criteria set forth by the task force are cognitive-behavioral in orientation." And I believe that he is correct in surmising that "therapies emphasizing process rather than behavioral outcomes will be put in jeopardy by the dissemination of these results." This has already happened where third-party payments are made for managed care mental health treatment because insurance companies are requiring short-term, empirically supported treatments.

From my experience, however, this trend is not all bad. The psychotherapy industry needed some checks and balances put in place. When I started working on the acute care psych unit of a large general hospital in the mid-1980s, I observed that some psychotherapy was ineffective and sometimes harmful. At times I was appalled both at the harm done and the money wasted. Competency review, accountability, and efficiency in psychotherapy practice were long overdue. I am therefore not a managed care handwringer, even though I believe managed care has gone over the edge. I would also say that the wedding of managed care companies with empirically supported therapy researchers was a logical and foreseeable outcome.

Unfortunately, the pressure for empirically supported treatments came too late for one group that I became closely involved with: the families caught in the "memory retrieval" therapies for abuse cases and the resulting hysteria of the 1980s. Memory retrieval is useful and occurs in most therapies, but the pursuit of memory recovery using unvalidated, and now largely discredited, techniques resulted in unending suffering for many individuals and families. Witnessing many instances of these ill-fated interventions was a part of my training in how not to be a therapist. Even now, despite empirical evidence that these therapies are not effective and can be harmful, they are still being used.

I was reminded of the resistance of some therapists to utilizing outcome research when I read an article by J. T. Stocks (1998) in which he stated that recovered memory therapy is a dubious technique. Irate practitioners wrote in and dragged out all the old arguments of the past decade to defend their discredited techniques. One writer expressed concern that Stocks's (1999) article "could lead insurers to stop coverage for interventions involving memory recovery" (p. 494). She completely ignored the fact that, according to Stocks, "There is no empirical evidence to suggest that memory recovery therapy results in improved outcomes for clients. There is evidence that indicates that individuals deteriorate while receiving therapy involving memory recovery" (Stocks, 1999, p. 497).

It takes a long time for research to trickle down to clinicians, and sometimes harm is done as a result. I, for one, hope and even request that clinical training of all orientations be more grounded in research. I believe that manualized psychotherapy grounded in sound research has its place in training clinicians to treat specific disorders that have been shown to respond readily to such structured treatment. But that will not happen while professors resist such an approach.

Dr. Messer writes,

> Insofar as psychotherapy manuals are what we used to call books, I have no problem with them. If they were merely books, however, they would be presenting general theoretical principles and techniques of practice at a fairly high level of abstraction, not necessarily directed to any one specific disorder . . . [otherwise] such manuals can function as straitjackets, constraining therapist responses too rigidly.

When I was a newly trained therapist, I stumbled on a book by James F. Masterson (1983) that remains my favorite and most helpful technique builder. It contains verbatim transcripts of training supervisions that Masterson conducted. Like manuals, it contains actual dialogue for strategic interventions in therapy, in this case of borderline personality adults. I found that using it released me from a straitjacket rather than put me into one. I was in a straitjacket of inexperience and confusion as to how to put the theory I knew into words that would be meaningful to my clients. At times I used the Masterson book like a manual quite literally, and successfully, I think.

I see using manuals as comparable to using recipe books when I was a beginner cook. I searched for recipes to fill our family's needs and followed them to the letter. Soon I was able to improve on a recipe, improvise, and substitute ingredients. Cooking became a creative endeavor, satisfying to the cook and to the partakers. Cookbooks still are very useful at times. Similarly, manuals can be essential for the beginning therapist and a valuable resource for the experienced therapist. So I am not as dismayed as Dr. Messer about manuals, though I appreciate the merits of his points.

Regarding ESTs, I see their advent as the beginning of a process. As time goes on, a wider array of techniques will likely be empirically validated, while some will be seen for what they are: ineffective and even harmful. Contrary to Dr. Messer's concern that humanistic, dynamic, and experiential therapies will be left out, there is growing evidence to support such approaches; nevertheless, their manualization will require more creativity than has generally been shown by manual writers. I am optimistic that both humanity and rigorous evaluation can emerge, especially now that descriptive and qualitative methods have gained currency.

When I was a newly graduated MSW, I often feared that I did not have the skills for working on a hospital psych unit, even with the prescribed supervision. I steeped myself in technique, rightly believing that the more knowledge I had, the more I would be able to help my patients. As the years went by, I became more conscious of the importance of a therapist's personal attributes that activate his or her technical skill. As my skills became more natural and ingrained, I recognized I was growing in essential traits such as spontaneity, nondefensiveness, and an increased awareness of my clients' projections.

Eventually I reached the point of confidence in my skills and in my capacity to engage clients in a therapeutic alliance. Now I am less concerned about my abilities and more conscious of the clients' part in the therapeutic process. I find myself assessing a client's capacity to do the necessary work much more than wondering if I am up to it. This personal experience of the developmental process of becoming a therapist reflects some of the research Dr. Messer cites regarding the variance in therapy outcomes. Certainly the variance is accounted for very differently in seasoned versus novice therapists and in active versus passive clients.

I appreciated the careful account Dr. Messer provided regarding researchers' current findings about the personal qualities that might account for therapy outcome. I would have liked more discussion of the human dimensions the therapist and the client bring to the therapy. I found somewhat limited Dr. Messer's implication that there is a linear causality between the therapy and the therapist acting on the client, whether it be with an outcome or a process therapy.

I also found Dr. Messer's case study problematic. In describing the case of Jack, Dr. Messer seems to subscribe to the myth of therapist neutrality. In helping Jack decide whether to leave his wife for his lover, Dr. Messer says he approached the problem "in an impartial way." But his approach, in fact, was value-laden. By communicating to his client that either choice before him was valid, he implicitly promoted self-fulfillment no matter what the cost to others. One may not agree that a person should sometimes sacrifice his own fulfillment to honor vows and obligations to others, but one ought to realize that such an opinion is not neutral or objective.

According to Dr. Messer's case description, there was no DSM-IV disorder. But there was a moral disorder. Jack not only displayed chronic selfishness and narcissism, but his conduct constituted a form of abuse of his wife and children and of the integrity of the social order. The guilt he reported was appropriate and even healthy. Where did it go? If the fundamental unit of society, the family, can readily be disrupted by the sensual infatuations of husbands and fathers—or wives and mothers—with the blessing of psychotherapy, we are creating a society of narcissism wherein individuals' sense of entitlement reigns supreme, with the accompanying lack of empathy and concern for others.

I understand that Dr. Messer chose this case to illustrate the inadequacy of ESTs to address the dilemmas of many clients who seek therapy. But this case is not appropriate for payment of any mental health benefit by medical insurance. It would rightly be rejected by an insurance company and therefore any therapist involved in the case could use any approach he or she wished as long as the client could afford it. The client is not suffering from a psychological malady. He is struggling with a moral dilemma. Soliciting the help of a therapist to work through this dilemma might very well be a wise choice, but Jack should expect to pay for such help himself.

We have here in this brief case an example that not only challenges diagnostic practices and the new health maintenance organization (HMO) and EST regimens, but also challenges us to acknowledge the values that permeate pathology and change. I believe there is a place for ESTs; for process therapies; and, perhaps even more important, for moral therapies that take into account the inevitable links between psychic structure and social structure.

To return to the original query of his chapter—what's a nonbehaviorist to do?—Dr. Messer has given us an answer to his own dilemma: use brief psychodynamic therapy. Although this type of therapy can be applied to diverse diagnoses and also to non-*DSM-IV* diagnosed cases, such as his example, what about the pressure to use narrowly focused treatments for specific diagnoses? Then what is a nonbehaviorist or a behaviorist to do? That raises a multitude of questions for practitioners like me who are potentially open to ESTs (Arnow, 1999; Myers & Thyer, 1997):

1. Do therapists have an ethical obligation (even at times a legal obligation) to learn of and to treat their clients with ESTs?

2. How do we overcome our resistance to the perceived constraints of manualized therapy?

3. Do practicing clinicians lack exposure to the availability of manualized therapies?

4. Are there misconceptions regarding the perceived constraints of using these as guides for therapy?

5. Is there a lack of training opportunities in ESTs?

6. How long does it take to become competent in utilizing a manualized therapy? Is supervision available as there was in the clinical trials?

7. How can therapists respond to the proliferating number of manualized therapies? How do we choose? Are some of them junk?

8. How many specialties can we manage?

9. What do the managed care companies really expect? Do they care about quality of care or just about numbers—brief therapies and low payments to therapists?
10. Might this whole movement backfire because therapists become so overwhelmed by the demands of learning so many specialized therapies that out of sheer exhaustion they fall back on generic, less effective therapies to get by?
11. Do I really want to be a therapist?

References

Arnow, B. A. (1999). Why are empirically supported treatments for bulimia nervosa underutilized and what can we do about it? *Clinical Psychology, 55,* 769-779.

Letters: Recovered memories. (1999). *Social Work, 44,* 484-490.

Masterson, J. F. (1983). *Countertransference and therapeutic technique.* New York: Brunner/Mazel.

Myers, L. L., & Thyer, B. A. (1997). Should social work clients have the right to effective treatment? *Social Work, 42,* 288-298.

Stocks, J. T. (1998). Recovered memory therapy: A dubious practice technique. *Social Work, 43,* 423-436.

Stocks, J. T. (1999). Recovered memory therapy: Response to all. *Social Work, 44,* 491-499.

Issue 2

Assessment

Psychological Assessment

From Objectification Back to the Life World

Constance T. Fischer
Duquesne University

What is a chapter on psychological assessment doing in a book on psycho-therapy? Isn't psychological testing a decidedly separate endeavor from psychotherapy? Isn't testing supposed to yield data that other people use to make decisions about the testee? Indeed, aren't psychological evaluations widely criticized as not relevant to psychotherapy? The categories of the *Diagnostic and Statistical Manual of Mental Disorders* (*DSM-IV*; American Psychiatric Association, 1994) are totally independent of testing, so we don't need assessment for treatment, right? Moreover, doesn't clinical testing typically overemphasize pathology and often dehumanize the client in the process of collecting emitted and elicited responses?

Unfortunately, all of the above too often have been true. But a *shift in philosophy of science not only can allow psychological assessment to be relevant to psychotherapy; it can allow the assessment process to be therapeutic in its own right.* This approach to psychological assessment places priority on the life world—the everyday world in which we go about living, experiencing, conceptualizing, acting on, and being acted on. This realm of human involvement grows from our biological nature, but is not reducible to it.

Historically, in the absence of a sanctioned life-world orientation, our application of *natural science* methods to psychology too often has turned people into objects. A *human science* approach to psychology, however, can help to keep us in touch with our clients' richly human circumstances. In this chapter, I describe assessment practices in which clients participate as collaborators, try out alternative actions, and write commentaries on reports that individualize both descriptions and suggestions. I provide examples of the assessor exploring the contexts in which the client has and has not acted in certain ways, and of the assessor intervening in the client's habitual style to explore and to develop personally viable alternatives. At the close of the chapter, I address some issues that psychologists often have raised when hearing of these practices.

Natural Science and Human Science

We humans are objects like other objects *and* we are unlike other objects in that we also are subjects: We experience, reflect, plan, choose, and live always in relation to ourselves, others, and our environment. Laboratory methods are appropriate for studying our object nature, but other methods are also required to address the ways we relate to our world—the life world. About a century ago, when scholars were forming psychology into a discipline, they chose to model it after the natural sciences—the sciences of objects that obey the laws of nature. Those were exciting times in which the advances of the industrial revolution and of medicine forever changed culture and the way we think of ourselves. Early psychologists adopted the methods of the emerging natural sciences, despite pleas from philosophers such as Dilthey (1894/1977) that psychology should align itself with the sciences of spirit and mind (*geisteswissenschaften*), and of warnings from philosophers such as Husserl (1935-1937/1970) about the dangers of psychology becoming a technology. James's work on consciousness and religious experience (1902/1990) was underplayed, whereas his laboratory-oriented *Principles of Psychology* (1890/1983) became foundational for our discipline. Wundt's folk psychology (1912/1928) was largely ignored, while his laboratory explorations (e.g., 1874/1910) led to his being named the father of experimental psychology. Although psychology as a human science is one of the "new ideas" that this volume highlights, its forefathers go back to such major philosophers as Dilthey; Husserl (1913/1962); Heidegger (1927/1962); and, more recently, Merleau-Ponty (1945/1962) and Ricouer (1950/1966).

By now mainstream psychology has proved itself as a rigorous science and as a valuable contributor to the quality of life. That very success has allowed psychologists to relax a bit and to consider that nevertheless our research methods and many of our applications have not explicitly taken into account the subject qualities of being human—agency, consciousness, and so on. Psychology conceived as a human science (Giorgi, 1970) can attend to both the subject and object character of being human (Fischer, 1977); that is, although psychologists may also make use of traditional data, methods, and related theories, they do not have to pretend to ignore the role of empathy, values, choice, and so on.

In other words, psychologists who work within a human science frame address the life world, where we go about living, carrying our pasts into our futures. The life world is where we live in relation with whatever we attend to, at various stages and kinds of awareness. Psychologists who work within a human science orientation acknowledge that our efforts to find order in our lives, and in those of others, are necessarily perspectival—from our biographies, historical times and cultures, assumptions, values, interests, curiosities, avenues. As humans we can only know in human ways; we cannot uncover a nonperspectival, universal Truth. Thus, as researchers, therapists, or assessors working within a human science frame, our goals are not the old ones of approximating an independent reality, nor of explanation and prediction, but rather of developing consensual understandings and options for action. Our methods are rigorous and objective, but they do not *object*ify the client.

Human Science Psychological Assessment Practices: Back to the Life World

The Psychology Department at Duquesne University, since the 1960s, has developed philosophical foundations and research and clinical practices that address people as being subjects as well as objects. Our early work was grounded in European existential and phenomenological philosophy, and our later work has drawn on additional contemporary post-Enlightenment philosophy. Note that psychologists who work within a general human science frame draw on, and sometimes inform, many theories and research literatures. It has been with graduate students and colleagues at Duquesne that I developed a collaborative, individualized approach to psychological assessment.

When engaging in psychological assessment, I anticipate being able to describe patterns relevant to the purposes of the assessment, but I do not undertake to explain in terms of traits, categories, or causes. My work is radically empirical, however, in the original meaning: All evidence is directly available to the senses, not probabilistic or deductive. Life events are the primary data, which I explore in part through the tools of scores, research data, personality categories, and related theory. Our findings are not scores or categories, but rather are revised understandings, in relation to specific questions, of how the person has been going through life; findings include personally viable alternative pathways that the person might take. The assessment's life world orientation allows the client to participate actively throughout the assessment.

The following guiding principles and practices imply each other and often overlap. (For their philosophical grounding, see Fischer, 1979, 1998a; for the first publication calling for collaborative assessment, see Fischer, 1970; for an overview of progress, see Fischer, in press; for a how-to textbook with many examples and sample reports, see Fischer, 1985/1994.) Although there are legitimate occasions for conducting fairly cut-and-dried assessments, as in some of those for classification, collaborating with the client and individualizing reports to whatever extent feasible is always productive.

Collaborate and Contextualize

When I receive a referral from another party, I ask for the circumstances that led to the referral. For example, the request, "Provide assistance in differentiating impulse disorder from borderline personality disorder" turns out to have arisen from an intake worker's wondering whether to refer the person ("Mr. Smith") to a behavior modification group or to a therapist with an object relations orientation. Those particular options arose in light of the interviewer's noting a history of work terminations due to insistent challenges to supervisors. Mr. Smith had come to the mental health agency wanting medication for "nerves"—which the interviewer indicated to me meant being fearful of being fired again, having trouble sleeping, feeling uncharacteristically despondent about how others were viewing him, and being "paranoid" about bosses.

When Mr. Smith and I met, I described the above background that had been presented to me and asked for elaborations and corrections. I explained the two proposed diagnoses in terms of typical histories of growing up and of related current difficulties, and I explained their relation to the goals of the two therapy options. We also read the *DSM* criteria together. He already understood that medication decisions would be delayed while assessment and psychotherapy got under way. In response to my asking what else he might be interested in exploring as we went through the assessment, Mr. Smith eventually asked if it would be possible to learn anything about why other people say he is an angry person when in fact he is earnest and hardworking.

I asked for examples of his "challenges" to supervisors and for examples of times when he had "gone along" (his words) despite harboring doubts about administrators' wisdom. We came to some tentative formulations. Later, while sharing my impressions of the Minnesota Multiphasic Personality Inventory (MMPI) with him, I mentioned that his pattern (high K, L, naivéte scales) was like that of persons who are idealistic and who want the world to be a just place. He readily agreed, but said that other people often saw his idealism as rigidity. From examples that he provided, we agreed that he has been more relaxed about maintaining his standards when he has understood what I called "the big picture," including other persons' goals and their related tactics.

I also mentioned that his high scale 4 sometimes reflects a strategy that a person has developed to deal with inconsistent parenting—just breaking out and "doing it my way." He agreed that he had not been able to predict when either parent would be critical and punitive, but at that point he did not see any relation to his challenging or to being seen as angry.

During the Bender-Gestalt (for which the client copies nine geometric designs freehand), Mr. Smith hunched over his work, drew with dark lines, erased and sighed frequently, and took longer than most people to complete the designs. As he shoved the paper toward me and declared that if I wanted him to do his best I should have let him use a ruler, I felt as though he were both judging himself negatively and somehow blaming me. We sat in silence for a bit, and then I mentioned that actually his renderings were remarkably accurate. He sat up, and said, "Really?" I reassured him, but also mentioned that while he was working on the figures I had not realized what a good job he was doing; I explained that I had been distracted by his intensity and by what I experienced as his resenting my insisting that he follow standard instructions. He acknowledged being uncomfortable about my watching him as he worked and eventually recounted instances in which he had resented supervisors' looking over his shoulder. We found that he had not been resentful when supervisors had nodded at him while watching or when he knew that they generally approved of his work or would give him reasonable, constructive suggestions.

I mentioned that I had found myself kind of bracing in the face of what seemed like his being hostile, even though I also thought he was being even harder on himself. At first he said it was my problem if I thought he was hostile when actually it was he who was under attack. Then we agreed that perhaps we had stumbled onto an example of someone (me, in this instance) experiencing him as angry when he felt he was just working hard under duress. Later, after Mr. Smith had been working on the Digit Symbol subtest of the Wechsler intelligence scale, he acknowledged that he had wanted to wish me out of existence so that he could work in peace. We then agreed that annihilating me could indeed be seen as angry or hostile!

I acknowledged that my impression was quite the opposite when I accidentally dropped blocks from the Wechsler on the floor and Mr. Smith readily retrieved them for me and carefully placed them within my reach but away from the edge of the table. We then spoke of the many other occasions when he feels close to other people, nondefensive, and so on, and we explored what these occasions had in common.

Note that we used test material and score patterns as bridges into Mr. Smith's everyday life. Concrete situations allowed me to witness relevant events and allowed him to recall structurally similar events from other situations. My knowledge of personality and test patterns guided my explorations, but our understandings were based on actual life events—those occurring between us and those that Mr. Smith reported. Note also that my expertise was applied to understanding his life, in regard to the issues presented, and not to fitting him into categories. The assessment process has not treated him as an object or explained his behavior as pathologically driven, as outside his ken and control. Later, concrete examples like those above would appear in a written report; readers—Mr. Smith, the intake worker, the therapist, the prescribing physician—would all be in touch with the same examples rather than interpreting jargon in diverse ways, and in that process losing touch with Mr. Smith. Please also note that we have begun to see the relevance of the diagnostic options (impulse control, borderline personality disorder), even as we also see that such categories are extremely limited in helping us to understand and work with Mr. Smith.

Intervene

As we explore the presented issues via assessment materials, I am likely to interrupt my own procedures, as well as the client's taken-for-granted style of dealing with situations. I usually intervene at the *end* of a Bender, a Thematic Apperception Test (TAT) card, or a Wechsler subtest. I wait until that point so that both of us have a sense of process and so that I have samples to compare with others that were gathered in a standardized manner.

During a second assessment session, Mr. Smith's TAT stories had to do with people competing, ignoring each other, and trying to stay out of one another's way. I handed him a card (10) showing what is most usually seen as an older man and woman in an embrace or dancing closely. Mr. Smith began, "Well, there's a man and a woman . . ."; I interrupted, quietly, but with a teasing tone, "They only look close, they couldn't possibly be sharing an intimate moment— they're probably competing, or just ignoring each other!" We sat in silence for several minutes, Mr. Smith seeming to be musing. I asked, softly, "*Can* you imagine these people being in touch with each other, caring about one another?" In our ensuing discussion, Mr. Smith spoke of his ambivalence as he had pondered possible stories for the card; he explained to me that he wanted to tell a story of mutual comforting but that other story lines quickly inserted themselves—story lines having to do with one person feeling close while the other secretly derided the first person. We fell silent again, and then I suggested that he must often feel lonely, yearning for closeness but ultimately opting for the safety of distance. He nodded, his eyes welling.

As implied in this TAT example, the purposes of intervening are (a) for me to try out and revise my evolving hunches, (b) for the client to discover habitual assumptions and actions and their impact, (c) for us to explore viable options rather than stopping with identification of present patterns, and (d) for us then to identify "landmarks" that the client can use to sense that a change in course is called for. Intervention allows us to try out alternative client comportment until we find actions and styles that are personally viable. We tailor options by redoing a task, such as telling a TAT story, and by role-playing related life situations.

Here are some examples of intervention and exploration with other clients:

On the Rorschach, Harriet had hesitatingly reported a fight between two bears who were both injured. On the next card, instead of the usual humans cooperating on ordinary tasks, she reported, "Warriors from another planet; they make me laugh—they're too stupid to know that they're hermaphrodites." I pointed out a similar sequence with other cards and asked her what she already knew about a pattern of running from being afraid or from being in touch with the danger of being injured and then trying to hide through being silly, voicing put-downs, and so on. Harriet readily provided examples within her family and her personal relationships. We used life instances and the Rorschach instances to help her to recognize landmarks that could indicate that she had entered frightening territory. She could then look for turnoff points to change course if she found herself veering into silliness or offensiveness. One landmark she identified was an inclination to convert her fearfully tightened lips into a sneer. We agreed that she might then purposively transform the coming sneer into an expression of determination to stay her course while checking out whether she was indeed in dangerous territory. (Fischer, 1998a, pp. 467-468)

Another example:

When I asked Ms. Seale if she had questions of her own, she said that she wondered if we could find out why she is slower than workmates at learning new procedures. We then used tests to explore when and how she has been slow. We found through a Wechlser Adult Intellegence Scale–Revised (WAIS-R) subtest (Digit Symbol) and the Bender-Gestalt that Ms. Seale has waited for others to take initiative when she has felt that *"they* are supposed to be in charge." Whether from supervisor, therapist, or assessor, she had waited for instruction rather than either asking for clarification or jumping in to try out her hunches. We discovered that she also had been slow to act in other unfamiliar circumstances, finding herself afraid that she might be criticized. We also identified what I refer to as *when nots* of this problematic style—times when she adopted a nonproblematic approach: Ms. Seale reported that she "rough-houses" with her little nephews, argues with her younger sister, and has initiated new arrangements of the candy bars in the movie theater where she clerks. By looking into life contexts, we discovered some ways in which Ms. Seale surpasses, as well as exemplifies, her therapist's characterization of her as being "passive-dependent." Then, through role-playing revised beginnings of the Digit Symbol subtest, the Bender, and a therapy session, we developed starting points through which she could ask me and her therapist for clarification and could even venture her opinions. Ms. Seale spontaneously noted that from now on, when she uses the same active approach in her job setting, she no longer will be slower than all her office mates to learn new tasks. (Fischer, 2000, p. 5)

The following excerpt from discussion with a client begins with a hunch from her Rorschach (low Afr, and zd $= -4$):

Assessor: From some of your scores, I wondered if you have often avoided complex or emotional situations.

Client: No, that's *not* it!—What it *is*, is that I have the *courage to hang in.* I just choose something to hold on to 'til I get through the situation.

Assessor: Like you pressed so hard on your pencil but didn't check back against the card [Bender-Gestalt]? (Client nods slowly). So what we called "being determined" is also a way of keeping things simple, of getting through?

Client (after a long pause, then laughing): Like a horse with blinders plodding straight ahead! (Fischer, 2000, p. 4)

Similar past situations become available to the client in ways that interviewing alone could not afford. The use of assessment instruments allows *both* client and assessor to observe the person's going about an activity. Here is another example:

> Ms. Rose had wanted to know if we might discover how it was that her boss gave her low performance ratings for efficiency, although she gets more done than anyone else in the office by the end of the day. As I watched her copy the Bender designs, I wondered if my reaction was similar to that of her boss. Ms. Rose looked at each design for a good while, stretched, then held her pencil lightly with one hand and anchored the paper with just two fingers of the other. She drew parallel lines for the square, then half the circle, then finished the box, then the circle. She continued in her unorthodox manner through the nine designs. She never looked at me, and never looked back at the stimulus card after first observing it. When she had finished the designs, I was astounded to see that they were geometrically precise and neat, and that she had finished in considerably less than the average time. We laughed together as she realized that she similarly has created her own world in the busy office, where others can't see what she's up to as she does things out of order, stretches, seems oblivious to the clock, and so on; others hadn't noticed the nicely completed projects among the part projects arranged on her desk. Through our work, Ms. Rose already was finding that she could make sense of her circumstance; she had discovered how she had been contributing to others' perceptions of her. We then role-played doing the Bender again with her making comments that allowed me to know what she was doing and that she was indeed following directions. She remarked later that she was now "liberated" to both be herself and to win the approval of her boss. (Fischer, 1998a, p. 467)

Individualize Reports and Records

I next describe several forms of reports. All of them are intended to continue to affirm the client as an active agent, sometimes self-defeating, but also capable of changing course. As during the assessment, the reports focus on actual situations, whether from the assessment or reported from the client's larger life. The forms and styles sampled below will seem common*sensical*, but they are still not *common*. The traditional report format still prevails, with the assessor referred to in third person, if at all, and "results" being scores, categories, diagnoses, and unilateral advice. The latter typically is based on logical deduction from those results, for example, "This student's distractibility requires a structured environment," or "Indicators of psychotic functioning suggest referral for psychotropic medication." These suggestions may be solid as far as they go, but they are not yet about an individual and do not indicate particular ways the client and helper can pursue them.

First, I present some general principles of individualized writing that we follow in our assessment courses at Duquesne University. We write with verbs, in active voice, to evoke the person moving through the world; action language also evokes background context as the reader pictures the person in the described action. Past tense keeps readers mindful that previously habitual actions may be modified in the future. We also write in the first person, both to help the reader to imagine a concrete assessment situation and to own our personal participation in the impressions that emerged. For example, we might write, "While copying Bender designs, Ursula held the pen so firmly that twice she broke the lead, re-marking each time that she was just trying to 'get it right.' Later we noted the similarity to her children having complained that she has been 'heavy handed' with them as she tried to be a responsible parent." Compare those sentences with a previous finding: "The employee's forcefulness and controlling personal-ity do not suit her for supervisory responsibility."

Here is another example:

> As the Comprehension subtest items became more difficult, Mr. Schwartz pulled his chair back and wordlessly stared at me. I felt a bit intimidated, even fleetingly wondering if I really had to complete the Wechsler. Later, when we discussed the pertinence of his 4-6-9 MMPI constellation, Mr. Schwartz volunteered that he *has* frequently been called hostile, angry, and suspicious.

Note that here personality constructs were useful in the assessment process, but our "results" were actual life incidents to which the constructs helped us to gain access.

In writing reports, we take special care in selecting examples. Our criteria are relevance to presented issues and likelihood of evoking similar happenings from readers' lives—through which they understand the descriptions. We also take care to include examples of "when nots" of problematic comportment. For example, although at times I had been intimidated by Mr. Schwartz, at other times I found him to be considerate and helpful. The latter occasions are valu-able as places into which he could pivot from problematic stances. Including when nots in reports reminds all parties that the client can move into promising places and that "treatment plans" should be customized accordingly. To that end, we often organize reports by dynamic themes, for example, "Diego Pro-tecting Himself," "Diego Protecting Underdogs," and "Diego Trusting Himself and Others."

By asking clients to read and then to write comments on our reports, we in-crease client involvement, keep ourselves honest, and clarify for one another. Reports specify issues about which the client and the assessor ultimately agreed to disagree.

Report formats vary with intended readers. Some reports are letters to the client. We sometimes write fables for children which remind both parents and children of what we learned. Other reports follow a traditional format of describing explorations and findings, and may include diagnoses and technical appendixes with test profiles for psychologist readers. Sometimes we wait to write a report until we can summarize what was agreed to by client, therapist, and assessor in a joint meeting at which therapy goals were discussed in light of the assessment.

Here is an excerpt from a letter to a young woman, which summarized the understandings we came to in regard to her questions about how it could be that other people often see her as seductive and self-centered and at other times as vulnerable. The excerpt from the letter contains the section addressing being seen as self-centered and a summary with action suggestions.

> *Self-centered?* This characterization has come up when you've been into "do-ing things my way." We talked about such instances in relation to your unique way of going about copying the Bender designs. We discovered that it is when other people don't see where you're going, when you leave them out of what you're up to, that they may experience you as being self-cen-tered. However, you certainly care a lot about many other people (for exam-ple, I recall your crying at one point when expressing concern for members of your family).
>
> In my office, we talked about your understanding that you had had to form your standards and values very early in childhood, and that you have held others as well as yourself to black and white standards of conduct. You have handled complexity with agility (I think of how you accommo-dated your posture to the newly complex last block design). But you haven't liked ambiguity much at all—you have expected others to behave in certain exacting ways. Hence your impatience with teachers who didn't understand the bell curve, with waitresses who didn't know the routine, etc. We laughed in my office as you resisted my suggestions that other people live in their worlds, and that our standards for ourselves may not make sense for them. Not leaving room for other people's standards as legitimate for them, even if not what you choose for yourself, can indeed be seen as self-centered.
>
> *So what?* Of course you want to continue to be you! That's not an issue. However, when you're concerned about someone perceiving you as being seductive, intimidating, or self-centered, you might want to pause to con-sider our understandings of what may be going on in those instances. Most often, if it matters to you, you might then opt to slow down, to let the other person know where you're gong, much as you explained to me what you were doing on one of the assessment tasks (was it the TAT—the pictures about which you told stories?). On other occasions, you might want to slow down to consider more about the other person's life circumstance (not un-like your sensitivity to your family and to your learning-disabled kids), and to consider how his or her choices make a certain sense in that circumstance. *Landmarks for considering a slowdown or a change in your course include moments when you're beginning to feel righteously judgmental or insistent on Your way.* One alternate route would be to bypass your impulse for the moment, and ask yourself if who you are is really at risk in the situation; usually you'll dis-cover that nobody's in your way, and that the bypass gets you along your way quite efficiently and with less disruption.

Note that we see in this excerpt, as well as in earlier ones, that first-person reference to the assessor's involvement and to the dyadic nature of the assess-ment reminds all readers of the life-world context in which the reported under-standings evolved. These references also remind us that to be most useful, an as-sessment report should pose suggestions in terms of pivot points in the client's life-world travels.

The following excerpt is from the end of a fable that Michele Julin and Kathleen Gaydos (then graduate students) wrote to accompany their report on school-referred 6-year-old Bobby and his mom. The lioness is his school teacher, the flighty bird is his mom, and the baby elephant is Bobby. The title of the fable is "The Jabby Jungle"; Bobby had used the word "jabby" several times during the Wechlser to indicate something that could hurt him.

> The baby elephant needed the little bird whenever he left his friends and the lioness. He looked to the little bird to help him remember the rules he had learned from the lioness, because little baby elephants can't always remember.
>
> But the baby elephant would often be confused and not know quite where the flighty little bird could be. Sometimes the little bird was perched on his back so lightly that baby didn't even know it. One day the baby elephant wanted the little bird to guide him, and got so confused that he threw his head back and trumpeted as loud as he could, and stomped and stamped, shaking his jungle home, so that she would know where he was and that he was lost and needed help. Usually when he did this the little bird gave him some peanuts to calm him down or flew away for a little while. But this time, instead flying away or giving him peanuts, she flew in front of him where he could see her. The little bird looked at the bright-eyed baby elephant and noticed that he was not so big. A baby elephant is strong, but the little bird had realized how important she was to him and how he depended on her to guide him firmly through the jabby jungle. She had lived in the jungle longer and the baby elephant trusted her to see ahead for him. The little bird saw that she should be a guide in front of him on the tip of his trunk, so that he could listen to her and follow her. (Fischer, 1985/1994, p 209)

Other sample reports from a wide range of settings also are available in Fischer (1985/1994).

Questions and Clarifications

Question: I can see how this approach manages not to objectify the person in the negative sense of treating the person as an object whose actions are determined by external or underlying forces, but how is the positive sense of scientific objectivity assured? *Response:* Descriptions and suggestions are based not on one person's perspective, but rather are objective in that they are based on documented observations (scores, behaviors, self-reports) that are open to questioning by other professionals, as well as by the client. Individualized assessment practices are as rigorous as laboratory traditions in specifying project goals, access, and context in relation to findings. They are more objective than traditional test-oriented reports in meeting the original demand of objectivity: being able to point to evidence observable in life rather than in subjective impressions alone or in theory or constructs. I might also mention in this regard that the method of "clinical inference" within a human scientific frame is likewise more objective in the classic meaning of being anchored to reality rather than to theory or subjectivity:

Rather than relying heavily on mathematical theory and logical deduction or on the constructs of a particular personality theory, individualized assessment moves hermeneutically among direct observation, reported history, understandings of life contexts, test scores, recollections of other clients and personal acquaintances, personality theory, client opinions, research data, and so on, back and forth and around, repeatedly, until each has informed the other and the evolved understanding of the client's life world is coherent.

Question: But what about validity? How can you demonstrate that your approach is valid when it doesn't lend itself to statistical verification? *Response:* The appropriate study would be one that addresses outcome satisfaction. There are such studies, for example, Finn and Tonsager (1992), which documents client satisfaction with MMPI feedback, even when that feedback includes negative information. Actually, individualized assessment meets a strong test of validity— whether concrete suggestions based on the assessment prove to be successful. This practical validity does not pretend to once-and-for-all accuracy, but rather assumes that the findings are a progress report—a report of progress to date. Client and helpers will continue to revise understandings and actions in light of how the suggestions fare and in light of inevitably changing circumstances. The life world is always in flux.

Question: What you have said here about human science is not all that different either from other social sciences, or even some neurophysiological views, or from the way some mental health professionals practice, is it? *Response:* That is right. Most of our graduate programs continue, however, to train in terms of an at least implicit model of materialism, realism, and positivism (Truth is knowable, and is ultimately about material, countable characteristics). Hence many graduates are hesitant to practice outside of this model of science. Individualized, collaborative practices often are regarded as compassionate add-ons, but not as psychology as such. Thinking through our philosophical assumptions may allow practitioners to more systematically expand their own individualized and collaborative efforts. One way or another, practitioners are increasingly open to this approach. For example, Stephen Finn and his colleagues (Finn, 1996; Finn & Tonsager, 1997) explicitly pursue collaborative assessment at their Center for Therapeutic Assessment in Austin, Texas, where managed care companies not only pay psychotherapy rates for the practice but also refer clients for therapeutic assessment.

Question: But isn't this approach appropriate only for articulate, reflective, fairly well-functioning clients? *Response:* No. Once common ground and contexts are established and the client understands that he or she will participate as a consultant about his or her own life, the process works in most assessment situations. The assessor does have to work harder to be present to and to explore the client's life world rather than "just" to gather responses to instruments and interviews. But of course, as with any approach to assessment, the same clients are more difficult to work with collaboratively, for example, many forensic cases, and other persons who do not willingly come to the assessment, and persons who are limited intellectually and verbally. Still, to whatever degree the process is individualized, to that degree we have a better understanding of the particular person.

Question: With emphasis on description of comportment rather than on scores and categories, aren't human-science assessment reports awfully long and time consuming and hence not cost-effective? *Response:* Descriptive reports indeed often are longer and, I think, more demanding to compose. Even when that is the case, however, because all participants (client, assessor, other readers) are "on the same page," they can address the same events with similar understandings, which goes a long way toward cost-effectiveness. In addition, the assessment process also includes tailored suggestions that the client regards as viable and the client and helper can continue to tailor the suggestions in response to trying them out. Moreover, when the emphasis of reports is on outcome (understandings and individualized suggestions) rather than on test-based development of conclusions, then reports can be brief, mostly itemizing the agreed-on suggestions. In fact, Stephen Finn (at the Center for Therapeutic Assessment in Austin) and Patricia Piercy (a Pittsburgh colleague) have been conducting collaborative custody evaluations and finding that the process is less contentious than usual, that the report can be considerably briefer than the usual sort that documents at length the grounds for findings, and that the need for further court hearings is obviated.

Question: This practice of assessment does seem growthful for clients. Do you distinguish collaborative assessment from psychotherapy? *Response:* Yes. This approach is therapeutic, much as short-term therapy is—clients come to recognize habitual patterns as no longer being necessary, and they try out alternatives. Even when the assessment concludes, for example, that a person is indeed neurologically compromised, maximal viable alternative problem-solving approaches are identified. But longer-term psychotherapy allows for fuller exploration of one's history and relation to families; it allows fuller use of the interpersonal nature of psychotherapy; it allows for deeper and fuller self-discovery, integration, and so on. Psychologists at the Center for Therapeutic Assessment find, however, that clients not only self-refer, but frequently return for further exploration via review of prior assessment findings or for further collaborative assessment.

Question: Are you sure these practices are ethical? If they're not widely taught, are they truly professional? *Response:* Yes, the practices are well grounded in philosophy, are empirical (they make use both of norms and research and of direct observations of comportment), and are accountable. The sources of findings are clear, and the suggestions are concrete, testable, and revisable. Beyond that, human science practices encourage fulfillment of the American Psychological Association's (APA) code of ethics: ("Psychologists ensure that an explanation of the results is provided using language that is reasonably understandable to the person assessed or to another legally authorized person on behalf of the client"; 1992, §2.09)

Emphasis on attending to context also encourages adherence to APA's (1990) *Guidelines for Providers of Services to Ethnic, Linguistic, and Culturally*

Diverse Populations. More to the point: Professional ethics are our consensus of how our practices will be moral; morality has to do with attending to the well-being of the other and of community. We attend to the well-being of our clients when we engage them as active participants in understanding and revising their lives. For that matter, morale is related to morality; for both client and assessor, collaborative assessment enhances well-being in the form of self-assurance, self-respect, and enthusiasm. This good morale is not always the case when we have to administer batteries of tests; submit technical reports; and give feedback in terms of traits, categories, and the normal distribution.

Question: The excerpts from assessment sound commonsensical; is special training required to engage in collaborative, individualized assessment? *Response*: Many people are finding their own ways of revising the practices we were taught, and we learn from one another. In my department, which follows a scholar-practitioner model of training, we try to optimize human science assessment training through several means. Students take the tests that they administer, so that they experience something akin to what clients experience and realize how the instruments limit and guide responses. We encourage exploration of philosophy, arts, the classics, and expressive writing as avenues to understanding human dilemmas and possibility. We encourage attunement to cultural, economic, and familial contexts by requiring that some assessments be conducted in clients' homes. Students often work in teams to share perspectives, consult on choice of examples, and offer moral support. Through all assessment courses, we ask ourselves what in the client's actual life the test constellations might point to (see Fischer, 1998b, for a life world approach to teaching the Rorschach). We draw on life world research as well as on experimental/statistical research in our efforts to understand clients. As mentioned, students practice staying in life world frames by discussing assessment findings and implications conjointly with the client and therapist. Again and again, we find that until we can address our assessment findings directly with clients and clients' helpers; we literally do not yet know "what in the world" we are talking about!

Refrain

Giving philosophical priority to the life world allows us to be more directly relevant and helpful to our clients. Within a human science framework, the assessment process itself can be transformative, and subsequent psychotherapy and other efforts to serve can be individualized with and for the client.

References

American Psychological Association. (1990). *Guidelines for providers of services to ethnic, linguistic, and culturally diverse populations.* Washington, DC: Author.

American Psychological Association. (1992). Ethical principals and code of conduct. *American Psychologist, 47,* 1597-1611.

American Psychiatric Association. (1994). *Diagnostic and statistical manual of mental disorders* (4th ed.). Washington, DC: Author.

Dilthey, W. (1977). *Descriptive psychology and historical understanding* (R. Zaner & K. Heigas, Trans.). The Hague: Nijhoff. (Original work published 1894)

Finn, S. E. (1996). *Manual for using the MMPI-2 as a therapeutic intervention.* Minneapolis: University of Minnesota Press.

Finn, S. E., & Tonsager, M. E. (1992). The therapeutic effects of providing MMPI-2 test feedback to college students awaiting psychotherapy. *Psychological Assessment: A Journal of Consulting and Clinical Psychology, 4,* 278-287.

Finn, S. E., & Tonsager, M. E. (1997). Information-gathering and therapeutic models of assessment: Complementary paradigms. *Psychological Assessment, 9,* 374-385.

Fischer, C. T. (1970). The testee as co-evaluator. *Journal of Counseling Psychology, 17,* 70-76.

Fischer, C. T. (1977). Historical relations of psychology as an object-science and subject-science: Toward psychology as a human-science. *Journal of the History of the Behavioral Sciences, 13,* 369-378.

Fischer, C. T. (1979). Individualized assessment and phenomenological psychology. *Journal of Personality Assessment, 43,* 115-122.

Fischer, C. T. (1994). *Individualizing psychological assessment.* Mahwah, NJ: Lawrence Erlbaum. (Original work published 1985)

Fischer, C. T. (1998a). Phenomenological, existential, and humanistic foundations for psychology as a human science. In M. Hersen & A. Bellack (Eds.), *Comprehensive clinical psychology,* C. E. Walker (Ed.), Vol. 1: *Foundations* (pp. 449-472). London: Elsevier Science.

Fischer, C. T. (1998b). The Rorschach and the life-world. In L. Handler & M. Hilsenroth (Eds.), *Teaching and learning personality assessment* (pp. 347-358). Hillsdale, NJ: Lawrence Erlbaum.

Fischer, C. T. (2000). Individualized, collaborative assessment: Practices and foundations. *Journal of Personality Assessment, 74*(1), 2-14.

Giorgi, A. (1970). *Psychology as a human science: A phenomenological approach.* New York: Harper & Row.

Heidegger, M. (1962). *Being and time* (J. Macquarrie & E. Robinson, Trans.). London: SMC Press. (Original work published 1927)

Husserl, E. (1962). *Ideas: General introduction to pure phenomenology* (W. R. Boyce Gibson, Trans.). New York: Collier. (Original work published 1913)

Husserl, E. (1970). *The crisis of European sciences and transcendental phenomenology* (D. Carr, Trans.). Evanston, IL: Northwestern University Press. (Original work published 1935-1937)

James, W. (1983). *Principles of psychology* (2 vols.). Cambridge, MA: Harvard University Press. (Original work published 1890)

James, W. (1990). *The varieties of religious experience.* New York: Vintage Books. (Original work published 1902)

Merleau-Ponty, M. (1962) *The phenomenology of perception* (C. Smith, Trans.). New York: Humanities Press. (Original work published 1945)

Ricouer, P. (1966). *Freedom and nature: The voluntary and involuntary* (E. Kohak, Trans.). Evanston, IN: Northwestern University Press. (Original work published 1950)

Wundt, W. (1910). *Principles of physiological psychology* (E. B. Titchener, Trans.). New York: Macmillan. (Original work published 1874)

Wundt, W. (1928). *Elements of folk psychology* (E. L. Schaub, Trans.). New York: Macmillan. (Original work published 1912)

Commentary

Collaborative Psychological Assessment: Becoming Psychological Hermeneuts

Stevan Lars Nielsen
Brigham Young University

Given Dr. Fischer's title, which contemplated the goal of moving psychological assessment "from objectification back to the life world," I anticipated an antiscientific bias at odds with traditional psychometrics. Happily, my skepticism was misplaced. Her suggestions present an understandable, practical, and compelling approach to day-to-day psychological practice with application beyond the specific example she describes of collaborative assessment with psychotherapy clients. I anticipated an antiscientific bias because I was formerly afflicted with strong antiscientific, antipsychometric biases myself when I was introduced to psychological assessment during my first year of graduate school. I remember wanting to get on with something more important, such as learning and doing psychotherapy. Psychological assessment seemed an unnecessary evil. But I misjudged the intent of Dr. Fischer's title and her goal of integrating psychological assessment with psychotherapy.

My own view of psychological assessment changed when I went into practice and discovered a wide group of willing consumers who wanted psychological assessments—*and were willing to pay for* psychological assessments. In addition to the surprise of willing consumers with money came sobering realizations about the sometimes weighty consequences of psychological assessment. Most of my current assessment practice consists of forensic evaluations to which judges attend when deciding whether defendants are competent to proceed to trial or should remain in custody at our state hospital.

I came to this project unfamiliar with Dr. Fischer's work on assessment (see Fischer, 1985, 1992, 1998b) and her perspectives on qualitative, humanistic, and existential elements of psychotherapy and psychological research (see Fischer, 1998a, 1999). I am delighted to say that as I became more familiar I have discovered an approach that is both humanistic and scientific. I agree with Dr. Fischer's contention that a collaborative approach is most likely to benefit clients. I propose that it yields a common ground on which both psychometrically oriented test developers *and* decidedly humanistic, existentially oriented psychotherapists may stand together. A key benefit from the collaborative approach is that the science of psychometrics is preserved. I believe that collaborative assessment is one of the clearest manifestations I have yet seen of a hermeneutical approach to psychological practice.

Collaborative Assessment as Client-Centered Hermeneutics

Dr. Fischer's description of collaborative assessment suggested that we who do psychological assessment are, like it or not, aware of our role or not, in the role of hermeneuts translating our obscure psychological doctrines to willing and unwilling proselytes. Furthermore, the approach she describes is neither mundane nor highly controversial, but rather stimulating and full of potential reward as an expansion from the necessarily scientific world of psychometrics to our own life worlds as practitioners.

Dr. Fischer's description of collaborating with Mr. Smith is one important example of how psychological assessment might be interpretive. It describes a mutual, bidirectional learning process applicable to communicating about psychological assessment in many other contexts. The translation was bidirectional, Dr. Fischer to Mr. Smith and Mr. Smith to Dr. Fischer. The collaboratory communication from Mr. Smith to Dr. Fischer provided her with important tacit understanding (see Polanyi, 1962) of his world, which clarified her interpretation, which improved her understanding, which clarified her interpretation, and so forth. Mr. Smith's life world was a vital part of the assessment picture. Really skilled interpreters work to become so familiar with the culture of those with whom they work that they step at least partially into and become part of the cultures involved. Collaboration as Dr. Fischer describes it required that she step into Mr. Smith's life world. This mutual interpretative process may vary greatly depending on clients and context; clients and context establish the hermeneutical problem.

I stumbled into an understanding of this with court testimony about my use of the Rorschach Inkblot Technique (Exner, 1993; Rorschach, 1942). I had been asked by the court to evaluate a defendant's competency to stand trial. It was my opinion, in part because of results from the Rorschach Inkblot Technique, that the defendant was competent to stand trial. I had been warned by the prosecuting attorney that the defense attorney would likely mount an aggressive attack on my expertise and testimony. The defense attorney asked about the procedures I used and almost immediately asked if my use of the

Rorschach was "really any different from use of Tarot cards or reading tea leaves?" I got my Rorschach cards and I said something like this,

> We know from having shown this image many, many times that about 70% of those who look at this ink blot report seeing a butterfly or a bat. Frequently reported images like these are called "popular responses." If someone reports seeing an average number of these popular images, it suggests that the person is able to appreciate reality as most people see it. The defendant reported seeing a bat when he looked at this card and reported seeing five other popular images on other cards. Reporting six images is average.

As I explained that about 70% of examinees see a bat or butterfly in the card I presented to the jury, all eight members of the jury nodded; five or six jury members smiled. The defense attorney noticed their smiling and nodding agreement and immediately changed the subject. I had stumbled into an important realization about the hermeneutics of psychological assessment: Interpreting clearly to the client accounts for most of the successful outcome in any psychological assessment. In this case the client was the jury. Jury members' responses to my explanation dramatized the importance of interpreting to the client at hand. The goal in court as well as during collaborative assessment as described by Dr. Fischer is clear translation and effective interpretation.

I am a willing convert to the collaborative model proposed by Dr. Fischer. I close with a cautionary note, although not by way of disagreement: The culture of psychological assessment, including but not limited to psychometric science, has important rules the violation of which yield invalid and potentially unethical counterfeits to psychological assessment. Many elements of psychological assessment cannot be tied directly to psychometric science, such as impressions about nonverbal elements of the client's behavior, judgments about grooming and verbal fluency, the client's willingness to cooperate, and so forth. Nonetheless, what can be tied to psychometrics should be tied to psychometrics. Psychological assessment should, additionally, be guided and controlled by the formal doctrines set forth in ethical principles and codified in ethical rules. Some of these principles and rules are themselves tied to psychometric principles. Most such rules have their foundation in core values espoused by governing organizations (see the American Psychological Association's "Ethical Principles of Psychologists and Code of Conduct," 1992).

Let me return briefly to the example of my court testimony. I interpreted results from the Rorschach Inkblot Technique to the jury based on simple, scientifically derived psychometric information. It was information of known reliability and validity. It seemed to have generated special attention in jury members. Without the psychometric foundation provided in the research of psychometrically oriented Rorschachers (see Exner, 1993, 1995; Exner & Weiner, 1995), I would have had nothing to say, or I would have been presenting unsupportable conjecture, or I would have been making up whatever I said. Psychometric foundations were critical to that presentation.

In conclusion, Dr. Fischer's presentation encourages me to believe that if the science and ethics of psychological assessment are respected, a collaborative approach to psychological assessment can integrate the often competing, contradictory life worlds that converge as we practice our disciplines.

References

American Psychological Association. (1992). Ethical principles of psychologists and code of conduct. *American Psychologist, 47,* 1597-1611.

Exner, J. E. (1993). *The Rorschach: A comprehensive system: Vol. 1. Basic foundations* (3rd ed.). New York: John Wiley.

Exner, J. E. (1995). *Issues and methods in Rorschach research.* Mahwah, NJ: Lawrence Erlbaum.

Exner, J. E., & Weiner, I. B. (1995). *The Rorschach: A comprehensive system: Vol. 3. Assessment of children and adolescents* (2nd ed.). New York: John Wiley.

Fischer, C.T. (1985). *Individualizing psychological assessment.* Monterey, CA: Brooks/Cole.

Fischer, C. T. (1992). Humanizing psychological assessment. *Humanistic Psychologist, 20,* 318-331.

Fischer, C. T. (1998a). Being angry revealed as self-deceptive protest: An empirical phenomenological analysis. In R. Valle (Ed.), *Phenomenological inquiry in psychology: Existential and transpersonal dimensions.* New York: Plenum.

Fischer, C. T. (1998b). The Rorschach and the life world: Exploratory exercises. In L. Handler & M. Hilsenroth (Eds.), *Teaching and learning personality assessment.* Mahwah, NJ: Lawrence Erlbaum.

Fischer, C. T. (1999). Designing qualitative research reports for publications. In M. Kopala & L. Suzuki (Eds.), *Using qualitative methods in psychology.* Thousand Oaks, CA: Sage.

Polanyi, M. (1962). *Personal knowledge: Towards a post-critical philosophy.* Chicago: University of Chicago Press.

Rorschach, H. (1942). *Psychodiagnostics: A diagnostic test based on perception* (P. V. Lemkau & B. Kronenberg, Trans.). New York: Grune & Stratton.

Issue 3

Biologization of Psychotherapy

The Biologization of Psychotherapy

Understanding the Nature of Influence

Richard N. Williams
Brigham Young University

Martha, a young wife and mother of four in her mid-20s, had the classic symptoms of depression—blunted affect, thoughts of suicide, difficulty performing the ordinary tasks of daily living. Her doctors were having trouble getting the levels of her five or six medications just right, smoothing out the highs and the lows. Martha hated the substantial weight gain induced by the drugs and the feeling they gave her of being not fully in touch with things. Martha underwent two courses of electroconvulsive shock treatments. After the electricity and the drugs, Martha was still in a difficult family situation, married to a husband who although demanding of affection was not able to settle down to the business of supporting his family. Martha's history of moving her family every year or so following financial disasters and the history of her own family and her brother's legal troubles were still intact. Her experiential future lay before her virtually undisturbed by anything that had happened to her brain.

Rose, a woman about the same age, but without many of the other contexts Martha had to cope with, was also depressed. On learning that her depression was simply a medical condition, produced by some imbalance in neurotransmitters, and receiving a prescription for a single medication, Rose was much relieved. She had been afraid that there might really be something wrong with her relationships or that perhaps she was actually doing something wrong. She could now continue her relationships and pursue her life's agenda just as before without the need for much soul searching and self-examination.

These cases illustrate that when persons have severe emotional difficulties—pathologies—these always have moral and relational contexts, histories, and futures inextricably imbedded in them. Indeed, pathologies of this sort require contexts to be what they are. They do not exist without them. Furthermore, there are moral and social implications associated with the possibility that psychological disorders have biological causes. Our received understandings of the relation of the biological to the psychological support the commonsense intuition that if our psychological disorders or, indeed, psychological life itself, arise strictly or even chiefly from biological bases, then that moral and social concern that has for centuries defined our very humanity is in doubt. My intent is to investigate the now well-established phenomenon of the biologization of psychopathology and psychotherapy to make clear where our faith in biology as an explanation is most problematic and to point out important consequences of conceptualizing persons in biological terms. This is facilitated by a careful consideration of the nature and meaning of constructs of causation and influence.

The Trend Toward Biologization

I use the term "biologization" as a generalized description of an unambiguous and well-recognized trend (e.g., Gazzaniga, 1995) in all branches of psychology to account for human behaviors, including intentions, preferences, emotions, cognitions, and even pathologies in biological terms. Questions regarding the relationship between mind and matter have long been important in the Western intellectual tradition, from its earliest stirrings in the work of the pre-Socratic atomists (see, e.g., Regnell, 1967), through the classical period of Plato and Aristotle (see, e.g., Robinson, 1989), and onward through the Enlightenment. The essential dualism of mind and body, the legacy of modern thought, and certainly of psychology, from the early Enlightenment, derived chiefly from an ontological reading of Descartes' (1641/1986) epistemologically useful distinction between thought and extended matter, came to be a philosophical issue of lasting impact.

Although the dualism of mind and body seems obvious and experientially inescapable, dualisms are metaphysically problematic. If we are searching for a single, ultimate explanatory principle—following the Greek metaphysical project (Williams, 1990)—dualism suggests that there are really two. This not only runs counter to the oldest assumptions of our intellectual tradition, but necessarily complicates explanations since we are required not only to deal with two fundamental realities but to come to grips with an account of how these two very different realities might possibly interact.

Clearly, mind-body dualism implies two things likely to be regarded as problematic and unacceptable to the mainstream psychology of our time. First, if minds constitute an ontological category apart from bodies, the methods of natural science imported by psychologists from 19th- and early 20th-century natural science for the study of persons may not be effective in rendering an acceptable understanding of the principle subject matter of the discipline, to wit, psychological phenomena seemingly involving the mind. Second, any dualism in which mind stands as its own reality implies the dreaded "ghost in the machine" (Ryle, 1949). To allow for an intelligence not clearly and ultimately natural in every sense to be the animating principle of human beings opens the door for souls, spirits, and other seemingly supernatural entities. Instead, the field has sought to be thoroughly naturalistic and monistic, reducing one reality to the other.

Reductionism in psychology seeks to show that there is only a single causal substrate underlying human behavior. Biology is so alluring to psychology because it holds out what has heretofore been, and will likely continue to be, a false promise of real scientific credibility, unambiguous causes, and, concomitantly, freedom from the mentalism, volition, and spiritualism that have, in the minds of many, impeded progress in our discipline for decades. Thus psychology at the end of the 20th century is enamored with materialism, confident that at last we have achieved an explanatory ground sophisticated enough and firm enough to please the contemporary mind.

The Problem of Reductionism

Once one decides that naturalistic and materialistic monism is the ontological foundation grounding all understandings of human behavior, one still must deal with the overwhelming reality of the experience of mental life. It seems we experience thought and not brain activity. The solution of preference is to reduce the psychological to the physical. This reduction, unfortunately, often takes the form of an unexamined presupposition—that is, many psychologists just assume that when the ultimate story of human behavior is known, it will be written in the language of biology. With this presupposition in place, the discipline has been rather unconcerned about the issue, opting to go about the work of normal science, developing and believing only those theories and models that can easily be brought into conformity with known or presumed biological realities or adapting theories and models (sometimes rather drastically) until they do. This strategy is distinctly anti-intellectual.

I will not here attempt a thorough critique of reductionism in general, since a number of comprehensive discussions are available (e.g., Agazzi, 1991; Charles & Lennon, 1992; Dupre, 1993; Lennon, 1990; and chapters in books by Eccles & Robinson, 1984; Robinson, 1985, 1998). I will, however, highlight the essential strategies and the problems that attend them, paying attention in particular to the implications of these problems for psychology.

The essence of reductionism in psychology is the claim that "X is really just Y." (Slife & Williams, 1995). That is, when X, a psychological or mental phenomenon, is seen in the proper light, understood fully or adequately, it will be not what it has seemed to be but what it more basically and truly is, namely Y, a biological phenomenon. No program of reductive thinking could be seriously pursued absent the assumption that the reduction were necessary to arrive at an understanding better or truer in an ontological sense. Once we understand that X is really Y, then we do not need the category X in our explanations of the world (Robinson, 1995).

It is also inherent in reduction that X is really just Y. This is to say that Y is in some important sense more simple or basic, closer to the essential reality, than X is. It is important to show X to be *just* Y. Otherwise we might be misled by the *appearance* of X. This intellectual drive to get down to the simplest substrate is at the core of Ockhom's Razor as well as all claims to parsimony, a virtue to which contemporary psychology is strongly committed. The sticking point of the drive for parsimony has always been that a reductive explanation, Y, must be simpler than X but adequate to the explanatory task for which X currently exists. It must adequately account for everything that X accounts for, and it should do so without destroying or dismissing phenomena that used to fit in category X (Robinson, 1995).

The insurmountable conceptual problem in achieving a satisfactory reduction is, of course, the absence of a set of criteria by which the reduction is judged to be adequate, that is, whether Y has distorted phenomena of the "X" class too much, or whether something essentially important about "X-like" phenomena is left unaccounted for. This amounts to a judgment as to whether only unnecessary complexity has been removed. Such judgments and criteria can only be grounded in a particular ontological perspective, or "paradigm" (see Kuhn, 1970; Yanchar & Slife, 1997). Thus what appears to be unnecessarily complex and unjustifiably abstract in one metaphysical system may be quite simple, concrete, and absolutely essential in another. For example, it may seem unnecessary to speak of a self or of human agency within naturalism, but it is inescapable within an ontology not composed entirely of material entities. If biological reduction is to be more than simple prejudice, persuasive criteria must be invoked to justify the reduction on grounds other than those entailed in a prior ontological commitment to biological materialism. No criteria have been established that allow us sensibly to judge parsimony or the truth value of a reduction, nor, it appears, can they be.[1]

Types of Reductions

Dupre (1993) provides a taxonomy for understanding reductive strategies. "Diachronic" reductions take place over time as one theory replaces another because a new theory is seen to be capable of explaining all the previous theory explained, and more, often achieving greater parsimony in the bargain. An example of this might be the way in which germ theory replaced earlier theories of disease. Of more importance to the present chapter are "synchronic" reductions, wherein one concurrently existing theory replaces another. The biologization of psychology is an example of synchronic reduction. The question is how the reduction of the higher-order theory or construct takes place. Some theories are reduced by what Dupre (1993, p. 98) refers to as "derivation." In reduction through derivation, the original higher-ordered theories and their constructs, or the phenomena they are intended to explain, are altered to the point that the reducing theory is seen to offer a better (i.e., simpler and less complex) explanation. For example, if theory X (the higher-order one) were to contend that humans are agents and must exercise their agency to overcome a psychopathology, theory Y might effect a reduction by simply defining agency as the ability to avoid noxious forces in one's life. Avoiding noxious forces *can* be explained by simple avoidance mechanisms based on primitive conditioning and physiological processes. Theory Y can then claim to adequately account for curative functions in terms of simply biological mechanisms and processes, and the reduction is accomplished.

Reduction by derivation is a genuine reduction because theories based on a simpler ontology (e.g., naturalism) replace theories based on a higher-level ontology (e.g., agentive persons). But the reduction is accomplished by language and consensus about language use. It is a breach of logic to seriously claim that simply because a phenomenon *can* be explained by a theory, the theory adequately does explain it. Here the analysis ends in the criterion problem. On what basis do we judge whether a nonagentic account is adequate or whether it simply defines out of existence the constructs it ought to explain and substitutes one it wants to explain?

A form of reduction stronger than derivation is elimination. Eliminative reductions seek to replace one theory and its attendant ontology with another. An eliminative biological reduction would take the position that minds really are just brains, and not only is the concept of mind unnecessary in explanations of behavior, but the mind in fact does not exist in any way that cannot be entirely accounted for by brains and the ontology of brains. This type of reduction is defended in various contemporary sources, including P. M. Churchland (1981, 1985), P. S. Churchland (1986), and Stitch (1983). Eliminative reduction is the most serious and severe sort. Its consequences in psychology are substantial because they strike right at the heart of our understanding of persons—of what we take ourselves to be and to be about. To conclude that our thoughts, emotions, and behaviors are most essentially and fundamentally biological processes strips them of the meaning they have historically had. Biological events cannot mean what agentic acts mean. Biological entities cannot "mean" at all, in the sense we use the term. Following a biological eliminative reduction, mental, emotional, and moral actions and events are epiphenomenal on biological events and at most serve an instrumental function helping us carry out in some way whatever we were bound to carry out anyway (see Gollwitzer, 1999). From the perspective of eliminative reduction, psychopathologies are ontologically indistinguishable from physical pathologies. The justification for this reductive position, as is the case with derivative reductions, would need to come from scientific data. If the reductive theory were true, the epistemology underlying natural scientific method would be the only type that would satisfy or persuade a well-trained brain. Various sources suggest that at the present time there is no body of research that can convincingly establish the validity of an eliminative biological reduction (e.g., Valenstein, 1998). Others argue against the viability of the reduction on conceptual grounds (see, e.g., Dupre, 1993; Robinson, 1998). I evaluate the problems entailed in such validation in later sections of this chapter.

Lacking precise empirical evidence sufficient to establish the validity of the stronger eliminative reduction, yet still adhering to a thoroughgoingly materialist philosophy, some scholars have staked out a range of more moderate positions.[2] These positions all take advantage of what is known as the "supervenience thesis" (Dupre, 1993). Early articulations of this thesis are usually ascribed to Moore (1922), Hare (1952), Kim (1978), and Davidson (1980). The term "supervenience" is meant to convey that one realm of phenomena (e.g., the mental) depends entirely on another (e.g. the biological) even though explicit and evident relations between the two are lacking (Dupre, 1993, p. 96). As the definition makes clear, reduction based on assumptions of supervenience stops short of eliminating an entire domain of phenomena. But it is an unconvincing and problematic position for three reasons. First, it is a conflicted agnostic position; it must assume to be true precisely what it accepts as unproven and perhaps even in principle unknowable—the dependency of one realm on the other. Second, a supervenience position itself reduces to an eliminative position (Dupre, 1993) since if one domain relies entirely on the other, fundamental descriptions must be given in terms of the more basic domain. Supervenience is a necessary condition for eliminative reduction. Once this is clear, the only reasons not to replace the higher-level domain with the lower are purely pragmatic or romantic. Finally, since supervenience is a necessary condition for an eliminative reduction it must, in the final analysis, rely on the same data as an eliminative reduction to establish its validity.

The concept of supervenience, albeit in a slightly altered form, also constitutes the philosophical underpinnings of the approach taken by various versions of what may be called "postmodern" and constructionist psychologies toward the mind-body question. These positions oppose explanation in terms of souls and other "ghosts," affording them no ontological status or place in explanation. But they are also genuinely hesitant to pursue a reductive explanatory strategy, realizing that such a strategy destroys persons and meaningful actions, as well as the social processes that constitute them. Thus they attempt to stake out for themselves nonreductive materialist positions. Some of the most explicit articulations of this position are found in the writings of the "discursive psychology" movement (see, e.g., Harre, 1998; Harre & Gillett, 1994).

Sophisticated positions constructed on some type of supervenience hypothesis acknowledge the stultifying effects of eliminative reductions on meaningful human life. They also admit that human life, to all appearances, is meaningful. Human beings possess rational propensities and are capable of moral concern and action. How these propensities evolved from the material substratum is impossible to explain given the present state of the cognitive and neurosciences. For nonreductive materialists, it is not important how these human qualities did arise. The project of psychology is to understand them as we find them and to help persons, including clients in psychotherapy, develop them in the interest of living a fully functioning life. This strategy amounts to taking out what Daniel Dennett (1978) refers to as "intelligence loans." The idea of an intelligence loan is that we deal with people as if they were what they seem to be—meaning-making, purposive, moral beings—although we understand that human behaviors and human beings are, in fact, natural phenomena (something we cannot yet establish scientifically, especially not at a level where biological language and strictly biological therapeutic interventions suffice). This maneuver has the collateral benefit of allowing us to deal with people in therapy at the level of their moral discourse while not having to really take the moral dimension of life seriously because it is a mere placeholder to facilitate our work until the naturalistic story is known—until the eliminative reduction can be effected.

Another pragmatic advantage of the nonreductive materialist position described here and, at the same time, one of its most intellectually problematic features is that it need not concern itself about the lack of data supporting the naturalist assumptions on which it is based. It is a position born of acknowledged ignorance and resting firmly on continuing ignorance. There is an irony that "hardheaded" psychologists who routinely call for hard research to support virtually every hypotheses or treatment recommendation and who are driven by the need to match therapies to treatments based on hard data from empirical outcome studies are so easily persuaded that the lack of hard evidence for the most fundamental tenet of their most far-reaching ontological commitment poses no particular problem—certainly not one sufficient to cause them to challenge their assumptions about human nature. Since we lack the methodological wherewithal to establish the validity of the materialist assumptions of this position, we obviously lack the methodological wherewithal to conduct a crucial test that would falsify the position as well. All research becomes "suggestive," and suggestive findings satisfy the desire for verifications,[3] while lacking any real power to falsify. The logic of this position on science merits serious critical examination.

Judging from the lack of references on the topic in psychological literature, most psychologists are not familiar with the concept of supervenience or the philosophical issues at stake. Psychologists have come to this position, it seems, without doing the hard conceptual work that would justify it. It is, to be sure, a comfortable position. It protects psychologists from dealing with uncomfortable constructs such as souls and agentic minds; preserves the scientific potential, if not the actual scientific status, of psychology, which has political and economic as well as intellectual benefits; and relieves psychologists of the burden of defending their most fundamental understandings of human reality as true. It must be kept in mind, however, that this type of materialist position is still an eliminative reduction waiting to happen. It lives intellectually and conceptually beyond its means based on the credit afforded by intelligence loans. And as a weak form of eliminative reductionism, it is just as deeply destructive of human agency, meaning, and morality, just not obviously so.

This hidden materialistic assumption running through contemporary clinical theories and practices allows us to operate under a storefront advertising a commitment to the meaningfulness of human existence and the power of agentic persons to control and direct their lives without having to actually hold these positions. What cannot be so easily concealed is the nihilism of a purely materialist account of human life and human concerns. It must certainly be the case that therapists' ontological assumptions influence their practice in various, sometimes subtle and sometimes obvious ways.[4] Surely in any sustained and significant therapeutic interaction, the client will overtly or covertly derive from the experience an understanding of his or her nature and capabilities. In this way, the reductive nature of contemporary psychotherapeutic theories and practices will find their way consequentially into the lives of clients.

The Case for Biologization

I now return to the evidentiary basis and arguments usually marshaled in favor of biologization. Before I do so, however, it is important to make clear one analytical point. To argue against biologization, the giving over of psychology to biology and, concomitantly, reducing the mental and psychological to the physical and chemical, is not to claim that brains and chemical processes are irrelevant to psychological life. By all accounts, healthy brain function is facilitative of mental health and happiness. What is at issue is the reduction of things mental to things physical and the related problem of the nature of the influence of the one realm on the other.[5]

Post Hoc Inference. It is interesting to observe how evidence for the biological bases of various psychopathologies is presented in the literature. A recent comprehensive treatment, *Neuropsychology for Clinical Practice* (Adams, Parsons, Culbertson, & Nixon, 1996), illustrates a distinction unavoidably present, but not explicitly acknowledged, between the evidentiary bases of distinctly different types of pathologies. Early chapters deal with psychological disorders associated with known and obviously physiological conditions, such as traumatic brain injury, Alzheimer's disease, epilepsy, multiple sclerosis, alcoholism, and Parkinson's disease. The relationship between brain and central nervous system (CNS) conditions and psychological consequences in these cases is generally noncontroversial because both can be established fairly directly. Later chapters, however, deal with disorders such as Attention-Deficit/Hyperactivity Disorder (ADHD) and learning disabilities. Here the logic used to implicate physiology is of a very different sort. It is indirect and clearly inferential. For example, in the chapter on ADHD (Culbertson & Krull, 1996), Mirsky's (1987) conceptualization of the disorder and its relationship to the brain is presented. The post hoc inference proceeds in this fashion: Since ADHD involves attention, the reticular formation of the brain is clearly implicated. The model goes on pulling brain structures into the model by virtue of the fact that certain regions have been known to be associated with certain psychological functions that seem to be somewhat abnormal in ADHD clients.[6] This inference strategy is very different from the more usual, straightforward connection of brain trauma to behavioral deficit. Furthermore, the logic behind the inferences does not justify the conclusion that one is actually uncovering the physiology of ADHD. A counterexample makes this clear. A concussion often involves vomiting. Since the stomach is obviously involved in vomiting, the stomach, or some problem with it, is implicated as a cause of the concussion and associated behaviors.

This form of logical argument might be overlooked if it were an isolated incidence. But it seems to be common in the literature on biology and psychopathology. Zuckerman (1999, pp. 266-268), for example, using similar logic, argues that many neurotransmitters must be involved in alcoholism. This type of argument is unsatisfactory because there are no controls built into it. That is, one might argue that since alcoholism is something people do, involving choices, muscle actions, emotional factors, and social conditions, virtually the entire brain and nervous system must be involved. Thus we have scientific-sounding arguments that are essentially circular and tautological.

Post Hoc Ergo Proptor Hoc. The reasoning underlying the implication of neurotransmitters in various psychological disorders, including depression, is problematic in a similar way. Valenstein (1998) traces the history of the development of psychoactive drugs. He notes a sense, apparent in the field, that a bad theory of how biological factors produce psychological disorders is somehow better than no theory at all. He also notes that explanations of the disorders usually amount to descriptions of chemical reactions, not explanations of how the chemical reactions might produce the disorder. The overarching logic underlying claims that certain disorders have chemical causes, based on the chemical effects of certain drugs on neurotransmitters, is simply this (see also Slife & Williams, 1995, chap. 5): When we administer the drug, the neurotransmitters are put in state X and the depression is ameliorated; therefore the neurotransmitters being in state Y (not X) was the cause of the disorder. Again, a counterexample is obvious and compelling. The administration of aspirin to a flu sufferer results in a diminution of flu symptoms and aspirin-enriched blood; therefore, the flu must have resulted from a lack of aspirin in the bloodstream. Once again it appears that a scientific-sounding explanation takes on more credibility than it deserves, and certainly more than current empirical work can justify.

Argument From Deficit. In summary of his analysis of the logic and research behind the development of psychoactive drugs and the theories that locate in the brain the problems treated by the drugs, Valenstein (1998) concludes that, as of 1998, "no biochemical anatomical, or functional signs have been found that reliably distinguish the brains of mental patients" (p. 125). I am convinced that a much stronger statement could be made. There is, in fact, no evidence that a single meaningful, directed, telic behavior has ever resulted directly from any physiological state. Absent the sort of a priori evidence of particular physical differences between the brains of clients and nonclients that would make an affirmative case, biological thinkers have relied on a style of argument that may be described as "argument from deficit" (Slife & Williams, 1995, chap. 5). The argument proceeds in general this way: We do know that damage to the brain (or some other abnormality in the CNS) results in a particular deficit in behavior; therefore normal brain (or other physiological) structure or function is responsible for normal functioning. Once again, a counterexample is helpful. Absent a set of functional vocal cords, one is assured of diminished capacity as an orator; having a normal set of vocal cords cannot, however, on the basis of this evidence, be established as the cause of becoming a skilled orator, or even of speaking. Where our body of research evidence of a relationship between physiology and behavior is the strongest, it rather clearly shows that neurological deficits result in behavioral constraints. This, however, cannot be taken as legitimate evidence for the viability of a biological reduction, nor, indeed, as evidence of causality at all. Since to constrain (i.e., prevent) behavior is the logical opposite of causing it, argument from deficit can never support the project of biologization. Perhaps the strongest theoretical statement such evidence will legitimately permit is that a functional nervous system is a necessary condition for behavior and, perhaps, even that a "normal" nervous system is advantageous to normal functioning. This, however, seems to be little more than a banal truism.

The Ontological Gap. The biologization of psychology amounts conceptually to the proposition that events in one ontological domain can be produced by events in another. Psychological events, including emotions, preferences, reasons, and motives are essentially nonphysical, temporal, historical, meaningfully contextual, and, most often, directly experiential. Conversely, biological events and structures are essentially physical and chemical, ahistorical, nonmeaningful and only environmentally contextual, and, most often, not directly experiential. Thus we seem to be faced with two distinct ontological realms. The assumption has been too easily made in psychology that physical (biological) phenomena—consisting of meat and chemicals contained entirely in the tissues of the body in the present—can have a fairly direct causal influence on nonphysical phenomena—consisting of ideas and desires always oriented outside the tissues and across the temporal dimension. There are no theories of how this might happen, of how physical events can move or shape mental ones. All extant attempts at theoretical explanation of how physical entities and events can produce mental ones are nothing more than affirmations that, given materialistic assumptions, they surely must, or models that simply reiterate (in a circular fashion) that they surely do. The burden of proof here again lies with those who would claim biological causality.

Ontological Drift. One attempt at bridging the ontological gap described above is perhaps well intentioned, but nonetheless ill fated. Instances of the attempt are seen most often in trying to explain the effects of genes on behavior. It is generally granted that a complex behavior is unlikely to result from a single gene. One likely does not have, for example, a gene for scoring high on IQ tests, for drinking alcohol, or even for being violent. Attributing such things to a combination of genes does nothing to surmount the problems presented by the ontological gap. Nor does it strengthen the case for biological determination of behavior; it simply adds complexity. A related conceptual maneuver designed precisely to bridge the gap between body and mind or behavior is to invoke the concept of "tendencies," or "predispositions." In his treatment of "diathesis," Zuckerman (1999) reminds his readers that "although we may speak in terms of an inherited trait or behavioral disposition, we do not inherit traits or dispositions as such" (p. 6). We inherit simply genetic material composed of chemicals. Attributing particular behaviors and other mental phenomena to such chemicals ensnares us in the conceptual problem presented by the ontological gap.

However, it has become relatively common in psychology to attempt to bridge the gap by allowing the concept of a tendency or predisposition to drift from one ontological state to another. This is generally a two-stage process. First, the predisposition is reified, given an independent existence by speaking as if tendencies were things people have rather than descriptions of the flow of their lives. The second step is to grant some causal power and include the predisposition in causal explanations as if it were present as a factor in the phenomenon under examination. Thus the gene as a predisposition drifts between its ontological state as chemical and its ontological state as a contributing cause, transcending its own ontology and acting as bridge between the realm of physiochemical reality and psychological reality. Its apparent explanatory power, however, is strictly and merely rhetorical.

Another explanatory tack illustrating ontological drift is to explain human behavior, including psychological disorder, as arising from an "interaction" of biological and environmental events. Most of what psychologists might mean by "environment" is certainly outside the tissues of the body. Things such as a person's level of stress, treatment by other people, income, and childhood experiences are not, ontologically speaking, physical or bodily phenomena. Thus to speak of such things as "interacting" with physical, biological conditions is simply to ignore the ontological gap, for there simply is no ontological ground on which two such different things could meet. Nonetheless, the term "interaction," at least in our casual professional conversations, is allowed to drift freely between ontological states. If in more reasoned conversations "interaction" is used in a metaphorical sense simply to convey the belief that behaviors and disorders arise in complex situations composed of both bodies and experiences, then there is no ontological drift because there is no causal status granted to "interactions." But the position that behaviors and disorders arise in a nexus of physical and experiential factors is unproblematic because it is immediately apparent how such factors might come together. They come together due to the rational action of a sentient person. However, the legitimation of the person in just this way is what most theories invoking biological-environmental interaction are meant to deny and just what one opposed to biologization wants to preserve.

Heritability. Many explanations of the effects of genes on behavior demonstrate a misunderstanding of the nature of heritability itself. Indices of heritability are derived from measures of the variability of a trait manifest in populations in which genotype and relevant characteristics of the environment can be specified, controlled, or manipulated. Simply put, *heritability* is the proportion of variability in the trait that can be attributed to genetic rather than environmental sources. Several points deserve mention. First, heritability can only be determined under conditions in which the factors just mentioned can be tightly controlled. This is not possible for ordinary populations of human beings. The fall-back strategy is to rely on "experiments of nature" (Zuckerman, 1999), which usually entail the study of twins reared apart. However, a valid index of heritability requires, however, an assumption of the additive, and thus independent, effects of both environment and genetics. If either contaminates the other, or if either is not really comparable across subjects (persons), a valid index of heritability cannot be derived. Twin studies simply lack sufficient control to meet these conditions. A simple example will suffice. Even if twin brothers were separated at birth, one reared in Indiana and the other in Florida, the fact that they were (genetically, with an adequate diet available to both) both 6'4" tall and weighed over 200 pounds by the ninth grade would make it difficult to determine whether or how much of their interest and level of achievement in athletics might be due to genes.

It should also be kept in mind that heritability is an index of the variability of the occurrence of a particular trait in a population. It says nothing about the level (high or low) of that trait. Thus the fact that a trait that is highly heritable says nothing of the level of the trait in the population and even less about the expected level of the trait in any individual case. When interest is in a dichotomized variable, which can take on only two values (present or absent) rather than a continuous one, true heritability indices cannot be calculated. Researchers use indices of concordance to estimate heritability, but all schemes for estimating heritability encounter the problem just described.

Finally, it should be kept in mind that the heritability of a trait is irrelevant to the question of whether the trait can be changed or influenced by environmental or other interventions. The variability of highly heritable traits within the population may remain constant, but the level of the trait may be extremely sensitive to environmental and even agentic influences (Lewontin, 1991; Robinson, 1992). For these reasons, the biologization of psychology is unlikely to be achieved by the weight of evidence that any particular behavior has a high heritability. There are few implications of heritability for therapy. As Lewontin (1991) sums up the evidence, ". . . there is at present simply no convincing measure of the role of genes in influencing human behavioral variation" (p. 33).

Causality and Influence in Psychopathology and Psychotherapy

In spite of the fact that the clinical areas of psychology have adopted what has been called the "medical model," psychological theorists would be well served to give more careful attention to the way causality is handled in the field of medicine. Current medical thinking asserts the obvious, that disease is much more than the presence of a pathogen. A disease is not the result of the simple effects of a single cause or the end result of a chain of causes. Rather, medical disorders are the body's reaction in the presence of a host of relevant conditions. Earlier thinking about disease simply as a result of pathogenic forces was based on a particular worldview, an ontology of sorts, in which the universe of things could be neatly sorted into two categories, namely, causes and effects (Lewontin, 1991). This type of thinking and the atomism inherent in it have been replaced by more intricate models of systems of the universe itself (e.g., Bohm, 1980).[7]

The separation of causes from events is the legacy of psychology from particular readings of a distinctly Newtonian physics and logical positivism, but it is certainly not a view found on the cutting edge of ancient or modern thought. Aristotle could see the folly of separating causes from events. For him, a cause was part of an explanation adequate to render understanding of an event or thing. Thus a cause is better thought of as a description of how things happen along with the necessary conditions for them to happen, rather than as the name of some independent force that makes them happen. For example, contrary to the modern reading of efficient causes as blind forces of nature, Aristotle's example of an efficient cause was a skilled craftsman who takes material and, understanding the form and purpose of a thing, fashions it to be what it is supposed to be. Our modern understanding has become blind to an important aspect of causality as Aristotle meant it. The Greek word used by Aristotle was *aitheia*, meaning roughly, "to be responsible for." That notion of responsibility, with its implied rationality and meaningfulness, has been lost from the concept of causality that informs contemporary thinking on the issue, at least in psychology.

More recently, many (e.g., Bohm, 1957; Lewontin, 1991) have argued that what we take to be causes are not divorced from the things and events that we take to be effects. A cause is thus more a property of an event, part of the ontology of the events, than a separate entity with its own ontological status outside the event. For example, a germ is simply a germ; the cause of a disease can be found in the intricate interplay of all facets of the context in which a germ and person meet. Rather than looking outside the system for the cause (or inside the germ or the person), the cause is found and understood only in noticing how embodied persons react to and take account of the conditions imposed by the presence of the germ and vice versa. Causes, even in the physical world, are holistic and contextual. Rather than attempting—with virtually no hope of success—to reduce persons to material biological things, psychologists should be interested in maintaining the status of persons as persons and in understanding how persons take account of their external and their internal material circumstances. And through it all, we should keep in mind that psychotherapists treat persons, not disorders. This simple concept, I suspect, would have made a substantial difference in the outcomes of therapy for Martha and for Rose.

This expanded view of causality entails a more careful understanding of the nature of influence. Too often, the concept of influence has been used in psychology as simply a soft form of determinism—as a way of hedging one's metaphysical bet in the absence of hard evidence of hard determinism in human behaviors. There are at least three ways in which the term "influence" can be deployed in accounting for the mind-body relationship in human phenomena, including psychopathology. Influence may be strictly *causal,* that is, there may be a direct connection of physical states to mental ones. The best case for this may be the psychological deficiencies that accompany certain known physiological conditions, such as those resulting from traumatic head injury. Where there are no neural pathways undamaged and in place, certain behavioral events will not occur (unless and until there is some compensation and rerouting of the nerve pathways). But although this is "causal" influence, for all the reasons outlined above, caution must be taken in trying to move from evidence of this type of influence to a strict reductive materialism.

Another aspect of the mind-body relationship may be thought of as *conditional* influence. Bodily conditions may constrain human action. This type of influence is obvious in the relationship of outward bodily conditions to persons' actions. Many conditions, ranging from amputations to headaches, provide conditions to which persons will naturally be expected to adapt their behavior. The result of conditional influence will be seen as constraints and limitations, but there is no reason to assume that these constraints operate without the intelligent contribution and cooperation of persons. Such influences operate in a manner like "input" to an intelligent system. These influences, when properly understood, are not reductive.

It seems also that influence may occur in the form of what may be called *consequential* influence. Many factors in persons' lives are influential because of their anticipated consequences. Such consequences are symbolic and anticipatory, requiring intelligence and a sense of purpose in human life. Without an explicit or implicit sense of purpose, anticipation of consequences would be impossible. Although it is more difficult to connect this type of influence directly to bodily conditions, it is clearly active in the lives of persons seeking to live successfully. The mere existence of physiological conditions that introduce conditional constraints in a person's life will also introduce consequential influences as intelligent persons seek to take account of the conditions (physical, social, and moral) of their lives and set a course of action deemed worthy by them.

In summary, why must psychotherapists resist the biologization of psychotherapy? Simply because the moral integrity of the enterprise hangs in the balance. However well intentioned we are, however well we may attempt to bracket our own intellectual understandings during therapy, however strong our intention not to let on to clients that we believe them to be natural organisms, the belief that all that is human reduces to mere matter will erode our sensitivity to the moral tenor of life. We cannot see the sublimely good in persons, nor can we maintain a belief in their potential, if we are haunted from the periphery of our intellect, or from our training, by the thought that this person before us is at some level merely a natural object. To give the human over to the biological is to lose forever the sense of the sacred. It is to abandon the project of helping persons live lives, which are in the richest sense, worth living.

Notes

1. In the minds of most psychological scientists, no doubt the answer would be that these issues ought to be decided on the basis of the hard data accrued by careful scientific work. This response is problematic, however, because given limitations not exclusive to the social sciences but certainly prominent within them it is doubtful that a conclusive test could ever be performed. For such arguments, see, e.g., Bernstein (1983), Bohman (1993), Polkinghorne (1983, 1988), Slife and Williams (1995).

2. One intriguing position on the mind-body issue not taken up here that purports to be monistic and yet not reductive is that articulated by Strawson (1994).

3. This view of science wherein its ability to verify certain theories and presuppositions exceeds its ability to falsify others is curious in view of work in the philosophy of science by Popper (e.g., 1959) and Lakatos (e.g., 1970).

4. There is a large literature on the effects on clients and client outcomes of the so-called "therapist variables." If something as subtle as therapists' values can have an influence on the course of therapy and its outcomes (see, e.g., Richards & Bergin, 1997), then we have reason to believe that something as subtle as what type of being the therapist thinks the client really is will surely be manifested in some form in therapy and in therapeutic outcomes.

5. Some might see no way to take biology seriously without conceding to a reductive explanatory strategy. Alternative ways of talking about the mind-body relationship abound, however. Recent alternatives include the "hardware-software" metaphor (Penfield, 1975), the "task-tool" metaphor (Harre, 1998), and the "lived body" (Merleau-Ponty, 1989).

6. Silk (1998) uses a similar line of reasoning regarding the biological foundations of personality disorders.

7. The project of reducing consciousness to the material in many ways runs counter to a trend in modern physics, as found, for example, in Bohm's (1980) work, to integrate consciousness into a larger order of the universe.

References

Adams, R. L., Parsons, O. A., Culbertson, J. L., & Nixon, S. J. (Eds.). (1996). *Neuropsychology for clinical practice: Etiology, assessment, and treatment of common neurological disorders.* Washington, DC: American Psychological Association.

Agazzi, E. (Ed.). (1991). *The problem of reductionism in science.* Boston: Kluwer Academic Publishers.

Bernstein, R. J. (1983). *Beyond objectivism and relativism: Science, hermeneutics, and praxis.* Philadelphia: University of Pennsylvania Press.

Bohm, D. (1957). *Causality and chance in modern physics.* Princeton, NJ: Van Nostrand.

Bohm, D. (1980). *Wholeness and the implicate order.* London: Routledge.

Bohman, J. (1993). *New philosophy of social science: Problems of indeterminacy.* Cambridge, MA: MIT Press.

Charles, D., & Lennon, K. (Eds.). (1992). *Reduction, explanation, and realism.* Oxford, UK: Oxford University Press.

Churchland, P. M. (1981). Eliminative materialism and the propositional attitudes. *Journal of Philosophy, 78,* 67-90.

Churchland, P. M. (1985). Reduction, qualia, and the direct introspection of brain states. *Journal of Philosophy, 82,* 8-28.

Churchland, P. S. (1986). *Neurophilosophy.* Cambridge, MA: MIT Press.

Culbertson, J. L., & Krull, K. R. (1996). Attention deficit hyperactivity disorder. In R. L. Adams, O. A. Parsons, J. L. Culbertson, & S. J. Nixon (Eds.), *Neuropsychology for clinical practice: Etiology, assessment, and treatment of common neurological disorders* (pp. 271-330). Washington, DC: American Psychological Association.

Davidson, D. (1980). *Essays on actions and events.* New York: Oxford University Press.

Dennett, D. C. (1978). *Brainstorms: Philosophical essays on mind and psychology.* Montgomery, VT: Bradford Books.

Descartes, R. (1986). *Meditations on first philosophy: With selections from the objections and replies* (J. Cottingham, Trans.). New York: Cambridge University Press. (Original work published 1641)

Dupre, J. (1993). *The disorder of things.* Cambridge, MA: Harvard University Press.

Eccles, J., & Robinson, D. N. (1984). *The wonder of being human: Our brain and our mind.* New York: Free Press.

Gazzaniga, M. S. (Ed.). (1995). *The cognitive neurosciences.* Cambridge, MA: MIT Press.

Gollwitzer, P. M. (1999). Implementation intentions: Strong effects of simple plans. *American Psychologist, 54*(7), 493-503.

Hare, R. M. (1952). *The language of morals.* Oxford, UK: Oxford University Press.

Harre, R. (1998). *The singular self: An introduction to the psychology of personhood.* London: Sage.

Harre, R., & Gillett, G. (1994). *The discursive mind.* Thousand Oaks, CA: Sage.

Kim, J. (1978). Supervenience and nomological incommensurables. *American Philosophical Quarterly, 15,* 149-156.

Kuhn, T. S. (1970). *The structure of scientific revolutions* (2nd ed.). Chicago: University of Chicago Press.

Lakatos, I. (1970). Falsification and the methodology of scientific research programmes. In I. Lakatos & A. Musgrave (Eds.), *Criticism and the growth of knowledge* (pp. 91-196). Cambridge, UK: Cambridge University Press.

Lennon, K. (1990). *Explaining human action.* London: Duckworth.

Lewontin, R. C. (1991). *Biology as ideology: The doctrine of DNA.* New York: HarperCollins.

Merleau-Ponty, M. (1989). *Phenomenology of perception* (Colin Smith, trans.). London: Routledge.

Mirsky, A. F. (1987). Behavioral and psychophysiological markers of disordered attention. *Environmental Health Perspectives, 74,* 191-199.

Moore, G. E. (1922). The concept of intrinsic values. *Philosophical Studies.* New York: Harcourt Brace.

Penfield, W. (1975). *The mystery of the mind: A critical study of consciousness and the human brain.* Princeton, NJ: Princeton University Press.

Polkinghorne, D. (1983). *Methodology for the human sciences: Systems of inquiry.* Albany: State University of New York Press.

Polkinghorne, D. (1988). *Narrative knowing and the human sciences.* Albany: State University of New York Press.

Popper, K. (1959). *The logic of scientific discovery.* New York: Basic Books.

Regnell, H. (1967). *Ancient views on the nature of life.* Lund, Sweden: C. W. K. Gleerup.

Richards, P. S., & Bergin, A. E. (1997). *A spiritual strategy for counseling and psychotherapy.* Washington, DC: American Psychological Association.

Robinson, D. N. (1985). *Philosophy of psychology.* New York: Columbia University Press.

Robinson, D. N. (1989). *Aristotle's psychology.* New York: Columbia University Press.

Robinson, D. N. (1992). Races and persons. *The World & I, 7*(2), 481-499.

Robinson D. N. (1995). The logic of reductionistic models. *New Ideas in Psychology, 13,* 1-8.

Robinson, D. N. (Ed.). (1998). *The mind.* New York: Oxford University Press.

Ryle, G. (1949). *The concept of mind.* New York: Harper & Row.

Silk, K. R. (Ed.). (1998). *Biology of personality disorders.* Washington, DC: American Psychological Association.

Slife, B. D., & Williams, R. N. (1995). *What's behind the research? Discovering hidden assumptions in the behavioral sciences.* Thousand Oaks, CA: Sage.

Stitch, S. P. (1983). *From folk psychology to cognitive science: The case against belief.* Cambridge, MA: MIT Press.

Strawson, G. (1994). *Mental reality.* New York: Cambridge University Press.

Valenstein, E. S. (1998). *Blaming the brain: The truth about drugs and mental health.* New York: Free Press.

Williams, R. N. (1990). The metaphysic of things and discourse about them. In J. E. Faulconer & R. N. Williams (Eds.), *Reconsidering psychology: Perspectives from continental philosophy* (pp. 136-150). Pittsburgh, PA: Duquesne University Press.

Williams, R. N. (1995). The priority of ontology in reductionist models: A response to Robinson. *New Ideas in Psychology, 13,* 17-23.

Yanchar, S. C., & Slife, B. D. (1997). Pursuing unity in a fragmented psychology: Problems and prospects. *Review of General Psychology, 1,* 235-255.

Zuckerman, M. (1999). *Vulnerability to psychopathology: A biosocial model.* Washington, DC: American Psychological Association.

Commentary

The Biologization of Psychotherapy: Understanding the Nature of Influence

Louis A. Moench, MD

Dr. Williams has given us a fine, fascinating, thought-provoking scholarly essay decrying what I as a clinician and nonscholar do best, though not most happily—relatively biological psychiatry. His theme is that if psychological disorders and psychological life arise chiefly from biological bases, the moral and social concern that define our humanity are in doubt. Such a biology-as-causation proposition constitutes a divorce between disorder of the mind (brain) and social and moral responsibility. He makes the point that emotional pathologies always have moral and relational contexts; require contexts to be what they are; and, in fact, would not exist without them

The same can be said for any human mind state or endeavor—not just pathological ones. I will tell you the context of my review of this chapter. I had just finished participating in meetings of three committees of the American Psychiatric Association in Washington, D.C.

The first, the Committee on Psychiatric Diagnosis and Assessment, oversees the production of the *Diagnostic and Statistical Manual* (DSM), a very reductionist document categorizing mental illnesses in purely descriptive terms with little reference to causation. The second, the Steering Committee on Practice Guidelines, produces the guidelines for treatments of psychiatric disorders, the guideline on panic disorder having stirred up a contentious debate over the short shrift given to the section on psychotherapy, some insisting the guidelines be strictly evidence-based and evidence favors biological treatment, others saying that the treatment of panic does not lend itself to hard evidence and that the empirical evidence for the effectiveness of psychotherapy for panic disorder is ample. The third, the Committee on Electroconvulsive Therapy (ECT), is rewriting the recommendations for the practice of ECT, which some claim to be sham therapy, making patients feel better by satisfying postulated latent masochistic desire, but which most knowledgeable professionals consider a biological therapy, and an effective one. (After all, though ECT receives bad press, when psychotherapy costs $100 to $150 per treatment hour, how can one fault a treatment that costs 7 cents per kilowatt hour?)

The previous weekend, I had attended a seminar on hormonal influence on mood states, where the presenter, a female psychoendocrinologist, asserted that the dimming of cognitive capacity resulting from the dwindling of estrogen at menopause, and not male antifeminine bias, is the real basis for the mid-career glass ceiling barring women from entering the top echelon of their professions.

That same afternoon, I participated in a political strategy session with a few others on influencing the state legislature to pass a bill for parity of coverage of mental illness. The legislature had been unwilling even to let the bill get to the floor without a provision restricting parity coverage to seven illnesses "known" to have a biological base, to be sure, I presume, that insurers would not be required to cover treatment of an illness for which the patient has some personal responsibility. (The irony is that insurers cover illnesses that clearly result from lack of personal responsibility, such as those from smoking or sexual promiscuity, as long as they do not affect primarily the mind.) More political strategizing that evening focused on countering a very determined lobby of out-of-state psychologists wanting privileges to prescribe psychotropic medicines—for many years the stated goal of the current president of the American Psychological Association.

Clearly, the biologization of psychology is present and pervasive. But is it bad? It is certainly not new. Freud, who gave us the concept of behavior governed by an unconscious mind and the establishment of the talking cure, was basically a mechanist. He conceived of the mind in terms of fluid hydraulics— forces applied here or drives emerging there, either expressed overtly or, if blocked by defenses, expressed through some diverted channel constituting symptom production.

Is the biologization of psychology winning out? Some evidence suggests not. Here are a few examples: (a) For about 30 years now, psychologists have rejected the medical model in their terminology. They treat clients, not patients. Clients have needs, not illnesses. (b) At Harvard, all psychiatry residents are newly required to participate in a course on spiritual needs in patients. (c) There has been a rapid rise of public enthusiasm for nonscientific treatments, for example, herbal remedies, New Age fascinations, EMDR, Eastern mysticism, massage therapy, iridology, reading auras, and so on.

These do not suggest to me an ascendancy of the biological over the mental, an acceptance that it is just matter and motion at issue. The president's theme at the American Psychiatric Association's annual scientific meeting for the year 2000 was "Mind Meets Brain." The current buzzword in both of our fields, I believe, is "biopsychosocial," a term coined by the internist George Engel in 1982 in an article not in a psychiatry journal but in the *New England Journal of Medicine*. He meant it as the way to conceptualize all illnesses, not just those of the psyche.

Dr. Williams gives us vignettes of two women who underwent biological therapy, Martha, who received a pharmacopoeia of medicines, and when they caused only side effects, ECT, and Rose, who received one medicine, which alleviated her symptoms of depression and let her pursue her life's agenda—and here comes the value judgment—"without the need for much soul searching and self-examination." He proceeds to explicate quite elegantly the metaphysical problem of dualism. How do two totally dissimilar realms interact (outside a meeting of research psychologists and clinical psychologists)? Seeing no other way, he reminds us that reductionism is employed to obviate the problem—attempting to simplify to the most parsimonious adequate explanation. That the favored explanation should be the material one should not surprise us if the other choice is immaterialism. Albert Einstein said "Things should be made as simple as possible; no simpler." Eliminative reductive materialism is simpler than possible. But I differ with Dr. Williams' contention that any partial reduction when pursued to its logical end is just a total reduction in the making.

I believe scientists are more tolerant of dualism than philosophers are, for example, in holding that light can be a wave and a particle. I believe people in general are more tolerant of ontological dualism than philosophers are—for example, in seeing that science and religion both can shed light on the world's origin and purpose. Dr. Williams' sense is that modern psychology disparages the mind. My sense is that Dr. Williams disparages the brain as nothing more than the road we travel on. Or at least he disparages our ways of knowing about the brain. Understanding how brain activity relates to meaning is indeed a formidable task. The psychiatrist Seymour Kety, winner of the 1999 Lasker Award in Medicine, famous for his twin and adoption studies of schizophrenia, uses this analogy: Suppose a book were found centuries from now when our language was no longer known. Anatomists, physiologists, biochemists, and sociologists would all try to explain its meaning, anatomists by noting its rectangular shape and measuring its dimension, physiologists by examining the way the pages were all bound on one side and could be turned from right to left, biochemists by analyzing the content of the ink and binding glue, and sociologists by counting the words—the number of four-letter words, Dr. Kety says, would quickly determine whether the book was a 20th-century novel.

The brain is no longer a black box or a book in an unknown language. The National Institute of Mental Health has called the 1990s the Decade of the Brain because about 90% of what we know about the brain we have learned in the past 10 years. Magnetic resonance imaging (MRI) scans show us quite elegantly the anatomy of a brain, including the generalized thinning of gray matter in schizophrenia even in drug-naïve adults. This reduction is correlated not with symptom severity but with diminished cognitive performance. That gray matter development accelerates in the later part of gestation whereas white matter growth is primarily postnatal supports the hypothesis that neurodevelopmental processes are involved in the gray matter thinning in schizophrenia (Gurr et al., 1999). Similarly, MRI consistently shows volume loss in the orbital frontal region and the amygdala in obsessive-compulsive disorder (OCD) (Szeszko et al., 1999).

Positron emission tomography (PET) scans show regional blood flow and metabolic activity variations from normal in selected brain regions under certain conditions of illness. For example, "hypofrontality," which diminished flow in the dorsolateral prefrontal cortex, is found in schizophrenia. Abnormally increased metabolism in the anterior caudate nucleus is found in obsessive-compulsive disorder (OCD). Scans demonstrate fluoxetine (Prozac) reducing the excess. But they also show behavior therapy producing this effect (Baxter et al., 1992). Thus a psychotherapeutic intervention appears able to influence the brain's regional metabolic activity just as a medication can.

How misleading and unfortunate it would be to attribute a schizophrenic person's distorted perceptions and illogical thoughts to a sick soul. How much more accurate and humane to recognize that a sick soul may arise from distorted perceptions and illogical thoughts. If we can first correct his hypofrontality, we can then be much more effective in helping his sickness of soul. How misleading and unfortunate to interpret an OCD patient's compulsion to repeat as a pathological need to control, or whatever theory we may propose, without recognizing disregulation of localized seratonergic neuron function as a treatable basis for compulsive repetition.

Eric Kandel, 1998 National Medal of Science winner, tantalized us in 1979 with demonstrations that environmental learning can create permanent strengthening of synaptic connections. This was shown only in the sea snail, Aplysia, because of its quite simple nervous system. But it provided a model for how psychological and biological mechanisms in a higher organism might intertwine. He observed, narrowing the ontological gap, "It is only insofar as our words produce changes in each other's brains that psychotherapeutic intervention produces changes in patients' minds" (Kandel, 1989).

In 1993, Kandel further demonstrated the cellular biochemistry of learning, showing in the postsynaptic cell the chemical cascade of calcium, kinases, and nitric oxide behind the process he labeled "long-term potentiation" or "LTP," enhancing neurotransmitter release from presynaptic cells, influencing neighboring neurons to generate new synaptic connections. He postulated that when the psychotherapist educates the patient, helping him or her learn new ways of getting along in the world, LTP takes place. New synaptic connections are the neurochemical correlate of new insights that occur in psychotherapy. Addressing the mind-body problem in light of Kandel's work, Glen Gabbard tells us,

> The subjectivity of the insight gleaned from psychotherapy, replete with memories, personal, meanings, defenses and underlying wishes cannot be explained or reduced by the mechanism of LTP. However, there is clearly an accompanying change in the brain that is associated with the acquisition of new knowledge. (Gabbard, 1994, p. 58)

Learning involves not just proliferating new synaptic connections (sprouting) but getting rid of the clutter of existing connections (pruning) so we can use the new ones in response to gene-programmed, chemical, and other environmental influences, a process that has been referred to as "neural Darwin-ism." This means the brain is much more plastic than we realized, selecting what it wants to keep and what it wants to throw away. Without plasticity, there would be no learning.

How do these biological principles guide therapy? Patients plea that we help them be "better"—feel better, think better, relate better, or hurt less. They are not concerned with the ontological gap. Dr. Williams pleas that we respect their humanity, the value of their choices, and the morality of their behavior. I can't respect their humanity, choices, or morality if I don't foster an environment through somatic treatment, psychotherapy, or both, for the best expression of their genetic endowment.

My expectations of a patient are informed by the PET scan, the MRI scan, the LTP, and the genetic data. I do not expect my schizophrenic patient with thinned gray matter to have a brain center that when stimulated will produce the Twenty-Third Psalm or the Gettysburg Address. Maybe the best he can do is address an envelope to a friend in Gettysburg. But with olanzepine he might en-close in it a meaningful letter.

What will be considered the most significant contribution of the 20th cen-tury? Will it be electricity, air and space travel, nuclear fusion, or the micropro-cessor? I doubt it will be any of the psychotherapies. I think it will be the under-standing of the synapse or the mapping of the genome. It really comes down to the question of whether we have free will. It appears we have much less than we thought and much more than we can handle.

References

American Psychiatric Association. (1994). *Diagnostic and statistical manual of mental disorders* (4th ed.). Washington, DC: American Psychiatric Association.

Baxter, K. R., Schwartz, J. M., Bergman, K. S., Szuba, M. P., Guze, B. H., Mazziotta, J. C., Alazraki, A., Selin, C. E., Ferng, H.-K., Munford, P., & Phelps, M. E. (1992). Caudate glucose metabolic rate changes with both drug and behavior therapy for obsessive-compulsive disorder. *Archives of General Psychiatry, 49,* 618-689.

Engel, G. L. (1982). The biopsychosocial model and medical education: Who are to be the teachers? *New England Journal of Medicine, 306,* 802-805.

Gabbard, G. O. (1994). Mind and brain in psychiatric treatment. *Bulletin of the Menninger Clinic, 58,* 427-446.

Gur, R. E., Turetsky, B. I., Bilker, W. B., & Gur, R. C. (1999). Reduced gray matter volume in schizophre-nia. *Archives of General Psychiatry, 56,* 905-911.

Kandel, E. R. (1979). Psychotherapy and the single synapse: The impact of psychiatric thought on neurobiological research. *New England Journal of Medicine, 301,* 1028-1037.

Kandel, E. R. (1989). Genes, nerve cells, and the remembrance of things past. *Journal of Neuropsychiatry and Clinical Neurosciences, 1,* 103-125.

Kandel, E. R. (1993, May). *Genes, synapses, and declarative forms of memory.* Lecture presented at the annual meeting of the American Psychiatric Association, San Francisco.

Szeszko, P. R., Robinson, D., Alvir, J. M. J., Bilder, R. M., Lencz, T., Ashtari, M., Wu, H., & Boggerts, B. (1999). Orbital, frontal, and amygdala volume reductions in obsessive-compulsive disorder. *Archives of General Psychiatry, 56,* 913-919.

Issue 4

Spirituality

The Phenomenon of Spirit in a Secular Psychotherapy

Sally H. Barlow
Allen E. Bergin
Brigham Young University

Many worlds of consciousness exist . . . which have a meaning for our life . . . the total expression of human experience . . . invincibly urges me beyond the narrow "scientific" bounds. Assuredly the real world is of a different temperament— more intricately built than physical science allows.

—*William James*

Many of us have had experiences during our psychotherapy practice that transcend ordinary secular terminology. At times, during moments Bergin (1998) has termed "meta-empathy," perceptions and feelings appear to be influenced by an alternate reality beyond that which is sense-perceivable. For example, I (SB) had an unusual experience when working with a particularly recalcitrant client. I had worked diligently to establish trust, but this young woman's issues predisposed her to secrecy and mistrust. Much was awry in her life and her genuine threats of suicide plagued me because they were corroborated by objective and projective assessments. During one particular session, while I was listening to her talk circuitously, I had a word come into my head. It felt so strange that I literally shook my head as if to dislodge the word. It was not anything I had considered, it did not appear to have popped out of my unconscious, nor would I have considered it a normal experience of heightened insight. On those occasions, I have been able to put a number of disparate facts together over time and then all of a sudden have experienced an "aha" in the midst of a session. It also did not feel as if it were a product of what Ogden (1990) refers to as "thoughts generated à la the schizoid position"—as if they have been put into one's head from the outside, but are actually projections. Though I am unable to describe precisely why this situation was different, I did experience it as spiritual. What seemed to appear in my head as if from nowhere was simply a word, gentle and revealing, that brought with it an entirely new avenue to explore. I determined to use it as the gift it was and said it out loud. My client was visibly shaken by it, as if somehow I had guessed her "secret." But her consequent relief was evident, and we began, finally, to truly talk. Her suicidality abated, and eventually she terminated treatment successfully. Once she had decided to talk about who she really was, she was able to face that and become who she wished to be.

A young man who had recently returned from military service sought help from me (AB) with a problem of compulsive masturbation and other sexual struggles. He had a Beck Depression Inventory score of 11 and was diagnosed as dysthymic with identity confusion. As I analyzed the problem, I decided to use a cognitive-behavioral approach, including rational-emotive therapy and self-regulation techniques. But during the fourth session, as I reflected meditatively on his lack of progress, the meta-empathic intuition came to me that "sex and masturbation are not the problem." I discussed the meaning of this thought with him for some time and we concluded that the real issues concerned his sense of self, his purpose in life, his relationships, and his plans for the future. This was a deeply spiritual and moving experience for both of us that resulted in a remarkable change in his demeanor and ability to take responsibility for himself. Two outside reviewers of the videotape of this session, which was part of a research project, concluded that a tremendous transformation occurred in the client during this hour, from a dysthymic state to an integrated sense of focus about self and life. The client maintained this throughout our treatment, which he finished successfully according to his report and objective measures.

We realize that the above examples, which we would like to refer to as "incidences of spirit," are not easily reconciled with the standards of care that have evolved in psychotherapy over the past 40 years, and that a number of rival hypotheses exist (e.g., simply a good interpretation demonstrating fine therapist attunement, one unconscious communication to another unconscious communication, and so on). Nevertheless, in this chapter we hope to address the very possibility of spirit, how spiritual reality compares and contrasts to other realities, definitions of spirituality and religiosity, the research on religion and spirituality, the implications for therapists—believing and unbelieving—and possible applications in the practice of psychotherapy. We do not and cannot offer irrefutable proof, declarative answers; but we do invite the reader to sit with these questions, to allow a space in therapy for these possibilities. Perhaps, somewhere between Rabbi Kushner's (1989) notion of a dead landscape ("A world without God would be flat," p. 206) and Albert Ellis's (1986) notion of a treacherous landscape ("Religious piety and dogma do much more harm than good," pp. 42-43), there exists true terrain—varied, alive, rich—to be explored.

The Possibility of the Spiritual Realm

Carl Rogers was one of the first research-oriented psychotherapists to acknowledge the importance of spiritual phenomena in therapeutic transaction. He referred to an "altered state of consciousness [in which] it seems that my inner spirit has reached out and touched the inner spirit of the other . . . our relationship transcends itself. . . . Profound growth and healing energy are present" (1980, p. 129). Similarly, Paul Fleischman, winner of psychiatry's Oskar Pfister award, noted,

> There is a healing spirit. By "spirit" I mean a mood, an intangible yet definable ambiance that underlies and facilitates the restoration of well-being. In some circumstances, the healing spirit alone can reverse psychopathology, but more often it participates in complicated processes that include technical, psychological, and medical intervention which are buoyed up by it. (1993, p. 17)

Can we even understand such mysteries? As Heschel (1991) states, "Wise is he who by the power of his own contemplation attains to the perception of the profound mysteries which cannot be expressed in words" (pp. 339-340). Why would we even attempt the partial understanding implied in this chapter as we use mere words to explain what place spirituality might have in mental health and psychotherapy? Perhaps because the domain of the "talking cure," which has been relied on by so many to cure their ills, must clarify as much as possible how it does work. Recently, religion and spirituality have been viewed as healthy rather than neurotic, in the position of "being let back into the therapy room"; thus an explanation of how the sacred and secular might combine appears warranted. Early writers of treatment efficacy lacked a precise vocabulary to describe just how psychotherapy works, yet they persisted, believing that something about the endeavor helped. It took decades of effort to achieve the position of approval and efficacy represented recently in the reviews of outcome research (Bergin & Garfield, 1994) and in the national survey of former clients conducted by *Consumer Reports* (Seligman, 1995). A similar developmental trail appears to be occurring for the integration of spiritual processes in standard clinical approaches.

Perspectives of Reality

When Sigmund Freud initiated the search for a scientific therapy, he embarked on a path that many would follow. His work was shaped by the dictates of a burgeoning scientific agenda that had brought about exciting advances in physics and biology, thereby setting an essentially humanistic/secular and mechanistic course for our exploration of the internal universe of the psyche. Though he wrote to Pfister, "In itself psycho-analysis is neither religious nor non-religious, but an impartial tool which both priest and layman can use in the service of the sufferer" (Meng & Freud, 1963, p. 17), he generally viewed religion as a failed social phenomenon that had not cured societies' ills (e.g., Freud, 1927/1961).

By contrast with the naturalistic assumptions made by Freud and the early pioneers who have influenced theory and practice throughout the 20th century, psychotherapists and psychotherapy researchers at the beginning of the 21st century may be on the verge of a spiritual perspective of psychotherapy. We believe that the human personality has inherent spiritual features, and these need to be taken into account in the change process. We note with satisfaction the growing body of literature (Koenig, 1998; Miller, 1999; Randour, 1993; Richards & Bergin, 1997; Richards & Bergin, in press; Shafranske, 1996) that attests to the importance of attending to religious and spiritual phenomena in personality, mental health, and psychotherapy. These endeavors represent a convergence of modern, postmodern, and spiritual perspectives that have become an international movement with considerable momentum, bolstered by recent critical examinations of the legacy of humanism and positivism (Slife & Williams, 1995).

How might this movement, alien to Freud's beginnings, impact psychotherapy and psychotherapy research? Certain assumptions that derive from the world's religious and spiritual movements challenge traditional philosophy of science and provoke us toward alternative perspectives about reality. These trends are subsumed broadly under *spiritual realism,* in contrast to *classical realism,* the positivistic philosophy that greatly influenced the fields of physics and biology and, as a consequence, psychotherapy research. *Critical realism,* the less absolutistic view that influences quantum physics and the most recent philosophy of science (see Richards & Bergin, 1997, pp. 23-33), is more consistent with our view. According to McDargh (1993), this spiritual reality perspective "is the broadest and most inclusive psychotheological perspective" (p. 177), though it "may not be radical enough" as it continues to hope that research methodologies developed à la positivism's worldview might eventually yield verifiable facts (p. 178). McDargh refers to two other psychotheological perspectives: *God relational* and *faith relational,* which focus more on the essential mystery of the human-divine interaction. They contain compelling arguments regarding such things as the clinician's need to determine (a) what is of God and what is of the unconscious, and (b) how a client is religious versus why the client is religious. We agree with McDargh's theoretical stance in that God's reality and our own spirituality may become known; we disagree, however, with his extreme critique of scientific methods that such methods will never reveal the sacred realm. Our view endorses methodological pluralism (Slife & Gantt, 1999), including spiritual experience as an additional mode for understanding reality.

A Spiritual Reality

We believe a spiritual strategy is the root common to science, religion, and other domains that is based on a theistic view of human nature. It provides a spiritual conception of personality, a moral frame of reference for guiding and evaluating psychotherapy, a body of spiritual interventions and techniques, and a spiritual view of both scientific discovery and the research process (Richards & Bergin, 1997, p. 11). Though still in its infancy when compared with naturalistic and secular orientations, the spiritual approach actually finds its origins in the very beginnings of human history. Many theorists in our culture have echoed the sentiments manifested in diverse world cultures in one form or another, ranging from theism to pantheism as well as the optimistic versions of existentialism. The seminal contributions of Gordon Allport, Erik Erikson, Abraham Maslow, Viktor Frankl, William James, George Kelly, Carl Rogers, and Jerome Frank, to name only a few, have combined to lay a foundation that rejects the reductionism that has led to little or no room for the higher reaches of human nature.

Continuing the search for spiritual factors established by such predecessors, we define *spirituality* as those invisible phenomena associated with thoughts and feelings of enlightenment, vision, transcendence, harmony, and truth. The *Webster's New Universal Unabridged Dictionary* (1996) describes spiritual as "of or pertaining to, or consisting of spirit, incorporeal . . . soul" (p. 1840). The definition for religious is, "of or pertaining to, or concerned with religion . . . imbued with or exhibiting religion; pious, devout, godly; scrupulously faithful . . . sacred rites, observances" (p. 1628). These definitions are helpful but in no way cover the entire array of what is meant by the words. In addition, they do not help elucidate the distinctions between the two. The term "religious" tends to cover those things that are found in beliefs, practices, and denominations and are perhaps more public. "Spiritual" covers more private matters that are universal. *Spiritual realism* assumes that God exists, "there is a spirit [in human beings], and the inspiration of the Almighty giveth them understanding" (Job 32: 8).

At the very least, a spiritual reality is shared by a large proportion of believers.[1] A recent Gallup Poll indicated that approximately 95% of the U.S. population believe in God, 70% belong to a church or synagogue, and 60% are actually on the rolls of a congregation. Though these statistics vary for the world at large (e.g., the proportion of Christians, Muslims, Jews, etc.), they nevertheless reflect the increasing trend worldwide towards an epistemology of belief (Richards & Bergin, 1997). Therapists are therefore more likely than ever to encounter patients who profess to believe in some type of spiritual reality. This premise, which undergirds the world's major monotheistic religions (Judaism, Christianity, Islam, Zoroastrianism, Sikhism), is perhaps represented more broadly as a spiritual presence by the world's Eastern religions (Buddhism, Hinduism, Jainism, Shinto, Confucianism, Taoism) and in science as a belief in a universal intelligence, referred to by Einstein (1934) as "a rationality or intelligibility . . . behind all scientific work of a higher order . . . a superior mind" (p. 11).

Does attending to a spiritual reality require that a therapist *be* "religious"? Notions of "belief and unbelief" in a "higher power" have divided the world since time's beginning and continue to divide it (Larson & Witham, 1999). As the spiritual reality has yet to yield clearly discernable measures, "believers" cannot readily hold up irrefutable evidence to the "unbelievers." This search for measures might be compared to the search for components in particle physics at the end of the 19th century. Though they were not fully known then, Max Planck's fin de siècle assertion that tiny invisible bundles of energy he called "quanta" existed opened up an entire universe of exploration (Planck, 1922). Such "visions" have led to incredible discoveries about the subatomic universe as well as astrophysics' latest assertion that the neutrino is a fundamental building block in the larger universe, yet no one has observed it directly. In psychology, the "ineffable but ineluctable background spiritual phenomena must also be inferred from observations" (Bergin, 1998, p. 8).

Still, there are wide philosophical gaps between the cynic and skeptic and the spiritually willing. Perhaps in the spirit of Kierkegaard's Knight of Infinite Faith, we invite the curious to consider the possibility that it might be true that there are several realities. In answer to the question, "Does a therapist necessarily have to be a believer?" we suggest that several levels of possibility exist that can benefit clients. In an appeal to the well-being of many clients who are themselves believers, we further invite professionals to consider that these clients often have mental health issues that inextricably link their internal representations of God with their sense of self and their manner of relating to others. Many religious clients enter psychotherapy reluctantly, fearing that therapists will "cure" them of their faith. Therapists need to be ecumenical in the largest sense; that is, to learn specifically about a client's denomination (at the very least, to ask, "Is that how your religious group does it?") as well as to invite the client to explore the isolated aspects of his or her religion, given that these religious systems are often "symbolic universes" (Berger, 1967) that remain unintegrated into other aspects of personality functioning. After all, the integration of the sacred and the profane has never been an easy task. Rizzuto (1993) notes, "Here the therapist needs great tact . . . to get the patient to talk about such private matters" (p. 22). The emotional significance of spiritual issues, with their considerable power to shape clients' psyches, will never emerge in therapy as important discourse if the client suspects that the therapist does not possess a way to understand and respect them. As McDargh (1993) suggests, what kind of empathy does a clinician convey who privately experiences the religious client as delusional at worst and deluded at best?

Research Findings

A substantial body of literature has accumulated regarding the positive correlations of intrinsic spirituality or devoutness with well-being, self-esteem, marital

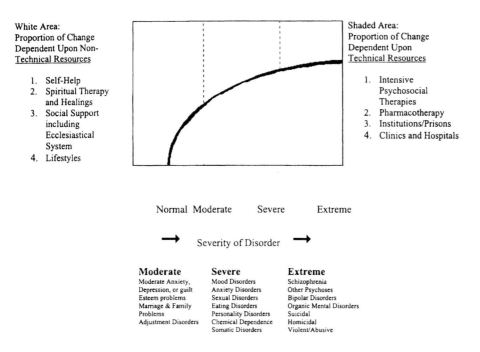

White Area:
Proportion of Change
Dependent Upon Non-
Technical Resources

1. Self-Help
2. Spiritual Therapy
   and Healings
3. Social Support
   including
   Ecclesiastical
   System
4. Lifestyles

Shaded Area:
Proportion of Change
Dependent Upon
Technical Resources

1. Intensive
   Psychosocial
   Therapies
2. Pharmacotherapy
3. Institutions/Prisons
4. Clinics and Hospitals

Normal Moderate   Severe   Extreme

→   Severity of Disorder   →

Moderate	**Severe**	**Extreme**
Moderate Anxiety,	Mood Disorders	Schizophrenia
Depression, or guilt	Anxiety Disorders	Other Psychoses
Esteem problems	Sexual Disorders	Bipolar Disorders
Marriage & Family	Eating Disorders	Organic Mental Disorders
Problems	Personality Disorders	Suicidal
Adjustment Disorders	Chemical Dependence	Homicidal
	Somatic Disorders	Violent/Abusive

Figure 4.1. Hypothesized Role of Personal, Social, and Spiritual Resources Versus Technical Resources in Treating Mental Disorders, as a Function of Severity of Disorder

SOURCE: Reprinted from Richards and Bergin (1997, p. 130). Copyright © 1997 by the American Psychological Association. Used with permission.

satisfaction, family cohesion, and positive mood (Richards & Bergin, 1997). Another large data set demonstrating similar positive effects of religious spirituality and activity on pathological social conduct and in support of appropriate social behavior has also been accumulated. Nevertheless, negative, or at the very least neutral, effects do appear in some studies examining certain correlations with religiousness (e.g., perfectionism). Mixed effects also result (Pargament & Brant, 1998), as in the research on coping where it was found that religious people experienced both help and hindrance from their religious systems when coping with a real life tragedy, for instance, the Oklahoma bombing. Whether positive, negative, or indifferent, the increased attention on the impact of spiritual and religious phenomena has led to a new zeitgeist, despite the early discouragement noted by Levin and Chatters (1998), who suggest that this period of "consciousness raising" needs next to move to genuine scientific progress. There are various ways to do this (McCullough & Larson, 1993), including the development of more qualitative studies (Richards & Bergin, 1997).

Assessments of spiritual methods of therapeutic intervention are growing as well. The findings have led to a reevaluation by many mainstream mental health professionals regarding the role of religion and spirituality (Bergin 1980a,

1980b, 1980c; Ellis, 1996; Jensen & Bergin, 1988; Propst, Ostrom, Watkins, Dean, & Mashburn, 1992; Worthington, Kurusu, McCullough, & Sanders, 1996). As research begins to accumulate, the appropriate uses of psychotherapy and religious/ spiritual intervention, separate and overlapping, will be better understood through empirical study. Figure 4.1 illustrates the hypothesized role of personal, social, and spiritual resources versus technical (traditionally professional) resources in treating mental disorders as a function of the severity of the disorder.

No longer viewed as simply neurotic manifestations, religious and spiritual beliefs, both in and outside of mental health interventions, are being taken seriously in their own right. These research endeavors cover a number of techniques and theories, from cognitive (e.g., Propst et al., 1992) to psychoanalytic (e.g., Kainer, 1993). They also cover a range of methodologies, from controlled experimental designs to single case studies. Medical education often includes spiritual curriculum, apparently responding to the large percentage of patients who believe in God and prefer physicians who acknowledge this (Larson, Lu, & Swyers, 1996). Recent texts in psychology and psychiatry also attest to this proliferation of interest in spirituality and psychotherapy (Koenig, 1998; Randour, 1993; Richards & Bergin, 1997; Shafranske, 1996). Though these movements in psychotherapy intervention and training are promising and merit further development, the few good outcome evaluations conducted thus far reveal only limited advantages for such methods when compared with standard techniques (McCullough, Pargament, & Thoreson, in press).

Implications for Therapeutic Interventions

Given our premise of a spiritual reality, we assume that every human interaction has the potential for a spiritual component. What does this really mean? There are ethical questions and dangers that psychotherapists need to be sensitive to before they embark on spiritual strategies. For instance, "dual relationships, or blurring boundaries between religious and professional roles, usurping or replacing religious leaders, imposing religious values on clients or being insensitive to their values, violating work setting (church-state) boundaries, and practicing outside the boundaries of professional competence" (Richards & Bergin, 1997, p. 17) represent just a few of the problems. These potential abuses of power and influence and inappropriate treatment can range from innocuous to lethal. Certainly, there are contraindications for spiritual interventions. For any therapist who believes spiritual interventions are indicated, the guiding principles of client autonomy and freedom, sensitivity and empathy, flexibility and responsiveness to client values and needs must be paramount (Richards & Bergin, 1997).

Psychotherapy Goals. A clinical application of a spiritual strategy requires awareness of worldviews about religion and spirituality generally, and the client's denomination specifically. During the assessment phase, clients need to be viewed multidimensionally, including biological, social, emotional, cognitive, systemic, spiritual components. The overall purpose of psychotherapy is to promote health. Spiritual strategies suggest that some of the meaning that is constructed during this process of promotion of health will involve dealing with difficult issues, such as tragedy, pain and suffering (learning from trials and tribulation, the presence of evil), and mistakes (forgiveness and repentance). A spiritual strategy includes strengthening a person's reliance on his or her value-based lifestyle that promotes lasting change, continued growth, and inoculation against future distress (Larson & Larson, 1994).

Matching, Common Therapy Goals. Here we must consider the important and robust literature that states that when the client and therapist are united in common goals, the psychotherapy outcome is more likely positive, as well as that body of literature on matching that suggests that better outcomes result when therapist and client are matched on certain variables (Bergin & Garfield, 1994). Therefore a spiritual strategy would not be utilized if the client had no interest. To illustrate this notion, a 2 x 2 table can be envisioned where the factors of client religious/spiritual (yes/no) and therapist religious/spiritual (yes/no) create 4 cells that further explicate how matching might occur at the most rudimentary level.

Therapist Role. Just as therapists must examine their own prejudices about other potentially difficult topics (e.g., free will vs. determinism), they must also examine their stance toward religious and spiritual phenomenon. A number of writers (Freedman & Enright, 1996; Kochems, 1993; Larson, Pattison, Blazer, Omran, & Kaplan, 1986) suggest that many therapists appear to be phobic about the topic of religion, in contrast to being quite open about a number of other so-called uncomfortable topics (death, sex, anger, etc.). They further note that psychotherapists and psychotherapy researchers need not be religious in the denominational sense but rather might need to recognize that their endeavors involve spiritual aspects. The fear of spiritual content thus may need to be overcome, just as former fears of sex and anger were overcome.

Perhaps, at the very least, these issues argue for better matching between clients and therapists. As noted above, matching is that empirically robust phenomenon that suggests that better client outcomes result when client problems and personality styles are matched with therapist expertise and what has come to be called "common factors," or personality attributes and the like that therapists possess. This does not necessarily mean that therapists must be "true believers," only that they are willing and open to the exploration of spiritual themes in therapy.[2] In fact, the 2 x 2 table envisioned above could be expanded to a 3 x 3 table that included another factor: open to the client's or therapist's religious/spiritual experience though not personally believing. This reflects the very real differences that exist between knowing a religious/spiritual system (an openness to finding out about it), being available to the spirit of God (an openness to the possibility of spirit), and possessing faith that it represents truth (believing in that religious/spiritual system).

In addition to research on matching, there is a robust literature on the therapeutic alliance, with its subtle and obvious components, which also predicts positive outcome. The success of this alliance is partially based on the client's willingness to tell the therapist what he or she is really thinking and feeling. As humans, we are most likely to obfuscate certain topics, which the age-old adage, "Never talk about religion and politics," reflects. Therefore it behooves a therapist to honestly examine his or her stance regarding religion and spirituality and whether or not the client can feel comfortable discussing such topics. Richards and Bergin (1997) have listed the characteristics of the effective ecumenical psychotherapist that reflect, among other things, the therapist's attitudes of sensitivity, flexibility, and respect for the client.

Good-enough therapists tailor interventions to a broad conceptualization of the client. Once the therapist understands the client's religious or spiritual system, spiritual interventions could include discussing spiritual themes; examining relationships to deity; using spiritual relaxation techniques; encouraging clients to pray; encouraging forgiveness; examining incongruous feelings, thoughts, or actions and a client's espoused values; consulting with the client's religious leaders, given written permission; and using religious and spiritual literature as bibliotherapy (Alter, 1994; Ball & Goodyear, 1991; Kelly, 1995; McDargh, 1993; Richard & Potts, 1995; Worthington, Dupont, Berry, & Duncan, 1988). Only therapists who are religious or spiritually oriented themselves can use some techniques, but therapists who are sensitive and respectful can utilize many.

As therapists develop ever-increasing skills to listen to their client's struggles, they will be able to discern cultural manifestations of the client's denomination from doctrinal beliefs. For instance, in a study by Bergin (1993), healthy and unhealthy aspects of the Mormon religion were determined (see Table 4.1). No doubt these distinctions between healthy and unhealthy aspects hold true for other religious systems and cultures as well.

As we await empirical evidence regarding the efficacy of spiritual strategies and the development of even clearer guidelines for appropriate uses of those spiritual interventions, we encourage therapists to continue to develop meta-empathy, or that type of empathy that includes a spiritual perception factor, that is,

> the ability to synthesize ordinary clinical observations in a creative way that all good clinicians do, but it goes beyond that empirical process to include an openness to inspirational impressions that convey spiritual insights or convictions about the individual that differ from ordinary diagnostic impressions or treatment hunches. (Richards & Bergin, 1997, p. 136)

The cases noted earlier illustrate our view, embedded as they are in spiritual realism, that spiritual resources do exist beyond ordinary, day-to-day clinical

TABLE 4.1 Religious-Spiritual Values, Lifestyles, and Mental Health: An Interview and Assessment Guide

Adaptive-Healthy Values and Lifestyles	*Maladaptive-Unhealthy Values and Lifestyles*
1.A. Intrinsic Sincere Congruent Lives religion Personal faith	1.B. Extrinsic Role-playing Incongruent Uses religion Normative faith
2.A. Actualizing Growth oriented Self-regulated agency Experiential-creative Self-renewing, repentant Integrates ambiguity and paradox	2.B. Perfectionistic Righteous performances Over-controlled inefficacy Ritualistic-stagnant Self-punitive, depressed Anxious about the unanticipated
3.A. Reforming-renewing Change oriented Benevolent-reforming power Tolerant Egalitarian	3.B. Authoritarian Rigid Dogmatic-absolutistic Intolerant-prejudiced Controlling-dominating
4.A. Interpersonal-social orientation Networking-familial-kinship Cooperative Open-authentic-integrity Self-sacrificing	4.B. Narcissistic Self-aggrandizing Competitive Manipulative-deceptive Self-gratifying
5.A. Nurturing Tender-protective Warm-faithful-intimate Caring Facilitating growth Empathic	5.B. Aggressive Angry-abusive-violent Antisocial-unfaithful Sadistic Power seeking Insensitive
6.A. Reconciling Forgiving Humble Appropriately direct Problem solving	6.B. Dependent Pleasing-submissive Compliant-masochistic Passive-aggressive Conflict avoidant

SOURCE: Reprinted from Richards and Bergin (1997, p. 109). Copyright© 1997 by the American Psychological Association. Used with permission.

insights. There are clear ways therapists must and must not respond once having received these gifts of the spirit that will enhance the therapeutic and spiritual encounter between two humans engaged in the endeavor of psychotherapy. For instance, one would not announce God has spoken to him or her on behalf of the client. As this field of inquiry develops, we will learn the nuances of dealing appropriately with such meta-empathy that promote rather than thwart the client's health. Some good guidelines do exist (see Alter, 1994; Koenig, 1998; Randour, 1993; Richards & Bergin, 1997).

Remaining Questions

There are a number of issues yet to be clarified in this area where the boundary between the therapeutic and the religious is still largely uncharted terrain. For instance, what exactly is the role of the clinician? Is a spiritually alert therapist donning the hat of the minister? (Kehoe & Guntheil, 1993, have illuminating things to say about this.) Does God become part of what is "interpreted" in the therapeutic endeavor? (Spero, 1985, wonders how God will feel about this.) Where does faith enter and empiricism exit? Where is the line between the actively psychotic hallucination and the genuinely received vision? How will we as a profession (once called healers, now called helpers) truly grapple with those psychological terms (e.g., self-esteem, consciousness) that used to be the domain of the religious (e.g., morality, the soul)? We look forward to the exploration of these and other important issues that will more clearly map the terrain of the mortal and the divine.

Conclusion

The enormous benefits of science appear to us to be only one part of life's knowledge base—the elegance of physics, the beauty of mathematical theorems, the startling awe that the double helix engenders—all of these remarkable achievements of science may be matched, perhaps exceeded, by the spiritual universe, even though it is as yet less measurable in the traditional sense. We look forward to the day when spiritual realism and its beneficial by-products are as knowable and known as neutrinos or the DNA sequence. The humbling experience of grappling directly with another person's suffering instills in us an enormous respect for the wisdom of science (traditional psychotherapy research) and the beauty of spiritual reality, a spiritual essence that is not bound by time or space. We believe that some day both sides of this seemingly dialectical epistemology (classical realism vs. spiritual realism) will be circumscribed by a larger synthesis, perhaps comparable to the unifying theory in physics regarding the four major forces that has thus far eluded the finest minds. In that particular search, we know that weak and strong nuclear forces, gravity, and electromagnetism all exist—but we have yet to develop a theory that explains how they all coexist, or cohere and decohere together.[3] Such unifying truths, in physics and in psychotherapy, will benefit individuals in psychotherapy, ameliorate society's ills (e.g., violence), and act as a catalyst that will enable humans to transcend the pain that is often a necessary part of human experience.

T. S. Eliot's (1950) words bring us full circle, back to Heschel (1991), "Words strain/crack and sometimes break, under the burden/Decay with imprecision/will not stay in place/Will not stay." But as the deeply Anglican Eliot reminds us later in this poem, "Four Quartets," "We shall not cease from exploration/And the end of all our exploring/Will be to arrive where we started/And know the place for the first time/Through the unknown, remembered gate . . . /And all shall be well" (pp. 121, 145). We concur and conclude with Rizzuto (1993),

> Religion has nothing to fear from psychotherapy. A person who has made some peace with his or her inner world is well disposed to hear human or divine communications. . . . Human history is a long and painful record that religion without self-examination can be a terrifying justification for the vilest of tortures and destruction. However, religion as an integrated transformation of human predicaments, suffering and hope into a socially sound faith that allows for sublimation of personal developmental joys and pains may be an essential component of individual and societal health. (p. 33)

And psychotherapy has nothing to fear from religion. As we endeavor to articulate the border between these two, the age-old conflicts, the mistrust, as well as indifference, can be set aside in service of the alleviation of suffering.

Notes

1. We realize the dangers inherent in citing a "majority rules" argument; witness the ensuing tragedy when Nazi Germany used such reasoning.
2. In Propst et al.'s (1992) ingenious study, however, the therapists did not have to profess belief in order to deliver the cognitive-behavioral therapy (CBT) religious treatment protocol.
3. Some scientists have suggested that the enigmatic features of both quantum mechanics and consciousness infer a relationship shared by both. Perhaps quantum effects reside in the brain, or perhaps there is a role for consciousness in the interpretation of quantum mechanics.

References

Alter, M. (1994). *Resurrection psychology: An understanding of the human personality based on the life and teachings of Jesus.* Chicago: Loyola Press.

Ball, R., & Goodyear, R. (1991). Self-reported professional practices of Christian psychologists. *Journal of Psychology and Christianity, 10,* 144-153.

Berger, P. (1967). *The sacred canopy.* New York: Doubleday.

Bergin, A. E. (1980a). Behavior therapy and ethical relativism. *Journal of Consulting and Clinical Psychology, 48,* 11-13.

Bergin, A. E. (1980b). Psychotherapy and religious values. *Journal of Consulting and Clinical Psychology, 48,* 95-105.

Bergin, A. E. (1980c). Religious and humanistic values: A Reply to Ellis and Walls. *Journal of Consulting and Clinical Psychology, 48,* 642-645.

Bergin, A. E. (1993). *Adaptive/healthy vs. maladaptive/unhealthy religious lifestyles.* Unpublished manuscript, Brigham Young University.

Bergin, A. E. (1998, June). *The spirit of psychotherapy research.* Invited address at the annual international meetings of the Society for Psychotherapy Research, Snowbird, UT.

Bergin, A. E., & Garfield, S. (1994). *Handbook of psychotherapy and behavior change* (4th ed.). New York: John Wiley.

Einstein, A. (1934). *Essays in science.* New York: Philosophical Library.

Eliot, T. S. (1950). *The complete poems and plays.* New York: Harcourt Brace Jovanovich.

Ellis, A. (1986). *The case against religion: A psychotherapist's view and the case against religiosity.* Austin, TX: American Atheist Press.

Ellis, A. (1996, August). Discussant. In A. P. Jackson & S. L. Nielsen (Chairs), *Religiously oriented REBT: Reconciling the sacred and the profane.* A symposium presented at the 104th annual convention of the American Psychological Association, Toronto, Ontario, Canada.

Fleischman, P.R. (1993). *Spiritual aspects of psychiatric practice.* Cleveland, SC: Bonne Chance Press.

Freedman, S., & Enright, R., (1996). Forgiveness as an intervention goal with incest survivors. *Journal of Consulting and Clinical Psychology, 64,* 983-992.

Freud, S. (1961). *The future of an illusion.* New York: Doubleday. (Original work published 1927)

Heschel, A. J. (1991). The mystical element in Judaism. *An introduction to Judaism: A textbook and reader* (pp. 339-340). Louisville, KY: Westminister/John Knox Press.

Jensen, P., & Bergin, A. E. (1988). Mental health values of professional therapists: A national interdisciplinary survey. *Professional Psychology: Research and Practice, 19,* 290-297.

Kainer, R. (1993). The transcendent moment and the analytic hour. In M. L. Randour (Ed.), *Exploring sacred landscapes: Religious and spiritual experiences in psychotherapy* (pp. 154-171). New York: Columbia University Press.

Kehoe, N., & Guntheil, T. (1993). Ministry or therapy: The role of transference and countertransference in a religious therapist. In M. L. Randour (Ed.), *Exploring sacred landscapes: Religious and spiritual experiences in psychotherapy* (pp. 55-80). New York: Columbia University Press.

Kelly, E. (1995). *Religion and spirituality in counseling and psychotherapy.* Alexandria VA: American Counseling Association.

Kochems, T. (1993). Countertransference and transference aspects of religious material in psychotherapy. In M. L. Randour (Ed.), *Exploring sacred landscapes: Religious and spiritual experiences in psychotherapy* (pp. 34-54). New York: Columbia University Press.

Koenig, H. G. (1998). *Handbook of religion and mental health.* San Diego, CA: Academic Press.

Kushner, H. (1989). *Who needs God?* New York: Summit.

Larson, D., & Larson, S. (1994). *The forgotten factor in physical and mental health: What does the research show?* Rockville, MD: National Institute of Healthcare Research.

Larson, D., Lu, F., & Swyers, J. (Eds.). (1996). *Model curriculum for psychiatry residency training programs: Religion and spirituality in clinical practice.* Rockville, MD: National Institute for Healthcare Research.

Larson, D., Pattison, E., Blazer, D., Omran, A., & Kaplan, B. (1986). Systematic analysis of research on religious variables in four major psychiatric journals, 1978-1982. *American Journal of Psychiatry, 143,* 329-334.

Larson, E., & Witham, L. (1999, September). Scientists and religion in America. *Scientific American,* pp. 89-93.

Levin, J., & Chatters, L. (1998). Research on religion and mental health: An overview of empirical findings. In H. Koenig (Ed.), *Handbook of religion and mental health.* San Diego, CA: Academic Press.

McCullough, M., & Larson, D. (1993). Future directions in research. In H. Koenig (Ed.), *Handbook of religion and mental health.* San Diego, CA: Academic Press.

McCullough, M., Pargament, K., & Thoreson, C. (in press). *Forgiveness: Theory, research and practice.* New York: Guilford.

McDargh, J. (1993). Concluding clinical postscript: On developing a psychotheological perspective. In M. L. Randour (Ed.), *Exploring sacred landscapes: Religious and spiritual experiences in psychotherapy* (pp. 172-193). New York: Columbia University Press.

Meng, H., & Freud, E. (Eds.). (1963). *Psychoanalysis and faith: The letters of Sigmund Freud and Oskar Pfister.* New York: Basic Books.

Miller, W. (Ed.). (1999). *Integrating spirituality into treatment: Resources for practitioners.* Washington, DC: American Psychological Association Press.

Ogden, T. (1990). *Matrix of the mind: Object relations and the psychoanalytic dialogue.* Northvale, NJ: Jason Aronson.

Pargament, K., & Brant, C . (1998). Religion and coping. In H. Koenig (Ed.), *Handbook of religion and mental health* (pp. 111-128). San Diego, CA: Academic Press.

Planck, M. (1922). *The origin and the development of the quantum theory* (Nobel Prize Address, June 2, 1920). Oxford, UK: Oxford University Press.

Propst, L., Ostrom, R., Watkins, P. Dean, T., & Mashburn, D. (1992). Comparative efficacy of religious and nonreligious cognitive-behavioral therapy for the treatment of clinical depression in religious individuals. *Journal of Consulting and Clinical Psychology, 60,* 94-103.

Randour, M. L. (Ed.). (1993). *Exploring sacred landscapes: Religious and spiritual experiences in psychotherapy.* New York: Columbia University Press.

Richards, P. S., & Bergin, A. E. (1997). *A spiritual strategy for counseling and psychotherapy.* Washington, DC: American Psychological Association.

Richards, P. S., & Bergin, A. E. (in press). *Psychotherapy and religious diversity: A guide for mental health professionals.* Washington, DC: American Psychological Association.

Richards, P. S., & Potts, R. (1995). Using spiritual interventions in psychotherapy : Practices, successes, failures, and ethical concerns in Mormon psychotherapists. *Professional Psychology: Research and Practice, 26,* 163-170.

Rizzuto, A. (1993). Exploring sacred landscapes. In M. L. Randour (Ed.), *Exploring sacred landscapes: Religious and spiritual experiences in psychotherapy* (pp. 16-33). New York: Columbia University Press.

Rogers, C. (1980). *A way of being.* Boston: Houghton Mifflin.

Seligman, M. (1995). The effectiveness of psychotherapy: The Consumer Reports Study. *American Psychologist, 50,* 965-974.

Shafranske, E. (Ed.). (1996).*Religion and the clinical practice of psychology.* Washington, DC: American Psychological Association.

Slife, B. D., & Gantt, E. (1999). Methodological pluralism: A framework for psychotherapy research. *Journal of Clinical Psychology, 55*(12), 1-13.

Slife, B. D., & Williams, R. (1995). *What's behind the research? Discovering hidden assumptions in the behavioral sciences.* Thousand Oaks, CA: Sage.

Spero, M. (1985). The reality of the image of God in psychotherapy. *American Journal of Psychotherapy, 39,* 75-85.

Webster's new universal unabridged dictionary. (1996). New York: Barnes & Noble.

Worthington, E., Dupont, P., Berry, J., & Duncan, L. (1988). Christian therapists and client's perceptions of religious psychotherapy in private and agency setting. *Journal of Psychology and Theology, 16,* 282-293.

Worthington, E., Kurusu, T., McCullough, M., & Sanders, S. (1996). Empirical research on religion and psychotherapeutic processes and outcomes: A ten-year review and research prospectus. *Psychological Bulletin, 119,* 448-467.

Commentary

The Phenomenon of Spirit in a Secular Psychotherapy

Lorna Smith Benjamin
University of Utah

Barlow and Bergin's chapter provides a marvelous summary of major issues on the theme of how spirituality and therapy are related. It shows that there is a large body of scientific data on the subject. From the review, we learn that people who work comfortably within their faith do better and feel better in many respects than people who do not. The review also notes which specific types of religiosity seemed to facilitate mental health (adaptation) and which do not. For that purpose, Table 4.1 is particularly interesting. It provides pastors and ministers and counselors, as well as therapists, with a well-articulated system for classifying specific religious concepts as enhancing or interfering with therapy.

For example, let us consider a religious woman who might be seen by a secular therapist as harmed by her religion. Suppose this prototypic woman has a controlling, domineering, and abusive husband who sadistically beats her on a regular basis. He demands that she submit to his every whim and claims she deserves his condemnation; he reiterates that she should try harder to please him. Suppose the woman complies—she accepts blame and tries ever harder to meet his demands. She discloses to the therapist her belief that God says she should be submissive to her husband and that it is good and right for her to be forgiving, faithful, and self-sacrificing. At this point, the secular therapist can be at a loss. He or she might conclude that the patient's depression and her devastatingly low self-esteem are made worse by her husband's constant denigration and abuse. No wonder she feels helpless and trapped and naturally despairing. The secular therapist would like to help the patient have more regard for her own dignity and to assert to her husband her own rights and needs to be treated fairly and well. The secular therapist might hesitate to challenge her belief that the present marital pattern is mandated by God. The professional norms might silence the therapist on this point. The therapist might feel frustrated by the patient's religion since it appears to support a situation that is making therapy work far more difficult.

My preferred method of dealing with such a problem has been to seek consultation within the patient's own faith. If an appropriate authority within the patient's faith can convey an alternative, healthier prospective, the religious belief can begin to enhance rather than interfere with therapy. But what if there is no such available consultation? Suppose the therapy founders on perceived incompatibility between the patient's religious belief and therapy goals. I think it is perfectly consistent with therapy norms to ask people to explore the problem religious perspective the same way they might explore any other situation that comes up in therapy, as when there are difficulties with somebody at work, with a child, with a parent, and so on. Given that I favor interpersonal definitions of psychopathology (Benjamin, 1996), such situations are examined by considering their "input," the person's "response," and the impact on the self. Each relationship needs examination in terms of its associated behaviors, affects, and cognitions. Relationships with institutions and institutional figures can be approached in the same manner. In this illustrative case, the therapist might inquire, "Tell me more exactly what your (religious institution) says about (how husbands and wives should behave, how people should react to poor treatment, the higher goals within the religion, etc.). How do you feel about that?" And so on.

Of course, the therapist cannot and should not enter into ecclesiastical debate. The idea here is just to give the patient an opportunity to explore and perhaps reconsider his or her assumptions. Favorable resolution is more likely if the inquiries are oriented in the direction of eliciting principles of love and caring—which are nearly universal in religions, except in cults of evil, such as Satanism. Once the patient has embraced the idea that love, kindness, and caring are major values in his or her religion, Table 4.1 becomes extremely valuable. The values there mark tolerance, cooperativeness, forgiveness, and love as religious goals that are, from the perspective of mental health, adaptive. They surely also are compatible with the goals of most therapy approaches, if not techniques.

Perhaps the belief that science and religion are incompatible began with John Locke (1690/1952), who contributed, among other things, to a better understanding of the meaning of empiricism. He did remark that miracles could (empirically) prove the existence of God. This framework is implicitly invoked by Barlow and Bergin in the beginning of their chapter as they describe opening oneself up to sensing the unusual, the spirit, as an aid to therapy. Such experiences of understanding that surpasses ordinary senses are striking and memorable. For me, such mystical moments are fundamentally no more amazing than much of what comes under the heading of more familiar everyday human activity. Consider the development of a baby. We understand that process in some depth through decades of advances in science. Even so, is not that process truly awesome? Does not the depth and richness of the scientific description of the development of a baby, of the immune system, of DNA make everyday sense data all the more amazing?

Science is descriptive at best. It explains "how" with ever-increasing degrees of resolution. But the scientific "hows" can never be peeled back to the level of "why." Religion is the human activity that attempts to explain "why." This perspective would challenge Locke's suggestion that miracles prove the existence of God. Instead, I would argue that much that is accessible to ordinary senses is miraculous and neither the familiar nor the unfamiliar proves the existence of God. And neither the familiar nor the unfamiliar proves that God does not exist. Science simply cannot prove or disprove the existence of God because it can do no more than describe. Science helps us describe our universe in ever-escalating detail. Yet even as we "sense" more and more, we are no closer to understanding the "why" than we were before Locke (1690/1952) and Poincaré (1905/1947) and others who shaped the rules of scientific method.

Hume (1758/1952) noted that scientific descriptions are utterly dependent on the faith that what happened before will happen again. His example noted that the rising of the sun tomorrow is by no means guaranteed. We expect that it will rise tomorrow because we *have faith* in our description of the relations among the solar system that are based on past observations. But nothing *guarantees* the sun and the planets will continue in the future as they have in the past. Science rests on this faith. My own personal interpretation (faith) is that science does an ever more detailed job of describing God's amazing work.

Now, if it is acknowledged that science necessarily stops at the level of description, then it becomes easy to "reconcile" the type of spirituality (religious activity) described by Barlow and Bergin with secular therapy. Table 4.1, which lists frequently observed adaptive and maladaptive religious values, clearly is consistent with norms embraced by therapists of many different persuasions. Many of the adaptive religious values listed in the table are consistent with the idea that good attachment is central to human well-being. The role of attachment in human adjustment is well established by a mushrooming scientific literature (Baumeister & Leary, 1995). A therapist and a therapy that embrace the positive religious values in Table 4.1 surely is going to be consistent with the science of attachment and achieve the goals marked by the the *Diagnostic and Statistical Manual of Mental Disorders* (*DSM-IV;* American Psychiatric Association, 1994), namely to diminish suffering and enhance function.

Barlow and Bergin provide a huge service to psychotherapy as they mark the vital, powerful, and benign spirit that is implicitly present in most psychotherapies. One need not subscribe to any particular religious or therapeutic catechism to recognize and enhance the connections between the loving religious spirit and good therapy outcomes.

References

American Psychiatric Association. (1994). *Diagnostic and statistical manual of mental disorders* (4th ed.). Washington, DC: Author.

Baumeister, R. F., & Leary, M. R. (1995). The need to belong: Desire for interpersonal attachments as a fundamental human motivation. *Psychological Bulletin, 117,* 497-529.

Benjamin, L. S. (1996). An interpersonal theory of personality disorders. In J. F. Clarkin (Ed.), *Major theories of personality disorder* (pp. 141-220). New York: Guilford.

Hume, D. (1952). Enquiry concerning human understanding. In R. M. Hutchins (Ed.), *Great books of the Western world* (pp. 451-509). Chicago: Encyclopaedia Britannica. (Original work published 1758)

Locke, J. (1952). An essay concerning human understanding. In R. M. Hutchins (Ed.), *Great books of the Western world* (pp. 93-400). Chicago: Encyclopaedia Britannica. (Original work published 1690)

Poincaré, H. (1947). Science and hypothesis. In D. J. Bronstein, Y. H. Krikorian, & P. P. Wiener (Eds.), *Basic problems of philosophy*. New York: Prentice Hall. (Original work published 1905)

Issue 5

Culture

Psychotherapy as an Instrument of Culture

Lisa Tsoi Hoshmand
Lesley University

In examining how psychotherapy serves as an instrument of culture, I will draw on a cultural and narrative view. The usefulness of this view is illustrated with a case that follows. Implications of this perspective are further discussed in terms of the need for cultural inquiry, issues of social control, and the therapist's role in an activity that is inherently moral in nature.

Cultural and Narrative Views of Pyschotherapy

The cultural view of psychology situates psychotherapy as a cultural practice among other cultural forms and types of social discourse. One may place the psychotherapy enterprise on a continuum from folk psychology and self-help movements on one end to social science and social philosophy on the other. Psychotherapy also may be considered one of the preferred practices among the professions in the United States, with the "therapeutic" being a common part of social discourse. Whether it is regarded as a healing art or a science-based practice, it has a culturally distinct character that reflects the larger sociocultural and political context in which it took shape in the 20th century.

Previously I proposed that a cultural understanding of psychology could serve as a second-order, integrative theoretical framework for the discipline and other interpretive social sciences (Hoshmand, 1996). Culture provides meaning systems, forms of discourse, action alternatives, and scripts for living (Shweder, 1995). As the source of beliefs, values, and personal worldviews, culture offers individuals and groups identity and developmental potentials just as it constrains and controls human choices (Markus & Kitayama, 1991). The cultural view of psychology acknowledges that the theories and ways by which psychologists describe people involve cultural metaphors and societal beliefs because we are rooted in our own cultures (Bankart, 1997; Goldberger & Veroff, 1995). In this view, all forms of intersubjectivity, including the interactions and knowledge associated with psychotherapeutic practice, derive from cultural sources. This perspective differs from a purely scientific view of psychology that assumes psychotherapy is based only on research-tested theories and objective knowledge (though it is in part the case, as with certain behavioral approaches). It also means that it is not sufficient to claim legitimacy for psychotherapy by aligning it only with science as commonly defined.

After all, science involves rhetoric and persuasive argumentation and may be considered a specialized, rather privileged, form of cultural discourse with particular assumptions and ways of knowing. In understanding the enterprises of science and psychotherapy in terms of praxis (Hoshmand & Martin, 1995; Hoshmand & Polkinghorne, 1992), we can demystify them as human activities that have come to be valued by society. This introduction is by way of saying that we need to place psychology and psychotherapy in their historical and social context and to see them as evolving along with sociocultural change and internal changes in the profession—to the extent that we are able to learn from our own praxis as embedded theorists, researchers, and practitioners.

The definition of science has changed, particularly among the interpretive disciplines or semiotic sciences that rely heavily on everyday language and intersubjective ways of knowing. Bruner (1990) made the distinction between scientific, paradigmatic knowing and narrative knowing that refers to the natural human capacity for story-form organization of knowledge. Both modes of knowing are needed for the development of psychology. Psychotherapy in particular relies on narrative knowing, and the narrative metaphor has revolutionized theories of identity and life span development (Coupland & Nussbaum, 1992; Hermans & Kempen, 1993; Shotter & Gergen, 1989). Support for psychotherapy as a "talking cure" has come from social constructionism, qualitative research, and therapeutic practice itself. There is a growing literature that includes philosophical, theoretical, and research work (Hermans & Hermans-Jansen, 1995; Martin, 1994; Neimeyer & Mahoney, 1995; Polkinghorne, 1988; Sarbin, 1986; Sexton & Griffin, 1997) as well as more practice-oriented writings by those advocating a narrative view of therapy (Eron & Lund, 1996; McLeod, 1997; Monk, Winslade, Crocket, & Epston, 1997; Smith & Lund, 1997; White & Epston, 1990).

A cultural, narrative view of psychology and psychotherapy allows us to draw on other intellectual resources such as anthropology, sociology, cultural studies, discourse analysis, and the humanities. These areas of knowledge enable us to develop historical, dialogical, and contextual understanding of psychotherapy as a cultural practice. The cultural, narrative formulation of the therapeutic enterprise also has allowed feminists and critical theorists to critique the assumptions and sociopolitical implications of particular therapeutic theories and practices (Brown, 1994; Fox & Prilleltensky, 1997). Those who consider psychotherapy applied philosophy may further think of it in terms of moral social philosophy that addresses questions of the virtuous person, the good life, and the good society (Hoshmand, 1998; MacIntyre, 1981; Taylor,

1989). For example, using Taylor's moral philosophy as an argument for a cultural view of the moral, Sugarman and Martin (1993) formulated in psychological terms how the therapeutic conversation constitutes a moral conversation. Thus the possibilities of enriching our understanding of psychotherapy with a cultural-historical and narrative perspective are tremendous.

The utility of these interrelated ideas can be illustrated with a case that may be familiar to some of the readers.

Gloria Revisited

Most students of counseling and psychotherapy who have been schooled in the work of Carl Rogers have watched the film produced by Shostrom (1965) on Rogers's interview with the client "Gloria." Briefly, Gloria presented in the recorded session as a young, newly divorced mother who questioned whether sexual involvement with the men she dated would impact negatively on her children, especially her 9-year-old daughter. As Gloria responded to Rogers's attentive listening and reflection, she proceeded with her own questioning and became more self-reflective. This increased client reflexivity may be considered the goal of narrative, experiential therapies where the role of the therapist is to facilitate the client's own interpretive, reflecting process.

According to Rogers, therapeutic movement occurs in a climate of genuine acceptance, therapist authenticity, and an indwelling on the deep meanings of the client's experience. During such movement, there would be a change from construing life in rigid "black-and-white" terms toward more tentative ways of construing one's experience and meanings. This is consistent with the narrative construction of therapeutic process in that the therapeutic conversation provides an opportunity for the client and the therapist to co-construct and explore a range of relevant meanings. Rogers also proposed that in the process the client would move from an external locus of evaluation to recognizing her own capacity for making judgments and choices. We can observe Gloria's narrative account of her dilemma and how she searched for answers with a detailed analysis of the interview transcript (referenced by the indexed interchanges).

Early in the session, Gloria depicted the value base of her concerns, namely that she wished to be open with her daughter, Pammy, but had to lie about her sexual relationships after the divorce from Pammy's father, so as to preserve her daughter's innocence and ideal image of her as a mother. She contrasted the notion of a "sweet mother" with being "sexy," "ornery," and "really a devil," ashamed of her "shady side" (3.1-3.2), thus showing a dichotomizing tendency resembling the way Rogers characterized what tends to happen at the beginning of therapy. She felt guilty about having to lie to her daughter and sometimes wanting to have sex with men without a love relationship—"I want to be honest and yet I feel there is some areas that I don't even accept" (3.5). Gloria wanted reassurance that her honesty would not harm her daughter (5.6). In the process of Rogers facilitating her self-reflection, she revealed her own valuing of personal authenticity—"I want to approve of me always, but my actions won't let me. I want to approve of me" (4.1). Both she and Rogers discovered that she had internal standards of her own, including her belief that sexual intimacy should occur only when there is genuine love and respect (4.2-4.6). The further differentiation of meanings eventually extended to the concept of an "imperfect person" and a "full woman" (5.7), both deserving of acceptance and love.

To apply the cultural and historical framework, we should remember that Gloria came to Rogers as a client in the mid-1960s when the sexual revolution had begun and the women's liberation movement was just gathering force. She was aware of the new perspective on women's sexuality and the implicit liberalism of therapists; "Through therapy I'll say . . . I know this is natural. Women feel . . . sure, we don't talk about it a lot socially, but all women feel it" (5.3). Yet Gloria herself was a child of the previous decades when sex was taboo and prudence in sexual relationships was still a cultural norm. Early in the interview, she expressed the fear that her daughter would regard her negatively, just the way she had felt about her own parents making love; that "it was dirty and terrible and I didn't like her [Gloria's mother] anymore" (2.5). She commented later that her picture of normalcy was affected by her parents' "narrow attitude about sex" (5.7). Furthermore, American society in the 1950s expected men and women to uphold family values, even as it encouraged individualism and personal choice. As a female, Gloria's identity was derived largely from the traditional role of being a good mother. She stated, "I want to be a good mother so bad" (3.9). She referred to working outside of the home as one of those "exceptions" to being a good mother.

The cultural, narrative perspective also requires that we deconstruct the value assumptions in social discourse, including therapeutic conversations. If the 1960s was a time for expressive individualism and liberal sexual stances, Gloria was not ready to adopt a simplistic "feel good" worldview. She expressed disappointment with herself, stating "I like it when I feel that no matter what I do, even if it's against my own morals or my upbringing, that I can still feel good about me. And now I don't" (3.8). When she questioned herself, Rogers did not entirely hear her moral voice. He suggested, "Perhaps the person you're not being fully honest with is you" (5.2), assuming apparently that if she truly felt right about going to bed with a man, then she would not have any concerns.

In this instance, Rogers as therapist redirected Gloria to her "self" (as construed in liberal ideology) rather than affirming her moral deliberation and responsible questioning. She in turn followed his lead, as many clients do in deference to their therapists, stating, "Right. All right. Now I hear what you're saying. I want to work on accepting me then. I want to work on feeling all right about it. That makes sense. Then that will come natural and I won't have to worry about Pammy" (5.2). She and Rogers then returned to the concept of self-acceptance that they had constructed in dialogue. Nonetheless, Gloria continued with her moral questioning: "But, when things do seem so wrong for me and I do have an impulse to do them, how can I accept that?" (5.2). She reaffirmed the cultural values from her own socialization while pondering her desires: "I've had sex for the last eleven years. I'm, of course, going to want it, but, I still think it's wrong unless you're really truly in love with a man, and my body doesn't seem to agree. And so I don't know if I'm to accept it" (5.3).

In choosing possible ways of being, Gloria was caught between the social mores of the 1960s and the values and gender roles of her parental culture. She found it necessary to rework her self-narrative to integrate the possibility of acknowledging her sexuality while trying to be a good mother to her children. In the process of self-questioning, which turned into reflexive self-talk, she could only appropriate from her own culture and socialization what was available for American women to fashion their identities at the time. What would have happened if a feminist therapist were available to Gloria then? How might the session with Rogers be different if Gloria had been born two decades later and come to him for therapy in the 1980s? By posing these two questions to the case, we can further consider how the stance of the therapist and the embedding sociocultural context can have mutual influences on what occurs in therapy.

A feminist therapist might be expected to empower Gloria to reframe her choices in ways that acknowledge her own needs as well as her socialization experience. Gloria would try to look for ways of being responsible to both herself and her daughter without feeling as much guilt or conflict. This does not mean removing the sociocultural givens and constraints. She would still have to make choices, with the knowledge that her actions would be judged by others, including her parents, and that her decision could impact on her children. More important, the feminist lens directs us to Gloria's moral sense as a woman and to hearing her moral voice as being imbued with caring and the values she placed on relationships. She said in reference to her daughter, Pammy, "I don't want her to turn away from me" (3.3). The internal conflict reflected her obligation to her children: "I only notice it so much when I pick it up in the children, then I can also notice it in myself" (4.4).

For Gloria, guidance and affirmation from a person she trusted as a benevolent authority was essential: "I get encouraged when I read in a book from somebody I respect and admire—this is the right thing" (6.9). She longed for acceptance and unconditional love—fatherly approval in a deeply respectful way as she had experienced with Rogers. She had felt cheated and hurt by not having experienced her father as caring and accepting or having her parents know her in an authentic way (8.8-9.0). She tried to be a responsible mother in carefully evaluating the risk of harm to her daughter, someone she obviously cared for dearly and with whom she wanted to maintain an authentic relationship (5.8). The relational context remained the key to her moral outlook.

The degree of moral conflict Gloria apparently felt might not be as acute if the context were different, as in the 1980s or later, because of changes in attitudes and beliefs about women and sexuality. Nonetheless, her interpretation of the situation and the framing of her identity issues would always be reflective of her upbringing and sociocultural context. In a narrative mode of therapeutic interaction where client reflexivity is the goal, the therapist has to exercise reflexivity and empower the client in considering the full range of meaningful options available. Given that the therapeutic encounter can be an occasion for people to consider their moral responsibilities, the issue becomes the degree to which the therapist's intentions are transparent and how the therapist uses this social influence.

A feminist or critical theorist would further encourage the client to question certain cultural assumptions when they appear to have an oppressive effect. Critical hermeneutics requires deconstructing cultural givens and other assumptions we appropriate from our shared social condition. The goal then is not necessarily prejudging the appropriateness of particular choices but fostering a questioning attitude that may free an individual from feeling overly constrained or vulnerable to externally imposed standards. Gloria was not a passive agent or someone who is unable to raise moral questions of her own. Yet she was looking for an authoritative source of support in risking harm to her daughter by being truthful: "I don't quite want to take the risk of doing it unless an authority tells me that" (6.1). In spite of her responsible self-questioning and sense of values, she evaluated herself as immature (morally) and wished that she had the maturity to make her decisions and live by them (6.10).

Toward the end, Gloria thoughtfully explained the complexity of assessing her inner choices with respect to the different pulls she felt—"How can I know which is the strongest? Because I do it, does that mean that's the strongest?" (7.6) and "How do I really know when I'm following my true feelings if I have conflicts afterwards, or guilt afterwards?" (7.7). Her queries pointed to the limitations of an emotivist ethics and the inadequacy of individual gratification as a basis for personal choices, leaving her with a "hopeless feeling" and wishing for inner peace. Even if we can hope that the reflexive talk was engendering Gloria's moral self, this therapeutic dialogue as a moral conversation was unfinished as a segment of self-engendering moral discourse that potentially will continue.

Yet another instructive scenario would be to assume that Gloria was a second-generation Asian American (such as Chinese or Japanese) coming to therapy in the 1990s. A somewhat similar conflict might be presented, as the client would be caught between the contemporary Euro-American culture and her parental cultural heritage. Assuming that her parents were not highly acculturated into Western values and attitudes, there would be some shame attached to her divorce and an expectation that she would place her children above her individual needs. Though remarriage is not completely out of the question, sexual relationships for a single divorced woman would not be condoned. To the extent that Gloria had been socialized in the values of her parental culture and to the extent that she lived in an Asian-American community, her conflict would accentuate her own issues with her cultural identity and developmental dynamics as a woman.

A culturally sensitive approach to working with Gloria in therapy would have to address the question of her bicultural identity. Persons with multicultural backgrounds can appropriate values and meanings from more than one culture, thus increasing both the likelihood of conflict and the availability of multiple sources of meaning. The latter may afford clients a certain degree of interpretive flexibility in contemplating their choice of action or constructing their narrative identity. Although stage models of cultural identity development tend to suggest a linear progression—from rejecting one's ethnic-minority culture to appreciation of one's own group at the expense of others to an eventual appreciation and integration of different cultures—persons with more than monocultural socialization are often in a dialectical state. In this sense, the valuation and moral reflection could be continuous, interacting with the saliency of choices at a given time.

For the same reasons, it is not certain how an Asian-American Gloria would respond to a feminist therapist. The reach of feminists to ethnic-minority women has not been easily achieved. Womanhood in Asian cultures is deeply rooted in family, duty, and chastity. Though there is contemporary awareness of the rights of women, ideas for how to be assertive about one's rights tend to differ from the image of militancy left by certain American feminist activists. And although sexual liberation became attached to the women's movement, it counters the ideal of a virtuous female in more traditional Asian cultures. On the other hand, kindness and the ethic of care are not foreign to the Asian female. An Asian-American woman could relate well to the language of connection. Gloria could be empowered to see herself as a maturing female with the opportunity to develop the strengths of personhood that could be derived from her bicultural background.

The cultural, narrative views of identity development and therapy as a moral conversation bring together contributions from cultural psychology, social constructionism, and critical and feminist theory, as well as a historical perspective in understanding the case of Gloria as discussed here. In the remaining sections of this chapter, I focus on three particular conceptions of therapy and the functions it can serve.

Therapy as Cultural Inquiry

The first dimension of therapy that I would like to emphasize is its relevance to cultural understanding. All therapists have to engage in culture learning with a client because there are significant cultural, social, religious, and other forms of diversity within groups of common ethnic origins as well as between groups. The field of counseling and psychotherapy has become more sensitive to the need for culturally valid practice. Space does not permit a review of the relevant literature on the subject. Suffice to say that the cultural view of psychotherapy supports culture learning by therapists in assessing the history of acculturation and process of cultural identity development for a given client and in working with other forms of diversity brought by a client.

Another aspect of cultural inquiry that has not been emphasized sufficiently consists in using therapy as the vehicle for cultural analysis and critical inquiry on the sociocultural and political context in which therapeutic theory development and practice take place. The therapeutic conversation allows therapists and clients to explore cultural meanings and paradigms of living in addition to addressing more obvious social influences. In this process, there is differentiation of coconstructed meanings, which if performed with sufficient reflexivity, enables a mutual acknowledgment of their cultural sources such that the therapist may engage the client in evaluating the underlying assumptions and values involved. In other words, both parties become cultural observers and potential cultural critics through reflective conversation.

Just as anthropologists have helped to describe the cultural sources and manifestations of psychological dysfunction (e.g., Castillo, 1998), therapists in the role of participant observers can try to comprehend the cultural labyrinth in which clients present with their lived experience. For example, to work with a native Hawaiian client, one has to learn about the native cosmology and appreciate the culture loss experienced by the client as a result of Americanization of the islands. Issues of wellness are closely linked to the Hawaiians' relationship with nature and the land, which has to be experienced as harmonious. Problems of identity and social adjustment in Hawaiian youth have much to do with the history of colonization and the downward socioeconomic displacement of Hawaiian families. Even though we may not have been trained as cultural historians, a knowledge of history and an awareness of sociocultural changes would be helpful in understanding the cultural and social embeddedness of our clients in relation to our theory and practice.

A historical perspective on the development of any given form of therapy can illuminate the conditions that contributed to its rise and fall, as well as its impact on the larger culture. For example, the popularity of psychoanalysis in the United States in the early decades of the 20th century could be attributed in part to American reactions against Victorian sexual morality and somatic solutions to psychiatric disturbance. Additional factors for its popularity came from the religious appeal of its confessionlike therapeutic interaction as well as the fertility of Freudian theory for inner-directed aspects of culture such as the work of artists and writers. Psychoanalysis, as grafted onto more liberal American ways of thought, resulted in the institutionalization of psychotherapy as a form of practice by the elite as a service for those who could afford it as a talking cure. The decline of Freudian ideas since the 1960s in turn was brought about by feminist and other social critique (Hale, 1995; Torrey, 1992). The Freudian denigration of women and the therapeutic assumption of individual happiness as the greatest good led to charges of promoting social inequity and narcissism. Though it had sewn the seeds of self-absorption for the therapeutic forms of the 1960s, the elitism and theoretical assumptions of Freudian psychoanalysis were no longer in tune with the liberalism of more recent decades.

The role of the therapist as a cultural observer and evaluator extends to studying cultural trends that impact on contemporary popular consciousness in an information age of globalization. Gergen (1995) and Smith (1995) have commented on both the positive and negative potentials of the postmodern age. Do we as theorists and practitioners assume the view of a "saturated self" (Gergen, 1991) thriving in the rich offerings of a multicultural society or are we concerned with an "empty self" (Cushman, 1990) struggling to live in a fragmented society? How do young people fashion their identities and their sense of reality from participation in virtual chat rooms inhabited by persons at different developmental levels who express different worldviews? These are questions that theorists and practitioners can address through both formal and informal research. Therapy provides an opportunity for cultural inquiry, as we can learn about the cultural messages and metaphors impacting our clients, as well as the cultural scripts in which clients participate vicariously or directly.

The concern of cultural critics is that the popular culture and media tend to distort social realities while offering powerful images of the successful, beautiful person, as well as materialistic portrayals of the good life. Psychotherapists are in a position to examine the effects of such cultural messages on people. Whether in young men from socioeconomically disadvantaged backgrounds who feel disempowered from achieving the American dream or young women from privileged backgrounds who despair at achieving beauty as defined by the popular media culture, these distortions can create psychological difficulties and maladaptive behaviors. How therapists can help clients to overcome inappropriate cultural pressures or to transcend the realities of societal double binds becomes an issue.

As professionals, we tend to ignore the interrelationship between the mainstream culture and the culture of therapy and other recovery movements that are paraprofessional or grassroots in nature, when in fact the continuity of therapeutic practice with the larger culture is more seamless than assumed (Cravens, 1997). Sarason (1993) observed that the neglect of religious affiliation as a psychological phenomenon to be studied reflects a lack of understanding for the importance of community in human attempts at transcendence. It appears that the existential search for meaning in contemporary life is challenged by the artificiality and fragmentation of a society driven by materialistic concerns and mistrust of differentness. Many therapists are aware of the desire for spirituality and meaningful connection in those who seek therapy and wellness. It is of interest to note, for example, that the community psychologist Newbrough (1995) has been collaborating with Dokecki (1995), who wrote about ethical, generative practice, to articulate the concepts of community and spirituality (Holmes, 1999). Such efforts, as well as holistic health movements, represent attempts to reckon with existential concerns in the context of current realities.

It is important to recognize that cultural inquiry is dynamic in at least two ways. One is that because sociocultural change is continuous, culture learning and cultural analysis have to consider such changes. A common problem in cross-cultural psychology and the application of cultural knowledge to practice is the tendency to stereotype unfamiliar cultural groups and to assume that all members of a given group share the cultural traditions that are documented often by the more educated or elite members of their society of origin. This problem becomes more acute in the case of societies that have undergone major changes with modernization and Westernization (Hoshmand & Ho, 1995). In such instances, therapists have to be prepared to learn about cultural change and take into account varying degrees of acculturation. More people are becoming bicultural, if not multicultural, in their identities as societies become more globalized (Sampson, 1989).

The second way in which cultural inquiry is dynamic concerns the fact that cultural analysis and critique potentially can constitute a form of social influence and intervention. Therapists and the public are not passive participants in social, cultural, or political discourse. Voices of cultural dissent and critique have the potential of modifying the existing culture. Cultural observers and commentators shape the social and cultural realities that they study and evaluate. Thus reflexivity, or accounting for one's own philosophical biases, is essential. This point is taken seriously by critical theorists and feminists who view therapy as a form of rhetoric that represents institutionalized societal values and serves largely the function of social control (Cloud, 1998; Cushman, 1995; Mirken, 1994).

Therapy as Social Control

To recognize the implications of therapy as a cultural force, one has to place therapeutic theories and practices in ideological context. Every therapeutic school of thought comes with particular assumptions about human nature and the relation between the self and others, assumptions that are reinforced in therapeutic discourse. Social historians such as Lasch (1979) considered the therapeutic as a cultural force that had unfortunate ideological import for American society. He associated the preoccupation with self and personal fulfillment in therapy with a general narcissism in the culture. It is not hard to see the connection between the "Gestalt Prayer" of Perls (which celebrated the notion of self and other being separate and not mutually accountable) with what has come to be called the "me generation."

Other criticisms of the ideological influence of therapy come from communitarian concerns about the likely implications of therapeutic self-absorption for social relations and social responsibility. Individualism and consumerism, which have been liberal manifestations of the American ideological makeup (Kallen, 1924/1998), promote a cultural motif that allows the intrapsychic to become an increasingly prevalent way of defining and coping with problems of living. Social philosophers such as MacIntyre (1981) considered the preoccupation with self-identity to be a symptom of modern society in which alienation is acute. Bellah, Madsen, Sullivan, Swidler, and Tipton (1985) cautioned that the therapeutic mode of thought may perpetuate a culture of separatism that emphasizes individual gain at the expense of communal commitment and participation in public life.

The politically conscious further warn that the personal consolations offered by therapy may discourage people from seeking collective political solutions to social problems, including challenging the established structures of
power. Although not all psychological difficulties stem from sociopolitical
problems, the fear is that overusing therapeutic rhetoric in the public sphere
may perpetuate the status quo. Issues of class are an example of the social in-
equities that therapists need to address (Hill & Rothblum, 1996). When behavioral control is exercised in the name of therapy, we need to question if it is simply serving a function of symptom control for system's problems that require
more complex societal intervention. Psychological discourse, both in terms of
theories that build on unquestioned cultural assumptions and practices that
serve social control functions, may promote the status quo (Prilleltensky, 1994).

Cultural inquiry, including achieving a certain level of ideological consciousness, must go hand in hand with understanding when and how therapy
may constitute a cultural force of its own with social control functions. Some
feel that the postmodern age has continued to perpetuate the cultural symptoms
of modern society (Cloud, 1998; Giddens, 1991). From receptivity to the elite
practice of psychoanalysis to popular self-help movements, we have become a
therapeutic society. Being a product of modern capitalist society and liberal constructions of identity in Western society, therapy as an enterprise can only
evolve within the constraints of its own cultural and ideological givens. This is
likely the case for as long as the therapeutic prevails as a cultural practice with
hegemonic influence on the larger culture. However, globalization and the inevitable diversity of a pluralistic society offer hopes for breaking the hegemonic
hold of dominant cultural practices. The narrative turn in psychotherapy suggests that restorying may be possible. This possibility depends on how the participants in cultural restorying (deconstructing and reconstructing) would go
about such a process.

Psychological knowledge and practice may serve the aims of a democratic
society to the extent that we are able to question unjust social conditions and unhelpful practices and to empower diverse individuals and groups in effecting
cultural changes that will support what is generative and life giving (Etzioni, 1996;
Kekes, 1993; Prilleltensky, 1999). A therapeutic enterprise that is self-reflective
and self-generative could play a transformative role in culture and society.

Therapy as Experiments in World Making

One of the hopeful postulates of narrative, social constructionist views of therapy is that new meanings can emerge from creative revisions of life stories, thus
transforming personal identity and future life scripts. The emphasis on meanings, also a reflection of contemporary longings for a meaningful existence,
represents a swing of the pendulum from behavioral approaches to interpretive
views of psychological problems. Even critical theorists acknowledge that it

takes a psychologically empowered client to be an active agent in solving larger social problems (Cloud, 1998). World making, however, requires not only meaningful dialogue and restorying, but also effective action. A cultural-historical view of therapy as a vehicle for improving the human condition must not overstate the power of narrative reconstruction alone.

Yet, because therapy is believed largely to be a talking cure, we tend to stay with the metaphor of discourse in considering the metaphysics of living. There is something liberating about the notion that narrative therapeutic means can open up a space for new stories and new possibilities of living. We would like to assume that the creative ability to imagine greater depths of meaning and potentials for living is enhanced in the narration of personal realities in a therapeutic context. Those who emphasize the respectful, empathic engagement with the other in this phenomenological encounter would attest to the increased client reflexivity that we observed in Rogers's session with Gloria. The client in this case was caught in a changing cultural world, and the therapist half knowingly tried to help her with an experiment in living. Though Gloria began with asking for an authoritative response to her moral questions, she eventually found some authority in her own voice. Although therapy as a moral conversation is not conclusive, the inherently moral nature of the therapeutic encounter (Prilleltensky, 1997) means that the profession has a moral responsibility in participating in world making.

In a multicultural, globalized society, cultural negotiation is necessary to arrive at shared value commitments that point to collective courses of action. By their emphasis on the social good, communitarians have appealed to social discourse as the mechanism for negotiating cultural horizons. The therapeutic conversation may be thought of as a micro example of cultural negotiation that is engendering of selfhood and intentionality. A client not only entertains multiple cultural scripts of living, saturated with meanings and action alternatives, but also encounters cultural contradictions and conflicts. Differentness between the therapist and the client could further enhance the differentiation of understanding and more discriminating interpretations of social reality. In this respect, the critical theorists seem right to be cautious about the hegemonic influence of the therapeutic as a cultural force.

What is the likelihood for any dominant discourse to be amenable to critical cultural and social change? Therapy as an instrument of culture can be valid to the extent that it reflects pluralistic cultural forces in a diverse world. The therapeutic is but one of a cacophony of voices interpreting, creating, and altering social realities. Therapy may serve a social control function, just as it could be a vehicle for empowering clients to tell stories that cannot be told in ordinary life. Rather than being considered as a special type of therapeutic approach, empowering, emancipatory, and communitarian practices (McWhirter, 1994; Prilleltensky, 1999; Zimmerman, 1995) could be endorsed as a common therapeutic ethic.

Professional training in therapeutic psychology can be informed by cultural studies, social philosophy, feminist theory, and critical hermeneutics.

Therapy research should ally with the work of sociologists and community psychologists to complete the ecological picture of living inhabited by our clients. Theoretical and philosophical training as part of the graduate education experience must include practicing hard conversations in cultural negotiation and value analysis. The yields of such conversations would then have to be implemented in reflective practice, thus linking theory and practice. To bring about this type of generative practice, we need to model reflexivity and collaborative attitudes and provide skills of cultural inquiry and critical analysis in world making.

Finally, lessons from therapy as cultural inquiry and experiments in world making can be shared as critical ethnographies of cultural coexistence. They represent an untapped source of grounded knowledge that can inform therapeutic theory building. Although discourse remains one of the most powerful social practices of human society, it is the enactment of discursive realities that changes history and shapes our future course. If theories of therapeutic practice can encompass cultural pragmatics and at the same time critique cultural prescriptions for living, therapeutic psychology may yet contribute to human understanding in a more socially and culturally conscious way.

References

Bankart, P. (1997). *Talking cures: A history of Western and Eastern psychotherapies.* Pacific Grove, CA: Brooks/Cole.

Bellah, R. N., Madsen, R., Sullivan, W. M., Swidler, A., & Tipton, S. M. (1985). *Habits of the heart.* New York: Harper & Row.

Brown, L. S. (1994). *Subversive dialogues: Theory in feminist therapy.* New York: Basic Books.

Bruner, J. (1990). *Acts of meaning.* Cambridge, MA: Harvard University Press.

Castillo, R. J. (1998). *Meanings of madness.* Pacific Grove, CA: Brooks/Cole.

Cloud, D. L. (1998). *Control and consolation in American culture and politics: Rhetoric of therapy.* Thousand Oaks, CA: Sage.

Coupland, N., & Nussbaum, J. F. (1992). *Discourse and life-span development.* Newbury Park, CA: Sage.

Cravens, H. (1997). Postmodern psychobabble: The recovery movement for individual self-esteem in mental health since World War II. *Journal of Policy History, 9,* 141-154.

Cushman, P. (1990). Why the self is empty: Toward a historically situated psychology. *American Psychologist, 45,* 599-611.

Cushman, P. (1995). *Constructing the self, constructing America.* New York: Addison-Wesley.

Dokecki, P. R. (1995). *The tragicomic professional: Basic considerations for ethical reflective-generative practice.* Pittsburgh, PA: Duquesne University Press.

Eron, J. B., & Lund, T. W. (1996). *Narrative solutions in brief therapy.* New York: Guilford.

Etzioni, A. (1996). *The new golden rule.* New York: Basic Books.

Fox, D., & Prilleltensky, I. (Eds.). (1997). *Critical psychology.* London: Sage.

Gergen, K. J. (1991). *The saturated self: Dilemmas of identity in contemporary life.* New York: Basic Books.

Gergen, K. J. (1995). Exploring the postmodern: Perils or potentials? *American Psychologist, 49,* 412-441.

Giddens, A. (1991). *Modernity and identity: Self and society in the late modern age.* Stanford, CA: Stanford University Press.

Goldberger, N. R., & Veroff, J. B. (Eds.). (1995). *The culture and psychology reader.* New York: New York University Press.

Hale, N. G., Jr. (1995). *The rise and crisis of psychoanalysis in the United States: Freud and the Americans 1917-1985.* New York: Oxford University Press.

Hermans, H. J. M., & Hermans-Jansen, E. (1995). *Self-narratives: The construction of meaning in psychotherapy.* New York: Guilford.

Hermans, H. J. M., & Kempen, H. J. G. ((1993). *The self: Meaning as movement.* San Diego, CA: Academic Press.

Hill, M., & Rothblum, E. (1996). *Classism and feminist therapy: Counting costs.* Binghamton, NY: Haworth.

Holmes, J. R. (1999). A community psychology perspective on spirituality by J. R. Newbrough with Robert T. O'Gorman and Paul R. Dokecki. *Descriptive Psychology, 26,* 38-39.

Hoshmand, L. T. (1996). Cultural psychology as metatheory. *Journal of Theoretical and Philosophical Psychology, 16,* 30-48.

Hoshmand, L. T. (Ed.). (1998). *Creativity and moral vision in psychology: Narratives on identity and commitment in a postmodern age.* Thousand Oaks, CA: Sage.

Hoshmand, L. T., & Ho, D. Y. F. (1995). Moral dimensions of selfhood: Chinese traditions and cultural change. *World Psychology, 1,* 47-69.

Hoshmand, L. T., & Martin, J. (Eds.). (1995). *Research as praxis: Lessons from programmatic research in therapeutic psychology.* New York: Teachers College Press.

Hoshmand, L. T., & Polkinghorne, D. E. (1992). Redefining the science-practice relationship and professional training. *American Psychologist, 47,* 55-66.

Kallen, H. M. (1998). *Culture and democracy in the United States.* New Brunswick, NJ: Transaction. (Original work published 1924)

Kekes, J. (1993). *The morality of pluralism.* Princeton, NJ: Princeton University Press.

Lasch, C. (1979). *The culture of narcissism.* New York: Norton.

MacIntyre, A. (1981). *After virtue.* London: Duckworth.

Markus, H., & Kitayama, S. (1991). Culture and the self: Implications for cognition, emotion, and motivation. *Psychological Review, 98,* 224-253.

Martin, J. (1994). *The construction and understanding of psychotherapeutic change: Conversations, memories, and theories.* New York: Teachers College Press.

McLeod, J. (1997). *Narrative and psychotherapy.* London: Sage.

McWhirter, E. H. (1994). *Counseling for empowerment.* Alexandria, VA: American Counseling Association Press.

Mirken, M. P. (1994). *Women in context: Toward a feminist reconstruction of psychotherapy.* New York: Guilford.

Monk, G., Winslade, J., Crocket, K., & Epston, D. (Eds.). (1997). *Narrative therapy in practice: The archaeology of hope.* San Francisco: Jossey-Bass.

Neimeyer, R., & Mahoney, M. (Eds.). (1995). *Constructivism in psychotherapy.* Washington, DC: American Psychological Association.

Newbrough, J. R. (1995). Toward community: A third position. *American Journal of Community Psychology, 23,* 9-38.

Polkinghorne, D. E. (1988). *Narrative knowing and the human sciences.* Albany: State University of New York Press.

Prilleltensky, I. (1994). *The morals and politics of psychology: Psychological discourse and the status quo.* Albany: State University of New York Press.

Prilleltensky, I. (1997). Values, assumptions, and practices: Assessing the moral implications of psychological discourse and action. *American Psychologist, 47,* 517-535.

Prilleltensky, I. (1999). Critical psychology foundations for the promotion of mental health. *Annual Review of Critical Psychology, 1,* 95-110.

Sampson, E. E. (1989). The challenge of social change for psychology: Globalization and psychology's theory of the person. *American Psychologist, 44,* 914-921.

Sarason, S. B. (1993). American psychology and the needs for transcendence and community. *American Journal of Community Psychology, 21,* 185-202.

Sarbin, T. R. (Ed.). (1986). *Narrative psychology: The storied nature of human conduct.* New York: Praeger Press.

Sexton, T. L., & Griffin, B. L. (Eds.). (1997). *Constructivist thinking in counseling practice, research and training.* New York: Teachers College Press.

Shostrom, E. L. (Producer & Director). (1965). *Three approaches to psychotherapy: Part 1. Carl Rogers* [Videorecording]. Corona del Mar, CA: Psychological Films.

Shotter, J., & Gergen, K. J. (Eds.). (1989). *Texts of identity.* London: Sage.

Shweder, R. (1995). Cultural psychology: What is it? In N. R. Goldberger & J. B. Veroff (Eds.), *The culture and psychology reader.* New York: New York University Press.

Smith, C., & Lund, D. Y. (1997). *Narrative therapies with children and adolescents.* New York: Guilford.

Smith, M. B. (1995). Selfhood at risk: Postmodern perils and the perils of postmodernism. *American Psychologist, 49,* 405-411.

Sugarman, J., & Martin, J. (1993). The moral dimension: A conceptualization and empirical demonstration of the moral nature of psychotherapeutic conversations. *The Counseling Psychologist, 23,* 324-347.

Taylor, C. (1989). *Sources of the self: The making of the modern identity.* Cambridge, MA: Harvard University Press.

Torrey, E. F. (1992). *Freudian fraud: The malignant effect of Freud's theory on American thought and culture.* New York: HarperCollins.

White, M., & Epston, D. (1990). *Narrative means to therapeutic ends.* New York: Norton.

Zimmerman, M. A. (1995). Psychological empowerment: Issues and illustrations. *American Journal of Community Psychology, 23,* 581-599.

Commentary

Psychotherapy as an Instrument of Culture: A Clinician's View

Lynne A. Bennion, PhD
Brigham Young University

As a clinical psychologist who is in the habit of offering and thinking about in-dividual psychotherapy, I first approached Dr. Hoshmand's chapter as a po-tential source of ideas about how to better my work with my clients and my su-pervision of trainees' therapy caseloads. From this viewpoint, although I did not read many ideas that were new to me, Dr. Hoshmand articulated several notions that I believe cannot be overemphasized, including the great importance of respectfully seeking to understand a given client's cultural background and his or her particular view of this culture or cultures; developing our own reflexivity and self-awareness as therapists; and expanding our understanding of cultural studies, social philosophy, and feminist and narrative perspectives.

As I considered Dr. Hoshmand's insightful discussion of the role of the ther-apist as a cultural observer and evaluator, and particularly as I read her sections on therapy as social control and therapy as experiments in world making, my lens shifted. I realized how one-sided my perspective has become, as reflected in my very approach to this chapter: I have considered at some length how I and my clients make sense of our cultural backgrounds, but given little thought to how our engagement in traditional therapeutic interventions may have a broad or significant influence on our cultures. The most novel and compelling ques-tions that I experienced in response to this chapter were the following: Given the argument that a psychotherapist has a unique perspective on culture, how much of my resources ought I to devote to disseminating what I am learning about cul-ture through my own practice? To influencing my professional organizations based on my experience? To other forms of influence or activism with the aim of questioning "unjust social conditions and unhelpful practices, and . . . effecting cultural changes that will support what is generative and life giving"?

From my perspective, this chapter makes a compelling invitation for psychotherapists to "encompass cultural pragmatics and at the same time critique cultural prescriptions for living." I would be most interested in hearing Dr. Hoshmand and others build on this general introduction and invitation by elaborating more specific ways in which culture and the practice of psychotherapy are mutually influential and more specific ways in which psychotherapists can help clients manage or transcend harmful cultural influences. I agree that both quantitative research and "narrative knowing" are critical to this exploration.

I believe we will find that the interactions between culture and the practice of psychotherapy are complex. Consider, for example, the convergence of the following factors: the managed care movement, prominent "helpers," and the portrayal of psychotherapy in movies and television shows. Arguably, the managed care movement has influenced the development of measures of psychotherapy outcome (e.g., Lambert et al., 1996) that measure reduction in symptoms and postulate an empirically derived "recovery" score; the number of therapy sessions that are practically available to some clients; and, for many clinicians, a search for circumscribed, short-term treatment goals. Prominent helpers in the media, such as Ann Landers and Dr. Laura, offer quick advice in response to a very small sample of information about an individual and his or her situation. When movies and television portray therapists positively, they tend to show them offering relatively simple but magical insights that quickly resolve the clients' problems. These and other societal factors may contribute to a cultural focus on short-term, solution-oriented therapy without acknowledgment of other therapeutic forms or goals.

Suppose an individual who is making sense of such societal factors has grown up with a largely British heritage like mine and a grandmother whose mottos include, "You'd better get on your pony," "Pull your socks up," and "It could be worse." Cultural and familial values that stress the importance of hard work, suppression of negative emotions, and a practical approach to solving problems might converge with larger societal influences. When we also take into account a client's unique developmental events, we begin to appreciate the complexity of factors that a client is affectively assessing or creatively construing.

I would prefer an even greater endorsement of clients' ability to creatively invent meanings to impose on cultural themes than Dr. Hoshmand suggests. For example, she states that Gloria "could only appropriate from her own culture and socialization what was available for American women to fashion their identities at the time." I prefer an even stronger recognition of clients' ability from the very beginning of experience to engage in what Rychlak (1977) referred to as the "transcendental dialectic." Thus I would add to Dr. Hoshmand's statement, "A client not only entertains multiple cultural scripts of living, saturated with meanings and action alternatives, but also encounters cultural contradictions and conflicts" the notion that both client and therapist are actively creating constructs that were never literally input by cultural influences.

As a clinician, I would heartily welcome both narrative and empirically based discussions of how individuals make sense of cultural factors and how we as psychotherapists can assist and support them in formulating beliefs and behaviors that create more freedom, opportunity for healthy connection with others, sense of meaning, and capacity for happiness—or whatever additional goals we and our clients can agree on! Making more complex and specific inquiries will be more useful than making broad generalizations.

For example, much has been written about the tendency of the media to portray unrealistic, unattainable, stereotypical feminine ideals (e.g., Paff & Lakner, 1997; Wolf, 1991). In my clinical experience, the weight loss and body image concerns that are in part influenced by media portrayals tend to be initial factors in the development of eating disorders. Additional factors (e.g., difficulty regulating and soothing intense affect, concerns about parental intrusion and autonomy, the physiological effects of starvation) seem to help maintain well-entrenched eating disorders. I believe we already have some useful theories and empirical data about etiological and treatment considerations with eating-disordered clients and that it is unlikely we will discover a simplistic panacea for eating disorders. Nevertheless, I welcome the continued exploration of specific questions about etiology and recovery that include a consideration of the client's personal constructs about his or her culture.

For me as a clinician, specificity and an appreciation for complexity would also be useful in future discussions of how psychotherapy impacts society. I continue to believe that my own actions have quite a small impact on broader society. After reading Dr. Hoshmand's chapter, however, I feel even more strongly the responsibility to consider how I may contribute to or ameliorate suffering, prejudice, or discrimination through my actions as a psychologist and to consider how I can be ethical on a larger scale. I imagine that my concern for my clients' welfare will usually "do no harm" to broader society, but wonder how I can assess this possibility.

As an example of one way in which psychologists may impact American culture, in 1997 the American Psychological Association (APA) Council of Representatives adopted the *Resolution on Appropriate Therapeutic Responses to Sexual Orientation* (APA, 1997). Among other important points, this resolution refers to societal ignorance about and prejudice toward same-gender sexual orientation; the extensive debate in professional literature about the efficacy, benefits, and potential for harm of therapy that seeks to reduce or eliminate same-gender sexual orientation; and various aspects of the APA "Ethical Principles of Psychologists and Code of Conduct" (APA, 1992).

Psychologists have offered various responses to this resolution and to the debate about appropriate interventions with gay, lesbian, or bisexual individuals. For example, Yarhouse (1998) argues that multicultural diversity challenges psychologists to respect the moral and religious values and convictions of their clients and affirms the client's right and ability to choose among various treatment options, including therapy aimed at curbing same-sex attraction or behavior. In contrast, Tozer and McClanahan (1999) argue that therapists should not acquiesce in a client's desire to change his or her orientation and should celebrate and validate lesbian, gay, and bisexual persons and their relationships.

These authors appeal to some of the same ethical principles (e.g., respect for people's rights and dignity), but apply them differently as they concern themselves with the client's welfare.

We psychologists interpret ethical principles according to our own cultural and personal values. I hope further attention will be given to the historical and ideological contexts that have influenced the very ethical principles APA has established and, more particularly, to the way we attempt to apply them in culturally sensitive ways. I agree with Dr. Hoshmand's statement, "Therapy as an instrument of culture can be valid to the extent that it reflects pluralistic cultural forces in a diverse world." I encourage continued, respectful, specific exploration of the interplay between culture and the profession of psychology and concur with the suggestion that we include cultural studies, social philosophy, feminist theory, and critical hermeneutics in our graduate programs.

References

American Psychological Association. (1992). Ethical principles of psychologists and code of conduct. *American Psychologist, 47,* 1597-1611.

American Psychological Association. (1997). *Resolution on appropriate therapeutic responses to sexual orientation.* Washington, DC: Author.

Lambert, M. J., Burlingame, G. M., Umphress, V., Hansen, N. B., Vermeersch, D. A., Clouse, G. C., & Yanchar, S.C. (1996). The reliability and validity of the Outcome Questionnaire. *Clinical Psychology and Psychotherapy, 3,* 249-258.

Paff, J. L., & Lakner, H. B. (1997). Dress and the female gender role in magazine advertisements of 1950-1994: A content analysis. *Family and Consumer Sciences Research Journal, 26,* 29-58.

Rychlak, J. F. (1977). *The psychology of rigorous humanism.* New York: John Wiley.

Tozer, E. E., & McClanahan, M. D. (1999). Treating the purple menace: Ethical considerations of conversion therapy and affirmative alternatives. *The Counseling Psychologist, 27,* 722-742.

Wolf, N. (1991). *The beauty myth.* New York: Doubleday.

Yarhouse, M. A. (1998). When clients seek treatment for same-sex attraction: Ethical issues in the "right to choose" debate. *Psychotherapy 35,* 248-259.

Issue 6

Managed Care

Managed Care Programs

What Do Clinicians Need?

Donald E. Polkinghorne
University of Southern California

Psychotherapy is a method for treating certain distressful physical and psychological symptoms through the use of therapeutic conversation between a therapist and a client. Although conversational healing has been employed in various cultures and historical periods (Frank, 1974; Torrey, 1986), it made its entry into modern Western medical practice a little over a century ago. During its first 60 years, psychotherapeutic theory and practice remained relatively stable in comparison with the enormous changes that began to appear in the 1960s.

In the past four decades, the early synthesis of psychotherapeutic practice has come apart. Psychotherapy has been transformed into a multitude of highly diverse practices. This transformation has been brought about by changes both in the community of psychotherapists and in the cultural context in which psychotherapy is practiced. Psychotherapists themselves developed new theories and techniques and adapted their practice to research findings generated by advances in experimental and correlational designs and statistical sophistication. Changes in the social and cultural context, such as the growing acknowledgment of psychotherapy as an acceptable form of treatment for people suffering from psychological distress, have increased the recognition of the importance of psychotherapy in the health care system. The introduction of psychotropic medications in the 1960s and the continued refinement of these drugs have made possible psychotherapeutic interventions with clients who previously were too depressed or disturbed to participate in healing conversations. Genetic research has uncovered biological links between relatives of clients with syndromes of schizophrenic and bipolar symptoms. The finding that there are genetic propensities for certain mental disorders has challenged certain theoretical explanations provided by psychotherapists, for example, the double-bind theory of the etiology of schizophrenic symptoms.

Perhaps the most significant societal change to affect the theory and practice of psychotherapy in the United States has been the recent makeover of how payments are made for psychotherapeutic services delivered in the health care system. A change in the financial arrangements for paying for health care would seem not to relate directly to the theoretical bases of psychotherapy or to the manner in which it is practiced. This financial makeover has, however, produced consternation and anger among numerous psychotherapists and challenged many of the assumptions that have guided the practice of psychotherapy.

Because of the spiraling costs of health care, the nation's health care system has become increasingly dominated by organizations expected to control the supply of services to the public (Newman & Reed, 1996). The mechanism through which the changes in health care financing is affecting psychotherapy theory and practice is the introduction of a third party in what was previously a two-party dialogue between psychotherapist and client (Metzl, 1998). The third party is the organization that pays for the psychotherapy. It is present as a case manager, an algorithm, or a concurrent review. Its function is to ask questions of the therapist. These questions are in the form of, "Is this psychotherapy session necessary?" "Can you (the therapist) demonstrate its necessity?" "Is what you are doing proven to bring about symptom relief?" "Is there a less expensive treatment that can bring about the same relief?" The third party can not only ask questions of the therapist but, depending on whether the answers satisfy its criteria for certifying services, can also restrict or withhold payment for a client's psychotherapeutic services.

Not all psychotherapy is delivered under the auspices of the health care system. Nevertheless, psychotherapists whose practice is conducted outside the health care system have also been affected by the changes in the way the health care system manages the provision of psychotherapeutic services. Managed care has provided the impetus for an examination of the taken-for-granted assumptions that have guided psychotherapy practice and theory.

Psychotherapy Before Managed Care

The changes in psychotherapy practice brought about through the influence of managed care are but the latest to occur during its over 100+ years as a method of treatment. In the years since the advent of psychotherapy, the essential notion of psychotherapy—a healing conversation—has retained its central position. Within its nonessential aspects, however, significant changes have occurred.

In the first 60 years after its origin, the manner in which psychotherapy was carried out followed the design developed by Freud. Before Freud, psychotherapy was primarily conducted in asylums or private inpatient clinics as part of milieu rest therapy. Freud moved the practice of psychotherapy out of these residential settings and made it an office-based specialty. He conducted what today would be called long-term therapy; that is, he did not set up in advance a limited number of sessions of treatment, but worked with patients until their symptoms were removed. In traditional psychoanalysis, patients met with a therapist several times a week. Patients would lie on a couch and talk about their childhood, their dreams, or whatever came to mind. The psychoanalyst interpreted these thoughts and helped patients resolve unconscious conflicts. This type of therapy often took years and was very expensive.

Freud held that for the conversation to produce a reduction in symptoms, patients needed to come to transfer to the therapist feelings originally directed at their father or other persons associated with their symptoms. The focus of the healing conversation was on a patient's early childhood repressions and consisted of the client's free associations and the therapist's interpretations. Freud held that psychotherapy was appropriate for treating only patients with neurotic symptoms, not those with psychotic symptoms. Patients with psychotic symptoms were thought to be unable to establish a relationship with the therapist of sufficient depth to generate transference. Significant theoretical revisions, such as object relations and ego therapy, were developed in the 1930s (Mitchell & Black, 1995). These were refinements of the psychoanalytic framework developed by Freud. Until the 1960s, classical Freudian psychoanalysis, or one of its variants, was virtually the only form of psychotherapy available, and the terms "psychotherapy" and "psychoanalysis" were virtually synonymous.

Beginning in the 1960s, the psychoanalytic hegemony began to break apart, and by the 1980s psychoanalysis had become marginalized within the general practice of psychotherapy. An explosion of new approaches to conducting psychotherapy appeared. The general thrust of this explosion was to increase the diversity of ways in which psychotherapy was conducted. Behavioral therapy with its desensitization techniques emerged from the academy and took parts of therapeutic practice out of the office with its in vivo practices. May, Rogers, Maslow, and others gathered in Old Saybrook, Connecticut, in 1963 to announce a growth-oriented approach to psychotherapy. Their approach became known as humanistic psychology and was identified as a third force in psychotherapy. These two new approaches to psychotherapy produced their own subdivisions, and therapies such as Gestalt therapy, phenomenological therapy, and person-centered therapy, among many others, were developed. Psychotherapies designed to treat specific disorders appeared—for example, therapies for sexual dysfunction, for eating disorders, for alcohol addiction, and for drug addition. In addition, therapies based on new theories were proposed—for example, scream therapy, codependency therapy, Transactional Analysis, and inner child therapies. It seemed that a therapy was developed for every trouble and a technique for every taste. By the end of this period of psychotherapy development, Karasu (1986) was able to identify over 450 different therapies.

The use of psychotherapy was extended from the treatment of dysfunctional behavior and distressful systems to a practice aimed at increasing people's level of positive functioning. Approaches were developed to assist people to become more fully functional and to achieve optimal performances. People sought out psychotherapy as a means to make their lives more productive and their relationships more meaningful. Growth centers intended to assist people to achieve self-actualization appeared as nonoffice settings for the practice of psychotherapy. The traditional one-to-one delivery of psychotherapy was augmented by therapy delivered to couples, families, and groups. Work with groups became the treatment of choice for people with addictions and for troubled families or marriages. Psychotherapy and counseling spread from hospitals and private psychiatric offices to new settings—elementary schools, high schools, colleges, prisons, mental health clinics, military bases, businesses, and churches and synagogues. With more opportunities for individuals to receive help for their problems and more affordable treatments, psychotherapy became increasingly popular.

Despite the development and use of these multiple modes for providing psychotherapy, aspects of the standard approach employed by Freud's legacy continued to inform the manner in which most psychotherapy was delivered. One-to-one, office-based, unlimited sessions continued to be the basic way in which therapy was delivered. But under economic influence and scheduling convenience, Freud's three sessions per week evolved into one session per week. It is interesting to note with regard to the current debate about time-limited therapy that some treatment during this period did take place under time-limited conditions. For example, the 48-hour weekend group marathons and the 28-day residential alcohol and drug treatment programs.

At the beginning of this period, one of the venues in which psychotherapy was provided was the publicly funded state mental hospitals and the few private mental hospitals. A development that began to affect the role of psychotherapy in important ways was the introduction of psychopharmacological drugs for the treatment of psychological symptoms. Schizophrenic hallucinations were found to be less intrusive in patients' thoughts when Thorazine was administered. Further drug developments led to belief that long-term hospitalization would no longer be necessary for the care of severely mentally disturbed people. States closed a large number of their mental hospitals and released patients with the understanding that they would be able to function outside the hospital by taking medication. Community mental health centers were planned as a place where psychotherapy could be provided as a supportive treatment for previously hospitalized patients and as a preventative treatment for people experiencing distressing psychological symptoms. Unfortunately, the plan for community centers to serve people who could not afford to pay for psychotherapeutic services was never fully implemented.

The recent advent of managed care has brought to focus the effect of the manner of financing on the way psychotherapy is currently conducted. But the way in which psychotherapy was financed in the period 1960 to 1980 also had a significant effect on how it was practiced during that time. At the beginning of the period, relatively few insurance packages included payment for psychotherapy services. Most psychotherapy clients paid their own fees. Thus, only those people with significant financial resources could afford psychotherapy. As psychotherapy became more accepted as a suitable adjunct to health care, insurance plans began to include psychotherapy as one of the services it supported. At this time, insurance plans indemnified holders to reimburse providers for their services. Many of these plans were quite generous in their psychotherapy coverage. For example, the insurance plan covering federal employees reimbursed 80% of the cost for 20 psychotherapy sessions per year. The therapist and client together determined the number of sessions needed; insurers exercised little direct control over the decision. This fiscal arrangement allowed health care providers significant autonomy in their work with clients. Therapists could render any service they felt appropriate and receive payment with no questions asked.

At first, only psychotherapy delivered by a physician (psychiatrist) was eligible to be reimbursed. A major effort was undertaken by the American Psychological Association (APA) to include psychologists as insurance-eligible providers. Eventually, psychiatrists found it hard to maintain their monopoly (Sarason, 1981). They tried arguing that it was not ethical to allow upstart professionals who lacked "proper" training to deliver psychotherapy without supervision by psychiatrists. Nevertheless, psychologists prevailed and gained the right to practice without psychiatric supervision and to receive payments directly from insurance companies (Humphreys, 1996).

Strategies used by the APA in its struggle to gain access to the financial bonanza doled out by the insurance companies remain in effect. One move was to make psychologists look more like physicians. A doctoral degree was now required and graduates of master's level psychology programs were no longer accepted as "real" psychologists. Under pressure from state psychological associations, licensing legislation was passed that limited the use of the term "psychologist" and the use of techniques employing psychological principles to those who had doctoral degrees from approved or accredited psychological programs. The APA was accused, by many of its academic members, of functioning as a guild the purpose of which was to gain access for its professional members to insurance payments. The APA continued its efforts to position psychologists as members of the health care profession by arguing for hospital privileges with the authority to commit disturbed people for hospitalization.

While gaining acceptance as legitimate members of the health care profession with its dependence on third-party payers as the source of its funding, psychology set itself up for the troubles it was to experience when health care financing became, beginning in the 1980s, more stringent in its payments and more likely to interfere in therapeutic practice. Some, Szasz (1961), for example, argued that the medicalization of psychotherapy tended to make psychological distress appear symptomatic of diseases, analogous to physical diseases. Szasz preferred that psychological symptoms be understood as being derived from problems of living. By identifying themselves as health care providers, psychotherapists seemed to position themselves as treating mental diseases just as physicians treated physical diseases. That is, sets of symptoms were understood as indicators of an underlying disease. If one reads the symptoms accurately, that is, if a correct diagnosis is made, then it is possible to know what particular techniques are required to remove the cause of the symptoms. Thus psychotherapy came to rely on a diagnostic nosology—*The Diagnostic and Statistical Manual of Mental Disorders* (*DSM*; American Psychiatric Association, 1994).

During the 1960s and 1970s, seeing a psychotherapist for treatment of mental distress and for personal growth became more acceptable. Before the 1960s, people often viewed the need for psychotherapy as a sign of personal weakness. Those who received therapy seldom told others about their treatment. During the period of diversity, the stigma attached to psychotherapy decreased significantly. It became more common for people to consider seeing a therapist for an emotional problem, and recipients of therapy became more willing to disclose their participation in therapy to friends. Psychotherapy became a topic of immense public interest. In the scientific community and in the media, people assessed methods of therapy and debated which approaches were best for particular problems and disorders. The increased openness toward psychotherapy produced a greater demand for therapists and allowed for experimentation in alternative forms of therapeutic treatment.

By the end of the period of diversification, psychologists wrestled control of psychotherapy from psychiatrists. Psychiatric practice became more centered on administering the newly produced psychotropic drugs, whereas psychotherapy became more and more the province of the burgeoning number of clinically trained psychologists. Psychotherapy had attached itself to the health care system, and the insurance companies comfortably supported it. Psychotherapists were seen to be providing a valuable and worthwhile service to the community. Psychotherapy had entered into what can be considered, in retrospect, its golden age.

The Advent of Managed Health Care

Until the 1960s, the general social understanding was that one should not make a profit caring for the ill or infirm. General hospitals were run by nonprofit organizations such as religious, charity, or community organizations. Hospitals for the care of the mentally ill were the responsibility of state governments. Although the incomes of physicians were among the highest in the society, the general understanding was that physicians were motivated primarily by service to the health needs of people and that income was only of secondary interest. Physicians, symbolized by television's Dr. Welby, were kind and generous providers, supplying services without charge to those who could not afford to pay.

During the 1960s, a turn in the approach to providing health care began to happen. States began passing legislation that allowed for the creation of for-profit hospitals. Groups of physicians organized themselves into corporations and built their own hospitals, to which they would refer their patients. As stockholders in these for-profit hospitals, the more profit these physician hospitals made, the more money the physicians made. For-profit psychiatric hospitals were created for the residential care of adolescents and for residential alcohol and drug treatment programs. In the beginning, the management of these hospitals was in the hands of the physicians who provided the patient care. The physicians began to be replaced by executives and accountants whose background and training were in business and profit making, however. These managers were attuned to extracting the greatest payment from insurance companies for the least cost required to deliver covered services.

Although people still professed that the treatment of people's health care needs should not be a source of profit, in practice, health care was becoming more of a profit-making business. The notion that a person's misfortune from illness or accident should not be taken advantage of by others to make money became less the governing ideal. It has been replaced by the "financial biopsy." To receive care, a person has to have ability to pay (or have insurance that will pay). Although stories of injured people who are refused service at a hospital because they cannot pay are abhorrent, they are all too often accurate. One of the most important questions of an intake interview is, "How are you going to pay for the treatment?" Even psychotherapists practicing out of their offices, as well as those who had joined together in group practices, incorporated themselves as businesses. Thus, before the advent of managed care, health care was already becoming a business run for profit.

By the middle of the 1970s, medical costs were spiraling out of control under the indemnity, or fee-for-service, system employed by the insurance companies. In the United States, the primary purchasers of insurance are employers, not individuals. As health care costs rise, insurance companies simply raise their rates to cover the added costs, and employers pass on the added costs to consumers. At the beginning of the 1990s, under competition from foreign manufacturers, American business began a corporate belt tightening. Downsizing and reengineering led to layoffs of many workers, including white-collar middle managers. Corporate hierarchies were leveled and production was outsourced, often to foreign workers. American industry was in a period of cost containment and reexamination of ways in which costs could be reduced. One of the costs that had grown out of control was the health insurance for employees. Health care costs were rising at over three times the rate of inflation and they had come to consume over 14% of the American gross national product.

Something had to be done to reduce health care costs. Several presidential administrations attempted to address the problem of rising health care costs, but did not succeed. A national debate on health care reform occurred during the 102nd Congress (1993-1994). Various proposals were considered, including a Canadian-style, government-run health care and a cost control design administered by the government. Both plans were designed to cover the health care costs for every citizen. Neither of the plans became law. Instead, the insurance companies were mandated to reduce the nation's health care costs.

The insurance companies replaced the old indemnity policies, which simply paid for procedures according to policy limits. They adopted a process of examining claims so as to allow payment only for procedures they determined were medically necessary. This meant that decisions about which treatments were needed by patients and who should deliver these treatments were moved out of the hands of the providers and given to utilization review boards set up by the insurance companies. That is, the insurance companies themselves took over the management (or micro-management) of the delivery of health care. Within the mandate to control costs, the purpose of health care was reduced from assisting patients to obtain optimum recovery to doing what was medically necessary for patients to return to a functioning level. Once this reduced purpose was accomplished, additional care was slow to be authorized (Tuttle & Woods, 1997).

All health care providers—physicians, dentists, rehabilitation therapists, and others—have been affected by the changes in health care financing. Among those most affected are psychotherapists. Insurance companies suspected that much of what was being paid for in psychotherapy did not meet the criteria of medical necessity but was simply designed to help people grow or improve. The insurance industry did not hold that helping people achieve self-actualization or deal with problems of living (*DSM's* V codes) was part of their mandate. Although people go through periods of psychological distress, such as anxiety and nervousness, such conditions did not sufficiently impair their lives to any great extent. They were still able to "love and work," just not as effectively as they might (Johnson, 1995). Thus psychotherapeutic care was only required when a person was too dysfunctional to work or perform activities of daily living (ADLs).

The practice of psychotherapy affected by managed care involves both the provision of psychotherapy as part of milieu residential treatment and treatment provided in office settings. Issues include how many sessions are allowed in the treatment of a client (short-term, or brief, therapy versus long-term therapy), what credential or license is necessary to deliver psychotherapy, and the ethical responsibilities psychotherapists have to their clients and to the corporation that pays for their services.

Limitations on Residential Treatment

One of the most significant ways to lessen costs associated with psychotherapy was to sever treatment from residential stays. Residential care in hospitals or psychiatric treatment centers is the most expensive form of mental health care. Efforts to control mental health care costs have emphasized reducing the number of patients admitted to hospitals and residential treatment centers as well as lessening the length of stay. Costs of inpatient mental health treatment are in the range of $500 per day and higher compared with outpatient treatment in the range of $65 per session. Because of their high costs, residential treatment programs have come under close examination by those managing the costs of mental health treatment. Managed care programs have developed stringent criteria for inpatient coverage. These criteria typically include evaluating the medical necessity of the stay. What this means is that a patient can be covered for inpatient care if, and only if, there is no less restrictive level of care that can be safely offered. Johnson (1995) has described the typical criteria used by managed care organizations to authorize inpatient (IP) care for patients with severe psychological symptoms:

1. A patient must be acutely suicidal or dangerous to others. This danger to self or others must be life threatening, in that there is a plan 'to commit suicide or assault and a strong desire to carry it out.' A patient who makes small cuts on herself or himself without an intention to commit suicide is not appropriate for an acute level (inpatient) of care. Likewise, a patient who often thinks of suicide but has no active plan and intent is not a candidate for inpatient care (see Brink, 1998).

2. A patient must have a serious mental disorder and show significant deterioration, in spite of competent and comprehensive outpatient care; the level of functioning must be deteriorating to the point that the patient's life is significantly impaired. In other words, there must be a deterioration in ability to function, reflected by decreasing Axis V Global Assessment of Functioning (GAF) scales. Low GAF scales in and of themselves do not necessarily support inpatient treatment, because it is possible for a chronically mentally ill person to not function well, but this would be characteristic and not an acute exacerbation.

3. A patient must be unable to perform activities of daily living (ADLs), such as feeding and caring for oneself. A patient who has delusions that interfere with his or her ability to eat and sleep and perform ADLs is appropriate for inpatient treatment. A patient who hallucinates but is not acutely disorganized (i.e., can find his or her way around, get food and shelter, etc.) is appropriate for a less intensive level of care.

Patients who meet one of these criteria, but after a few days of treatment no longer meet it, lose their certification to continue their stay. The concern that there might be a relapse is not considered sufficient for remaining in the inpatient facility because the threat is now potential, not actual. The 28-day alcohol and drug treatment programs and the adolescent residential programs that flourished in the 1970s were not able to offer evidence to the insurance companies that their results were better than outpatient treatment (Miller & Hester, 1986). These expensive and highly profitable residential programs and the psychotherapy provided by them have all but disappeared because without insurance payments they are no longer viable (Roback et al., 1999).

Limitations on Number of Psychotherapy Sessions

Managed care companies have not only engaged in strict inpatient reviews, but have come to administer reviews of outpatient care as well. One of the areas of greatest contention between psychotherapists and those who manage the provision of outpatient (office-provided psychotherapy) is the number of sessions authorized for payment. Case reviewers for managed care companies decide how many sessions of therapy each person should receive. Usually a case reviewer will authorize only a small number of sessions at first. If the therapist and client wish to continue beyond this number, the therapist must get approval from the case reviewer for additional sessions. If the client wishes to continue after reaching the authorized maximum, he or she must pay the full cost of the additional therapy.

Austad (1996), in her book *Is Long-Term Psychotherapy Unethical?*, argues that the need for long-term therapy is a myth and that it is based on the concept that, like cancer patients, psychotherapy clients should stay in treatment until all disruptive pathology has been eliminated through character restructuring (Cummings, 1991). This restructuring cannot be rushed; uncovering the deep repressed origin of the pathology takes a considerable length of time, at least a year or more. Howard et al.'s (1991) study found, however, that of those who made mental health outpatient visits in 1980, the median number of visits was two and the average number was slightly over eight. They also reported that most of the improvement by clients happened during the first eight sessions and less improvement per session occurred in subsequent sessions.

The position of managed care companies is that their mandate is not to promote personal growth or to help people get through the ordinary psychological distresses that do not prevent performance of the activities of work or daily living. Thus many of the reasons for which people sought psychotherapy in the period of the 1960s and 1970s would not be covered. The *DSM-IV* (American Psychiatric Association, 1994) states that to be classified as a mental disorder, symptoms must be a manifestation of a dysfunction in the individual (p. xxi). Yet Vessey and Howard (1993), who pooled the information from various epidemiological surveys, report that one half of people who had been in psychotherapy do not meet the criteria for a *DSM* diagnosis and thus would not meet the criteria for managed care payments.

Managed health care companies approach psychotherapy as a "stop-in" kind of care. Their view is that only clients who are sufficiently dysfunctional to meet the criteria of medical necessity should receive treatment and then only enough treatment to become functional. These clients may need to return for psychotherapeutic intervention a number of times throughout their lifetime. Also, the only kind of psychotherapy interventions that are authorized for therapists' use are those that have been empirically demonstrated to reduce clients' symptoms and return them to functionality (Rainer, 1996). Treatments that have not been empirically validated (or that are not empirically supported) are considered experimental treatments and do not qualify for payment.

A recent innovation in payment for psychotherapy offered by some managed care companies is to pay therapists a set fee to meet with a client for up to a specified maximum number of sessions, depending on the nature of the problem, free of interference from case reviewers. For example, a managed care firm may pay a therapist $200 to hold up to eight sessions with a person. If the client uses all eight sessions, the therapist would lose money. But if treatment is completed after two or three sessions, the therapist makes a profit. This relatively new system is controversial because it creates a financial incentive for the therapist to shorten the length of treatment.

Credentials and Organization of Providers of Psychotherapy

Into the 1960s, the only professionals licensed to provide psychotherapy were physicians. One of the strategies used to add psychologists to those authorized to provide psychotherapy was to hold out the doctoral degree as a requirement for licensure. Master's level practitioners, who were excluded from the new credential laws, then organized and appealed to state legislatures to accept them as authorized providers of psychotherapy in limited areas of practice. For example, the California legislature added master's level psychotherapy licenses for Marriage, Family, and Child Counselors (changed to Marriage and Family Therapists in 1999) and for Licensed Clinical Social Workers. As part of their cost-cutting strategies, managed care organizations have tended to hire these master's level practitioners because they can be paid less for providing psychotherapy services than doctoral level psychiatrists and psychologists (Stein & Lambert, 1995).

Smith and Glass's (1977) meta-analytic study concluded that psychotherapy efficacy was unrelated to therapists' credentials or level of academic degree. (They also concluded that the length of therapy was unrelated to its success and that the type of therapy provided was unrelated to its effectiveness.) The famous study by Strupp and Hadley (1979) comparing the effectiveness of university professors to professionally trained and credentialed psychologists in treating problems (such as neurotic depression or anxiety reactions) found them, in general, equal. But Stein and Lambert (1995) reported that more experienced therapists have somewhat better outcomes than new or inexperienced therapists, and Seligman (1995) reported that in the *Consumers Report* study clients preferred psychotherapy with doctoral level psychologists over master's level therapists. Nevertheless, managed care organizations have not been convinced that the difference in effectiveness of doctoral level providers is enough to justify the added expense.

Managed care organizations also control costs by referring their insured only to those providers of psychotherapy who have agreed to accept reduced fees and who are willing to demonstrate that they are following acceptable diagnosis and treatment protocols. The organizations argue that they cannot achieve cost savings or control the quality of care if they are not in control of which psychotherapists provide the service. The organizations screen psychotherapists who apply to be on their list of preferred providers. Therapists who do not conform to the managed care protocols or who do not achieve desired outcomes can be dropped from provider panels.

Managed care firms maintain that they need one provider for each 1,000 people they insure. If there are many providers in the area, then the managed care company has no need to recruit additional therapists. If the demand for therapists' services increases in an area, then the managed care firm can recruit more providers, usually those who can provide specialized services and can complement the core provider group. If the firms lose contracts or employers reduce benefit packages, the provider network is likely to be reduced. Presently, there are 300,000 practicing psychotherapists and 25,000 new psychotherapists are licensed each year. Based on the 1:1000 ratio, managed care firms estimate they will need only one half to one third of the presently licensed psychotherapists to deliver the required services. Tuttle and Woods (1997) give the following description of the present situation:

> The "psychebusiness" experienced unprecedented growth during the 1960s, 1970s, and 1980s. We are now undergoing the purposeful downsizing of a business that is part of industrialization. Therapists are going out of business, accepting lower or flattened incomes, working part-time for agencies, or becoming employees of managed care systems. This is part of a political and social climate in which all forms of service delivery are subject to cynicism and to questions as to whether the service is needed, and if so, how it can be delivered more efficiently. (p. 21)

A recent working group reported to the APA (Spruill, Kohout, & Gehlmann, 1997) on the implications of changes in the health care delivery system: "The focus of our [doctoral level] training will need to be changed because it is unlikely that professional psychologists in the future will be solely, or even primarily, direct service providers, the role that is most familiar today" (p. 7). The report suggests that psychologists of the future are more likely to be engaged in training and supervising other mental health professionals, in the design and evaluation of programs, in the design of quality management activities, in the development of treatment planning modules, and in outcome assessment.

Ethical Issues

Conducting psychotherapy under the auspices of a managed care firm presents psychotherapists with new challenges to their professional ethics. Austad (1996) proposes that psychotherapists need to balance an individual-oriented ethic with a societal ethic. She holds that therapists have primarily emphasized an individual-oriented ethic in their work with clients. The individual ethic is client centered and focuses on issues related to serving a client's needs. Issues arise around patient confidentiality, release of information, informed consent, sexual misconduct, practicing out of one's area of expertise, and so on. Much of the criticism of managed care is focused on the threat that managed care poses to the ethical treatment of a therapist's individual clients. For example, Bilynsky and Vernaglia (1998) identify three areas in which managed care threatens therapists' ethical responsibility to their clients: (a) in patient care, (b) in the handling of patient data, and (c) in issues surrounding membership in a managed health care organization. Austad (1996) points out that although these individual-oriented ethical concerns are of great importance, their focus is on what is best for the individual the therapist is serving at the time, for example, getting the most therapy possible for the client. Therapists' commitment to their individual clients may cause them to neglect the competing societal need for making the distribution of psychotherapy fair so everyone who is entitled to it has equal access. From this ethical perspective, it is better to give some therapy to everyone than to give abundant therapy to a few.

Metzl (1998) discussed the delivery of psychotherapy when it was provided on a fee-for-service basis. He writes, "Prices for treatment rose to the point where those who needed help the most were often unable to afford it" (p. 346). He suggested that managed care could potentially extend psychotherapeutic coverage so as "to effectively alleviate pain in many diverse patient groups regardless of social class or level of functioning" (p. 346). He accuses the fee-for-service system of frequently alleviating only the pain of the affluent. Austad (1996) challenges psychotherapists to undertake the dual responsibilities of ethical treatment of their individual clients and opening up the delivery of services to those who were left out of the fee-for-service system and the over 40 million Americans who are not provided for in the managed care system.

Summary

Cummings (1995) reports that many professional psychology leaders during the past several years gave assurances that managed care was "paradoxically a gimmick that would go away and a threat that would be defeated" (p. 10). Instead, Cummings holds that it was the "greatest resocialization of psychologists to occur since the explosion of clinical psychology in the post World War II era" (p. 10). Management of health care has succeeded in its mandate to cut health care costs by reducing the amount of care delivered and by reducing the cost of the health services that were retained. The change in financing health care in the United States appears to be not a temporary change but a permanent one.

The managed care industry is not a finished product. It is still being created. Its configuration is not finished and it will continue to modify itself in the future. As the ill treatments that are the product of its policies are becoming apparent, federal and state governments are exerting pressure for changes that recognize patients' rights. It has become a billion-dollar industry in which its excessive executive salaries and corporate profits no longer reflect the notion that money should not be made off people's injuries and illnesses.

Spruill et al. (1997) report that managed care enrollment in Oregon more than doubled in a recent 4-year period (1993 to 1997) and is estimated to be at

92% of residents with health insurance. They also report that the experience in Oregon has already occurred or is in the process of occurring in all the other states. Managed care has become a central concern for almost all who practice psychotherapy (Tuttle & Woods, 1997). PsychInfo lists over 4,600 articles about managed care published since 1990. It is no longer enough to point to research that shows that psychotherapy is effective; now it must be shown to be cost-effective (Fraser, 1996). Psychotherapists now talk about money and marketing; the "filthy lucre" (as Norman O. Brown, 1986, calls it) has entered the therapeutic dyad along with giving care and comfort to those in need.

Metzl (1998) criticizes managed care companies for overlooking the cost-effectiveness and benefits of greater access to psychotherapy. He writes that managed care companies "are in the process of drastically cutting back the level of care offered to many patients suffering from mental illness, and thus radically revising a previous standard of care" (p. 348). He reports that they have offered almost no evidence that their cutbacks in psychotherapy are not antitherapeutic or dangerous. Such evidence would be routinely demanded in other settings, such as the testing requirement of the federal Food and Drug Administration (FDA) in decisions of new medications.

In the 1960s, American psychotherapy associated itself with the nation's medical health care system. As a result, instead of patients paying their therapists out of their own pockets, more and more third-party organizations became the source of payments for psychotherapy services. In the beginning, payers entered the psychotherapeutic relationship as silent partners, but with the changes in financing health care that began in the 1980s, psychotherapy was dragged along into a new pecuniary system in which the third party has become a very vocal partner in determining who will be provided psychotherapy, who will provide it, what will be done in the sessions, and how many sessions will be allowed.

Adjusting to Managed Care

Managed care has required psychotherapy to justify many of the assumptions that guide its practice. These assumptions were (a) long-term treatment is necessary to produce effective client change, (b) successful and safe psychotherapy requires therapists with doctoral degrees, (c) removal of psychological symptoms requires changes in personality through the resolution of childhood conflicts, (d) psychotherapy can be productive only if strict client confidentiality is maintained, and (e) treatment of clients suffering from alcohol or drug addiction requires milieu residential treatment. Some of these assumptions had guided psychotherapeutic practice since Freud had advocated them; others had been added during the period of diversity. Most of these assumptions did not stand up to the scrutiny demanded by managed care. In general, it was the research conducted by psychologists themselves that was used to undercut these long-held convictions.

The inability to convince managed care firms that they needed to finance the kind of psychotherapy that had been practiced in the period of diversity lessened the standing and authority of psychotherapists to determine how they would practice. Other issues also contributed to weakening the authority of psychotherapy to determine its own mode of practice. Dawes, a leading psychotherapy researcher, produced a very influential and damning book (1994) about the scientific basis of psychotherapy. He subtitled his book *Psychology and Psychotherapy Built on Myth*. The overzealous commitment by some psychotherapists to repressed memories of childhood abuse as the cause of their clients' problems raised public and judicial concern about the sophistication of therapists. Forensic psychology also came under criticism. Hagen's (1997) *Whores of the Court* cited studies that found that 60% of the time psychological professionals incorrectly predicted which violent criminals would repeat their offenses. Wilson (1997) accused psychological experts of introducing implausible excuses, such as those used in the Twinkie defense and in the psychosexual abuse defense used for the Menendez brothers. A state legislator in Arizona introduced a bill that would require psychological experts to wear a magician's hat when testifying in court.

The loss of control over their practice of psychotherapy and concomitant authorization of only some modes of treatment have led some therapists to believe that managed care is destroying the practice of psychotherapy. Shore, a cofounder of the Coalition of Mental Health Professionals and Consumers, sent a letter to the APA Council of Representatives on January 23, 1995. The letter stated that managed care

> is destroying much of what our profession has built over the past 100 years and is defying the values we believe are essential for quality care. I, as many others, feel I cannot practice ethically or with any sense of personal dignity under a managed care system. Many good psychologists are being forced out of work because they refuse to under-treat people or to comply with the betrayal of their patient's trust. Others are already preparing to leave the field, demoralized and in utter despair because of what is happening to patients, treatment, morals, ethics, to themselves as human beings and as professionals. . . . We are working against great odds to try to stop a giant from destroying all we hold dear. (quoted in Austad, 1996, pp. 36-37)

Woolfolk (1998) argues that the humanistic tradition of psychotherapy as self-exploration and personal growth should not be lost in the movement to a "psychotechnology represented by short-term, manualized treatment" and the effort to "'medicalize' psychotherapy [and] to reduce it to a healing technology based on somatic medicine" (p. xvii).

Psychotherapy Outside the System of Managed Care

Managed care corporations have cut mental health care costs by substantially limiting who is eligible to receive psychotherapy. In general, only those people for whom it is a medical necessity are certified to receive psychotherapy, and they are treated only until they obtain a minimal level of functionality. The people who meet these criteria are only a relatively small portion of the people who sought psychotherapy in the 1960s and 1970s. It can be argued that psychotherapy is least effective with the relatively psychologically dysfunctional clients funded by managed care. Freud recognized that clients needed a sufficient level of functionality to engage in a relationship with a therapist. It may be that people excluded by managed care from psychotherapy provisions are the very ones for whom psychotherapy is most beneficial and for whom the risk of damage from psychotherapy is less.

Although these results are not included in the purview of managed care, psychotherapy can serve to improve the quality of clients' lives; to assist them through troubled times; and to prevent some minor symptoms from festering into major, dysfunctional symptoms (those that will be covered by managed care). Psychotherapy can significantly help during times of crisis and stress—for example, the loss of a loved one, the loss of employment, marriage and family tensions, the stress of adolescence, sorting out issues affecting major life decisions, and other problems of living. Psychotherapists should not abandon these clients simply because they have been removed from the health care payout roles. It may be that, as Szasz (1961) recommended, psychotherapy needs to conceive of itself primarily as an educational service and only secondarily as a health care treatment.

Service for client needs not covered by managed care will require sources of funding outside the present health care system. Community and nonprofit service agencies can provide support for this broader range of clients. Private and group practices based on sliding scale charges and low fees for service are other possibilities. At a recent workshop on how psychotherapists can support themselves outside the managed care system, the speaker suggested that therapists explain to clients with high incomes that part of their fee goes to provide service to clients who are able to pay only minimal amounts. In a recent article in *USA Today*, a psychotherapist (Schwarzchild, 1999) wrote about his decision to "get out of the managed care system before it gets me." He wrote,

> I don't know whether I'll be able to make a living on my own terms. I can't compete financially with nothing-out-of-the-patient's-pocket insurance plans. Instead, I'll have to offer that old-fashioned commodity managed care companies seem to have forgotten about: real service to my customers.

Psychotherapists need not "follow the money" into the managed care system. Although remaining outside will result in diminished incomes from the level achieved before managed care, staying in the system is also resulting in diminished incomes. Leaving managed care can allow practitioners to retain the values that led them to become psychotherapists and to exercise their own professional judgment about how best to serve their clients.

Psychotherapy Within the System of Managed Care

A recent trend in the managed care system is the development of capitated practice groups. Under the capitation system, mental health benefits are separated out from medical benefits provided by a managed care entity. The managed care entity contracts out to a provider group all the mental health services for the dependents covered by the company. In capitation plans, the provider group agrees to provide all the mental health services necessary for a flat fee. The provider group makes its own decisions about how many psychotherapy sessions to deliver and who should receive them. The external managed care aspect is eliminated and the group can decide how best to serve the mental health needs of the group under its care. It can provide psychotherapy for problems in living and preventative mental health programs. The only limit placed on the providers is the resources they can afford to provide under the flat fee for which they contracted. Because a provider group has to periodically return to the managed care entity to have its contract renewed, it needs to provide services of high enough quality that group members under their care are satisfied.

Cummings (1995) notes that adjusting to practice under managed care has not been easy after the struggle for so many years to attain autonomy only to see the rules of the game change. Cummings proposes that to succeed as a provider in the new system will require that psychotherapists make a paradigm shift from a dyadic model to a catalyst model. The dyadic model has the following characteristics: (a) few clients are seen, but for lengthy courses of treatment; (b) treatment is continuous, often weekly; (c) the therapist is the vehicle for change; (d) therapy is the most important event in the client's life; (e) therapy continues until healing occurs and the client is terminated as "cured" to some degree; (f) individual and group psychotherapy in the office are the main modalities by which healing takes place; and (g) fee-for-service is the economic base for practice. The catalyst model, required for practice in the managed care system, has the following characteristics: (a) many clients are seen for brief episodes of treatment very often in nontraditional modes, (b) treatment is brief and intermittent throughout the life cycle, (c) the therapist is merely a catalyst for the client to change, (d) therapy is an artificial situation like an operating room and significant changes occur and keep occurring after therapy has been interrupted, (e) the client has recourse to therapy as needed throughout the life cycle, (f) every healing resource in the community is mobilized, and (g) prospective reimbursement or capitation free the therapist to provide whatever psychotherapeutic services are needed regardless of the client's ability to pay.

The initial interaction between psychotherapy providers and managed care companies was a confrontation between two different sets of values—doing what is necessary to serve the needs of clients versus saving money by doing only what is medically necessary. Providers damned managed care executives as uncaring profit mongers and prayed they would simply go away. Managed care firms accused psychotherapists of being unreasonable and unwilling to give up their cherished assumptions to assist the nation in gaining control over the ruinous spiral of health care costs. It has become apparent that psychotherapists and managed care firms are going to have to live together. Both sides will have to listen carefully to each other and to compromise their positions so that they will progress toward a goal of providing responsive, effective, and efficient psychotherapeutic care for everyone in need.

References

American Psychiatric Association. (1994). *Diagnostic and statistical manual of mental disorders* (4th ed.). Washington, DC: American Psychiatric Association.

Austad, C. S. (1996). *Is long-term psychotherapy unethical?* San Francisco: Jossey-Bass.

Bilynsky, N. S., & Vernaglia, E. R. (1998). The ethical practice of psychology in a managed-care framework. *Psychotherapy, 35*(1), 54-77.

Brink, S. (1998, January 19). I'll say I'm suicidal. *U. S. News & World Report* [On-line]. Available: http://www.usnews.com/usnews/issue/980119/19mana.htm

Brown, N. O. (1986). *Life against death: The psychoanalytical meaning of history* (2nd ed.). Middletown, CT: Wesleyan University Press.

Cummings, N. A. (1991). Brief intermittent psychotherapy throughout the life cycle. In C. S. Austad & W. Berman (Eds.), *Psychotherapy in managed care: The optimal use of time and resources.* Washington, DC: American Psychological Association.

Cummings, N. A. (1995). Impact of managed care on employment and training: A primer for survival. *Professional Psychology: Research and Practice, 26*(1), 10-15.

Dawes, R. M. (1994). *House of cards: Psychology and psychotherapy built on myth.* New York: Free Press.

Frank, J. D. (1974). *Persuasion and healing* (rev. ed.). New York: Schocken.

Fraser, J. S. (1996). All that glitters is not always gold: Medical offset effects and managed behavioral health care. *Professional Psychology: Research and Practice, 27*, 335-344.

Hagen, M. A. (1997). *Whores of the court: The fraud of psychiatric testimony.* New York: Regan Books.

Howard, K., Orlinsky, D., Sanders, S., Bankoff, E., Davidson, C., & O'Mahoney, M. (1991). Northwestern University-University of Chicago psychotherapy research program. In L. Beutler & M. Crago (Eds.), *Psychotherapy research* (pp. 65-81). Washington, DC: American Psychological Association.

Humphreys, K. (1996). Clinical psychologists as psychotherapists: History, future, and alternatives. *American Psychologist, 51*(3), 190-197.

Johnson, L. D. (1995). *Psychotherapy in the age of accountability.* New York: Norton.

Karasu, T. B. (1986). The psychotherapies: Benefits and limitations. *American Journal of Psychotherapy, 40*, 324-342.

Metzl, J. M. (1998). Psychotherapy, managed care, and the economy of interaction. *American Journal of Psychotherapy, 52*(3), 332-351.

Miller, W. R., & Hester, R. K. (1986). Inpatient alcoholism treatment: Who benefits? *American Psychologist, 41*, 794-805.

Mitchell, S. A., & Black, M. J. (1995). *Freud and beyond: A history of modern psychoanalytic thought.* New York: Basic Books.

Newman, R., & Reed, G. M. (1996). Psychology as a health care profession: Its evolution and future directions. In R. J. Resnick & R. H. Rozensky (Eds.), *Health psychology through the life span: Practice and research opportunities.* Washington, DC: American Psychological Association.

Rainer, J. P. (1996). Introduction to the special issue on psychotherapy outcomes. *Psychotherapy, 33*(2), 159.

Roback, H. B., Barton, D., Castelnuovo-Tedesco, P., Gay, V., Havens, L., & Nash, J. (1999). A symposium on psychotherapy in the age of managed care. *American Journal of Psychotherapy, 53*(1), 1-16.

Sarason, S. B. (1981). An asocial psychology and a misdirected clinical psychology. *American Psychologist, 36*, 827-836.

Schwarzchild, M. (1999, August 2). Getting out before the system gets to me. *USA Today* [On-line]. Available: http://pqasb.pqarchiver.com/USAToday/

Seligman, M. E. P. (1995). The effectiveness of psychotherapy. *American Psychologist, 50*(12), 965-974.

Smith, M. L., & Glass, G. V. (1977). Meta-analysis of psychotherapy outcome studies. *American Psychologist, 32*, 752-760.

Spruill, J., Kohout, J., & Gehlmann, S. (1997). *Final report of the American Psychological Association working group on the implications of changes in the health care delivery system for the education, training and continuing professional education of psychologists* (#96MO2052201D). Washington, DC: American Psychological Association.

Stein, D. M., & Lambert, M. J. (1995). Graduate training in psychotherapy: Are therapy outcomes enhanced? *Journal of Consulting and Clinical Psychology, 63*, 182-196.

Strupp, H. H., & Hadley, S. W. (1979). Specific versus nonspecific factors in psychotherapy. *Archives of General Psychiatry, 36*, 1125-1136.

Szasz, T. S. (1961). *The myth of mental illness: Foundations of a theory of personal conduct.* New York: Paul B. Hoeber.

Torrey, E. F. (1986). *Witchdoctors and psychiatrists* (rev. ed.). New York: Harper & Row.

Tuttle, G. M., & Woods, D. R. (1997). *The managed care answer book for mental health professionals.* New York: Brunner/Mazel.

Vessey, J., & Howard, K. (1993). Who seeks psychotherapy. *Psychotherapy, 30*(4), 546-553.

Wilson, J. Q. (1997). *Moral judgment.* New York: Basic Books.

Woolfolk, R. L. (1998). *The cure of souls: Science, values and psychotherapy.* San Francisco: Jossey-Bass.

Commentary

Managed Care Programs: What Do Clinicians Need?

Lynn D. Johnson
The Brief Therapy Center, Salt Lake City, Utah

To my chagrin, I worked inside a managed care program for 8 years. It began as an inpatient managed care program for one of its clients in 1985. Late that year, I was hired as a psychologist consultant to the process. I continued through early 1994. During this time, I spent a half day to a full day each week helping design processes and consulting on specific cases. The rest of the time I directed the Brief Therapy Center in Salt Lake City and saw private patients. By that time, my practice was entirely outpatient, except for an occasional consult to inpatient programs. I developed successful alternatives to inpatient care for my acutely distressed patients, those needing detoxification, and teenagers in crisis.

Managed care was something I believed in because, as a psychologist, I was skeptical about the value of inpatient care as opposed to high-quality outpatient care. We focused on reducing care that was restrictive or of questionable value, such as chemical dependency programs of 28-day duration. We helped people transition to less restrictive levels of care; we helped therapists plan for effective transition plans. We encouraged empowerment of patients and found outpatient resources to help them function as independently as possible. I was pleased and happy with what we were doing. The insurance plans saved money, the patients were encouraged to do as much as they could for themselves, and the only people who were unhappy were those who had ridden the boom of for-profit inpatient mental health from the late 1970s to the late 1980s.

Interestingly enough, there was a huge range of average lengths of stay from hospital to hospital, from 10 days in one facility to 42 days in another. Reading the case records suggested the main difference was not in the acuity of the patient but rather in the dedication of the facility to keeping people inpatient. I felt I was doing righteous work—always a dangerous position.

Then something bad happened. The company—by this time having been purchased by a nationwide insurance company—began offering outpatient management. Again I was supportive, since I had always believed in the power and usefulness of brief psychotherapy. We found occasional egregious manipulations of the system to justify in our minds intruding into the outpatient arena. One therapist seemed particularly gifted at seeing people with relatively low levels of disorder for two to three times a week, years at a time. An analyst in New York had seen a fellow for 6 years, three times a week, for generalized anxiety disorder. But the patients were beginning to make progress. So at first I thought I was doing good by empowering patients and reducing psychotherapy processes that encouraged dependency and produced equivocal or limited benefits. My own experience with psychoanalysis made me think there was much less there than met the eye, and I felt good about what I was doing.

But I began to have doubts. It seemed that the vast majority of cases did not really need us butting into the process. We occasionally did good, but more often we were tampering with the process. And I knew enough about statistics to know that the result of tampering is to increase the variance. The review process was very expensive, and the budget for it came out of the total outpatient dollar, which meant that therapists were subsidizing what we were doing.

And I began to notice in my own private practice that reviews were getting more and more absurd, inane, and intrusive. Originally we in managed care thought we were doing good. By this point, my feelings about managed care had shifted. Now, they were only trying to save money. And managed care became managed costs. I came to think that I was not learning anything new and was not contributing any value. Clinicians lost control of the process and MBA types ran the show. I left the ship with some of the other high-principled rats.

Justification for Managed Care

I have spoken frankly with several medical directors of managed care plans about outpatient management. It has always been clear to those at the top of managed care that outpatient reviews are a loss leader. They are done to make the client happy, not to actually save money. That is because they violate the Willie Sutton rule, namely, there is no money in outpatient care.

We managed inpatient care because that was where the money was, and I did it for my own selfish agenda of emphasizing what I believe are the real helpful aspects of psychotherapy, namely, helping people make the best possible decisions about their own behavior, their lives, and the way they treat others. Since the average number of sessions in all outpatient care is around six, it is foolish to think that we are going to reduce a mean that low by management. Instead, managed care is sold to the customer through the attraction of "quality assurance." Since quality is a word with a lot of positive valence in business, that is a good selling point. And the outpatient care contract is just window dressing. All the money is saved on inpatient care.

What Do Clinicians Need?

I see several needs that we as clinicians have, needs that the academic side of psychology can help us with. I break those into two general areas. First, living with managed care, and, second, replacing managed care.

Living With Managed Care

First, pragmatically, what are the best ways of obtaining the visits we need? It seems to me that simulations and decision-making strategies would help us with that. In my own case, I have used objective measurements and that has tended to produce good results. I administer an objective measure—say, the Beck Depression Inventory—and I know the cutoff scores, in the case of the Beck, a score of 10 or less being full recovery. Sophisticated users already notice I am using a strict and very conservative level. Now, when I show a Beck to the managed care companies, they are more cooperative. Is this the best strategy?

How can we do better therapy in less time? How can we have the best impact on our clients in the least time? What are the best treatments for difficult and complicated problems, such as eating disorders? How can we communicate that knowledge to the reviewers and decision makers inside managed care? How have the National Council on Quality Assurance (NCQA) standards impacted outpatient quality? Can academic psychology have an impact on standards that, in my view, are irrational and ill informed?

The so-called validation process bears little or no resemblance to actual clinical results. We need more naturalistic approaches to looking at what works, and we need to validate treatment with patients as they enter a general clinic, not patients specially selected to test a process. Experienced clinicians often focus on the more general factors of alliance, mobilizing hope, mobilizing behavior change, and so on and seem less and less tied to specific models as they gain experience.

What Is the Post-Managed Care World?

Second, how can academic psychology help us move into the post-managed cost world? What academic studies examine vehicles of treatment, unanticipated costs to managed care, or alternative treatment delivery systems? Why not research the cost-benefit ratio of managing outpatient care? I think there is no benefit from it, and my evidence would be that the amount saved by the decline in number of sessions is more than consumed by the overhead of the management system. But I do not know this to be true. Research could enlighten us.

Researchers and academicians too often write to themselves. Where are the articles in *Harvard Business Review* on the cost-benefit ratio of outpatient psychotherapy? Where are the articles comparing medication-focused and psychotherapy-focused treatment in terms of costs, improvements in productivity, reduction in absences, and so on? When they are written, they are published in places where the decision makers about managed care will never read them. Let us write articles that will be read by decision makers, not only by other psychologists.

The Pragmatics

The problem is that I have seen nothing of value come from the academic community. Personally speaking, I am saddened and discouraged by the lack of an intelligent response to managed care. It is as if psychology has been willfully foolish, like an alcoholic refusing to sober up. Some of our leaders have reacted to managed care by indignation and anger. My experience in marriage counseling leads me to conclude that anger and indignation are some of the most useless strategies in influencing others. There was a good deal of angry demand for 50 sessions of therapy a year. What a foolish position! It may well be that some people need 50 sessions a year, although in 20 plus years of practice I have never seen someone 50 times in a year. But to demand it? That demand is guaranteed to alienate the decision makers and marginalize psychology as a discipline.

A better alternative would have been to develop actuarial models of treatment, suggesting that the mean number of sessions will always be at or about six and allowing for clinician judgement in that context. If a clinic can keep the mean number of sessions at a reasonable number, what is the harm in seeing one patient 50 times a year? Of course, that means that we must be skilled in very brief (single-session), effective interventions.

It would seem that we have ignored our social-psychologist peers who could have helped us strategize methods of influencing the decision makers. I call for conferences featuring consulting psychologists, industrial-organizational (IO) psychologists, and social psychologists together with clinicians to dialogue about how to influence social processes. We have not used our own resources.

Issue 7

Individualism

Individualism and Modern Psychotherapy

Frank C. Richardson
Timothy J. Zeddies
University of Texas at Austin

Men and women today are haunted by a sense that in the midst of plenty, our lives seem barren. We are hungry for a greater nourishment of the soul. In the England of today, a businessman turned philosopher, Charles Handy, has won a widespread following with his writing. Capitalism, he argues, delivers the means but not the point of life. Now that we are satisfying our outer needs, we must pay more attention to those within—for beauty, spiritual growth, and human connection. "In Africa," Handy writes, "they say there are two hungers . . . the lesser hunger is for the things that sustain life, the goods and services, and the money to pay for them, which we all need. The greater hunger is for an answer to the question 'why?,' for some understanding of what life is for."
—David Gergen, editorial, *U.S. News & World Report,* August 23, 1999

"Jackie" called a university telephone counseling service and stated that she was stressed, anxious, and afraid that her future was ruined. She had just withdrawn, with no penalty, from a required course in her premed curriculum that had given her difficulty. She had already made an appointment at the university counseling center but was feeling so much distress and panic that she wanted to talk to someone immediately.

Jackie's telephone counselor, a psychology graduate student, encouraged her to explore her experience of dropping the class, her goals and values concerning personal achievement, and her view of herself. She said she had very high expectations for herself and feared she would disappoint her parents, even though she indicated that they had been understanding and supportive about her dropping a class. The counselor reassured her that this self-imposed pressure was experienced by many ambitious, high-achieving people. He suggested that she might need to learn better skills for coping with stress and anxiety and that the current situation might present a good opportunity to acquire such skills. He also praised Jackie's decision to seek counseling.

A few days later, the counselor discussed this call with the counseling service supervision group. He reported feeling uneasy that offering her understanding, support, and insight might have prevented him from giving her some kind of more tangible help. He described feeling very sympathetic with her sense of being all on her own in a competitive and lonely "rat race," something quite familiar to him and many others he knew. And he commented critically about what seemed like too much of a "knee jerk" reflex on his part to endorse her seeking therapy as the key to dealing with her problems.

The supervision group zeroed in quickly on the fact that the counselor seemed to have feelings of helplessness and anxiety similar to Jackie's and to feel pressured to respond to her distress and request for help. They suggested that Jackie was employing a communication style and way of relating best described as "projective identification"[1] and encouraged the counselor to interpret his own thoughts and feelings as reflecting a tendency to become unhelpfully entangled in the caller's flawed way of coping with her situation. They also reiterated the importance of not reaching for concrete, direct interventions when dealing with panicky callers. Instead, they reaffirmed, what clients really needed was increased openness to and awareness of the sorts of feelings that were driving their high anxiety and faulty coping.

After this discussion, the counselor still felt troubled and dissatisfied. He could not shake an image of Jackie as emotionally isolated and stressed out in a hypercompetitive social universe that might never be any more hospitable or comfortable than it was today and might get worse. It just did not seem to him that his anguish about her situation really came from being inappropriately caught up in her problems. He felt uncomfortable about how therapy was assumed in the discussion to be a kind of savior, an all-sufficient cure for what ailed Jackie. He wondered if the notion of projective identification might not increase her isolation and make matters worse by putting all the responsibility for alleviating her stress on her as a solitary individual.

Psychology and psychotherapy are in some ways a unique 20th-century phenomenon. They are an intimate part of the warp and woof of our turbulent era. Because of their entanglement in culture, it seems to many thoughtful observers that psychology and psychotherapy both creatively address emotional problems in living and inadvertently perpetuate ideals and practices of our way of life that may actually contribute to those very problems. One way to address this problem is to examine the many ways that modern psychotherapy theory and practice are embroiled with that distinctively modern moral outlook that goes by the name of "individualism" (Bellah, Madsen, Sullivan, Swidler, & Tipton, 1985) or "liberal individualism" (Sandel, 1996; Sullivan, 1986). We suggest that such individualism is the "disguised ideology" (Richardson, Fowers, & Guignon, 1999) of the modern therapy enterprise. Much that is worthy and much that is questionable about modern psychotherapy stems from these underlying values, which operate as a driving ethical force in all our activities.

From Premodern to Modern

Most of us have a sense of how people in premodern or traditional societies took for granted that they belonged to a hierarchical and meaningful cosmic drama, or order of being. As a result, men and women acquired meaningful roles to play in everyday life as well as on the cosmic plane. Moreover, they acquired what Anton Antonovsky (1979) calls "a sense of coherence" that helps make "affectively comprehensible" the uncontrollable and tragic aspects of human life. Much of this sense of belonging and purpose was lost with the rise of a neutral, "disenchanted" (as Max Weber famously put it) view of the universe as made up of inherently meaningless objects in causal interaction with one another. In this new world, our experiences of beauty, purpose, and goodness tend to be regarded as merely human fabrications that must be located in a private, purely subjective realm. This idea of subjectivity gives birth to our distinctive modern emphasis on personal inwardness and inward depths, which is enriching but also tends to leave us deeply disconnected from one another and the social world.

This new scientific outlook is reinforced by the distinctive moral temper of the modern age, one we might describe as antiauthoritarian and emancipatory. The conception of a disengaged subject of scientific knowledge confronting a separate material universe resembles and reinforces the moral ideal of the autonomous and free modern individual who distances himself or herself from the past and the social world and seeks above all "to be self-responsible, to rely on one's own judgment, to find one's purpose in oneself" (Taylor, 1995, p. 7). This approach makes people the responsible center of their own moral universe. But it also risks emotional isolation and debilitating alienation by significantly downplaying lasting social ties, a sense of tradition, or wider purposes beyond individual self-realization.

Concerns About Psychotherapy

Much of the social commentary and cultural criticism of the past two centuries has centered on sorting out the good and bad, the worthwhile and the harmful, in this individualistic credo and way of life. In fact, over the past 50 years, a number of astute critics in social science and the psychotherapy field have voiced sharp concerns about the entanglement of psychology with questionable modern ideologies. In retrospect, it seems remarkable how sharp these critics' observations are, how much they are saying similar things, and yet how uncertain they were about what to do about the problems they identified.

In the 1960s, the sociologist Peter Berger (1977, p. 23) commented on a "social phenomenon of truly astounding scope," namely, the emergence of a new "psychological society" dominated by "an assortment of ideas and activities derived in one way or another from the Freudian revolution in psychology."

Traditional religious belief was losing its authority, and as it did so, psychotherapists, social workers, career counselors, psychiatrists, management trainers, organizational development consultants, and other specialists came to play a pivotal role in providing guidance and direction in our society. "Institutionalized psychologism," he remarks, can "commute along with its clientele" from bedroom to boardroom, offering help with personal emotional problems while also providing "nonviolent techniques of social control" to be used by bureaucracies in the private and public sectors.

Also in the 1960s, C. Marshall Lowe (1969) argued that modern people often experience a severe "crisis of values" because at the same time that the authority of traditional morals and customs is waning, the uncertainty and flux of modern life tends to prevent the crystallization of any new beliefs and values to serve as a basis for living. One result is that increasing numbers of people turn to counselors and therapists as "new moral authorities" or "secular priests" as guides who are asked to "make moral pronouncements in the name of science in the way the clergy was called upon for religious directives." But Lowe contends that we have lost both the guidance of tradition and the rugged individualism of earlier modern times. Thus we have a great "need for approval" and have become "other-directed" personalities to be evaluated by our "ability to adjust to contemporary social customs" (pp. 16-17). We are afflicted, in part, with problems of meaning and ethical judgment that psychology as an applied science really cannot address. About this time, Philip Rieff (1966) made a similar point, namely, that after psychoanalysis has lowered one's compulsions and increased one's options in living, one may face the dilemma of "being freed to choose and then having no choice worth making" (p. 93).

In the 1970s, Jerome Frank (1978, pp. 6-7) thoughtfully observed that as "institutions of American society, all psychotherapies . . . share a value system that accords primacy to individual self-fulfillment," including "maximum self-awareness, unlimited access to one's own feelings, increased autonomy and creativity." The individual is seen as "the center of his moral universe, and concern for others is believed to follow from his own self-realization." In Frank's view, these values are admirable in many ways, and modern therapies are often beneficial. Nevertheless, he notes, the implicit value system of modern psychotherapy "can easily become a source of misery in itself" because of its unrealistic expectations for personal happiness and the burden of resentment it imposes when inevitable disappointments occur. In his opinion, the literature of psychotherapy gives little attention to such traditional, possibly worthwhile, values or virtues as "the redemptive power of suffering, acceptance of one's lot in life, adherence to tradition, self-restraint and moderation."

In recent years, Philip Cushman (1990, p. 604) argues that our society defines the mature or ideal individual as a "bounded, masterful self" that is expected to "function in a highly autonomous, isolated way" and "to be self-soothing, self-loving, and self-sufficient." Unfortunately, Cushman thinks there is evidence that the inflated, would-be autonomous self almost inevitably collapses into an "empty self," whose characteristics of fragility, sense of emptiness, and proneness to fluctuation between feelings of worthlessness and grandiosity are often said to be the hallmarks of neurotic psychopathology in our day.

In their engaging (even if at times overwrought) treatise, *We've Had a Hundred Years of Psychotherapy and the World's Getting Worse,* James Hillman and Michael Ventura (1992) analyze our contemporary overpsychologizing of life and its struggles. They feel that psychotherapy, valuable as it can be, tends to reinforce some of the most problematic aspects of modern life, including a view of the person as a self-encapsulated entity, and places a heavy stress on inwardness. Therapeutic thinking tends to "internalize emotions." It takes powerful emotions and passions such as outrage and indignation over injustice, which can bind us to others and give us a sense of purpose, and converts them into inner feelings such as anxiety, hostility, or depression, which we ought to "process" and "work through" to free the inner citadel of the self from disturbance.

A corollary of internalizing emotions is a certain "developmental" perspective, the "principle content of American psychology," according to which personality and behavior are determined mainly by one's family relationships during childhood. This excessively narrow and inward focus, Hillman and Ventura feel, blinds us to the real social and cultural patterns that are a major source of human miseries. Hillman and Ventura worry that certain psychotherapeutic myths are "turning us into children." Although many individuals suffer harmful deprivations and abuses, a one-sided focus on inwardness can lock them into the viewpoint of a child who is preoccupied with issues of dependence on and need for protection from powerful parentlike figures, which encourages them to see themselves as victims rather than agents in their own life stories.

Finally, Robert Fancher (1995) argues that modern therapy systems claim to be based on some kind of "science" of psychopathology, but in reality reflect and surreptitiously promote a particular view of the good life, a value system, or a "culture." Concerning psychoanalysis, for example, Fancher writes,

> There is no inherent reason why internal dynamics, rather that one's place in society, must be the principle source of health or illness. For most of history, in most civilized cultures, the kind of internal fulfillment that psychoanalysis values has been suspect, and fidelity to "one's station and its duties" has generally been a higher value. (p. 124)

Liberal Individualism

Robert Coles (1987), when he toured the United States, found that no matter where he went, people were all too ready to speak in a psychologically charged vocabulary of their "problems" and "issues." "The hallmark of our time," he writes, is "lots of psychological chatter, lots of self-consciousness, lots of 'interpretation'" (p. 189). Psychology here means "a concentration, persistent, if not feverish, upon one's thoughts, feelings, wishes, worries—bordering on, if not embracing, solipsism: the self as the only or main form of (existential) reality." Robert Bellah and his colleagues (Bellah et al., 1985, p. 143) use the term "ontological individualism" to describe this widespread modern notion that the basic unit of human reality is the individual person, who is assumed to exist and have determinate characteristics prior to and independent of his or her social existence.

There is more to the modern outlook and modern ethics than just ontological individualism, however. Modern, or liberal, individualism[2] typically counterbalances its heavy stress on self-interest and self-realization with a serious ethical emphasis on regarding human agents as imbued with dignity and inherent worth and as possessed of natural rights. Clearly, ontological individualism's view of things runs a high risk of deteriorating into an amoral clash of will against will, power against power. To prevent such a calamity, the modern moral outlook supplements an uncompromising stress on autonomy and self-interest with a serious commitment to respecting individual dignity and rights. Needless to say, there is considerable tension between these two ethical poles of radical self-interest and obligation to respect the rights of others. We experience this tension in one form or another often in everyday life.

Liberal individualism links together the ideals of self-interest and respect for the rights of others in a unique modern approach to ethics. First formulated by the philosopher Kant, this approach centers on *formal* principles of *procedural* justice or fairness (Rawls, 1971). Such principles "constitute a fair framework within which individuals and groups can choose their own values and ends, consistent with a similar liberty for others" (Sandel, 1996, p. 11). In the mental health arena, we adopt this approach by talking about more or less "effective" therapeutic means to reaching ends that we often label "health" or "well-being," as if these ends were purely given by nature or chosen by clients without any outside influence. Therapists who think in these terms can blithely assume that they are merely facilitating a natural developmental process that is unaffected by their personal influence. But as Hoffman (1996) observes, this is simply not the case:

> When we interpret the transference, we like to think that we are merely bringing to the surface what is already "there," rather than that we are cultivating something in the patient and in the relationship that might not have developed in the same way otherwise . . . our hands are not clean. (p. 109)

Liberal individualism represents a sincere effort to affirm freedom without dissolving responsibility, to eliminate dogmatism without abandoning our moral duties to others. Nevertheless, this approach is one-sided. It is embroiled in the paradox of advocating a thoroughgoing *neutrality* toward all values as a way of *promoting* certain basic values of liberty, tolerance, and human rights. Our commitment to human dignity and rights is meant to be taken very seriously. But what is to prevent liberal individualism's neutrality toward all notions of the good life from extending to those basic values of liberty and human dignity as well, thereby undermining their credibility and motivational force (Sullivan, 1986, p. 39)? On a practical level, liberal individualism's insistent characterization of human action and motivation as exclusively self-interested is likely a self-fulfilling prophecy. The direct pursuit of security and happiness seems progressively to dissolve the capacity to respect and cherish others (Bell, 1978, p. xv ff.).

Disguised Ideology

We suggest that liberal individualism in modern times takes several different forms and that singly or in combination they comprise a great deal of the conceptual and moral underpinnings of contemporary psychotherapies. They shape the modern therapy enterprise at its core and make it the vital and highly regarded cultural force it is. As a result, however, therapy also shares in some of the blind spots and harmful aspects, as well as the virtues, of these modern ideologies.

Utilitarian Individualism. Bellah et al. (1985) identify two main forms of individualism in modern times. The first they term "utilitarian individualism," which "takes as given certain basic human appetites and fears . . . and sees human life as an effort by individuals to maximize their self-interest relative to these given ends" (p. 336). It assumes that the ends of human life are either inbuilt pleasures and satisfactions or whatever goals or desires we just happen to prefer. Human thought and action are essentially tools for effectively and efficiently pursuing survival, security, and satisfaction. The ego in Freud's original psychoanalytic theory is almost a pure utilitarian, pragmatic calculator of this sort. A utilitarian individualist vision also seems to lie at the heart of behavioral and cognitive therapies that seek to foster more effective controlling or self-controlling sequences of behavior and thought. Utilitarian individualist themes pervade the innumerable discussions of "mastery," effectiveness, and "realism" in the literature on psychotherapy.

All these therapies blend strong utilitarian motifs with at least a tacit sense of human dignity and rights. But it is easy to imagine how, as with liberal individualism in general, this self-interested, starkly instrumental picture of human activity might undermine its own ethical dimension. In our opinion, we need to pay close attention to the critique of one-sided instrumentalism in our society put forth by critical theorists (Habermas, 1973) and critical social scientists (Fox & Prilleltensky, 1997). They show how a calculating, means-end rationality may expand our instrumental prowess in certain areas, but its dominance in culture gradually destroys our ability to evaluate the worth of the ends we seek, to set priorities and needed limits in individual and social life, to achieve integrity as well as mastery, and to come to terms with the dark and tragic sides of human life.

Expressive Individualism. The second form of individualism Bellah et al. (1985) identify is "expressive individualism," which is guided by the belief that "each person has a unique core of feeling and intuition that should unfold or be expressed if individuality is to be realized" (p. 334). It arose out of the Romantic movement of the late 18th and 19th centuries as a reaction against the overly rationalistic, calculating, deadening aspects of utilitarian views and has reverberated throughout our culture down to the present day. Romanticism celebrates closeness to nature, instinct, mythical consciousness, beauty, and art. Romantic notions have a large presence in the world of psychotherapy. For example, in Kohut's (1977) widely influential self psychology the self follows a universal "narcissistic line of development" from birth to maturity. Its goal is a "healthy narcissism," which includes pride; assertiveness; vitality; joyfulness; creativity; and, eventually, mature wisdom and acceptance of one's mortality. Meaningful social ties are stressed by self psychology, but they play a quite ambiguous role in human development. Others, or "self-objects," serve mainly to mirror and confirm the individual's uniqueness and vitality in early development, and when autonomy is achieved to support the project of individual self-realization through creative activities. Kohut's approach and other contemporary psychoanalytic approaches emphasize the development of soothing and tolerant internal "objects" or "self-objects" in a way that partly obviates the need for real others, possibly undermining the very social ties needed for healthy development and a rewarding life (Cushman, 1990; Eagle, 1984; Richardson et al., 1999, pp. 249 ff.).

Expressivist notions of personal authenticity are enriching, but seem insufficient for a good or even a stable life. Expressive individualism incorporates liberal individualism's heavy emphasis on individual autonomy and preserves the deep gulf between the individual and social realms. As a result, it seems to purchase freedom at the price of a social and emotional isolation that ultimately makes freedom a burden or robs it of meaning. By itself, self-realization of this kind seems insufficient for overcoming egoism, resolving conflict, and achieving lasting social ties or a sense of purpose among mature individuals.

Existential Individualism. We suggest that a third kind of modern individualism figures prominently in therapy theory and practice. Like expressivism, existential viewpoints represent a protest against the scientism and technicism of our way of life. But existential individualism also is skeptical of the expressivist idea of getting in touch with core feelings or impulses as the main way to find integrity and direction in life. Sartre's (1956) classic formulation of existential freedom involves repudiating any notion of pregiven inner directives or objective values as inauthentic "bad faith." Instead, we must take a kind of total responsibility for the de facto choices that "invent" the ultimate values and "fundamental project" of our lives as a whole. Indeed, we should strive to realize both our own practical freedom and that of all others as well. Numerous modern therapy theories, including Gestalt and existential therapies, explicitly incorporate a version of this ideal of existential freedom. Other important theorists draw heavily from the existential perspective. For example, Roy Schafer's (1976) radical revision of psychoanalytic metapsychology advocates the ideal of accepting our ultimate responsibility as authors of ourselves, others, and our world through what he calls "optional ways of telling the stories of human lives." Schafer celebrates the "joyfulness" and "integrity" this kind of freedom and autonomy can bring.

The ideal of existential freedom contributes in a positive way to a sense of our being responsible, committed agents in all our activities. But it also greatly obscures how much our goals, values, and personalities are shaped by history and culture. It represents, in fact, a rather extreme version of ontological individualism. The kind of authenticity and integrity it promises rest mainly on opposition to arbitrary authority or copping out on responsibilities. As a result, existential individualism offers no way to articulate the superiority of one way of life over another. Thus it reduces our radical choice of ultimate values to a matter of simply registering brute preferences or arbitrarily settling on one option over others (Taylor, 1989). In fact, there seems to be no good reason why we *should* elect a life of authenticity or integrity at all or why we *should* nurture our own or others' existential freedom! Over time, this approach may actually undermine both genuine autonomy and meaningful ties and commitments to others.

Social Constructionism. In the wake of growing doubts about both the "scientific" aspirations of academic psychology and the individualist ideals that infuse modern psychotherapy, social constructionist viewpoints have gained increasing influence (Gergen, 1985; McNamee & Gergen, 1992). To get away from what they often call "self-contained individualism," constructionists insist that there is no universal decontextualized self or truth about the self. Rather, notions of self and world, as well as the meanings or values we live by, are social artifacts. They are not grounded in any kind of transcendent realities, natural or ethical, but are endlessly shaped and reshaped through ongoing "negotiations of meaning" in social life. Therapist and patient jointly coauthor a new narrative, a new form of life and feeling, for the patient's benefit. To facilitate this process, therapists should adopt a "thoroughgoing relativism in expressions of identity" (Gergen & Kaye, 1992, p. 199).

Social constructionism provides us with valuable insights into the cultural embeddedness and narrative structure of human activities. But it also seems surreptitiously to perpetuate many of the worst features of the very modern individualism it condemns. Social constructionism's moral relativism is troubling enough. But more fundamental is the problem that this kind of relativism only makes sense from a highly individualistic standpoint. No one but a thoroughly detached and disengaged self could claim to treat all moral commitments and beliefs as things on hand for endless revision and ironic play. Thus, Jane Flax (1990) points out inconsistencies in the work of postmodern thinkers who claim to dismantle modern notions of selfhood but still embrace a profoundly modern romantic/aesthetic vision of the "constant remaking of the self." They "presuppose a socially isolated and individualistic view of the self," which seems impossible to reconcile "with, for example, the care of children or with participation in a political community." It also happens to be "deeply antithetical to feminist views of self in relation to others" (pp. 216-217). It appears that constructionist therapy, like liberal individualism in general, employs relativism to undermine dogmatic or authoritarian influences while still confidently advocating its own ideal for human life as it were not relative at all.

Beyond Individualism

In our view, we should neither give in to relativism nor claim to have any final answers concerning the good life. Rather, we need to instigate a sustained dialogue about these issues, as both therapists and citizens, that will allow us to become less blind and more self-reflective about our way of life and also become wiser therapists, consultants, and educators. What follows is simply a contribution to that dialogue.

The Search for Community. Psychotherapists are generally on the lookout for ideas that make better sense of their clients' emotional struggles. In today's world, we need to expand our horizons and scrutinize those struggles in a wider social and moral context than has previously been employed. Common sense and a lot of good theory strongly suggest that the lack of a sense of connectedness, a feeling of wider belonging and purpose, and a feeling of making a difference in the world fosters chronic tension, chronic irritability and anger, emotional isolation, frustration, impatience, and cynicism or despair. These feelings and attitudes undermine individual well-being directly and also indirectly, by eating away at the social fabric of family, work environments, and community life. They are an emotional and spiritual drain on all of us. Not only does this situation foster stress, irritability, and sometimes more serious emotional problems. It also fails to provide people with emotional afflictions—all of us at times—in our lives, with the support, corrective feedback, guidance, and ethical challenge we badly need to break our isolation and return to a more constructive path.

How can we raise our consciousness about these influences and respond creatively to them as psychologists and therapists? As a way of bringing our dilemmas into focus, Alan Wolfe (1989, p. 2) analyzes what he calls the "withering away of civil society." He suggests that people in complex modern societies aspire to be "free to make choices about how to live their lives irrespective of the actions of others." But they tend to be *unaware* of the fact, further obscured by modern individualistic ideologies, that they are "dependent on everyone around them to make their societies work." Despite our increased freedom and sense of individuality, we have entanglements with and obligations to an increasing number of others "beyond family and locality." According to Wolfe (1989, p. 10ff.), liberal democracies tend to rely on either "individualistic moral codes associated with the market" or "collective moral codes associated with the state." But neither the "invisible hand" of the market nor the impersonal regulations of the bureaucratic state are adequate to the task. We hand over too much of our responsibility to such mechanisms and seek to escape into an ever-shrinking private world. In Wolfe's view, we need to depend less on "impersonal mechanisms of moral obligation" and seek instead to restore a civil society characterized by "ties of trust and solidarity." This includes learning again to appreciate what he calls the "gift of society" and giving central place to "the notion that ordinary people create moral rules through everyday interaction with others."

Amitai Etzioni (1996) argues that there can be "excessive liberty." Without limits on choice, provided first and foremost by some "shared moral convictions," neither a coherent sense of personal identity nor social peace is really possible. Thus we have "a need for a much thicker social order . . . reflecting the fact that all societies promote some shared values . . . [which] mobilize some of their members' time, assets, energies, and loyalties to the service of one or more common purposes" (p. 10). "Communitarian" thinkers like Etzioni seek to nourish shared values that are "largely voluntary" and envision not one overall community but a "community of communities" in a modern pluralistic society (p. 176). Thus Etzioni recommends that in the "next historical phase" we find a way to "blend the virtues of tradition with the liberation of modernity" (p. xvii). On a more individual level, he suggests that the familiar "golden rule," which appears in different forms in many cultural traditions, is too narrowly interpersonal and might be reformulated: "Respect and uphold society's moral order as you would have society respect and uphold your autonomy" (p. xvii). Such a notion fully acknowledges our dependence on others and society at the same time that it encourages individuals to cultivate excellence and develop their unique individual powers and gifts. These powers and gifts are often developed more fully in cultivating friendship and community, working out differences, and learning from others different from ourselves than in just "doing one's own thing." In these efforts, freedom and responsibility often mesh rather than conflict with one another, thereby bringing some of life's greatest satisfactions.

Spiritual Practices. There is a burgeoning interest today in spiritual practices, Buddhist, Christian, and others, and in their integration with counseling and psychotherapy practice (Miller, 1999). These spiritual notions and practices are sometimes treated superficially and employed to advance individual-centered aims of tranquillity or self-realization. But many creative thinkers draw on these practices explicitly to correct some of the deficiencies and blind spots in the modern therapy enterprise that have been discussed over the years.

For example, Jeffrey Rubin (1996) argues that psychoanalysis and psychotherapy are "self-centered." He points out that psychoanalysis "arose from the soil of the modern period" in which there was a "despiritualization of subjective reality" and a devaluation and even "pathologization" of the spiritual

(1997, p. 81). In Rubin's (1997) words, "self-maximization" now replaces "commitment to the life of the commons," and society is considered to be "essentially subordinate to the needs of individuals, who are all governed by their own self-interest" (p. 81), thus leading to a "depersonalized" view of and "narcissistic" relation to others.

Rubin (1996) feels that psychotherapy may be crucial for dissolving many kinds of intolerant and authoritarian behavior to which spiritual traditions sometimes fall prey. But by itself it does not provide standards for or wisdom concerning many important life decisions, and it fails to nurture the kind of "decentering from the centrality of our own cherished viewpoints" required for "ethics and tolerance." It would be desirable, therefore, to supplement psychoanalysis with the kind of "larger perspective fostered by spiritual [viewpoints], wherein one's own experience is viewed as a part of a more encompassing reality" (p. 86). He finds that Buddhist meditation can be of great assistance in giving up the kind of "attachment" that often causes suffering through excessive judgmentalness and fruitless efforts to control one's own experience and the behavior of others. It can "enhance self-observational capacities," increasing "attentiveness and self-awareness" in ways that benefit customary psychotherapy. But more than that, it can cultivate a unique ability to become less attached to experience, less "addicted to pleasing experiences and less afraid of painful ones" (p. 91).

According to Rubin (1997), such detachment enhances an "openness to experience" and "decreased defensiveness" (p. 91) that fosters ethical sensitivity to the needs of others and compassion for them. This kind of detachment fostered by spiritual practices is quite different from that of the separate, disconnected self of ontological individualism, even when that self is seen as having inward personal depth. For Buddhists, detachment occurs in the context of a more fundamental belonging to a wider, encompassing reality, one in which all events and experiences are integral facets of an infinite flux in which everything is profoundly interdependent with, and an expression of, everything else that exists. For Jews and Christians, decentering of the self takes place in the context of a vision of humans as created in the image of God and meant for fellowship with one another and the divine.

If one were to find such spiritual perspectives and practices credible, sincere engagement in them might foster a sense of detachment from compulsive self-interest and a sense of wider belonging that would nourish one's ability to attend with others to matters of the public interest and common good. It is true that engaging in meditation or prayer takes time away from outward activities with others. But presumably it is the quality and not the quantity of human interaction that strengthens a sense of community, and surely it would be desirable for most of us to lead less frantic, overextended lives.

Perspectives on Dialog. The writings of contemporary hermeneutic philosophers (Gadamer, 1989; Taylor, 1989), Mikhail Bakhtin and his interpreters (Bakhtin, 1984, Morson & Emerson, 1990), and others (Bruner, 1990; Etzioni,

1996) provide perspectives that are of great value in rethinking modern individualism. Both hermeneutics thinkers and Bakhtin argue passionately against
monological models of human experience that reduce human thought, feeling,
and action to the workings of solitary and disengaged agents. It is only through
dialogue and relationship, Bakhtin (1984) believed, that people can be most fully
human: "Truth is not born nor is it to be found inside the head of an individual
person . . . it is born between people collectively searching for truth, in the process
of their dialogic interaction" (p. 110).

In the hermeneutic/dialogical view, individualism obscures or screens
out many of the dense and deep realities of social life. It mistakes a map of the
city for city life. It makes things seem both less difficult and less wonderful than
they really are. In the hermeneutic/dialogical view, our starting point should be
"shared values," not purely "individual choices or formulations of the good"
(Etzioni, 1996, p. 93). It stresses our deep *belongingness* and *indebtedness* to the
cultural and historical context in which we find ourselves. As Taylor (1995, p. 40)
puts it, "We are aware of the world through a 'we' before we are through an
'I,'" so that "we always find ourselves as a we-consciousness before we can be
an I-consciousness." In this society, our proud individuality itself is the product
or construction of a certain way of life that has developed over a long period of
time. The idea of being connected and belonging to history in this way often
seems threatening to a modern sense of individuality and integrity. An ac-
quaintance of ours, a respected Jungian therapist, on hearing some of these
ideas said, "Well, it sounds interesting. But my school of therapy focuses on
individuating the person away from society." We suggest that a dialogical view
does not undermine individual responsibility and integrity, however, but gives
a different account of them.

Bakhtin (1984) and Taylor (1991) outline a conception of the human agent
as a "dialogical self" that nips in the bud individualism's tendency to sharply
divide the personal and social spheres of existence. Our language and practices
themselves reflect and embody our culture's ongoing, never-finished conversation about how to find a balance between things like spontaneity and order, gratification and restraint, irreverence and awe, and so forth. Most theories of personality or psychotherapy describe how personality is formed through
internalizing the perspectives or evaluations of others as part of the self, leaving
us with the problem of explaining how a central "I" relates to these introjected
elements. But in the dialogical view, a child does not first internalize beliefs and
values of others that he or she must then either give in to or reject. Rather, in
Taylor's (1991) words, "what gets internalized" is "the whole conversation, with
the inter-animation of its voices" (p. 312). The self is identified with and takes
seriously all sides of the continuing dialog or debate about things that matter to
people in his or her world. The self "arises in conversation" as it assimilates and
joins that conversation and struggle, thereby becoming a member of and participant in that human community or communities.

In this view, the self or human being is first and foremost a scene or locus
of dialogue. Through the medium of shared values and meanings, we overlap to

an extent with others and are meaningfully connected with them as co-participants in a common cultural discourse and debate. In this view, what I centrally am is an interplay or conversation among various commitments, identifications, or points of view. Focus, or a sense of identity, arises not through adopting one single standpoint or another but through achieving an attitudinal or conversational stance toward diverse meanings and perspectives, one that involves reinterpreting them and harmonizing them in an always somewhat original way.

This approach "partly decenters" the human self (Richardson, Rogers, & McCarroll, 1998, p. 510). But it may heighten rather than dilute individual freedom and responsibility. Modern individualism distances the self from cultural values and moral meaning to protect its autonomy, but leaves the self socially and emotionally high and dry, isolated to a point where it cannot find needed purpose and direction. The dialogical view portrays us as woven into the fabric of culture and history, less separate or unique than individualism maintains. But we are compensated for that loss by a potentially greater sense of significance in everyday life. We are responsible for making sense of and acting on the moral tensions and dilemmas that show up in our sector of the human realm. No one else can take responsibility, in that time and place, for us. As Bakhtin puts it, there can be no "alibi for being" (Morson & Emerson, 1990, p. 31).

Implications for Psychotherapy

At the dawn of a new millennium, the most important thing psychotherapists can do, we suggest, is to view emotional problems and struggles in a wider social and moral context than is usually employed. To accomplish this, therapists will need to expand their horizons; acquire new conceptual tools; and face up to the fact that psychotherapy cannot substitute for, or by itself restore, a vital cultural or community life.

Rethinking Ideals of the Good Life. A good place to start, in our view, is by acknowledging that the mental health field needs a new character ideal, or a new understanding of what it means to live a full or worthwhile human life. We would want that ideal to be as broad and inclusive as possible. Of course, it will still reflect some cultural and moral value commitments. The way to avoid dogmatism is not to jettison our indispensable ideals but to be willing to submit them to searching examination through dialogue. The core of a better character ideal beyond autonomy and unassailable individuality might be just the capacity for this kind of dialogue. Hermeneutic thinkers, as well as Bakhtin, outline a conception of dialogue according to which our deep convictions and profound openness to the views of others actually require and enhance one another, so that we are not forced to choose between dogmatism and disconnectedness. Our deepest ethical and spiritual convictions seem true to us. But there is nothing inherent in holding such life-giving convictions that requires regarding them as final or certain. Can anyone honestly claim more than a partial and imperfect grasp of the meaning of justice, salvation, enlightenment, compassion, authenticity, courage, and so forth?

Picturesquely, Bakhtin (1981, p. 290) describes how, in dialogue within and between us, each voice or position is "viewed" by others and glimpses its own image through the eyes of the other. Two things are necessary for this process to be carried through. The first he calls "outsideness," in which our standpoint is considered and evaluated from the point of view of another to the fullest extent possible. The second is allowing a partly new, temporary, unified perspective of our own to emerge. This approach harmonizes our profound need of others and their perspectives with the maximum integrity and self-responsibility on our part. And it suggests an ideal of the best sort of human functioning that goes beyond individualism without nullifying individualism's worthy features.

Broadening the Therapeutic Dialogue. William Doherty (1994) clearly and courageously encourages therapists to address the moral dimensions of emotional problems and therapeutic action that our individualistic focus has tended to obscure. Doherty gives the example of a young divorced father whose personal convenience and happiness would be better served by moving away from the city where his children live with their mother, thereby depriving them of much-needed fathering. He illustrates how only in a tortured and unconvincing manner—perhaps by encouraging reflection about what is really the "healthy" thing to do—does conventional therapeutic language speak to the man's dilemma concerning how both to pursue his own goals and to meet his responsibilities to his children.

It is likely, however, that both the conflicted father and his therapist in this situation have bigger problems. The client probably lacks a wider conception of life and the good life that defines his personal fulfillment, in part, in terms of carrying out the responsibilities of a father in today's world and thus lends real meaning to the sacrifices he must make to serve his children's welfare. He needs more than help in facing up to and clarifying a tough moral decision. He also needs somehow to deal with a serious vacuum of cultural pathways and guiding moral ideals, without which his own life and that of his family may be thrown into considerable disarray.

Philip Cushman (1995) goes further and encourages us to own up to the fact that psychotherapy, in part, is a kind of "moral discourse." We usually deny or evade this uncomfortable fact. For example, by distinguishing between a true and false self the healing technologies of Winnicott, Masterson, and others "present themselves as effectively removed from the realm of moral considerations and the larger world of history and politics" (p. 286). By "labeling certain behaviors and sensations as 'true,' therapists are making a political move" (p. 298). They are as much prescribing as describing a certain mode of living. But they do so surreptitiously in a way that "draws attention away from the sociohistorical forces that shaped the masterful, bounded twentieth century self, which is caught between isolation and engulfment, terrified of being unnoticed and yet determined to be independent" (p. 286).

Instead, Cushman (1995) suggests that therapists and clients can, when appropriate, "think critically" and "oppose the status quo" (p. 292). They are not limited to finding a place in our society, with its injustices, shallow consumerism, and excessive competitiveness. Indeed, it is the "job of the psychotherapist to demonstrate the existence of a world constituted by different rules and to encourage patients to be aware of available moral traditions that oppose the moral frame by which they presently shape their lives" (p. 295).

Cushman's bold proposal for broadening therapeutic dialogue has a liberal reformist bent. Others of us, without downplaying the need for reform, might place a bit more emphasis on personal responsibility, a sense of tradition, or spiritual practices. So, in the spirit of dialogue, we might rephrase Cushman's idea of broadening therapeutic conversation in the following way. First, we need to help clients, at times, see more clearly the ways in which their emotional struggles are engendered or perpetuated by questionable ideologies and faulty patterns in living in our current society, many of which seem to be a part of an exaggerated individualism. Raising consciousness about these matters may be essential to gaining needed insight and leverage for change. Second, it may be helpful, or even essential, at times, to gently challenge clients in an ethical sense. Drawing as much as possible on their own best values and traditions, we may need to challenge them to take greater responsibility for their complicity, like that of all of us, in our current shallowness and moral confusion and to join with others in trying to envision and fashion a better world. Sometimes, relief of pain or escape from narcissism can only come with a heightened sense of our obligations to others and a greater sense of meaning in carrying them out.

Notes

1. Projective identification refers to "the way in which feeling-states corresponding to the unconscious fantasies of one person (the projector) are engendered in and processed by another person (the recipient), that is, the way in which one person makes use of another person to experience and contain an aspect of himself. In association with this unconscious projective fantasy there is an interpersonal interaction by means of which the recipient is pressured to think, feel, and behave in a manner congruent with the ejected feelings and the self- and object-representations embodied in the projective fantasy" (Ogden, 1982, pp. 1-2).

2. It is important in this undertaking to remember that the political views of the conventional "liberal" and "conservative" camps in today's politics, from this perspective, are more alike than different. They are different versions of the same underlying modern individualistic doctrine. One advocates large-scale social programs and a high degree of personal or "lifestyle" autonomy, the other stresses reliance on broad market forces and celebrates individual economic freedom. Both political viewpoints make individuals and individual freedom the cornerstone of their approach, even though they understand these notions somewhat differently. Both tend to rely on large-scale impersonal mechanisms, either the state or the market, to sort out our differences and downplay more traditional notions of community, civil society, or reasoning together about the public interest or common good (Etzioni, 1996; Sarason, 1986; Wolfe, 1989).

References

Antonovsky, A. (1979). *Health, stress, and coping*. San Francisco: Jossey-Bass.

Bakhtin, M. (1981). *The dialogic imagination*. Austin, TX: University of Texas Press.

Bakhtin, M. (1984). *Problems of Dostoevsky's poetics* (C. Emerson, Ed. & Trans.). Minneapolis: University of Minnesota Press.

Bell, D. (1978). *The cultural contradictions of capitalism*. New York: Basic Books.

Bellah, R., Madsen, R., Sullivan, W., Swidler, A., & Tipton, S. (1985). *Habits of the heart: Individualism and commitment in American Life*. Berkeley: University of California Press.

Berger, P. (1977). *Facing up to modernity*. New York: Basic Books.

Bruner, J. (1990). *Acts of meaning*. Cambridge, MA: Harvard University Press.

Coles, R. (1987). Civility and psychology. In R. Bellah, R. Madsen, W. Sullivan, A. Swidler, & S. Tipton (Eds.), *Individualism and commitment in American life*. New York: HarperCollins.

Cushman, P. (1990). Why the self is empty. *American Psychologist, 45*, 599-611.

Cushman, P. (1995). *Constructing the self, constructing America*. Menlo Park, CA: Addison-Wesley.

Doherty, W. (1994, Winter). Bridging psychotherapy and moral responsibility. *Responsive Community, 4*, 41-52.

Eagle, M. (1984). *Recent developments in psychoanalysis*. New York: McGraw-Hill.

Etzioni, A. (1996). *The new golden rule: Community and morality in a democratic society*. New York: Basic Books.

Fancher, R. (1995). *Cultures of healing: Correcting the image of American mental health care*. New York: Freeman.

Flax, J. (1990). *Thinking fragments*. Berkeley: University of California Press.

Fox, D., & Prilleltensky, I. (1997). *Critical psychology: An introduction*. London: Sage.

Frank, J. (1978) *Psychotherapy and the human predicament*. New York: Schocken.

Gadamer, H.-G. (1989). *Truth and method* (2nd ed., J. Weinsheimer & D. Marshall, Trans.). New York: Crossroad. (Original work published 1960)

Gergen, K. (1985). The social constructionist movement in modern psychology. *American Psychologist, 40*, 266-275.

Gergen, K., & Kaye, J. (1992). Beyond narrative in the negotiation of therapeutic meaning. In S. McNamee & K. Gergen (Eds.), *Therapy as social construction* (pp. 166-185). London: Sage.

Habermas, J. (1973). *Theory and practice*. Boston: Beacon.

Hillman, J., & Ventura, M. (1992). *We've had a hundred years of psychotherapy and the world's getting worse*. San Francisco: HarperSanFrancisco.

Hoffman, I. Z. (1996). The intimate and ironic authority of the psychoanalyst's presence. *Psychoanalytic Quarterly, 65*, 102-136.

Kohut, H. (1977). *The restoration of the self*. Madison, CT: International Universities Press.

Lowe, C. M. (1969). *Value orientations in counseling and psychotherapy: The meaning of mental health*. Cranston, RI: Carroll.

McNamee, S., & Gergen, K. (1992). *Therapy as social construction*. London: Sage.

Miller, W. (1999). *Integrating spirituality into treatment: Resources for practitioners*. Washington, DC: American Psychological Association.

Morson, G., & Emerson, C. (1990). *Mikhail Bakhtin: Creation of a prosaics*. Stanford, CA: Stanford University Press.

Ogden, T. (1982). *Projective identification and psychotherapeutic technique*. New York: Jason Aronson.

Rawls, J. (1971). *A theory of justice*. Cambridge, MA: Harvard University Press.

Richardson, F., Fowers, B., & Guignon, C. (1999). *Re-envisioning psychology: Moral dimensions of theory and practice*. San Francisco: Jossey-Bass.

Richardson, F., Rogers, T., & McCarroll, J. (1998). Towards a dialogical self. *American Behavior Scientist, 41*, 496-515.

Rieff, P. (1966). *The triumph of the therapeutic*. New York: Harper.

Rubin, J. (1996). *Psychotherapy and Buddhism: Toward integration*. New York: Plenum.

Rubin, J. (1997). Psychoanalysis is self-centered. In C. Spezzano & G. Garguilo (Eds.), *Soul on the couch: Spirituality, religion and morality in contemporary psychoanalysis* (pp. 79-108). Hillsdale, NJ: Analytic Press.

Sandel, M. (1996). *Democracy's discontent: America in search of a public philosophy*. Cambridge, MA: Harvard University Press.

Sarason, S. (1986). And what is the public interest? *American Psychologist, 41*, 899-905.

Sartre, J-P. (1956). *Being and nothingness*. New York: Philosophical Library.

Schafer, R. (1976). *A new language for psychoanalysis*. New Haven, CT: Yale University Press.

Sullivan, W. (1986). *Reconstructing public philosophy*. Berkeley: University of California Press.

Taylor, C. (1989). *Sources of the self*. Cambridge, MA: Harvard University Press.

Taylor, C. (1991). The dialogical self. In D. Hiley, J. Bohman, & R. Schusterman (Eds.), *The interpretive turn: Philosophy, science, culture* (pp. 304-314). Ithaca, NY: Cornell University Press.

Taylor, C. (1995). *Philosophical arguments*. Cambridge, MA: Harvard University Press.

Wolfe, A. (1989). *Whose keeper? Social science and moral obligation*. Berkeley: University of California Press.

Commentary

Individualism and Modern Psychotherapy

Judy Norman
Brigham Young University School of Social Work

It seems bold, even courageous, of psychologists to speak to colleagues with a reminder that all clinicians ought to be working themselves out of a job—bold because Richardson and Zeddies further suggest that psychology (or the field of mental health) does not have all the therapeutic answers, or even the best answers sometimes, and courageous to begin to act as if they believe that. It is commendable that Richardson and Zeddies would speak of enlarging the professional dialogue and expanding the dialogue with patients concerning emotional conditions and issues in a way that helps patients value autonomy to a degree while simultaneously entering the larger community of connections to others, which dialogue was practiced more abundantly in the past. Perhaps in this collective professional humility, there is an opportunity to learn from not always having the answer, to professionally "suffer," or to grapple with uncertainty or lack of singular "rights" and "wrongs" in defining mental health and in delivering mental health interventions. Furthermore, professionals can learn not to escape so quickly from the anguish of being unable to readily help clients. We should not try to avoid professional growing pains that call for being still and listening to and observing patients whose backgrounds are so diverse and so uncommon that traditional psychotherapies may be, at times, inadvertently blurring clients and treating them as less diverse, thereby adding to psychic or interpersonal tension and conflict. In modern individualism, self-interest and self-actualization ideals without acknowledgment of social interdependence paves one way to isolation. In reflecting transitory societal values or inflexible professional philosophical norms describing the "good life" or "mental health," psychotherapies may be requiring unsatisfying personal goals that engender neither autonomy nor interdependence.

As encouraged by Dr. Richardson, the dialogue among ourselves and then with clients could include direct exploration of tradition, religion, neighborhood,

165

family, morals, and spirituality, so as to bring both personal *and* social meaningfulness into healthy interaction. What are some clinical applications for the dialogue suggested? A few examples might be helpful in examining how psychotherapy might foster both self-interest and other-interest in mutually compatible and complementary processes.

In research regarding posttraumatic stress disorder (PTSD) among Vietnam veterans, few traditional psychotherapies have been found to be consistently helpful. One strategy that seems to be helping more of these veterans is the Native American "sweats": purification rites wherein one is encouraged to tell one's story of trauma and, in particular, to tell the story so that others may benefit (Meichenbaum, 1994). Psychotherapists can assist individual clients in sharing personal stories and encourage additional story details that recount the patient's ability to survive *and* to describe examples of resourcefulness and perseverance so that others might benefit therefrom.

Related to this constructivist technique is the need for therapists to constantly use the *client's* own language, phrases, and metaphors and to avoid summative, paraphrased versions offered by the clinician. In eliciting stories of survival, for example, the psychotherapist may encourage reference to those persons who may have helped (rescuers, concerned family members, friends, strangers, church and synagogue congregations) to reinforce notions like, "I am not in this alone," "People are more generous than I had previously supposed," "Most people are good," thus accentuating personal accomplishment in the context of assistance from others. Community and individual capacity can be brought together in the same discussion. Thus narrative construction (Cushman, 1995; Lee & Greene, 1999; McCann & Pearlman, 1991; McNamee & Gergen, 1992; Meichenbaum & Fitzpatrick, 1993) could reflect the personal and the social.

In the treatment of unipolar depression, it is widely assumed and supported by research that a combination of medications and particular psychotherapies is the most effective intervention strategy (Covi & Lipman, 1987; Evans et al., 1992; Jarrett, 1995; Miller, Norman, & Keitner, 1989). It is also believed that proper nutrition, rest, and exercise, as well as a progressive return to levels of activity, including interpersonal activity, are important. Much literature includes reference to "pleasant activities" or "pleasant events" (when energy level has improved) as antithetical to being depressed (Lewinsohn, Hoberman, Teri, & Hautzinger, 1985; Lewinsohn, Sullivan, & Grosscup, 1980). Of course, pleasant events are those that are pleasing to the individual. Perhaps social activism or "cause advocacy" could be considered akin to "pleasant events" as the patient engages in political or social activism in chosen and meaningful behaviors that further psychological gain and allow for interactions with others in a cause that seeks to help others as well, for example, educating others about depression, discrimination, inaccessible resources, and so on.

Related to the idea of social activism as therapeutic strategy would be the early 20th-century efforts by social workers to help individuals function more effectively in society (in neighborhoods, churches, synagogues, the workplace, institutions, and families), simultaneously improving society's responsiveness to individuals. Perhaps psychotherapists do not practice responsibly when direct clinical practice is not complemented by some effort to improve the community in which the patient lives, such as involvement in one's profession around issues of patient rights and care, legislative activity, specific efforts toward social equality and social justice. As Richardson and Zeddies suggest, acknowledging "powerful emotions and passions such as outrage and indignation . . . can bind us to others." Dialogue that includes morals must include discussion of the morality of social injustice by clinicians and as part of educating clients about psychiatric conditions that may be caused by or sustained by environmental factors. All psychotherapy models and strategies have limitations, and clinicians can so admit routinely.

Historically, assessing the role of culture, ethnicity, and diversity was too often tied to the impact these might have on clients and their illness and coping, without an awareness that these factors might hold answers as viable and useful as the scientific, researched, and experientially based answers offered by psychotherapy. Thus meditation, yoga, prayer, and spiritual pathways, as well as tradition, religious communities, spiritual advisors, and healers are potential contributors to mental health. This could be a way of helping patients remain comfortable in their communities and comfortable with the offerings of knowledgeable, experienced, *and* effective mental health practitioners.

In the introduction to their chapter, Richardson and Zeddies note Charles Handy's observation, "Capitalism . . . delivers the means but not the point of life." Psychotherapy may indeed have the capacity to deliver the means whereby clients can negotiate life, however its place may not be to decide the point of life, life's meaning, or even a uniform definition of health. Rather than expecting that individuals be the sole "responsible center of their own moral universe," professional dialogue might commence to include "such traditional, possibly worthwhile, values or virtues as 'the redemptive power of suffering, acceptance of one's lot in life, adherence to tradition, self-restraint, and moderation.'"

The authors quote Robert Fancher (1995), who wrote, "There is no inherent reason why internal dynamics, rather than one's place in society, must be the principle source of health or illness" (p. 124). So let psychotherapy scrutinize emotional struggles in a broader social and moral context, not to undermine but to strengthen, even embrace, the "social fabric of family, work environment, and community life," not abandoning the cause of autonomy but cultivating many excellences, intellectual, moral, and social. May the dialogue continue.

References

Covi, L., & Lipman, R. S. (1987). Cognitive behavioral group psychotherapy combined with imipramine in major depression. *Psychopharmacology Bulletin, 23*(1), 173-176.

Cushman, P. (1995). *Constructing the self, constructing America.* Menlo Park, CA: Addison-Wesley.

Evans, M. D., Hollon, S. D., DeRubeis, R. J., Piaseck, J. M., Grove, W. M., Garvy, M. J., & Tuason, V.B. (1992). Differential relapse following cognitive therapy and pharmacotherapy. *Archives of General Psychiatry, 40*(10), 802-808.

Fancher, R. (1995). *Cultures of healing: Correcting the image of American mental health care.* New York: Basic Books.

Jarrett, R. (1995). Comparing and combining short-term psychotherapy and pharmacotherapy for depression. In E. E. Beckham & W. R. Leber (Eds.), *Handbook of depression* (2nd ed., pp. 435-464). New York: Guilford.

Lee, M-Y., & Greene, G. J. (1999). A social constructivist framework for integrating crosscultural issues in teaching clinical social work. *Journal of Social Work Education, 35*(1), 21-37.

Lewinsohn, P. M., Hoberman, H., Teri, L., & Hautzinger, M. (1985). An integrative theory of depression. In S. Reiss & R. Bootzin (Eds.), *Theoretical issues in behavior therapy* (pp. 331-359). New York: Academic Press.

Lewinsohn, P. M., Sullivan, J., & Grosscup, S. J. (1980). Changing reinforcing events: An approach to the treatment of depression. *Psychotherapy: Theory, Research, and Practice, 47*, 322-334.

McCann, L., & Pearlman, L. A. (1991). *Through a glass darkly: Understanding and treating the adult trauma survivor through constructivist self-development theory.* New York: Brunner/Mazel.

McNamee, S., & Gergen, K. J. (1992). *Therapy as social construction.* London: Sage.

Meichenbaum, B. (1994). *A clinical handbook/practical therapist manual for assessing and treating adults with post traumatic stress disorder.* Waterloo, Ontario, Canada: Institute Press.

Meichenbaum, D., & Fitzpatrick, D. (1993). A constructionist narrative perspective on stress and coping. In L. Goldberger & S. Breznitz (Eds.), *Handbook of stress: Theoretical and clinical aspects* (2nd ed., pp. 706-723). New York: Free Press.

Miller, I. W., Norman, W. H., & Keitner, G. I. (1989). Cognitive-behavioral treatment of depressed inpatients: Six- and twelve-month follow-up. *American Journal of Psychiatry, 146*, 1274-1279.

Issue 8

The Scientist-Practitioner Model

The Patient-Philosopher Evaluates the Scientist-Practitioner

A Case Study

Hendrika Vande Kemp
Fuller Theological Seminary

I am a clinical psychologist trained in the scientist-practitioner model and teaching in an American Psychological Association (APA) accredited Boulder model doctoral program. I am also a historian of psychology who privileges the "philosophical roots of psychology" (Klein, 1970; Watson, 1963) over experimental roots emphasized by historians in the Boring (1929) tradition. I especially like the *Intellectual History of Psychology* by Robinson (1976), who anchors modern psychological problems in four ancient philosophical questions: the problem of knowledge, the origins of reason, the problem of conduct, and the problem of governance. I bring these preferences, and a commitment to liberal education, to my assessment of the scientist-practitioner model.

The Focus

The essence of the scientist-practitioner model can be summarized in a single sentence: "Scientist-practitioner psychologists embody a research orientation in their practice and a practice relevance in their research" (Belar & Perry, 1991, p. 7). My purpose is to assess how well various mental health professionals lived up to this ideal in one particular complex situation, using philosophical and theoretical concepts to illuminate both the failures and the successes.

The Case

The case is based on my personal experiences as a consumer of a variety of psychological and medical services (Vande Kemp, 1993, 1997). On July 12, 1989, the 1986 Honda Accord I was driving was totaled in a multiple-impact collision, at about 60 miles per hour, with a Freightliner and its 42-foot trailer. I experienced only a momentary lapse of consciousness and was released from the emergency room without a brain scan. I immediately sought chiropractic treatment for my painful whiplash injuries, and within 2 months entered therapy for posttraumatic stress disorder (PTSD). A neurologist treated my posttraumatic headaches with antidepressants, the effects of which resulted in a 6-day psychiatric hospitalization 11 months later for a Nardil-induced manic episode; other psychotropic drugs prescribed to treat the mania plunged me deeper into psychosis. Persistent headaches and symptoms of post-concussion syndrome (PCS) eventually led me to UCLA's Neuropsychiatric Institute (NPI), where neuropsychological testing and single photon emission computerized tomography (SPECT) documented a left frontal rotational injury. A personal injury lawsuit necessitated by California auto insurance law engendered extensive "testing" by defense examiners prior to a 2-week jury trial. I brought to this ordeal the "divided consciousness" of personal subjectivity and professional objectivity: Medical and legal necessity compelled me to educate myself about every aspect of my condition, requiring in-depth study of both scientific and clinical literature.

Mine was obviously a complicated clinical case. The assessment and treatment of the consequences of this motor vehicle accident (MVA) involved approximately three dozen professionals. Technicians performed the diagnostic spinal x rays, EEG recordings, SPECT, and MRI brain scans that were interpreted by other experts. A chiropractor and an orthopedist evaluated the whiplash injuries, which were treated by massage therapists and a physical therapist. Neuropsychologists administered test batteries for diagnostic and forensic purposes and provided cognitive rehabilitation therapy. Neurologists treated posttraumatic headaches and fatigue. Psychiatrists struggled with the side effects of psychotropic drugs. Clinical psychologists helped me cope with PTSD, PCS, and the stress of the personal injury lawsuit. A medical psychologist provided EEG neurofeedback.

Coming to Grips With the Case:
Essential Data and Guidelines

This MVA had multiple, complex consequences. A rotational brain injury produces cortical damage, and autopsies often reveal "widespread tissue disruption in the subcortical structures . . . owing to shearing forces affecting microscopic boundaries of moving and stationary brain structures" (Rubinstein, 1993, p. 110). For mild traumatic brain injury (MTBI), this "may involve disrupted axons with micro-hemorrhages, with subsequent macrophage activity" (p. 111). The injury to the brain is typically concomitant with damage to the body and the psychic trauma of the accident experience. Whiplash injury, PCS, and PTSD are often comorbid in MVA survivors, and in clinical and forensic practice it is common to encounter "at least 2 of these syndromes" (Miller, 1998, p. 10).

Posttraumatic Stress Disorder (PTSD) and Post-Concussion Syndrome (PCS) After Mild Traumatic Head Injury (MTBI)

In the past decade, neuroscientists and clinicians have clarified the relationship between PTSD and PCS and have clearly provided evidence to reject the traditional view (still stubbornly retained by Mayou, Bryant, & Duthie, 1993, and by Sbordone & Liter, 1995) that these disorders do not co-occur in MTBI cases. Comorbidity of MTBI and PTSD is common (Grigsby & Kaye, 1993; Wright & Telford, 1996), and there is a "tendency toward increased PTSD with the less severely brain injured" (Bontke, Rattok, & Boake, 1996, p. 95). Because there is some overlap of PTSD arousal symptoms and PCS (see Table 8.1), some authors focus on the difficulty of differential diagnosis (Bryant & Harvey, 1999b; Ohry, Rattok, & Solomon, 1996). This problem disappears if we base diagnosis only on the full range of essential symptoms, "the features that are generally required to make the diagnosis" (American Psychiatric Association, 1987, p. 21). Bryant and Harvey (1998) reported that PTSD occurs in 19% to 33% of MTBI cases after MVAs and found that although "impaired consciousness at time of a trauma may reduce frequency of traumatic memories in the initial month posttrauma, MTBI does not result in a different profile of longer-term PTSD" (Bryant & Harvey, 1999a, p. 15).

Bryant (1996) suggests that PTSD after MTBI may in part be due to pseudomemories that result from reconstruction of the trauma event. Such pseudomemories in MVA survivors may result from visualizations based on imagination (Burstein, 1986) and are dependent on vividness of visual imagery (Bryant & Harvey, 1996). Layton and Wardi-Zonna (1995) reported that "operation of a nondeclarative memory is a sufficient condition for the development of PTSD" (p. 2). "A 'window' of real or imagined experience resulting from loss of consciousness and posttraumatic amnesia after closed-head injury need not prevent PTSD from arising" (McMillan, 1996, p. 749; see also King, 1997).

Posttraumatic Headaches

Like many MVA survivors, I suffered from both acute and chronic posttraumatic headaches (PTH), a condition that may include features of tension, migraine, and cluster headaches (Sadwin, Rothrock, Mandel, Sadwin, & O'Leary, 1993). Such headaches represent unhealed injuries and may involve neuralgia,

TABLE 8.1 *DSM-III-R* Symptoms of Posttraumatic Stress Disorder and the Symptoms of Post-Concussion Syndrome[a]

Post-Concussion Syndrome	Posttraumatic Stress Disorder
Physical symptoms	**Re-experiencing the traumatic event**
Headache	Recurrent & intrusive recollections of the event
Sleep disturbance[b]	
Fatigue	Recurrent distressing dreams of the event
	Sudden acting or feeling that the event is recurring: illusions, hallucinations, dissociative (flashback) episodes
Dizziness	Intense psychological distress at exposure
Sensory sensitivity	
Cognitive symptoms	**Persistent symptoms of increased arousal**
Decreased information processing	Difficulty falling or staying asleep[b]
Poor attention & concentration[b]	Difficulty concentrating[b]
Decreased new learning & memory	Hypervigilance
Dysfluent problem solving	Irritability or outbursts of anger[b]
	Exaggerated startle response
	Physiologic reactivity on exposure to events that symbolize an aspect of the traumatic event
Behavioral-affective symptoms	**Persistent avoidance of stimuli associated with the traumatic event**
Irritability[b]	Efforts to avoid thoughts or feelings associated with the trauma
Depression	Efforts to avoid activities or situations that arouse recollections of the trauma
Loss of self-confidence	Inability to recall important aspects of the trauma (psychogenic amnesia)
Anger outbursts[b]	Markedly diminished interest or participation in significant activities
Social alienation[b]	Feelings of detachment or estrangement from others[b]
Anxiety	Restricted range of affect
	Sense of a foreshortened future

Notes: [a]Symptoms of post-concussion syndrome are from Kay, Newman, Cavallo, Ezrachi, and Resnick (1992).
[b]Symptoms common to posttraumatic stress disorder and post-concussion syndrome.

neuropathy, trigger points, and pain referred from other parts of the body (Parker, 1995). The reported incidence of such headaches ranges from 28% to 100% of cases in assorted clinical samples (Sadwin et al., 1993, p. 144). Paradoxically, "the severity of the head injury seems to be inversely proportional to the severity of the head pain," and patients with MTBI frequently suffer severe pain (pp. 144-145). I suffered for 4 years from continuous posttraumatic headaches.

Posttraumatic Dreams

Barrett (1996) described the typical pattern of posttraumatic nightmares in which "the initial dreams are fairly close to literal reenactment of the trauma with the twist that an additional horror, averted in real life, is added to the dream reenactment" (p. 3). Over time, "the dream content begins to make the trauma more symbolic and to interweave it with concerns from the dreamer's daily life" (p. 3). Hartmann (1996) assumed that ordinary PTSD dreams and nightmares are part of connecting "traumatic events with other themes in the person's life" (p. 109) and argued that the "repetitive posttraumatic nightmares" of Vietnam War veterans should be relabeled "memory intrusions" (p. 105), as they constituted "encapsulated memories" that might intrude at any stage of sleep. Such encapsulated memories may follow other types of trauma as well.

Although some approach traumatic dreams from a traditional psychoanalytic perspective (e.g., Lansky & Bhey, 1995), this view was challenged after World War I by Rivers (1920), who established that "the most trying and distressing symptoms" of war neurosis were "due to the attempt to banish from the mind distressing memories of warfare or painful affective states" (p. 187). Rivers helped soldiers integrate their traumatic war experiences into the fabric of their lives. Few psychologists have studied posttraumatic dreams after MVAs, but in my own experience over the past decade there have been occasional intrusive flashback scenes that Hartmann (1996) might describe as "encapsulated memories" and numerous traditional nightmares with pseudo-memories that appear to serve integrative and connecting functions as the crash experience is assimilated into my personal narrative (Vande Kemp, 1993).

Head Trauma and Psychotropic Drugs

Head injury survivors appear to be especially vulnerable to the effects of psychotropic drugs. Four errors occurred in the early management of my medications: (a) The prescribing doctors did not take an adequate medical history, thus remaining unaware of my well-documented drug sensitivities, allergies, and paradoxical responses as well as the mitral valve prolapse that was a contraindicator for tricyclic antidepressants; (b) they did not appear to know that drug effects are potentiated by head injury (Rubinstein, 1993; Sadwin et al., 1993) and inappropriately prescribed Elavil, Nardil, Klonopin, Restoril, Mellaril, and Trilafon; (c) they did not monitor the medication with follow-up visits, in contrast to the NPI neurologist who carefully monitored white blood cells levels after prescribing Tegretol for neuropathic pain; and (d) they prescribed antidepressants in the absence of depression. Professionals far too quickly diagnose depression without ruling out organic disease, when there are at least 50 medical syndromes, including MTBI, with symptoms that mimic depression (Hall, 1980; Hoffman, 1982).

An additional problem arose later in my treatment. I was taking Elavil and amantadine to help counter fatigue and Tegretol for neuropathic headaches. Each of these medications has an appetite suppressant effect—that is, it produces anorexia—and I had lost about 10 pounds in a year. I reported this unexpected weight loss to my neurologist, who swiftly checked for and found other drug reactions and promptly changed my medications. The defense neuropsychologist argued on the basis of this drug-induced appetite loss that I suffered from anorexia nervosa. I in fact met none of the essential *DSM-III-R* (American Psychiatric Association, 1987) criteria: "refusal to maintain minimal normal weight for age and height; intense fear of gaining weight or becoming fat, even though underweight; a distorted body image; and amenorrhea (in females)" (p. 65). The *DSM* explicitly declares, "The term anorexia is a misnomer since loss of appetite is rare" (p. 65).

Practical Diagnosis and Differential Psychology

The misdiagnosis in my case was one of multiple violations of "scientist" standards by the defense neuropsychologist. He and the Catholic defense attorney argued that I suffered from an obsessive-compulsive disorder because I was "rigid," a conclusion they based merely on the fact that I taught at Fuller Theological Seminary, which is an evangelical, multidenominational Protestant institution. They further substantiated this diagnosis with my alleged "lack of generosity," which they inferred from the fact that I was paid $200 to lead a 14-hour weekend retreat for a church group rather than donating these professional services. The neuropsychologist implied that my time as a professional psychologist was not worth $15 per hour, although he was charging $400+ per hour for his comparable services. This judgment reflected an unhealthy personal narcissism and a violation of the ethical principles relating to "respect for people's rights and dignity" (American Psychological Association [APA], 1992, 1599-1600), "nondiscrimination" (p. 1601), and "human differences" (p. 1601). When evaluating my performance on cognitive tasks, he repeatedly compared my test performance to his own: He could not conceive of the possibility that my intelligence, even after a head injury, might exceed his. My own eminent forensic neuropsychologist testified with wry amusement that, in his case, it did. The first practitioner remained unaware of how his "personal characteristics" affected his "professional interactions" (Belar & Perry, 1991, p. 9). He ignored research evidence indicating that head injury impairs "attention, memory, and a broad range of information-processing skills" without lowering intelligence (Berg, Franzen, & Wedding, 1987, p. 23). He interpreted standard tests without comparison to my past performance or requisite job skills: Even a small decline in accuracy will have serious consequences for a historian of psychology or statistical researcher. He also failed to recognize that normative data on standard tests, when applied to "individuals whose prior functioning is at the very highest levels," often erroneously presents them as "perfectly intact" (Kastl & Podboy, 1993, abstract).

The Differential Effects of Reification and Accurate Labeling

Once these professionals established their questionable diagnoses, they engaged in extensive reification. The original neurologist erroneously concluded that I had migraines. She then labeled me a "migraneur" and attributed my pain to the "low pain threshold of migraneurs," relying on an opinion for which there is fundamentally no research evidence (Martin, 1993). By then I felt truly mystified (Laing, 1965). I felt that my very being was attacked when the defense neurologist described me in his report as a "spinster": Such obsolete language suggests obliviousness to professional guidelines regarding gender sensitivity and gender discrimination (see Vande Kemp & Anderson, 1999) and ignorance of basic sociological variables.

I discovered the positive effect of labels at monthly support groups sponsored by the Southern California Head Injury Foundation (SCHIF), where participants introduced themselves as "head injury survivors" and thereby normalized various otherwise disorienting experiences. It was also helpful to have my therapist attend a workshop on MTBI, which provided us with another orienting name, extensive information, and parameters for reality testing. Another helpful use of labels occurred in a meeting sponsored by Citizens for Reliable and Safe Highways (CRASH): They refuse to speak of "accidents" because most truck crashes are in fact preventable. I was also helped by Gendler's (1984/1988) evocative "portraits" of Suffering, Pain, Shock, Alienation, and Terror, which provided words for feelings I had been unable to express.

Four Dimensions of Reality in Clinical Practice

When psychologists discuss "reality" and how it can be known, they generally do not make explicit that the term has multiple noninterchangeable referents. The philosophically aware scientist-practitioner takes into account the multifaceted nature of reality by approaching it with diverse epistemologies grounded in the empirical and rational components of the hypothetico-deductive method and in the empathic, intuitive components of phenomenological understanding.

Impersonal Reality

Psychologists must attend to the external, *impersonal*, tangible reality we typically regard as the domain of the natural sciences. This is the reality that appears to be most convincingly and permanently "out there," although it is neither static nor fully knowable. In this sphere of reality, we can comfortably search for "facts." Thus the accident reconstruction specialist concerned himself with the size and weight of both car and truck, their paths of motion and speed, and the direction of the multiple impacts. Such material "facts" were based on various ostensibly objective mechanical measurements as well as the more subjective testimony of accident witnesses. Obviously, the process of verifying these facts is not without problems: I, for example, have no memory of the crashes making any noise, and without witnesses would have had to rely on Berkeley's Permanent Perceiver to report them (see Watson, 1963, pp. 178-180). Defense attorneys presented a version of the events that contradicted my testimony and the testimony of the truck driver and three witnesses. The kinesiologist reconstructed the forces operating on my neck and brain by relying on empirical data about the effects of acceleration forces on the body (Sweeney, 1992). The defense argued that these forces were no stronger than those of an amusement park rollercoaster. This was either a serious failure in reality testing or deliberate lying in the sincere belief that manipulation of facts helps to "convey a 'true picture'" (Bok, 1978, p. 85). These experts provided no evidence to buttress this opinion, violating the ethical mandate that the forensic expert examine "the issue at hand from all reasonable perspectives, actively seeking information that will differentially test plausible rival hypotheses" (Committee on Ethical Guidelines for Forensic Psychologists, 1991, p. 661).

Interpersonal Reality

Psychologists must also be concerned about the relational, *interpersonal* reality that is constantly being created and renegotiated, and it is typically tested by applying the principle of consensual validation (Cameron & Magaret, 1951; Carson, 1969). The fact that this dimension of reality is constantly under construction (Gergen, 1994) does not render it unknowable: What has been negotiated can be observed, reported, or inferred.

A significant interpersonal issue for the MTBI survivor is the social isolation that is alleged to be a common feature of PCS (Kay et al., 1992). Psychologists might do better to speak of the new interpersonal world inhabited by the survivor. Assessment of a head injury survivor's social reality should include extensive inquiry into the person's current networks, even when these are not typically classified as social. Defense experts were invested in presenting me as socially isolated: The defense neurologist literally fabricated my social history; the defense neuropsychologist selectively omitted in his assessment summary all positive statements in the computer-generated test reports. This psychologist violated numerous ethical principles applying to the proper use of psychological tests (APA, 1985; 1992) and ignored the goal of the scientist-practitioner model that "case/problem conceptualization be grounded in valid assessment procedures and scientific literature" (Belar & Perry, 1991, p. 9).

The roles of patient and plaintiff propelled me from a world centered on work, family, friends, church, and professional activities into an entirely new phenomenal world in which protracted periods were spent receiving medical treatment, exercising, sleeping, commuting to UCLA/NPI, and coping with extensive paperwork. I was forced to interact with my attorneys, defense attorneys, judge, jury, accident witnesses, police, diverse expert witnesses, and health and auto insurance company representatives. Old networks of professional colleagues and church leaders drifted to the periphery as I reduced my teaching load and eliminated virtually all extracurricular activities to concentrate on rehabilitation, teaching, and writing. I became increasingly detached from siblings and others who were unable to enter my phenomenal world. A dear friend abandoned me during my manic episode. Other casual friends became more intimate and provided support during my period of temporary insanity and the extreme stress of my personal injury trial. These relationships proved to be actual movements of grace, altering "life radically for the better" (Hiltner, 1972, p. 39) and evoking gratitude. My therapist's grace emerged when, after a period of empathic failure, he realized that the craziness was not me but was being done *to* me, and that I needed his companionship in "the pit." He tearfully apologized and supported me in discontinuing Mellaril and Trilafon and "firing" my neurologist and psychiatrist.

Intrapersonal Reality

Psychologists must also concern themselves with *intrapersonal, intrapsychic* reality. Many early psychologists and epistemologists regarded personal, inner experience as more real than experiences of the external world. This assumption seems strange to the 21st-century mind, but without it philosophers would never have engaged in the heated debates concerning solipsism and "the problem of other minds" that are central to philosophical psychology (Watson, 1963). For the pre-Watsonian psychologist, "the introspective method constitutes direct and immediate contact with the subject matter, while what we now mean by objective observation was then only an indirect or mediate one. After the [Watsonian] revolution the meanings are reversed" (Samelson, 1981/1988, p. 415). Practitioner psychologists must assess several intrapersonal realities in persons with MTBI.

The Disrupted Sense of Self. Kay (1986) reports that the "sense of self is totally disrupted" following MTBI, and it is "more devastated after minor, than more severe head injury because the deficits encountered after minor head injury are unexpected and not apparent to anyone else" (p. 8). When colleagues, friends, family members, and experts continue to expect the MTBI survivor to perform at previous levels, this arouses a great deal of anxiety and the fear of going crazy, because survivors are often unable "to communicate to others the devastating nature of their inner experience" (p. 9). They now live in a world "where all the rules of thinking, feeling, and behaving are suddenly violated, for no apparent reason, and no one else is taking notice" (p. 9). My therapist educated himself about MTBI because he desired to use "scientifically validated interventions that follow logically from the case/problem conceptualization" (Belar & Perry, 1991, p. 9).

After a serious MVA, the self is disrupted in other ways. In my accident, I encountered fate and death, which Tillich (1952) described as the relative and absolute threats to being itself. I reconstructed my identity in the later struggle with pain and my psychotic "descent into hell" (Daim, 1954/1963). In addition to Tillich's (1952) *spiritual* perils of emptiness and loss of meaning, I encountered the *moral* risks of guilt and condemnation as we attempted to determine responsibility for the accident, recoup medical costs, obtain compensation for pain and suffering, and decide whether to sue for malpractice. I confronted all these existential crises in a single multifaceted, prolonged experience.

Pain and Its Consequences. When health psychologists write about pain, they consistently focus on pain management (e.g., Martin, 1993; Rubinstein, 1993; Sadwin et al., 1993) and define pain merely as illness. The philosophically grounded practitioner will join the sufferer in a search for the meaning of pain. Pain, by its very nature, "demands interpretation" (Bakan, 1968, p. 66), because it confronts us with mystery in a realm we thought we understood, the world inside our own skin. Pain is "a state of existential distress to which [one] responds as a person" (Buytendijk, 1943/1962, p. 162). It is one of the invisible realities of life that entirely transforms the experience of space and time (Leder, 1984-1985) in Heidegger's (1889-1976) sphere of temporality: "The connectedness of meanings that is present in *Dasein's* practical activities of everyday life" (Slife, 1993, p. 257; see also Hellstrom & Carlsson, 1996). Ultimately, we can manage physical pain, but we cannot restore the person to the prepain existential state: the awareness of the world as a place in which pain exists is a permanent acquisition.

The philosophically grounded practitioner also acknowledges that psychological components of pain are essential qualities and not simply complications to treatment. Members of the International Association for the Study of Pain (IASP; Merskey & Bogduk, 1994) no longer distinguish between objective and subjective pain. But they attribute pain in the absence of tissue damage to a *psychological origin*, leading health psychologists to postulate and search for a "chronic pain personality" to which pain without tissue damage could be attributed. That leaves patients not only with chronic pain but also with guilt and shame about their essential being. Fortunately, this trend is disappearing.

Martin (1993) concluded, "The extensive literature on headaches and personality does not support the clinically derived concept of a migraine or headache personality" (p. 68). Labbe, Goldberg, Fishbain, Rosomoff, and Steele-Rosomoff (1989) also found no support in the literature for a chronic pain personality and suggested that trait personality measures are inappropriate for the measurement of pain. They speculated that "high scores on psychogenic attitudes are a state phenomenon for most patients" (p. 389) and that test scores will change when pain no longer constitutes the center of the patient's universe (see also Demjan & Bakal, 1986).

Philosophical psychologists[1] must begin with the awareness that pain is a perceptual phenomenon with separate cognitive and affective components. For us, pain may well be the psychological phenomenon par excellence. Persons suffer from chronic pain *because* their psychological functioning is designed to make this possible; and pain is one experience that is by its very nature not dependent on a stimulus external to the brain or mind. Case or problem conceptualization is not complete without taking into account this aspect of our nature that makes it possible, apparently, to experience something that does not exist. Psychologists accomplish a rather remarkable philosophical feat when they speak of "hallucinations" or "illusions" of pain, when pain in fact is never grounded in a stimulus external to the body. "In connection with pain, we are at the margin between stimulus and response, right *in* the organism" (Bakan, 1968, p. 62). Experience itself has "no epistemological connotation. What is diagnosed as an hallucination may be phenomenally as real as something judged to be a percept" (MacLeod, 1970, p. 259). Pain, like memories and hopes, can be included among the experiences to which medieval scholars attributed "intentional inexistence": Their existence is implicit in a mental act, which always has a goal (intention) or content. Thus Brentano (1838-1917) and Meinong (1853-1920) argued that "what the mind knows or perceives exists independently of the acts of knowing and perceiving" (Robischon, 1967, p. 485). Brentano posited the ontological status of "immanent objectivity," which inheres in all contents or referents of mental acts, whether or not they have external counterparts (Sullivan, 1968) The new realists of the early 20th century built on Brentano's ontology. They coined the term "subsistents" to refer to the contents of experience (or of mental acts), which "do not come tagged as 'real' or 'unreal'" (Smith, 1982/1988, p. 460). The unrelenting headache pain that I endured for 4 years was no less real than the truck that hit my car or the oxygenation and EEG patterns in my brain.

Transpersonal Reality

The fourth dimension or mode of reality of concern is the *transpersonal*, which encompasses our relationship with God or a higher being and a spiritual realm, which may or may not be posited to contain personal beings. Scientific psychologists often dismiss this realm out of hand rather than simply acknowledging that they are not equipped to judge whether it exists or not (see Vande

Kemp, 1986). Nearly 4 centuries ago, Bacon (1620/1967) asserted, "Things which strike the senses outweigh things which do not immediately strike it, though they be more important. Hence it is that speculation commonly ceases where sight ceases, insomuch that of things invisible there is little or no observation" (p. 205). Locke (1632-1704) spoke of three kinds of things that could be known with decreasing degrees of certainty: "We know ourselves by intuition. We know God by reason (demonstration). Everything else that can be said to be known and that, in fact, exists, is known by sensation" (Robinson, 1976, p. 213). God is, of course, among the nonveridical objects to which we can assign immanent objectivity, and Brentano judged Saint Anselm's (1033-1109) well-known ontological argument for the existence of God to be a demonstration only of God's intentional inexistence (Sullivan, 1968). I was pleasantly surprised, during my 6 days of psychiatric hospitalization, by a profound sense of the presence of God that permitted me to comfort myself with the words of the Psalmist: "If I take the wings of the morning and dwell in the uttermost parts of the sea, even there thy hand shall lead me and thy right hand shall hold me" (Psalm 139: 9-10).

An additional transpersonal issue arose out of the caring provided by my neurologist at NPI, who provided a sympathetic presence and a conservative approach to medications. My relationship with him elucidated Caruso's (1952/1964) notion that the healer is a Christ archetype, a role which poses the terrible temptation "to become God and play Christ" (p. 170), the most dangerous form of countertransference. Practitioners must realize that patients contribute to the deification of doctors by their total helplessness: A patient's desperate search for a healer who will "be God" can easily fuel a helper's identification with the Christ archetype, leading patient and helper into what Tillich (1957) calls "idolatrous faith," in which "finite realities [such as health and the absence of pain] are elevated to the rank of ultimacy," and "the act of faith leads to a loss of the center and to a disruption of the personality" (p. 12).

Conclusions

I have argued that in the assessment, treatment, or legal adjudication of a complex clinical case, the scientist-practitioner is obligated to master and apply the most recent scientific and clinical research in case formulation and treatment planning. In addition, the scientist-practitioner is obligated to bring to such case formulation a philosophically informed understanding of the multiple facets of the client's reality, entering each of these realities with the appropriate epistemological and empathic stance.

Note

1. For an introduction to some philosophical approaches to pain, see Grahek (1991), Morris (1991), Nelkin (1994), and Vande Kemp (1990).

References

American Psychiatric Association. (1987). *Diagnostic and statistical manual of mental disorders* (3rd ed., rev.). Washington, DC: Author.

American Psychological Association. (1985). *Standards for educational and psychological testing.* Washington, DC: Author.

American Psychological Association. (1992). Ethical principles of psychologists and code of conduct. *American Psychologist, 47,* 1597-1611.

Bacon, F. (1967). Idols of the mind. In L. G. Locke, W. M. Gibson, & G. Arms (Eds.), *Readings for liberal education: Part 1. Toward Liberal Education* (5th ed., pp. 201-209). (Original work published 1620)

Bakan, D. (1968). *Disease, pain, & sacrifice.* Chicago: University of Chicago Press.

Barrett, D. (1996). Introduction. In D. Barrett (Ed.), *Trauma and dreams* (pp. 1-6). Cambridge, MA: Harvard University Press.

Belar, C., & Perry, N. W. (Eds.). (1991). *Proceedings: National Conference on Scientist-Practitioner Education and Training for the Practice of Psychology.* Sarasota, FL: Professional Resource Press.

Berg, R., Franzen, M., & Wedding, D. (1987). *Screening for brain impairment.* New York: Springer.

Bok, S. (1978). *Lying: Moral choice in public and private life.* New York: Pantheon.

Bontke, C. F., Rattok, J., & Boake, C. (1996). Do patients with mild brain injuries have posttraumatic stress disorder too? *Journal of Head Trauma Rehabilitation, 11,* 95-102.

Boring, E. G. (1929). *A history of experimental psychology.* New York: D. Appleton-Century.

Bryant, R. A. (1996). Posttraumatic stress disorder, flashbacks and pseudomemories in closed head injury. *Journal of Traumatic Stress, 9,* 621-630.

Bryant, R. A., & Harvey, A. G. (1996). Visual imagery in posttraumatic stress disorder. *Journal of Traumatic Stress, 9,* 613-620.

Bryant, R. A., & Harvey, A. G. (1998). Relationship between acute stress disorder and posttraumatic stress disorder following mild traumatic brain injury. *American Journal of Psychiatry, 155,* 625-629.

Bryant, R. A., & Harvey, A. G. (1999a). The influence of traumatic brain injury on acute stress disorder and posttraumatic stress disorder following motor vehicle accidents. *Brain Injury, 13*(1), 15-22.

Bryant, R. A., & Harvey, A. G. (1999b). Postconcussive symptoms and posttraumatic stress disorder after mild traumatic brain injury. *Journal of Nervous & Mental Disease, 187,* 302-305.

Burstein, A. (1986). Two cases of lifelike visualizations based on imagination in posttraumatic stress disorder. *American Journal of Psychiatry, 143,* 939.

Buytendijk, F. J. J. (1962). *Pain: Its modes and functions* (E. O'Shiel, Trans.). Chicago: University of Chicago Press. (Original work published 1943)

Cameron, N., & Magaret, A. (1951). *Behavior pathology.* Boston: Houghton Mifflin.

Carson, R. C. (1969). *Interaction concepts of personality.* Chicago: Aldine.

Caruso, I. (1964). *Existential psychology: From analysis to synthesis* (E. Krapf, Trans.). New York: Herder & Herder. (Original work published 1952)

Committee on Ethical Guidelines for Forensic Psychologists. (1991). Specialty guidelines for forensic psychologists. *Law and Human Behavior, 15,* 655-665.

Daim, W. (1963). *Depth psychology and salvation* (K. F. Reinhardt, Trans.). New York: Frederick Ungar. (Original work published 1954)

Demjan, D., & Bakal, D. (1986). Subjective distress accompanying headache attacks: Evidence for a cognitive shift. *Pain, 25,* 187-194.

Gendler, J. R. (1988). *The book of qualities.* New York: Harper & Row. (Original work published 1984)

Gergen, K. J. (1994). *Realities and relationships: Soundings in social construction.* Cambridge, MA: Harvard University Press.

Grahek, N. (1991). Objective and subjective aspects of pain. *Philosophical Psychology, 4,* 249-266.

Grigsby, J., & Kaye, K. (1993). Incidence and correlates of depersonalization following head trauma. *Brain Injury, 7,* 507-513.

Hall, R. C. W. (1980). *Psychiatric presentations of medical illness.* New York: Spectrum.

Hartmann, E. (1996). Who develops PTSD nightmares and who doesn't. In D. Barrett (Ed.), *Trauma and dreams* (pp. 100-113). Cambridge, MA: Harvard University Press.

Hellstrom, C., & Carlsson, S. G. (1996). The long-lasting now: Disorganization in subjective time in long-standing pain. *Scandinavian Journal of Psychology, 37,* 416-423.

Hiltner, S. (1972). *Theological dynamics.* Nashville, TN: Abingdon.

Hoffman, R. S. (1982). Diagnostic errors in the evaluation of behavioral disorders. *Journal of the American Medical Association, 248,* 964-967.

Kastl, A. J., & Podboy, J. W. (1993, April). *Do neuropsychological tests adequately assess very high functioning individuals?* Paper presented at the annual convention of the California Psychological Association, San Francisco.

Kay, T. (1986). *Minor head injury: An introduction for professionals.* Washington, DC: National Head Injury Foundation.

Kay, T., Newman, B., Cavallo, M., Ezrachi, O., & Resnick, M. (1992). Toward a neuropsychological model of functional disability after mild traumatic brain injury. *Neuropsychology, 6,* 371-384.

King, N. S. (1997). Posttraumatic stress disorder and head injury as a dual diagnosis: "Islands" of memory as a mechanism. *Journal of Neurology, Neurosurgery & Psychiatry, 62,* 82-84.

Klein, D. B. (1970). *A history of scientific psychology: Its origins and philosophical backgrounds.* New York: Basic Books.

Labbé, E. E., Goldberg, M., Fishbain, D., Rosomoff, H., & Steele-Rosomoff, R. (1989). Millon Behavioral Health Inventory norms for chronic pain patients. *Journal of Clinical Psychology, 45,* 383-390.

Laing, R. D. (1965). Mystification, confusion, and conflict. In J. Framo & I. Boszormenyi-Nagy (Eds.), *Intensive family therapy: Theoretical and practical aspects* (pp. 343-363). New York: Harper & Row.

Lansky, M. R., & Bhey, C. R. (1995). *Posttraumatic nightmares: Psychodynamic explorations.* Hillsdale, NJ: Analytic Press.

Layton, B. S., & Wardi-Zonna, K. (1995). Posttraumatic stress disorder with neurogenic amnesia for the traumatic event. *Clinical Neuropsychologist, 9,* 2-10.

Leder, D. (1984-1985). Toward a phenomenology of pain. *Review of Existential Psychology and Psychiatry, 19,* 255-266.

MacLeod, R. B. (1970). Psychological phenomenology: A propaedeutic to a scientific psychology. In J. R. Royce (Ed.), *Toward unification in psychology* (pp. 246-266). Toronto: University of Toronto Press.

Martin, P. R. (1993). *Psychological management of chronic headaches.* New York: Guilford.

Mayou, R., Bryant, B., & Duthie, R. (1993). Psychiatric consequences of road accidents. *British Medical Journal, 307,* 647-651.

McMillan, T. M. (1996). Posttraumatic stress disorder following minor and severe closed head injury: 10 single cases. *Brain Injury, 10,* 749-758.

Merskey, H., & Bogduk, N. (Eds.). (1994). *Classification of chronic pain* (2nd ed.). Seattle, WA: International Association for the Study of Pain Press.

Miller, L. (1998). Motor vehicle accidents: Clinical, neuropsychological, and forensic considerations. *Journal of Cognitive Rehabilitation, 16*(4), 10-23.

Morris, D. B. (1991). *The culture of pain.* Berkeley: University of California Press.

Nelkin, N. (1994). Reconsidering pain. *Philosophical Psychology, 7,* 325-343.

Ohry, A., Rattok, J., & Solomon, Z. (1996). Posttraumatic stress disorder in brain injury patients. *Brain Injury, 10*(9), 687-695.

Parker, R. S. (1995, May/June). The distracting effects of pain, headaches, and hyper-arousal upon employment after "minor head injury." *Journal of Cognitive Rehabilitation,* pp. 1-22.

Rivers, W. H. R. (1920). *Instinct and the unconscious.* Cambridge, UK: University Press.

Robinson, D. R. (1976). *An intellectual history of psychology.* New York: Macmillan.

Robischon, R. (1967). New realism. In P. Edwards (Ed.), *Encyclopedia of philosophy* (Vol. 5, pp. 485-489). New York: Macmillan.

Rubinstein, D. (1993). Psychiatric aspects of minor brain injuries. In S. Mandel, R. T. Sataloff, & S. R. Schapiro (Eds.), *Minor head trauma: Assessment, management, and rehabilitation* (pp. 107-122). New York: Springer-Verlag.

Sadwin, A., Rothrock, R., Mandel, S., Sadwin, D., & O'Leary, L. (1993). Posttraumatic headache syndrome. In S. Mandel, R. T. Sataloff, & S. R. Schapiro (Eds.), *Minor head trauma: Assessment, management, and rehabilitation* (pp. 142-158). New York: Springer-Verlag.

Samelson, F. (1988). Struggle for scientific authority: The reception of Watson's behaviorism, 1913-1920. In L. T. Benjamin, Jr. (Ed.), *A history of psychology: Original sources and contemporary research* (pp. 407-424). New York: McGraw-Hill. (Original work published 1981)

Sbordone, R. J., & Liter, J. C. (1995). Mild traumatic brain injury does not produce posttraumatic stress disorder. *Brain Injury, 9,* 405-412.

Slife, B. D. (1993). *Time and psychological explanation.* Albany: State University of New York Press.

Smith, L. D. (1988). Purpose and cognition: The limits of neorealist influence on Tolman's psychology. In L. T. Benjamin, Jr. (Ed.), *A history of psychology: Original sources and contemporary research* (pp. 457-467). New York: McGraw-Hill. (Original work published 1982)

Sullivan, J. J. (1968). Franz Brentano and the problems of intentionality. In B. B. Wolman (Ed.), *Historical roots of contemporary psychology* (pp. 248-274). New York: Harper & Row.

Sweeney, J. E. (1992). Nonimpact brain injury: Grounds for clinical study of the neuropsychological effects of acceleration forces. *Clinical Neuropsychologist, 4,* 441-455.

Tillich, P. (1952). *The courage to be.* New Haven, CT: Yale University Press.

Tillich, P. (1957). *Dynamics of faith.* New York: Harper & Row.

Vande Kemp, H. (1986). Dangers of psychologism: The place of God in psychology. *Journal of Psychology and Theology, 14,* 97-109.

Vande Kemp, H. (1990). Psychology and the problem of suffering in the 1980s. *Journal of Psychology and Christianity, 9,* 5-17.

Vande Kemp, H. (1993). Adrift in pain, anchored by grace. In J. Lee (Ed.), *Storying ourselves: A narrative perspective on Christians in psychology* (pp. 261-291). Grand Rapids, MI: Baker Book House.

Vande Kemp, H. (1997, Spring). Personal reflections on trauma and head injury. *American Family Therapy Academy Newsletter, 67,* 38-42.

Vande Kemp, H., & Anderson, T. L. (1999). Humanistic psychology and feminist psychology. In D. Moss (Ed.), *Humanistic and transpersonal psychology: Historical and biographical sourcebook* (pp. 125-144). New York: Greenwood.

Watson, R. I. (1963). *The great psychologists: From Aristotle to Freud.* Philadelphia: J. B. Lippincott.

Wright, J. C., & Telford, R. (1996). Psychological problems following minor head injury: A prospective study. *British Journal of Clinical Psychology, 35,* 399-412.

Commentary

The Clinician Turned Philosopher

James M. Harper
Brigham Young University

Dr. Vande Kemp's own case study reminds every clinician to treat clients as we would desire to be treated. My experience is that too often the relationship between therapists and their clients becomes depersonalized in the name of science and objectivity. Although I do not believe that warmth, genuine caring, and science are incompatible, Dr. Vande Kemp's story reminds me that the people who come to my office are suffering, and if I do not respond to them with compassion, warmth, and empathy, my attempts to be a scientist-practitioner will matter little to them. And if their suffering does not affect me in some way, I will gradually lose touch with my own humanity and my own "aliveness" will diminish.

Lynn Hoffman (1992) described her personal experience with these ideas as follows:

> When unobserved, I would show a far more sympathetic side to clients than my training allowed. I would show my feelings, even weep. I call this practice "corny therapy" and never told my supervisors about it. But within the past few years I began to feel, "why not?" Others were making empathy credit-worthy again. (pp. 15-16)

Dr. Vande Kemp focused on many concepts that are clinically useful. First, the necessity of consulting and conferring with other professionals who may be treating the same client is extremely important but often neglected. Dr. Vande Kemp reminds us that approximately three dozen professionals were involved with her. She does not really tell us whether they effectively consulted and coordinated the overall treatment, but as I read between the lines I would guess not, at least not to the extent that it was helpful to her. It sounds as if each professional treated a part of her as a whole person, but what professional or what team of professionals, was responsible to her as a whole person? Likewise, do clinicians really see whole persons and their strengths, their resiliency, their endurance rather than simply assuming clients meet the characteristics of the diagnosis and labels we give them? To put this to the test, tell any therapist you want to refer a borderline client to him or her and watch the reaction. Do we get past what we know about borderlines to see a whole person, or does the word "borderline" constrain our vision?

Second, we must beware of the tempting pitfall of assuming that we understand a case on the basis of referral, diagnosis, and sketchy history taking or on the basis of our experience with other clients of similar diagnosis. In Dr. Vande Kemp's personal experience, some professionals reached conclusions without adequate history taking. When other professionals refer to me, they often ask if I want to know something about the people they are referring. In my opinion, it is good practice to meet clients first, hear their story, and then consult with the person who referred them. If it happens the other way around, I feel constrained by the information the other professional gives me.

Third, the question Dr. Vande Kemp raises about what data are essential and what guidelines should inform the collection process is a crucial one. To use a mental health test without carefully considering the purpose for and context in which it was developed often leads to a mismatch. In the name of science, we insist on adequate psychometric properties of validity and reliability, but no amount of validity or reliability can compensate for using a measure in a way it was not intended. In addition, relying solely on the results of a paper-and-pencil measure without corroborating the findings in our own experience of the client in session or in the reports of significant others in the client's life may lead to conclusions that do harm. Like physicians, we should seek first to do no harm.

Maturana (1988), a medical philosopher, made a distinction between two processes of listening for explanations. He called these "objectivity-without-parentheses" and "objectivity-in parentheses." Objectivity-without-parentheses is a stance in which the clinician assumes one objective reality to be valid independent of the clinician as an observer. Maturana and Varela (1992) describe the world everyone sees as a world that we bring forth with others. In postmodern language, the observer is also a participant and as such influences those being observed and the context in which the observation occurs (Gergen, 1985). Objectivity-in-parentheses is a stance in which clinicians assume they are participants in what is being observed and ask, What do I do to evoke the processes I am observing? And if I were to do something different, would the process I am observing be different, thus resulting in different conclusions? Is the client being resistant or have I as the clinician reached the limit of my flexibility and creativity?

Fourth, Dr. Vande Kemp's experience reminds us that being current in the literature is a challenge. Clinicians should not be all things to all clients. To do so is to fall victim to the Christ archetype that Dr. Vande Kemp warns us against. Virginia Satir (1987) said that at one point in her career she felt as if people saw her as a body with breasts everywhere that clients were demanding to suckle.

There is nothing wrong with telling clients you do not have adequate training to treat a particular problem and then referring them.

Fifth, therapy is an endeavor that always involves the clinician's personal issues. If being objective and scientific means keeping our own issues out of the therapy room, therapy will be an impossible task. Every case brings up personal issues in the life of the therapist, and the therapist's personal characteristics affect the therapy interaction. It is not the fact that personal issues arise that is the problem. The problem is when clinicians are unaware of the effect this has on their professional interaction. There is no excuse for clinicians' lack of awareness of how personal issues affect professional interactions. Yet too many training programs neglect the personal characteristics of therapists and give cursory attention to how the personal and family-of-origin issues of therapists enter every session. Instead, we focus on delivering empirically verified treatment protocols. But what about the "vessels" for the delivery of these treatments? Are they not an important component?

Last, Dr. Vande Kemp reminds us of the existence of multiple, simultaneous realities. She identified the impersonal, interpersonal, intrapersonal, and transpersonal realities. To be unaware of any one or more of these four realities is to constrain the experience of our clients. I am encouraged that the mental health field is finally beginning to give more credibility to the transpersonal reality, the spiritual life and experience of clients and therapists. In my experience, clients hope their therapists will be able to respect this part of their world and they are eager to explore it. It is therapists who have been uncomfortable with the spiritual reality of their clients. Dr. Vande Kemp did not address the multiple possibilities of reality for the 30 or so professionals she encountered. But clinicians have multiple realities as well.

Clinicians should be skeptical of any conclusion they hold too rigidly. Therapy is hypothesis testing, but when clinicians hold so rigidly to any given hypothesis that they have to force the experience of their client to fit the hypothesis, they will get stuck. In my opinion, the magic number of hypotheses is three. In supervision with trainees, I practice generating as many plausible hypotheses as possible, but we have to develop at least three.

In every therapy session, clinicians face the existence of multiple realities. Many lenses, multiple views, and inviting the expression of multiple voices is part of the therapist's world. Olson (1977) reviewed decades of research in which multiple family members were subjects and completed the same measurements. He concluded that family members' views were often different and rarely congruent with the therapist's views. Yet they were all useful and gave a more complete picture. Likewise, clients' realities, which Dr. Vande Kemp identifies, cannot be ranked in terms of which are more valid. They are separate realities, and clinicians who enter each of these realities will be more helpful to their clients.

Gregory Bateson (1972), an anthropologist who had much influence in early family therapy, explained objective reality in a dialogue with his daughter, Catherine:

Daughter: What does objective mean?

Father: Well. It means that you look very hard at those things which you choose to look at.

Daughter: But how do objective people choose which things they will be objective about?

Father: Well, they choose those things about which it is easy to be objective.

Daughter: You mean easy for them?

Father: Yes.

Daughter: But how do they know that those are the easy things?

Father: I suppose they try different things and find out by experience.

Daughter: So it's subjective choice?

Father: Oh yes. All experience is subjective. (p. 47)

I often ask clients or clinical supervisees what one or two important things stood out for them in a session. In this tradition, I summarize seven things that stood out for me in Dr. Vande Kemp's paper:

1. Always be in awe of your client's humanity and join with him or her as a warm human being.

2. Consult and confer, consult and confer!

3. Assume each client is unique and a different interpersonal journey for you as a therapist. Do not force your client into a mold because of diagnostic labels or because of your experience with previous clients. (This stance will also help to keep you from burning out.)

4. Do not assume your here-and-now reality as a clinician is your only reality and do not assume your explanations and conclusions are more valid or objective than your clients'.

5. You take your personal characteristics and issues into every therapy session. Seek to be continually aware of how these affect your professional interaction and be accountable for this.

6. Be aware of your clients' multiple voices and multiple realities and invite them to be expressed. If you are uncomfortable exploring any of their realities, realize they hope for your growth as their clinician so they can share their important experiences with you.

7. And perhaps most important, do not be distant, inhumane, or lacking in empathy under the guise of science and objectivity.

References

Bateson, G. (1972). *Steps to an ecology of mind.* New York: Ballantine.

Gergen, K. J. (1985). The social constructionist movement in modern psychology. *American Psychologist, 40,* 266-275.

Hoffman, L. (1992). A reflexive stance for family therapy. In S. McNamee & K. J. Gergen (Eds.), *Therapy as social construction* (pp. 7-24). Newbury Park, CA: Sage.

Maturana, H. R. (1988). Reality: The search for objectivity or the quest for a compelling argument. *Irish Journal of Psychology, 2*(1), 25-83.

Maturana, H. R., & Varela, F.G. (1992). *The tree of knowledge: The biological roots of human understanding.* Boston: Shambhala.

Olson, D. H. (1977). Insiders' and outsiders' views of relationships: Research studies. In G. Levinger & H. Rausch (Eds.), *Close relationships.* Amherst: University of Massachusetts Press.

Satir, V. (1987). [Videotape of workshop]. University of Utah, Salt Lake City.

Issue 9

Free Will/Determinism

Psychotherapy as Practical Teleology

Viewing the Person as Agent

Joseph F. Rychlak
Loyola University of Chicago

The Case of Melvin O.

In the mid-1950s, as I was beginning my career in clinical psychology, I had some success with a client I shall call Melvin.[1] Melvin was 28 years of age, and his presenting symptom was chronic anxiety that had dogged him for roughly 6 years previous to our contact. He had had therapy "on and off" during these years without achieving a cure. There were several minor ("free-floating") manifestations of this anxiety, but the major symptom involved a profound fear of—as well as the actual experience of—pseudo-heart attacks. During such attacks, his heart "pounded" rapidly and he broke into a sweat and suffered shortness of breath. Initially, he was rushed to the hospital a few times. His wife looked after him solicitously, driving him to his place of employment in the morning and picking him up in the late afternoon. Melvin was a television and radio repairman with an excellent reputation for doing good work. He was quite intelligent. People liked him. But his job was menial, working in the repair shop of an older man who treated him well but could not pay him very much. Melvin's wife found employment to help out financially, but always with an eye to meeting his daily schedule.

As I was an "insight-oriented" therapist, I spent the next 6 months (one session per week) reviewing Melvin's past life. Without going into detail, let me say that we traced his symptom onset to a time when he was studying to take an examination for a position with the federal government. Shortly before Melvin was to take this examination, his wife was called back to the Midwest to help her mother settle some family business. Melvin's mother-in-law was not ill, nor was the family business of pressing importance. Melvin, who had been dominated by his own mother, found his wife's departure during a time of pressure-filled challenge horrendous. He not only failed his examination but went on an extended drunk, which included, for the first time in his life, a sexual encounter with a prostitute. Not long afterward, he began developing increasingly debilitating anxiety symptoms.

Fortunately, Melvin's wife was understanding and even took some responsibility for what had transpired. The couple attended marital counseling for a time and, as I noted, Melvin was also seen individually. The marital problems were handled, but his anxiety symptoms never entirely left him. I was pleased to see that over the 6 months of our therapeutic contact Melvin's condition improved. He looked and acted more confident. He gained needed weight. His wife, whom I met with occasionally, said that he was taking on responsibilities that he used to avoid. From my perspective, and at the risk of sounding conceited, I had worked up a beautiful dynamic picture of his early life with a dominating mother; the marriage to a supportive woman who was also tied to her dominating mother; all coming together during a point of tension when anxiety was to be expected; followed by a collapse in self-confidence, guilt, and an overwhelming fear of what the future held. The case dynamic was neatly tied into a bundle of insight that I believed would complete the cure.

Unfortunately, the dramatic anxiety attacks were still occurring at the rate of about two per month (down from about seven or eight per month). I was stymied and beginning to sense some personal anxiety concerning my future as a therapist. What saved me was taking a chance with Melvin concerning how anxiety can be brought on through expectations that functioned as quasi-intentions. At the time, I was following Norman Cameron's (1947) "biosocial" approach to psychopathology. Cameron spoke of a "reaction sensitivity" in the development of symptoms, by which he meant an increasing expectation that the emotional state was going to occur, resulting in a snowballing effect to the point where what was feared actually took place (Cameron & Rychlak, 1985, p. 183). I stressed to Melvin that he was effectively intending to bring on his anxiety attacks in spite of himself. He had to become convinced that he was not going to die, so that there would no longer be an expectation of disaster simply because he felt a bit nervous from time to time.

One day Melvin came to our late afternoon session looking very tired. It seems that he had been required to help his boss on a special job, which kept him up most of the previous night. Based entirely on intuition—and a touch of desperation—I asked Melvin if he felt now the way he felt on days when an attack was likely to occur. He nodded his head, and I then proposed that we try to bring one on, an idea he was none too pleased with. I assured him that I would ordinarily not want to make him uncomfortable either. But I asked him if it would not be a good thing if he could intentionally bring on an attack with me present to help analyze how such things can happen willfully, just as I was contending? Would not this help convince him that he was actually in charge of what took place? He could see the logic here and agreed to "give it a try." I immediately pulled my chair up close to his—face to face—and began asking him questions aimed at drawing out any anxiety, such as how he was feeling in various bodily locations, and when tension or discomfort was mentioned in one area (e.g., tingling in the neck and shoulder area), I encouraged him to let this "grow" and merely "see" what would follow. When shortness of breath developed, I suggested that he observe how it had emerged from previous sensations, and so forth. It should be noted that this was in the mid-1950s and Stampflian or Wolpian techniques were not generally known or practiced. I surely had never heard of them.

After I helped Melvin to sense the mounting anxiety for several minutes, he manifested nervous discomfort and then came to a point where he suddenly shuddered, gasped, broke into perspiration, and slumped in his chair, letting out a groaning sound and aspirating air from his lungs. I was somewhat frightened when this happened because I had never witnessed this rapid outburst before. The thought occurred that he might *actually* suffer a heart attack. But he had been cleared by several physicians on this point over the years. So I encouraged Melvin to have another emotional release and then two more. In all, he had four such emotional crescendos—and never another one! The cure took me by surprise. Six weeks later he terminated therapy. About a year after that, he returned to tell me how well things had been going, but that now he was trying for a job with the federal agency once again and he had begun to feel a little "jumpy" about the upcoming examination. He had prepared well, but was afraid that his emotions would get hold of him again. I saw him for a few sessions, inviting his wife to join us on one occasion. With a little support and reassurance from both of us, he passed his exam without any return of symptoms. Several months later, he called to let me know he was doing very well, having increased his income enough to take a mortgage on a home, and also was planning to begin a family.

Teleology

How do we go about explaining why Melvin improved so dramatically? Was it because I somehow stumbled upon Stampfl's implosion therapy (Stampfl & Levis, 1967) and this is why a cure took place? Stampfl's principle of explanation is "experimental extinction," based on Mowrer's (1939) suggestion that a reduction in level of anxiety could serve as a positive reinforcement. This principle holds that the autonomic response of anxiety from which Melvin suffered would have to be extinguished before he could be further conditioned to problem-solve. So when I encouraged him to permit a reaction sensitivity to develop and no death took place—a positive reinforcement if there ever was one!—Melvin was then open to other more voluntary forms of conditioning enabling him to problem-solve.

Of course, this was not my guiding theory when I suggested to Melvin that we try to make him come up with an anxiety attack "at will." I looked at things from a teleological perspective. *Teleology* is the belief that people behave for the sake of intentions. There is a purpose in behavior, sometimes not entirely conscious, but it is "there" nevertheless (Rychlak, 1997, chap. 6). The more popular or familiar phrase for such behavior is "free will." Often the term "agency" is used to describe such purposive and freely willed behavior. People have free will if they can set the grounds (encompassing purposes) for the sake of which they believe or enact something. Another way of saying this is that people have free will if they could have behaved differently in some situation, all circumstances remaining the same. The suggestion here is that they control what happens rather than being controlled by the impersonal forces of their environmental situation. To have free will does not mean that we can do anything we like. We cannot leap over tall buildings at a single bound or buy anything that strikes our fancy regardless of price. Such physical or financial realities must be taken into consideration. But within these defining limits, there is always room for the person to do otherwise, all things remaining the same.

The tradition in psychology is to follow Newtonian science, which acted as a causal model for behaviorism in earlier years and can be seen in the computer modeling of today. Neither of these views accepts teleology, agency, or free will in human behavior. They are mechanistic accounts. Behaviors and beliefs are mechanically determined by a kind of billiard ball causation in which the direction taken is shaped by the past, formed into structures based on material substances, and then pushed along by forces that move the person efficiently, albeit blindly. The person cannot purposively select grounds for behavior, changing the order of things based on some personal intention. The teleologist views causation more broadly, as encompassing not only the billiard ball kind of cause but also the patterns of meaning that occur in life. People are thought to believe or behave "for the sake of" these meanings—which are the *reason* why they do what they do.

In the case of Melvin, this would suggest that—thanks to my interpretations—he had a background context of understanding that depicted how his anxiety arose in the first place, but he had not yet appreciated his actual responsibility in bringing the anxiety attacks about. Once he experienced the willful contribution he was making to his symptom picture, he realized that he did not have to participate in this self-defeating action. Nor did my interpretations have to be true, wholly or in part, for the final cure to take place. All that was necessary was a plausible context of meaning encouraging a willingness to look further into things in light of this frame of reference.

Teleological and Mechanistic Terminology

There is a running terminological hassle between the teleologists and mechanists of our profession. The difficulty stems from the fact that it is so easy to slip back and forth between these two models to explain any one case history—as my contrast of Stampfl and Cameron demonstrates. The mechanist suggests that the teleologist lacks parsimony, stacking 10 feet of intellectual fat above the "basic variables" that really and truly determined what took place. Melvin's cure was related not to intention but simply to the manipulation of anxiety responses, bringing them on in a situation where they could do no damage and hence were rapidly extinguished. The teleologist replies that without a context of meaning there would have been no such extinction. The mechanist retorts that meaning is not at issue. The teleologist insists that it is central. Each side then searches about to find case histories in support of their biases that are difficult for the other side to explain. The trouble is, this is easier said than done.

It may well be—and I am coming to believe that it is—impossible to resolve such questions in favor of one side or the other. For most of my formal education in psychology, I was browbeaten by the behaviorists to concede that reinforcement theories were proving without doubt that concepts like purpose, choice, and volition were quaint vestiges of medieval religiosity. I can recall only too well how Greenspoon's (1955) research claimed that people could be manipulated without their awareness. I was beginning my first teaching job at about this time, and his claims were heralded as the final death blow for all talk of free will or personal responsibility. Thanks to the subsequent work of people like Dulany (1962), DeNike (1964), Spielberger (Spielberger, Berger, & Howard, 1963), and Page (1972) it was established that only when the organism under conditioning is *aware* of the patterned connection between an operant response and its contingent reinforcer, or a conditioned and unconditioned stimulus—and is willing to *cooperate* with what is being suggested in the experimental design—does actual conditioning take place. Without awareness and a willingness to cooperate there is no conditioning to speak of (see Brewer, 1974). I have for over 40 years debated mechanistic colleagues, citing much research, and writing over 100 empirical articles in support of my Logical Learning Theory (Rychlak, 1994).

The aim here, of course, was to prove the mechanists wrong. I still believe that they are wrong in their characterization of human nature, but I am beginning to think that there is no real chance of settling this issue one way or the other through empirical research. There will always be two basic, contradictory views of human nature to consider on this matter of agency. I think that the context of debate has to shift in some way. If either side can put its own "construction" on what is taking place in research or therapy, or can "reconstruct" the terminology being used by its opponent, then a reasonable step to take would be to move from the theoretical to the practical. On one occasion, I challenged a mechanistic critic to name three or four experiments from the research literature that he claimed "accounted for" my teleological concepts (see Rychlak, 1995). I had little difficulty establishing that these efforts to subsume my teleological concepts mechanistically did not actually do so! I continue to offer this challenge to any critic who believes that current empirical research findings are any more successful at explaining teleology without distorting this concept beyond recognition (see my early exchange with Bandura on this very matter; Rychlak, 1979).

What Difference Does It Make?

We have arrived at the pragmatic question, "What difference does it make whether we consider people as agents or as machines?" I think there are at least three points to be made in this regard. My first point takes me back to Hawaii and the 1972 convention of the American Psychological Association. I participated in a symposium organized by Immergluck (1964), who had written a controversial paper titled "Determinism-Freedom in Contemporary Psychology: An Ancient Problem Revisited." Immergluck appreciated how important it was for human beings to believe in their personal agency. He said that even if we psychologists establish empirically that people are machines, "We will still persist to behave as if inner freedom were a fact, if not for those around us, then at least for ourselves" (p. 279). Immergluck held that even though it was illusory, our sense of free will is so central to what it means to be human that we cannot do without it.

I did not like the suggestion that free will is simply an illusion and argued vigorously against it. The findings on awareness and cooperation in conditioning were evidence enough for me. But at another level of analysis, there is some merit in Immergluck's argument. If we begin with a sense of what it means to be a human being, so much of life turns on the decisions, choices, and actions called willful intentions and purposes that to leave them out would be to lose, or at least greatly distort, the very thing that we are trying to understand. Concepts like commitment, humor, joy, vision, hope, sorrow, guilt, deception, regret, distrust, and so on make no sense if we are describing the actions of machines. Even if we "simulate" such human characteristics on a computing machine, this does not make them real. They are then mere imitations of human reality, lifeless copies mirrored by the machine program. After all, we can write programs that never manifest even a single one of these human characteristics. We put them as simulations into the machine because we need them to capture the nature of the organism that we are trying to help.

So my first point holds that whether we think of basic human behaviors as manifesting teleological characteristics through the use of mechanical illusions or as being the "real thing," we cannot do without them. I therefore argue that given two theories of equal capacity to explain some therapeutic outcome, we ought to select the one that genuinely frames the person in teleological terminology rather than the one that does a bad job by trying to stretch mechanistic description to cover these human manifestations. Why speak of illusions when we can speak of the real thing?

Moving to another point, it is common today to hear in therapeutic circles of clients as "victims" or "survivors," without appreciating the teleology involved. A victim is a person who has suffered some loss, usually as the result of the intentional actions of others. Breaking one's leg while skiing does not represent victimization, but being denied opportunities for self-improvement due to one's gender, race, or religious outlook is clearly victimization. In the former instance, a person simply twisted a leg in falling, but in the latter there are premeditations of others being pressed on the victim. If people were really machines, being moved about by blind natural forces, they could never be victimized, because any such manipulation would simply be another example of what always takes place. As machines, they have no capacity to "do otherwise," so they must continually follow the determinations of others.

Referring to clients as "survivors" is the same thing, albeit from a more positive perspective. A genuine survivor is capable of "doing otherwise" in various life situations, so that even in the face of some dramatic setback he or she is capable of dealing with the stress and strain. Such individuals do not "quit." They pick up the pieces and carry on. They strategize and plan for the future rather than getting bogged down in the present. To genuinely capture the psychology of survivors, we must rely on such telic descriptions. I think that if we honestly search our attitudes we will admit that we support and encourage all such indications of survivorship in our clients. If so, why not further this insight and begin talking more openly of people as telic organisms rather than as information-processing mechanisms?

The final point I want to make is the most important of all because it has many implications for the future of our societal culture as well as civilization in general. I refer to the concern being widely expressed today regarding the character of modern Americans, such as: Civil behavior is on the decline. People do not care about manners. Altruism is a thing of the past. Personal responsibility has lost its meaning. Selfishness is rampant. I have colleagues working as therapists who believe that, in the final analysis, this "sickness" of character deterioration is the most serious problem facing our nation today.

Well, if true, what do we do about it? Do we conclude that people are just being shaped badly today and the thing to do is to initiate a mechanical overhaul of some type? Or is a nonmechanical solution called for? In his widely discussed book, *Slouching Towards Gomorrah,* which examines the moral and spiritual decline of modern America, Judge Robert H. Bork (1996) suggests that "a religious revival" (p. 336) might help regenerate the character of this country. The closing phrase of the book conveys what Bork called the "optimism of the will" (p. 434) as a countermeasure resisting the society's seeming destination of reaching Gomorrah. Only through an intentional effort of this sort will our civilization survive.

Religion is, of course, a teleological enterprise if there ever was one. Even if we do not have "traditional" religions in mind, the very same notions of commitment and willful effort predominate. The effort is to improve one's selfhood (spirituality, etc.) and enrich interpersonal relations. People live with such aspirations, encouraged by clergy or, more informally, by various self-enhancement experts who draw immense crowds in search of personal enhancement. Surely we can see in the decision to seek out our counseling and therapy that many of our clients have the very same motivation—a deeply held prompting to behave for the sake of some framework that gives their lives meaning. One finds such promptings not in the mechanisms of the body, but rather in the conceptual formulations and intentions of the mind. This is a telic quest. Why not bring it to the fore more clearly in our work? Why not teach people that they are indeed teleological organisms and not robots?

If there is one realm of lived experience that thrusts responsibility on the individual, it is certainly the law. Machines are directed by laws, of course, but they are solely of the physical variety. As physical beings, we humans must also be determined by such "laws of nature." Thus the law of gravity determines what will happen when we miss a step in descending a staircase. But human beings have more arbitrary laws that determine their behavior in the sense of rules to follow. These laws are not stamped indelibly into physical reality. They can change as the ends for the sake of which they are adopted can change. The laws that we live by are of this stripe. There is considerable interest in the so-called rule of law today. Some say we place too much emphasis on the law and its minions, the lawyers. America has been called a litigious society. Whatever the case, so long as legal matters have relevance for the human image, I think we must examine them closely. What is most important in the present context is how the law views the individual human being—whether as a mechanical robot or a teleological agent.

Legal judgments are based on the assumption of human responsibility. The law assumes that the normal person can make choices among alternatives, evaluate the rightness or wrongness of an action, and direct her or his behavior accordingly. In other words, the law presumes that a person acts according to his or her free will. In 1937, Supreme Court Justice Benjamin Cardozo affirmed this presumption when he wrote in a decision for this court that the law is "guided by a robust common sense which assumes the freedom of will as a working hypothesis in the solution of its problem" (Fingarette, 1972, p. 79). The Supreme Court later reaffirmed this proposition by stating that a "belief in freedom of the human will and a consequent ability and duty of the normal individual to choose between good and evil" is a proposition "universal and persistent in mature systems of law" (LaFave, 1978, p. 333). Other courts have made the same point. The legal concept of responsibility flows from this decidedly telic assumption because it stipulates that "criminal responsibility is assessed when through 'free will' a man elects to do evil" (LaFave, 1978, p. 333). If the law, which is in effect the foundation on which our society is built, holds so firmly to the belief that human beings have the capacity for free will, how can we as responsible psychotherapists stand against this view—particularly since there is ample empirical evidence in support of it (see Rychlak, 1994)?

Conclusion

Putting everything together, I conclude that it is sensible and practical to frame our therapies in terms of a teleological image of the human being. This is frequently what we do informally. That is, we relate to our clients as if they were agents and rely on telic techniques such as active imagination or symptom scheduling, but when it comes to writing up the case history we slip into information-processing or engineering systems lingo. This needlessly distorts what really occurred and perpetuates an image of humanity that is incompatible with common sense, religious commitment, and legal responsibility. Clinical and counseling psychologists have been intimidated into using such quasi-mechanistic terminology (see Rychlak, 1998). It used to be stimulus-response and now it is input- output-theoretical formulations that are friendly to those in our profession who model engineers. Except for use in certain metaphorical allusions, such mechanistic theories have not proven very instructive to the average person.

We can revolutionize our profession if we have the confidence to throw off such inadequate—and often-enough ingenuine—formulations. Let us describe people as we find them—intentional beings behaving for a purpose. This is a simple, practical suggestion that can be quickly realized if we all willfully behave for the sake of gaining this end.

Note

1. In addition to changing my client's name, I have taken other measures to conceal his identity even though this is an old case history. But the core dynamics and therapeutic measures under description are accurate.

References

Bork, R. H. (1996). *Slouching towards Gomorrah: Modern liberalism and American decline.* New York: HarperCollins.

Brewer, W. F. (1974). There is no convincing evidence for operant or classical conditioning in adult humans. In W. B. Weimer & D. S. Palermo (Eds.), *Cognition and the symbolic processes.* Hillsdale, NJ: Lawrence Erlbaum.

Cameron, N. (1947). *The psychology of behavior disorders: A biosocial interpretation.* Boston: Houghton Mifflin.

Cameron, N., & Rychlak, J. F. (1985). *Personality development and psychopathology: A dynamic approach* (2nd ed.). Boston: Houghton Mifflin.

DeNike, L. D. (1964). The temporal relationship between awareness and performance in verbal conditioning. *Journal of Experimental Psychology, 65,* 521-529.

Dulany, D. E. (1962). The place of hypotheses and intentions: An analysis of verbal control in verbal conditioning. In C. W. Eriksen (Ed.), *Behavior and awareness: A symposium of research and interpretation.* Durham, NC: Duke University Press.

Fingarette, H. (1972). *The meaning of criminal insanity.* Berkeley: University of California Press.

Greenspoon, J. (1955). The reinforcing effect of two spoken sounds on the frequency of two responses. *American Journal of Psychology, 68,* 409-416.

Immergluck, L. (1964). Determinism-freedom in contemporary psychology: An ancient problem revisited. *American Psychologist, 19,* 270-281.

LaFave, W. R. (1978). *Modern criminal law: Cases, comments, and questions.* St. Paul, MN: West.

Mowrer, O. H. (1939). A stimulus-response analysis of anxiety and its role as a reinforcing agent. *Psychological Review, 46,* 553-566.

Page, M. N. (1972). Demand characteristics and the verbal operant conditioning experiment. *Journal of Personality and Social Psychology, 23,* 372-373.

Rychlak, J. F. (1979). A nontelic teleology? *American Psychologist, 34,* 435-438.

Rychlak, J. F. (1994). *Logical learning theory: A human teleology and its empirical support*. Lincoln: University of Nebraska Press.

Rychlak, J. F. (1995). A teleological critique of modern cognitivism. *Theory & Psychology, 5,* 511-531.

Rychlak, J. F. (1997). *In defense of human consciousness*. Washington, DC: American Psychological Association Press.

Rychlak, J. F. (1998). How Boulder biases have limited possible theoretical contributions of psychotherapy. *Clinical Psychology: Science and Practice, 5,* 233-241.

Spielberger, C. D., Berger, A., & Howard, K. (1963). Conditioning of verbal behavior as a function of awareness, need for social approval, and motivation to receive reinforcement. *Journal of Abnormal and Social Psychology, 67,* 241-246.

Stampfl, T. G., & Levis, D. J. (1967). Essentials of implosive therapy: A learning-theory based psychodynamic behavioral therapy. *Journal of Abnormal Psychology, 72,* 496-503.

Commentary

Human Agency in Psychotherapy: To Choose or Not to Choose . . . Is That the Question?

Diane L. Spangler
Brigham Young University

Rychlak describes reaching a plateau with a patient, Melvin, whose primary symptoms consist of panic attacks. Melvin had partially responded to treatment, but still experienced panic attacks twice a week. In an attempt to completely resolve the panic attacks, Rychlak formulated the idea that Melvin's expectation that anxiety was dangerous actually created the experience of high anxiety or panic. The antidote then was to change Melvin's expectation or beliefs about anxiety from life threatening to a more benign interpretation so that he no longer had an expectation of danger when feeling normal fluctuations in anxiety. To achieve this end, Rychlak asked Melvin to intentionally induce a panic attack so that Melvin could experience bringing on a panic attack willfully. Melvin did intentionally produce several panic attacks, which brought about the intended effect, and Melvin was essentially cured of his panic attacks.

Rychlak explains this effect by invoking a teleological perspective, or in essence explaining the effect in terms of free will, or agency—that is, that a person (in this case, Melvin) is a self-determining agent who has choices about what a given situation means and how she or he wants to respond to it. Rychlak discusses the importance of directly invoking and using patients' ability to choose in therapy. He then goes on to discuss how this teleologic view is antithetical to early behavioral theory and therapy and to more recent information-processing or cognitive theories and therapies.[1] Many modern cognitive-behavioral theorists and therapists disagree with Rychlak's characterization of cognitive-behavioral theories and therapies as deterministic (e.g., Bandura, 1989, 1998; see Barlow & Craske, 1994, for a cognitive-behavioral therapy for panic disorder that

205

emphasizes choice between alternative beliefs about anxiety) and contend that one of the primary objectives of cognitive-behavioral therapy is highlighting and encouraging clients' choice about thoughts, beliefs, and behaviors (e.g., Beck, Rush, Shaw, & Emery, 1979; Burns, 1980; Burns, Neilands, & Spangler, 1999).

As recently noted by Bargh and Chartrand (1999),

> contemporary psychology for the most part has moved away from doc-trinaire either-or positions concerning the locus of control of psychological phenomena to an acknowledgment that they are determined jointly by pro-cesses set in motion directly by one's environment and by processes insti-gated by acts of conscious choice and will. Thus the mainstream of psychol-ogy accepts both the fact of conscious or willed causation of mental and behavioral processes and the fact of automatic or environmentally triggered processes. The debate has shifted from the existence (or nonexistence) of these different causal forces to the circumstances under which one versus the other controls the mind. (p. 463)

What implications does a state-of-the-field that acknowledges both agentic and automatic processes have for psychotherapy?

What Do Humans (Patients) Have Agency Over?

The first glaring and very clinically relevant question is, what specifically do humans have agency over? If we, as clinicians, want to acknowledge and effect the agency of our patients as recommended by Rychlak, then we need to know what humans can authentically self-generate or choose, and the linkages be-tween such agentic acts and their effects. From Rychlak's chapter, it (ironically) appears that he, like cognitive-behaviorists, believes that people primarily have choice over their own meanings, intentions, and behaviors, but more limited control over environment or consequences. For example, he notes people are capable of "doing otherwise" and that "people have free will if they could have behaved differently." These statements imply choice over behaviors. With re-gard to personal meaning and purpose, he states that people possess "a deeply held prompting to behave for the sake of some framework that gives their lives meaning," that these are "conceptual formulations and intentions of the mind," and that "people have free will if they can set the grounds (encompassing pur-poses) for the sake of which they believe or enact anything." I assume from these statements that Rychlak believes that the conceptual formulations of the mind and purposes are self-generated and chosen. He also notes the limiting effects of environment and of capacity in his statement, "To have free will does not mean that we can do anything we like. . . . physical and financial realities must be taken into consideration." Beyond these statements, the scope of human agency, ac-cording to Rychlak, remains unclear. Are humans completely autonomous agents? That is, do humans (our patients) have deliberate choice over their every thought, every meaning, every purpose, and every behavior? Can the environment have a significant influence (and even determine) people's thoughts, purposes, or behaviors under some conditions?

Research clearly demonstrates that environment can have a marked influence on people's thoughts, behaviors, and goals under some conditions (e.g., Bargh, 1989, 1990; Bargh & Chartrand, 1999; Brewer, 1988; Carlston & Skowronski, 1994). Furthermore, many researchers have noted how impossible it would be to function effectively if we consciously and deliberately controlled every mental process dealing with every aspect of life, perception, environment, action, and so on (e.g., Bargh & Chartrand, 1999; Bateson, 1972; Baumeister, Bratslavsky, Muraven, & Tice, 1998; Posner & Synder, 1975). It would appear then that human agency exists on a continuum and is not an all-or-nothing process. For some processes and domains (i.e., deliberate processes), we may have much ability to choose. In contrast, for other processes and domains (i.e., automatic processes), we have limited ability to choose. Many more processes lie somewhere in the middle. Furthermore, some deliberate (or agentic) processes may set in motion automatic processes that serve agency. As clinicians, should our ultimate goal really be to insist on no automaticity of human mental function at all? If not, then how shall we aid our patients in deciding what is automatic and what is agentic? One area that remains to be addressed by Rychlak is a delineation of which of patients' acts, thoughts, "purposes," or "frameworks" are agentic and could or should be submitted to choice or change. In addition, whose perception that agency has occurred (the patient's or therapist's) will be used to decide whether or not an intention, belief, or act is agentic?

How Is Meaning Created in Humans (Patients)?

The answer to the question of how meaning is created hinges on the answer to yet another question, how is agency created and expressed? If meaning (the grounds for actions and agency according to Rychlak) can be chosen or personally constructed, then it would seem of paramount importance for clinicians to know how meaning is generated and crystallized. In other words, what are the mechanisms of human agency? Unfortunately, beyond stating that meaning and purpose exist and allow for agency, Rychlak offers little detail on the creation or parameters of meaning, purpose, or agency. But he does criticize theories and experiments that attempt to elucidate how meaning and "conceptual formulations" are created or expressed and refers to them as mechanistic, deterministic, robotic, and essentially devoid of human application or use. Can we conclude from this that Rychlak believes meaning and purpose have no mechanistic process involved in their making or expression? Then of what is meaning made and through what is meaning expressed? Furthermore, if meaning making or expression do have some physical mechanisms involved, does this assumption then require that the entire meaning process is deterministic? For example, to see or have vision requires that I have a properly functioning retina, optic nerve, visual cortex, and so on. But stating that these mechanistic structures underlie my ability to see is not the same as claiming that I have no choice whatsoever about at what I choose to look. Nor does it imply that the experience of vision is *only* composed of retina, optic nerves, and visual cortex. Additionally, knowing some of the structures and mechanisms contributing to vision allows for greater agency over what can be chosen; for example, I can choose to put on my glasses or choose to continue to have distorted vision. To apply this eye analogy to meaning asserts that arguing that meaning making and expression involve physical processes is not the same as asserting that humans have lost all ability to choose meaning, just as my retina does not dictate at what I choose to look. As similarly noted by Bandura (1998), "sensory, motor, and cerebral systems are tools people use to accomplish the tasks and goals that give meaning, direction, and satisfaction to their lives. . . . The human mind is generative, creative, and proactive, not just reactive" (p. 5). "The view that cognitive events are neural occurrences does not mean that psychological laws are derivable from neurophysiological ones" (Bandura, 1989, p. 1181).

How Can the Use of Agency Be Increased via Psychotherapy?

A final question particularly pertinent to clinical work is, how can the exercise of patient agency be increased by the therapist or therapeutic process? In Rychlak's case example of Melvin, simply pointing out to Melvin that he had a choice in how he viewed anxiety appeared to allow him to choose an alternative view. But Rychlak is not specific about the ways patient agency can be highlighted, exercised, and increased. Greater specification of how agency could be used therapeutically, how and when to bring about patient recognition of agency, how to bring about patient increases in use of agency, and a description of processes by which agency can be expressed could arguably be the most clinically useful additions Rychlak could make to his teleologic theory. In cognitive-behavioral therapy, primary emphasis on agency has come in the form of observing and identifying patients' existing meaning structures and behavioral patterns, deliberately demonstrating to the patient that she or he can choose alternative meanings and behaviors if desired, and offering a technology to aid in the realization of such alternative choices (e.g., Beck, 1995; Beck et al., 1979; Burns, 1980).

Are there additional ways to identify and encourage the use of patient agency? It is most likely (e.g., Bandura, 1989; Gollwitzer, 1999). One somewhat counterintuitive possibility may exist. Agency over some processes or domains may be increased by automatizing other processes. To return to the eye example, when I choose to open my eyes I invoke automatic processes of visual perception, encoding, and stimulus decoding. Because of these automatic processes, I have more agency to choose what I look at and how to decide the meaning of it. Could we not (and do we not) similarly employ automaticity in the service of our patients' mental health (see Bandura, 1989; Gollwitzer, 1999;

Kirsch & Lynn, 1999)? Would we not want Melvin's automatic response to normal fluctuations in anxiety to change from one where he anticipates death to one that is more benign? Although initially conscious choice may need to be invoked to change Melvin's automatic dysfunctional response to anxiety, should he need to deliberately process these possibilities every time he feels anxiety fluctuation in the future? Or would we rather he "get over" the catastrophic response and more automatically respond to anxiety as a normal part of life? As eloquently put by Whitehead (1911):

> It is a profoundly erroneous truism, repeated by all copy-books and by eminent people making speeches, that we should cultivate the habit of thinking of what we are doing. The precise opposite is the case. Civilization advances by extending the number of operations which we can perform without thinking about them. Operations of thought are like cavalry charges in a battle: they are strictly limited in number, they require fresh horses, and must only be made at decisive moments. (quoted in Bargh & Chartrand, 1999, p. 462)

Conclusion

Toward the end of his chapter, Rychlak asks, "Why not teach people that they are indeed teleological organisms and not robots?" My answer, as a cognitive-behavioral therapist is, we do! But that does not mean that some human mental processes are not essentially robotic. Humans are not either teleological or robotic but are both teleologic and robotic and more. Indeed, it is reasonable to argue that some human "robotic" tendencies allow for the capacity for humans to be teleologic. Of course, it is important to explore meaning systems, goals, and behavioral responses with our patients and highlight the choices they have in these domains. Psychotherapy of all types could potentially be greatly improved if there were far more elucidation of how agency is created, accessed, exercised, and increased, however. In sum, the major question lying before us now is no longer whether or not human agency exists but when, where, and how to tap into it and use it for the benefit of all.

Note

1. In his chapter, Rychlak draws exclusively from behavioral theorists from 1970 (i.e., 30 years ago) and earlier.

References

Bandura, A. (1989). Human agency in social cognitive theory. *American Psychologist, 44,* 1175-1184.
Bandura, A. (1998). Exercise of agency in personal and social change. In E. Sanavio (Ed.), *Behavior and cognitive therapy today* (pp. 1-29). Oxford, UK: Pergamon.

Bargh, J. A. (1989). Conditional automaticity: Varieties of automatic influence in social perception and cognition. In J. S. Uleman & J. A. Bargh (Eds.), *Unintended thought* (pp. 3-51). New York: Guilford.

Bargh, J. A. (1990). Auto-motives: Preconscious determinants of social interaction. In E. T. Higgins & R. M. Sorrentino (Eds.), *Handbook of motivation and cognition* (Vol. 2, pp. 93-130). New York: Guilford.

Bargh, J. A., & Chartrand, T. L. (1999). The unbearable automaticity of being. *American Psychologist, 54,* 462-479.

Barlow, D. H., & Craske, M. G. (1994). *Mastery of your anxiety and panic: Part 2.* Albany, NY: Graywind.

Bateson, G. (1972). *Steps to an ecology of mind.* New York: Ballantine.

Baumeister, R. F., Bratslavsky, E., Muraven, M., & Tice, D. M. (1998). Ego depletion: Is the active self a limited resource? *Journal of Personality and Social Psychology, 74,* 1252-1265.

Beck, A. T., Rush, A. J., Shaw, B. F., & Emery, G. (1979). *Cognitive therapy of depression.* New York: Guilford.

Beck, J. S. (1995). *Cognitive therapy: Basics and beyond.* New York: Guilford.

Brewer, M. B. (1988). A dual process model of impression formation. In T. K. Srull & R. S. Wyer (Eds.), *Advances in social cognition* (Vol. 1, pp. 1-36). Hillsdale, NJ: Lawrence Erlbaum.

Burns, D. D. (1980). *Feeling good: The new mood therapy.* New York: Signet.

Burns, D. D., Neilands, T., & Spangler, D. L. (1999). *Do negative thoughts cause negative emotions? A microanalytic study using structural equation modeling.* Manuscript submitted for publication.

Carlston, D. E., & Skowronski, J. J. (1994). Savings in the relearning of trait information as evidence for spontaneous inference generation. *Journal of Personality and Social Psychology, 66,* 840-856.

Gollwitzer, P. M. (1999). Implementation intentions: Strong effects of simple plans. *American Psychologist, 54,* 493-503.

Kirsch, I., & Lynn, S. J. (1999). Automaticity in clinical psychology. *American Psychologist, 54,* 504-515.

Posner, M. I., & Synder, C. R. R. (1975). Attention and cognitive control. In R. L. Solso (Ed.), *Information processing and cognition: The Loyola symposium* (pp. 55-85). Hillsdale, NJ: Lawrence Erlbaum.

Whitehead, A. N. (1911). *An introduction to mathematics.* New York: Holt.

Issue 10

Eclecticism

Eclecticism in Psychotherapy

Is It Really the Best Substitute for Traditional Theories?

Brent D. Slife
Jeffrey S. Reber
Brigham Young University

Eclecticism has become the dominant orientation in psychotherapy (Bergin & Garfield, 1994; Poznanski & McLennan, 1995). Indeed, more than two thirds of all clinicians and counselors now identify themselves with this orientation (Jensen, Bergin, & Greaves, 1990; Norcross, Prochaska, & Farber, 1993). Although eclecticism may mean different things to different therapists (Arkowitz, 1989, 1992; Arnkoff, 1995; Norcross & Newman, 1992), all eclectic therapists share a common problem and a common solution.

First, eclectics have a common problem with traditional single-theory approaches. They believe that no single theory can be comprehensive and open enough to deal effectively with the diversity of problems that clients present (Goldfried, 1980; Lazarus, Beutler, & Norcross, 1992; Norcross, 1986; Prochaska & DiClemente, 1986). Second, eclectics share a common solution to the problem: "selecting what appears to be best from a variety of methods, approaches, or styles" (Lazarus et al., 1992, p. 11). That is, eclectics borrow from a wide variety of therapeutic techniques and theories and combine them together in a given therapy so as to best tailor their treatment to the specific needs of the client (Lazarus, 1995; Thorne, 1973).

As an illustration of this problem and its solution, consider the following vignette:

> John, a psychoanalyst from the East Coast, recently accepted a position with a therapy group in a small West Coast city. Having enjoyed considerable success at his previous position, John approached his new job with anticipation and confidence. As the only psychoanalyst on staff, John was not surprised to find himself discussing and often defending his orientation in meetings. Sometimes, however, he was genuinely puzzled by his colleagues' comments. It was one thing, they seemed to say, to use psychoanalysis frequently, but quite another to use it exclusively.
>
> At first, John figured that his colleagues were trying to convince him to adopt another orientation. But as time went on, he soon realized that they weren't advocating another orientation, nor were they disputing psychoanalysis per se. They were questioning his exclusive use of one approach: Wasn't he open-minded after all? How could his perceptions of clients be trusted when he was so obviously biased by one theory? And what about theory in general? Wouldn't reliance on any set of abstractions take away from knowing the clients themselves? John seemed like such a nice guy. Why was he so intent on being rigid and inflexible and divorced from the reality of client care?
>
> Initially, John tried to ignore his colleagues' questions and comments, but he found this difficult for several reasons. First, he had to give his colleagues credit: Sometimes his clients didn't respond well to his treatment. John was particularly struck by a "profound experience" with a recent client, Anne, who abruptly threatened to terminate therapy with him. (We will describe her case later.) Could his reliance on a single theory be the problem? Was he closing himself off to other creative and possibly effective options?
>
> John's economic condition was a second reason he couldn't ignore his colleagues. Without his colleagues' respect and without their perception that he was unbiased and open to all effective treatments, John knew he would receive fewer referrals. Without respect and referrals, he might as well hang it up. To his surprise, John found himself putting down psychoanalysis in colleague conversations and playing up other modes of therapy. John also experimented with different approaches and through various workshops learned other techniques. Although John didn't admit this to his colleagues, he knew in his heart that he had become an eclectic.

Problems and Eclectic Solutions

John, like many therapists, came face to face with the primary dissatisfaction of eclectic psychotherapists: *Single theories are biased and bias is bad* (Slife, 1987). That is, single theoretical orientations are supposedly too narrow and too close-minded to accommodate the multiplicity of problems that clients present (Beutler & Clarkin, 1990; Lazarus & Beutler, 1993). They have only a limited set of categories and techniques available for diagnosis and treatment, and they constrain the therapist to an idiosyncratic perspective on human nature (Held, 1995). In

John's case, he was supposedly locked into an analysis of sexual tensions and unconscious repressions. But all single-theory approaches are viewed with the same suspicion. Behaviorists attend to a client's behaviors, whereas humanists are predisposed toward innate potentials, cognitivists are inclined toward cognitions, and systems therapists emphasize feedback mechanisms.

Given the idiosyncratic biases of any particular theory of therapy, the obvious questions are: How can therapy be more comprehensive? and, How can therapists be more open- rather than close-minded? The response of the eclectic literature is essentially twofold: theoretical integration and technical eclecticism.1 Theoretical integration has focused on the problem of comprehensiveness, whereas technical eclecticism has emphasized the problem of open-mindedness. Ultimately, both solutions are intended to provide the same practical end: that therapists have all the theories, categories, and techniques they need to address the varied problems their clients present.

The first solution, *theoretical integration,* is designed to increase comprehensiveness by combining theories and thereby multiplying the number of categories and techniques available to address clients' needs (Held, 1995; Prochaska & DiClemente, 1986; Wachtel, 1977, 1987). John, for example, tried integrating psychoanalysis with behaviorist theories in his move toward eclecticism, so that he could address not only issues of unconscious motivation but also problems of maladaptive behavior. His aim was to expand *one* set of limited categories and techniques into *two.* In this sense, theoretical integration seems to resolve the narrowness problem by combining theories into a more comprehensive whole.

The second solution, *technical eclecticism,* was created to avoid theoretical bias altogether (Held, 1995; Lazarus, 1995; Lazarus & Messer, 1991). Technical eclectics advocate the use of scientific method to discern the most effective techniques of therapy (Beutler & Clarkin, 1990; Held, 1995; Lazarus, 1995). Although these techniques may be originally rooted in single theories, technical eclectics assume they can be cut from these roots and assembled into multiple technique formats (see Slife, Reber, & Gantt, 2000). Because science is considered to be objective and theory-free, there is no danger that technical eclectics can be viewed as imposing their own favored biases on their clients. Indeed, the very purpose of the scientific method, from this perspective, is to suspend biases while providing clear access to the reality of psychological treatment (see Slife & Williams, 1995). By moving away from a theoretically based, biased therapy to a scientifically based, bias-free therapy, technical eclectics appear to have solved the problem of single-theory close-mindedness.

Ultimately, all eclectics—whether they integrate or avoid theories—value the same practical goals. Like medical practitioners, eclectics want access to all that is available for dealing with client problems and disorders. They want to be able to update their treatments with the latest and most effective techniques. They want to be flexible, discarding whole theories if necessary to help a client in need. Finally, eclectics want a genuine sensitivity to clients and their contexts, rather than the theoretical rigidity that leads therapists to ignore the person and focus on single-theory abstractions.

Why the Eclectic Solution Fails

Despite its noble intentions, we hold that the eclectic project ultimately fails (Slife et al., 2000). And despite its twofold approach to the problem, both approaches fail for essentially the same reason: Both approaches ultimately rely on precisely what they attempt to avoid—a single set of assumptions and thus a single theory. In the case of theoretical integration, multiple integrative theories are reduced to a single metatheory that guides the integration of theories or the use of techniques (Slife, 1987). That is, theories are not integrated arbitrarily or haphazardly; they are combined on the basis of some criteria of integration. A true integration, then, requires a metatheory that specifies when and why each set of techniques is used. This metatheory, just like the theories it integrates, is based on a single set of assumptions that not only brings coherence and organization to the therapeutic situation but also restricts its domain of application and inquiry.

If eclectic therapists operated *without* a metatheory, then they would be viewed as "unsystematic eclectics" (Lazarus & Beutler, 1993, p. 381; Norcross, 1986). In one sense, this approach would seem the ideal of eclectic flexibility and openness to clients' needs. But therapists have generally spurned haphazard, random, or nonpurposeful approaches to client treatment, considering them to be unethical and potentially dangerous. Objections to unsystematic eclecticism are well documented, even in the eclectic literature (Howard, Nance, & Meyers, 1986; Jensen et al., 1990; Lazarus & Beutler, 1993; Lazarus et al., 1992). The primary objection concerns its lack of coherence. As Jensen et al. (1990) put it, unsystematic eclecticism "is often equated with lazy, sloppy, or unorganized practices" (p. 124).

The only way to organize and bring coherence to practice is through some formal or informal theory or metatheory. Integrationist eclectics may have moved their theories—their integration of theories—to another level, the "meta" level, but there is considerable debate about whether these metatheoretical integrations are really any different from their theoretical cousins. After all, Freud, Rogers, and Skinner would all have claimed to be integrating components of various theoretical structures, yet we typically do not view their theories as eclectic integrations. This is because these traditional integrations were all brought under one set of assumptions, providing them coherence perhaps, but also restricting their domain and applicability. We currently see no evidence that the metatheoretical integrations of today are any different from the single-theoretical integrations of yesterday, at least regarding their biased and restrictive natures.

The restrictiveness of integrative eclecticism is the main reason most eclectics have recently flocked to the technical eclectic camp (see Lazarus, 1995; Lazarus & Beutler, 1993; Norcross, 1986). Their hope is that technical eclecticism will be the one "proven" way of avoiding bias, and thus single sets of assumptions, altogether. Unfortunately, as we demonstrated in a recent article (Slife et al., 2000), this hope will never be realized, though most eclectics have not recognized this yet. Their hope depends on science being an atheoretical system that guides therapists' selections of techniques without contributing its own theoretical baggage. However, as many philosophers of science have made quite clear this philosophy of science—indeed any philosophy of science—is itself based on a limited set of assumptions that invariably biases its practitioners (Bernstein, 1983; cf. Curd & Cover, 1998; Gholson & Barker, 1985; Kuhn, 1970).

In the case of traditional scientific method, practitioners are biased toward what is observable, rational, and replicable, because the scientific method is itself based on assumptions of empiricism, rationalism, and positivism (Slife & Williams, 1995). These assumptions constitute the metatheory of science and the selection criteria of technical eclecticism. It is thus not coincidental that techniques that are *not* based on these assumptions, such as those practiced in existential therapy, are rarely "validated" in technical eclecticism (Slife et al., 2000). Indeed, most existential therapies eschew technique altogether (e.g., Yalom, 1980). Consequently, most technical eclectic approaches are a combination of behavioral and social learning conceptions (e.g., Lazarus, 1995), both of which are based essentially on the same assumptions as that of positivism (see Slife & Williams, 1995).

The upshot of this theoretical exclusivity is that certain aspects of clients— those unobservable, irrational, and unreplicable aspects—are excluded from the technical eclectics' purview, as are those techniques and therapy orientations that do not fit with these assumptions of science. How, for instance, does a technical eclectic use an existential orientation that is antitechnique and thus not technical in the first place? In this sense, a positivist view of science constitutes a single metatheory of human behavior, with a unified set of assumptions that narrows the availability of theories and techniques and closes the therapist off to "nonscientific" interpretations of presenting problems. Ultimately, technical eclectics, like integrationist eclectics before them, fail to escape a single theory.

At this point, we must conclude that a single set of assumptions—a single theory—is inevitable. The thoroughness and tenaciousness of the eclectic project can give us confidence in this conclusion. This project has clearly attempted to avoid single sets of assumptions, but it is equally clear that these thorough and tenacious efforts have utterly failed. All therapists have an orientation, whether conscious or unconscious, formal or informal. All therapists are oriented toward their clients in particular ways and must assume certain things to act therapeutically.

In John's case, he was oriented by and biased toward the assumptions of psychoanalysis, and he knew it. At the same time, his eclectic-minded critics were no less biased, though they may have thought otherwise. They, too, operated with a particular set of assumptions that biased them. Whether they advocated some integration of single theories or some form of technical eclecticism, they failed to escape the very criticisms they leveled against John. In a sense, John was in a better position than his peers, because he at least recognized that he had an orientation, which he could (and did) evaluate. His colleagues, on the other hand, could not see any problems with their orientations, because they presumed they had none. Their attitude toward John, then, came not from the superiority of their own orientations, but from their ignorance of them *as* orientations.

The eclectic project fails, then, because it cannot overcome the original dissatisfactions of those who first proposed eclecticism. Because biases and single theories cannot be escaped, no "orientation," whether integrational or scientific, can be completely open or comprehensive. Indeed, all the classical single theorists could be said to have been originally eclectic in this sense. And they, like today's eclectics, are ultimately relegated to a single, related set of assumptions for the sake of coherency. Otherwise, practice occurs randomly and thus, as the eclectics themselves admit, irresponsibly and unethically (e.g., Lazarus & Beutler, 1993; Lazarus et al., 1992). How, then, can the original dissatisfaction of therapists with traditional theories be addressed? Over two thirds of all psychotherapists have rejected traditional single theories and searched for something better. Why? With eclecticism revealed to be a species of the same problem, is there some other way of addressing the dissatisfaction of so many therapists?

Reconstruing the Problem

We believe there is. But it requires a different analysis of therapy theory than psychologists have rendered thus far—an analysis that focuses on the *quality* rather than the *quantity* of these theories. The eclectic project focuses exclusively on the latter, attempting to facilitate greater openness and comprehensiveness through the greater quantity of theories or techniques. The assumption is that there are not enough theoretical categories or techniques available in a single theory, so why not make more of them available? Integrationist eclecticism focused on increasing the quantity of theories, whereas technical eclecticism emphasized increasing the quantity of effective techniques. The problem with this quantitative solution, as we have seen, is that all concepts and techniques must eventually be related together in some coherent way, making a limited and limiting set of assumptions necessary, similar to any theory.

What if, however, the dissatisfaction of therapists with traditional theories was never a *quantity* issue? What if all traditional theories have an overlooked *quality* that is problematic for most therapists? If this were true, then a wholly different solution would be implied, with a wholly different set of implications for therapy. We believe that this is the case, as we will attempt to show in the remainder of this chapter. In fact, all traditional theories of psychology, as diverse as they obviously are, have one relatively overlooked theoretical quality in common—they are all *atemporal*. That is, these theories were formulated to be *a*temporal, or "timeless" (transcendent and universal), and "not temporary," (i.e., not changeable; permanent). Indeed, it is this assumption of atemporality, we contend, that therapists are ultimately dissatisfied with, because atemporal theories cannot, in principle, be tailored to meet the unique needs of individual clients or facilitate open-mindedness in therapists.

Atemporality actually has a long history of wide popularity (see Faulconer & Williams, 1990). Philosophers such as Leucippus and Democritus, Plato and Pythagoras endeavored to create a philosophy that accounted for the world in terms of some set of fundamental, universal, and unchanging principles or laws. To be fundamental and unchanging, however, these principles or laws could not be experiential or physical, because experiential and physical things are constantly in flux. Lived experience—the world as we perceive it—is widely acknowledged to be changeable, but physical things, too, eventually change and deteriorate, though perhaps at a slower rate than experiential change.

The point for Plato and a long line of Western thinkers after him was that the immutability of fundamental truths had to be *outside* our physical and experiential world, and thus *in* a metaphysical (or "beyond physical") realm. This realm was envisioned as a changeless, transcendent realm, allowing for changeless eternal truths to transcend physical location and be available at any time or place. Natural laws and mathematical principles are prominent examples of such metaphysical entities. Although they may affect, indeed govern, the physical and the experiential, they are neither. The law of gravity, for instance, has never been experienced by the senses, nor does it consist of physical entities that one can observe. Certainly, *manifestations* of this law are physical and experiential (e.g., we seem stuck to the earth), but the *law itself*, the law that supposedly governs these manifestations, is not made of a substance and is never experienced through our five senses.

Consequently, all good theorists—whether from the natural or the social sciences—have presumed that these same atemporal, and thus metaphysical, characteristics are necessary for their theoretical conceptions. They all presume that a valid theory is unchangeable and permanent (or not temporary), as well as transcendent and universal (or timeless). Often ignored or overlooked is the fact that these theoretical conceptions can only exist in a metaphysical realm, because the experiential and physical realms could never, in principle, accommodate such theoretical entities without changing them or causing their deterioration. This is the reason that such theories are often referred to as abstractions: They must, of necessity, exist outside the real and practical world.

We submit that all the traditional theories of therapy have participated in this same atemporal tradition. That is, when Freud, Skinner, and Rogers formulated their theories, they just assumed without awareness that the principles of good theories were immutable, transcendent, and universal. Even a cursory examination of each reveals this to be true. Freud's theorizing, for example, is easily cast in this metaphysical light, with the unchanging, contextless, and nonphysical entities of id, ego, and superego. Similar to the abstractions of other theories, these entities can change in their *content*, but must remain immutable and universal in their basic *process*. Hence their process is always outside of any one practical context, because practical contexts shift and change. This, of course, is our traditional notion of the theory-practice separation, with practice being physical and contextual (concrete) and theory being metaphysical and contextless (abstract).

Humanists, too, have postulated atemporal conceptions, such as Maslow's hierarchy of needs and Rogers's organismic valuing principle, that are supposedly universal and transcendent in nature. Even the behaviorists, who have attempted to eschew all metaphysical entities, have succumbed to unobservable and immutable "behavioral principles" or the nonsensory entity of reinforcement history. That is, reinforcement history is never observed in conjunction with the behavior it is supposed to cause; it is always an assumed influence. Similarly, systems theorists, despite their emphasis on context, assume that contextless feedback mechanisms universally and immutably govern the behavior of all systems. Suffice it to say that a great proportion of mainstream psychologists have adopted, perhaps unknowingly, the atemporal approach to grounding and founding their theories and their research.

Could this hidden assumption—this conventional understanding of theory and practice—be the root of the dissatisfaction of so many therapists with so many traditional theories? Consider, first, that the very nature of atemporal theories is their contextlessness. That is, because they are universal entities that exist outside of particular concrete contexts, either experiential or physical, they are always general and abstract by nature. To be sure, they are thought to be tailorable to particular clients. Indeed, their nature is abstract and general, according to an atemporal perspective, so they *can* be tailored to any context. This requirement, however, implies that the theories themselves are never tailored. To be tailored, they must be *applied*. That is, they must have a whole other set of actions and translators, called applications, set in motion. This means that atemporal theories are only useful when one has the skill of application, and even then the application is never spelled out in the theory itself, because the theory is always and forever a universal abstraction outside any particular context.

Needless to say, this can be a frustrating arrangement, especially for the people who are most concerned with applying these theories in psychology, the therapists. Therapists must first learn a set of abstractions (e.g., id, reinforcement history, schema, feedback loop) that they have not and can never have any lived experience with. Then, these abstractions can never experience the particularities of what they are meant to illuminate—the therapeutic situation—because they must be universal and transcendent of particular situations by their very nature. Finally, these people must next learn a completely different set of skills—application skills—having little, if anything, to do with the intellectual skills they attained in learning the theories in the first place.

This frustrating arrangement might be tolerated if the theories themselves functioned as advertised, with changeless, timeless, and universal conceptions, applicable to everyone in every situation. But therapists have increasingly discovered the awful truth: The particularities of their therapeutic experiences reveal that these theories are *not* and can *never* be universal and timeless, as advertised. Because these theories were formulated by particular individuals in particular circumstances for particular client problems, their range of domain is too narrow. Indeed, if the abstractions of these theories are truly followed as they are supposed to be, they draw a therapist's attention away from the experiential and toward the metaphysical, emphasizing the abstract over the concrete. The truth of the client, after all, must be a changeless, metaphysical abstraction that is behind our changeable experience of the client. Moreover, because therapists would regard metaphysical abstractions as primary, they would tend to make the concrete particulars fit the universal abstractions, rather than the reverse, and the close-mindedness that the eclectics so rightly fear would be brought to fruition.

Reconstruing the Solution

Temporality, on the other hand, is an alternative theoretical *quality* that provides another approach to addressing the dissatisfaction of eclectics. It does not combine or suspend theories, but instead reformulates single theories in a way that allows them to be sensitive to context and change. Whereas *a*temporality demands a focus on transcendental universals and contextless abstractions, which ultimately result in narrowness and close-mindedness, temporality requires a focus on the particular context and the singularity of the client's situation, which makes possible the comprehensiveness and open-mindedness that eclectics desire.

There are elements of temporality throughout Western history, though they are perhaps less obvious than those of atemporality. The early Greek philosopher Heraclitus, for example, took issue with the permanency and abstractness of atemporal conceptions, claiming that the world is always changing and that there is no transcendental world of reality underlying or governing it. As he put it, "One never steps in the same river twice" (Leahey, 1992, p. 48). That is, the river is representative of a reality that is constantly in flux. To understand the "river," one not only attends to the similarities of the river at each "step" but also focuses on the differences or uniqueness of each event.

Franz Brentano in the late 19th century also expressed difficulty with the unchanging universals of atemporality. His focus was the changeability of our lived experience, because all things are known through this experience. Indeed, how do we know there is an unchangeable objective realm (atemporality) when no one—including scientists—has access to any realm outside his or her experience? Brentano contended that our experiences change constantly, depending on their historical context and present situation. Whether water feels cool or warm to the touch depends on whether our hand was previously immersed in cool or warm water. The context of the past is crucial to the sensations we feel, proving that "neither warmth nor cold really exists in the water" as an atemporal entity (Brentano, 1874/1973, p. 9). Warmth and cold exist in our contextual experience and thus change as the context of our experience changes.

More recently, 20th-century hermeneuticists and existentialists—such as Heidegger, Gadamer, Taylor, and Merleau-Ponty—have emphasized the uniquely embodied person in a world of contextual possibilities. Similar to the view of Heraclitus, persons are constantly in flux. There is a sense in which, like the river, the person can be the same (e.g., have an identity), but there is also a focus on the uniquenesses or differences of the person across time. Similar to Brentano's thinking, however, these changes are inextricably tied to particular contexts that precede, occur with, and follow the changes. In this sense, temporality locates true knowledge *in* a particular experiential context, unlike atemporality, which locates true knowledge in some metaphysical realm *outside* particular experiential contexts.

This change of "location" is important, because it implies that temporal knowledge is never knowledge of the abstract and theoretical (at least in the conventional sense); it is knowledge of the concrete and practical—which changes as concrete situations change. Temporal knowledge is never metaphysical; it is always part of and at least derivable from the lived experiential and physical world. This means that temporal knowledge never requires application or application skills, because it is always situation specific. It does not need to be brought "down" from the metaphysical world of abstraction and then translated into the experiential and physical world; it is already part of that physical world. In this sense, the particular is never forced to fit the abstraction, because there is no abstraction in which it must fit.

Temporal conceptions also differ from atemporal conceptions in their pretentiousness. Atemporal theorists assume the ultimate completeness and correctness of their explanations and theories, because they presume them to be universal across all people, situations, and times. Temporal theories, by contrast, are inherently humble. Temporal theorists can never assert completeness or permanence, because temporality assumes that the qualities of a thing originate, at least in part, from its relationship with other parts of its context. A kiss could be a greeting, an indication of future intentions, or a death sentence—all depending on the context. In other words, a change in context could mean a fundamental change in the thing itself, because the very qualities of a thing stem, to some degree, from its context.

This changeability has been one of the main stumbling blocks to the wider acceptance of temporality. Truth and knowledge have been so associated with atemporal stability, permanence, and completeness that temporal conceptions have been discounted and degraded. Nevertheless, this property of changeableness allows for flexibility, possibility, options, and alternatives. From an atemporal perspective, universal theoretical principles are the determinants of all aspects of the physical and metaphysical worlds. Because these principles cannot change and because they ultimately govern the physical and experiential, no possibility of change is possible. Temporal conceptions, by contrast, are filled with possibility; change and choice are always possible.

We should note, however, that change is not *necessary* with temporal conceptions. Temporal theorists distinguish between the unchange*able* and the - unchang*ing*. From a temporal perspective, concepts and things are *able* to change, unlike atemporal conceptions, but this ability to change—this possibility— never requires that they *have* to change. Consider a promise, for instance. A person can make a promise to another person and remain constant and unchanging in the fulfillment of his or her promise. From a temporal perspective, however, such a promise is only meaningful if the promiser does not *have* to keep the promise—if keeping the promise is truly a possibility rather than a necessity. That is, the person can be unchanging in keeping the promise, but not unchangeable in *having* to keep it. In this manner, many things may not change, including patterns of behavior among clients. Still, this unchang*ing* state does not have to mean that these patterns are unchange*able* and thus determined by unchanging theoretical principles.

Similarly, temporal theorists and philosophers have made the distinction between temporal and atemporal generalities. For the atemporal theorist, of course, generalities are inherently metaphysical and transcendent entities; they are never part of changeable physical or experiential contexts and so their universality and immutability is never threatened. Temporal generalities, by contrast, are always inherent in particular contexts, so their universality is always threatened by the next particular (in time or space). For example, a general conception of a client (e.g., a diagnostic label) may have been informative in the past, but this generality may be irrelevant to the next particular context. This is the reason temporal theorists must hold humble generalizations; they could be completely wrong in the next instant. Still, this humility does not mean that temporal generalities are not relevant to several different contexts. Indeed, some general conceptions *could* be relevant to all contexts—that is, be universal. But no mortal could ever know this with certainty because ever-new contexts await. Consequently, one must always be humble and open to the possible irrelevancy of a general conception in the next context.

Temporality, then, is an alternative quality of theories that allows for the comprehensiveness and open-mindedness that is so important to eclectics. Because temporality demands a focus on the experiential rather than the metaphysical, temporal theories are comprehensively sensitive to all clients and all contexts. Also, because temporal theories do not propose any changeless abstractions, they are inherently open, recognizing their potential invalidity in the service of the particular context.

Practical Implications

With some of the characteristics of temporality now described, we can begin to outline how replacing atemporality with temporality would affect therapy. We must offer one admonition at the outset, however: Many therapists, eclectic or otherwise, have already sensed the problematic nature of atemporality and have already moved, perhaps unknowingly, to a mode resembling temporality. In such cases, our endeavor here will be to catch theory up to practice. That is, we should not have to practice *in spite of* our atemporal theories. Our theories should facilitate our practice, yet this has rarely been the case with traditional theories. The abstractness of traditional theories has required "applications" to bridge the theory-practice gap. At the very least, then, our reconstruing of the problem of eclecticism should help us to bridge this gap.[2] But temporal theorizing may also effect a new therapeutic mind-set—for some therapists, at least—if not a new way of practicing altogether.

To explore a temporal versus an atemporal approach to therapy, let us return to John. Recall that John was particularly jolted from his usual orientation through his therapy work with Anne. John had assumed that this "jolt" meant that he ought to move toward some sort of eclecticism. For most therapists, eclecticism has seemed the only alternative to traditional theories. We have already shown how this seeming alternative is essentially a combination of atemporal theories, in which case eclecticism has the same atemporal problems as traditional theories but with magnified complexity. Eclecticism, then, cannot be the solution to the atemporal problems of traditional theories. Still, what John found unsatisfactory in his experiences with Anne is worth describing as prototypical of what many therapists have found unsatisfying in their therapies. Ultimately, we will contend that John's "profound" experience with Anne is the power of the concrete and particular (the temporal) to reveal the problematic nature of the abstract and metaphysical (the atemporal).

> Typically, John would not have taken a case like Anne's. From his friend's referral, Anne was merely another 50-year-old schizophrenic, with a history of a few delusions and probably a hallucination or two. John figured he could simply "maintain" her, keep her from the hospital if possible, and provide a listening ear when needed. Wouldn't his eclectic friends be pleased? Here was a case in which he was doing not psychoanalysis per se but more of a biological approach to therapy. John admitted to himself some disappointment with this approach, but he expected that very little relationship would be possible with a schizophrenic, and so his psychoanalytic training would be wasted anyway.

John's history taking of Anne confirmed the delusions and hallucinations, but he was surprised to learn how long ago they had occurred. Nevertheless, he thought to himself, "Once a schizophrenic, always a schizophrenic." John was fairly convinced that this disorder was primarily biological, so Anne's long "remission" did not mean that she had lost the schizophrenic gene. Because of this, John was surprised that Anne was not currently on medication. He referred her immediately, with his psychiatrist friend providing independent confirmation of John's diagnosis and Anne's need for meds.

After a month of therapy sessions with Anne, John sensed that something was wrong. He had settled into a routine friendliness with her: being helpful, keeping her on her meds, and generally aiding her everyday problem solving. In today's therapy session, however, he sensed that Anne was withholding and angry, but he couldn't get her to discuss it. He was about to let it go when she finally burst forth with all sorts of accusations of him.

"You don't really listen to me," she cried. "You treat me like the wall. I can't get *in* to truly speak to you."

John couldn't help but wonder silently, "Were her delusions finally acting up again?"

"There," Anne shouted, "I see it. You are not here with me. I have been symptom-free for 3 years, and you and all the other doctors still treat me like I'm an alien from outer space. Your arrogance is hard to stomach, so I am going to discontinue my relationship with you—if you can call it a 'relationship.' "

These last remarks hit John like a ton of bricks. Somehow her complaints had struck a chord with him. Possibly Anne was right: Even after a month, he had never really been *with* her. He had treated her more like an object to be managed than a person to be cared for. He had been friendly and warm, after a fashion, but he had never *really* established any sort of personal connection. Was she a symptom-free "schizophrenic" or a person?

To John's everlasting surprise, he found himself apologizing to Anne and admitting to her the correctness of everything she had said. He was surprised at this response to her because he had never truly apologized to a patient before. This was not only contrary to the "biological approach" he was taking with Anne, but contrary to the "psychoanalytic reserve" he had so carefully cultivated. Somehow her pain, as caused by him, had broken through all his "professionalism."

The wrongness of his "professionalism" was further confirmed after several more sessions. John not only got to know Anne, as opposed to getting to know "a schizophrenic," but Anne got to know John. Indeed, their relationship was wonderfully productive and authentically therapeutic, which spurred John to reflect back to conversations with his colleagues about his "biases." The odd thing was that he had been the eclectic in this case. He had not treated Anne in his typical psychoanalytic manner, but had instead opted for a more biological approach. The problem was that neither approach seemed to be helpful in truly "being with" Anne. Without Anne's aid in *his* "breakthrough," he would still have been stuck in the same old therapeutic mold.

Atemporality Versus Temporality. Before comparing the atemporal characteristics of John's therapy with Anne to temporal alternatives (see Table 10.1), two words of caution are necessary. First, we do not consider temporal therapy to be another "school of thought" or another set of techniques to try with clients. Temporal therapy is more radical than that. Temporal therapy is an attempt to capture what is already going on with good therapists—as we said before, to catch theory up to good practice. It is also an attempt to articulate an alternative to eclecticism for the many therapists who have been dissatisfied with atemporal approaches. Their dissatisfaction has not been the result of an insufficient *quantity* of atemporal qualities (i.e., eclecticism), but rather the result of the atemporal *quality* of such theories. Second, John is not meant to be representative of all therapists. He is, instead, an illustration of how atemporal theoretical elements can invade (and sometimes pervade) the therapy situation. Most therapists will rightly see themselves as less extreme than John and thus more a mixture of temporal and atemporal elements. But our intention here is not to characterize therapy but to illustrate atemporality in therapeutic action. In other words, we are not contending that atemporality *always* happens in therapy, but rather that the atemporality of our current theories does not prevent it from happening. Indeed, these theories and systems encourage it.

For instance, John first assumed that he knew Anne and her problems from the referral description (see point 1 of Table 10.1). Indeed, he had decided his diagnosis and her treatment before ever meeting her. This is the confidence or, as Anne put it, the "arrogance" of assuming the atemporality of one's theoretical conceptions. Whatever one's theory—in this case a biological theory—it is assumed to be universal across all people and all situations. Indeed, the genetic account of schizophrenia has thrived on atemporality, because biological principles are typically understood as requiring universality in a similar atemporal sense. If schizophrenia were culturally or contextually bound, then the atemporal principles associated with traditional biological accounts would be ruled out.

A temporal therapist, however, would not have assumed that he or she knew Anne and her problems from the referral description. Temporality does not rule out the importance of past experiences—this is part of the therapist's historical context for interpreting Anne—so a temporal therapist could not help but draw on these experiences in anticipating Anne's case. Still, the therapist's confidence about these anticipations would be tentative at best. Crucial to a temporal perspective is an openness to the possibility that Anne is qualitatively different from expected, completely different from any past experiences with similar referrals. In fact, a temporal perspective would demand that the therapist be open to Anne being different from *herself* across therapy sessions. Indeed, a moment-by-moment openness is the ideal for a temporal therapist, where the particularities of the client take precedence over any theoretical conceptualization.

This is not to say that conceptualizations and theories are unimportant to the temporal therapist. As just described, generalizations are not only possible with temporal conceptions, they are also expected across the various contexts of therapy. However, one of the big differences between temporal generalizations

TABLE 10.1 Atemporal Versus Temporal Therapy

Atemporal Therapy	Temporal Therapy
1. Because theoretical abstractions are universal, atemporal therapists confidently generalize their abstract knowledge of the client.	1. Because theoretical conceptions and expectations are held tentatively, temporal therapists are open to the possibility that the client is qualitatively different from what they expect.
2. Because the "real truth" of the client is an abstraction (e.g., schizophrenic), outside of the concrete and physical, a personal relationship with the concrete client is either not needed or impossible.	2. Because the experienced and physical client is truer than any theory of the client, a real relationship with the client is not only possible but also unavoidable.
3. Because conceptual principles are theoretically true and immutable, atemporal therapists selectively attend to client characteristics that support these principles.	3. Because characteristics of the client may be temporary, temporal therapists must be sensitive to momentary changes in the client's behavior.
4. Because unchangeable conceptual abstractions (e.g., laws) govern the physical, the client's behavior is ultimately determined and completely predictable.	4. Because contexts are changing, the client and the therapist are not determined but have genuine possibilities.
5. Because atemporal therapists know universal theoretical principles, they tend to effect a professional "arrogance" and directiveness in the treatment of their clients.	5. Because any conception of the client could be inappropriate in the next moment, temporal therapists are open to being wrong and thus effect a professional humility.

and atemporal universals is that the latter are presumed (because they transcend contexts) and the former have to be demonstrated (because they can only exist *in* contexts). That is, temporal generalities are never presumed because there is always the possibility that they will be irrelevant to the next context. There is also no assumption that temporal conceptions are bound to or self-contained within a particular context. Although they have to be rooted *in* contexts, there is no limit to the number of contexts in which they can be rooted.

A second instance of atemporality occurred when John assumed that a real human relationship with Anne was either not needed or not possible (see point 2 of Table 10.1). Anne was not a person but a schizophrenic. After all, John decided his mode of therapy well before he met Anne. Even after several sessions, he was not interacting with a physical, experienced person, but with the "real truth" of Anne—her disordered state—contained in a metaphysical sphere that cannot change. Anne, in this sense, had no possibilities; her symptoms could come and go, but her basic condition was atemporal and unchangeable (e.g., genetic). All John could do, according to this conception, was "manage" her, as though she were a changeless, inanimate object—as Anne put it, a wall.

Temporal therapists, however, cannot avoid relationships with their clients. Unlike John, who selected a mode of interaction that led to superficiality and manipulation, these therapists are tied directly to the concreteness of their clients. John had the "luxury" of initially focusing on the abstract or metaphysical Anne—the "schizophrenic." Indeed, John could even view this abstraction as the real truth of Anne. Temporal therapists, by contrast, have no such luxury because they have no such abstraction. Even their anticipations and conceptualizations, albeit abstractions in a sense, have to be reexamined and reaffirmed in the next concrete moment. Moreover, these therapists can never deceive themselves with the notion that their conceptualizations of Anne are somehow more true than the experienced Anne.

This is not to say that conceptualizations are not intimately related to experiences. Temporal therapists know that their conceptualizations are always derived *from* the concrete experiential and not the reverse (as in atemporality). Many therapists have been taught to give primacy to the abstract and theoretical, as though treatment begins with theory and then continues to application. Temporality, however, reverses this order, beginning instead with concrete experiences and only then moving to abstract concepts. We should also note that "experiences" from this perspective are never "objective data," in the empiricist or positivist sense. They are, rather, an interpreted reality that is just as concrete and just as experiential, but is as connected to the interpreter as the interpreted. In other words, temporal reality is holistically contextual, including not only the situation itself but also the conceptualizer of the situation (who is, after all, part of the situation).

This type of temporal contextuality allows Anne more degrees of freedom as a client. For instance, a temporal therapist would never impose a stereotype or category on her, at least not in the enduring sense. If a stereotype or a category were used, Anne would be able to "break" its hold immediately, maximizing her possibilities for change, because the therapist expects and looks for this change. In this sense, Anne would never be a "schizophrenic" for life. If she were seen as schizophrenic at all (as a temporal conception), it is far more likely that she would be viewed as a momentary schizophrenic. That is, virtually no one with the label of schizophrenia acts "schizophrenic" all the time. Moreover, no one with *any* diagnostic label acts in accord with that symptomology all the time. Consequently, no one can ever *be* a diagnostic disorder. This does not preclude the cautious use of some enduring labels, but the therapist can never view the label as the primary truth about the client.

As a third example of atemporality, consider that even if Anne's condition *had* changed, John would likely have overlooked it (see point 3 of Table 10.1). In fact, he did ignore her recent freedom from all symptoms in understanding her basic condition. Eventually, of course, Anne's particularity—her pain and her threat of termination—broke through John's universal conception of her. But there is no telling how many other signs of Anne's particular personhood were available to John, but ignored, before this session. After all, atemporal therapists are expecting basic immutability and thus sameness, so why look for change? Even after Anne's outburst, when she accused John of treating her like a "wall" (a thing without possibility of fundamental change), he still persisted in his atemporal perspective. Recall that John assumed that she must be totally predictable in her delusional world.

In contrast, one of the cardinal advantages of temporal therapy is that therapists are much more attuned to the momentary changes of their clients. Atemporal therapists focus on the continuities or samenesses of therapy, the characteristics of their clients that support the unchangeable universals of their theories or diagnostic systems. Hence they selectively attend to "defenses" or "reinforcements," depending on the theory, and depressive or schizophrenic episodes, depending on the diagnosis. Temporal therapists, however, see, and have available for therapeutic "grist," any number of momentary changes. Why did this so-called depressive move into contentment, however momentarily? Why is Anne acting like a schizophrenic or a nonschizophrenic at this moment? Indeed, the temporal therapist boldly asserts that no one acts depressed or schizophrenic all the time; there are always and inevitably brief moments of happiness and lucidity that are vital to understanding clients.

This predictability implies a fourth characteristic of an atemporal conception. Because all things are unchangeable, either because they are metaphysical or because the physical is governed by the metaphysical, the course of all things is completely determined and predictable. Atemporal theorists may not know all the factors of a particular situation. Still, they assume that some sort of atemporal principles ultimately govern such situations; otherwise, the principles would presumably be invalid. This deterministic assumption makes any self-generated changes (e.g., choices, agency, decision making) problematic, because the "self" has no real options. The person (client or therapist) cannot really do other than what the metaphysical principles say. This determinism means that all therapy techniques that facilitate the agency of a client are misguided, because no such agentic factors really exist. Given Anne's presumed biological condition of schizophrenia, John chose to "manage" Anne as best he could; she was an object without agency or possibility, at least regarding her basic condition.

A fourth major distinction then between atemporal and temporal approaches concerns the possibilities and necessities of treatment. Atemporality presumes that the laws or principles (inherent in the theory) determine Anne. This means that Anne must (of necessity) be the way she is, through the principles of her nature or her nurture, regardless of her context. Her personality is *fundamentally* the same and cannot be easily changed. Conversely, temporal therapists presume that Anne has possibilities inherent in her changing contexts. Because Anne cannot be separated from her context and because contexts inevitably change, problems and treatments inevitably change. The main therapeutic task, then, is not to create change—as traditionally assumed—but to recognize and channel ongoing change appropriately, because it is *already* occurring.

Many therapists may find the mutability of a temporal approach to be more hopeful, but question whether such changeability precludes predictability. That is, temporality may sound chaotic and thus violate a therapist's sense of the order and predictability of most clients. But much like the situation with the issue of generality (see "Reconstructing the Solution") there is a temporal predictability and atemporal predictability. The later, given the right information, can be perfect, because it is underlaid with determinism. From this]havior, just from the brief statement of referral. From a temporal perspective, however, such predictions would be precipitous (and could never be perfect), but are not entirely out of the question, because Anne's possibilities are always limited by her context, including her bodily context (e.g., Merleau-Ponty, 1962/1989).

For example, Anne may indeed be genetically predisposed to schizophrenia, but such a predisposition could never rule out the possibility of at least momentary lucidity. Anne's history is also considered part of her context, according to temporality. Her history, like her biology, presents both a set of limitations as well as a set of opportunities. In this sense, the context giveth and the context taketh away. Although context plays a crucial role in the changeableness of temporal conceptions (as it changes), context can also play a stabilizing role, allowing greater understanding and predictability of clients. The main point here is that there is no metaphysical force—outside the experiential and physical— to determine Anne's actions. But the lack of a metaphysical force does not mean that contextual factors do not delimit, and thus make predictable, Anne's behavior.

Knowledge of unchangeable, universal, and controlling abstractions leads to a fifth characteristic of atemporality, that of the therapeutic expert (see point 5 of Table 10.1). Because the therapist has learned these theoretical principles, he or she can be completely confident in their use. Although this use can take many forms, such expert approaches to therapy are frequently directive. The therapist can *never* realistically be wrong, at least on fundamental issues of theory, because the therapist has a complete knowledge of the universal, unchangeable principles. This is the reason that John, an experienced psychotherapist, had never really apologized. He could never really *be* wrong—except on trivial issues—and so there was never really anything to apologize for. His arrogance was part of his professionalism.

Temporal therapists can never assume the role of expert. John, of course, assumed this role because he supposed that his training has exposed him to theoretical principles—biological or psychoanalytic—that controlled all psychological functioning. He could *act* humble and *attempt* to be nondirective in style, but he still assumed that he knew these principles, and this assumption inevitably affected his relationship with Anne. Indeed, she saw him as quite arrogant. Temporal therapists, on the other hand, cannot make this assumption. They must assume a very healthy skepticism about any conception of the client they might hold. In fact, temporal therapists *expect* to be wrong, and thus have no problem humbly apologizing; they do it all the time. Instead of a professional arrogance, where resistance really is futile, temporal therapists effect a professional humility.

Conclusion

There is obviously more work to be done in fleshing out temporal therapy. Indeed, there is much more to temporality itself, such as the narrative tradition (e.g., Carr, 1986; Polkinghorne, 1988), than we have room to describe here. Still, we believe this approach holds great promise, because so many therapists have chafed for so long under the atemporality of traditional theories. Fully two thirds of all therapists have rejected their inflexibility and abstractness by moving to eclecticism. Unfortunately, eclecticism merely compounds these problems, either by offering a more complicated, integrated atemporality or by attempting to hide atemporality in method.

What many eclectic therapists do not realize, at least intellectually, is that they can challenge the atemporal *quality* of their theories. This challenge is itself a single philosophy and thus not an eclecticism per se. But this single philosophy allows for theoretical order without squelching important treatment possibilities and without directing attention away from the concreteness of therapy. Many therapists have been instinctively operating from this temporal mode already; many temporal adaptations of conventional atemporal theories have undoubtedly already occurred. Indeed, these adaptations could be what people really mean when they say they are eclectic. They do not mean an increased quantity of atemporal theories—as the eclectic tradition portrays it—they mean a humbler sort of theory that is open to change and modification, depending on client needs.

Of course, the change from atemporal to temporal can never be a simple replacement of one assumption with another. Traditional theories have been born and bred on atemporality; it is inherent in their very core. Still, many temporal insights of these theories were probably forced into an atemporal framework. After all, these insights were often born of therapeutic practice and experience. Because true principles and natural laws were considered to be atemporal, it was assumed without critical examination that the insights of countless therapy theorists had to be developed and presented within an atemporal framework. If our analysis is correct, then many traditional theories can be reworked and distilled of the genuine temporal insights they originally contained. This would allow therapists, for perhaps the first time theoretically, to move out of the metaphysical realm of abstractions and into the real world of client care.

Notes

1. Although the eclectic literature often suggests a common factors approach as a third form of eclecticism, it is subsumable under these other two approaches (Slife, Reber, & Gantt, 2000).

2. Indeed, no bridging should be necessary if we truly embrace temporality.

References

Arkowitz, H. (1989). The role of theory in psychotherapy integration. *Journal of Integrative and Eclectic Psychotherapy, 8,* 8-16.

Arkowitz, H. (1992). Integrative theories of therapy. In D. K. Freedheim (Ed.), *History of psychotherapy: A century of change* (pp. 261-303). Washington, DC: American Psychological Association.

Arnkoff, D. B. (1995). Theoretical orientation and psychotherapy integration: Comment on Pozanski and McLennan (1995). *Journal of Counseling Psychology, 42*(4), 423-425.

Bergin, A. E., & Garfield, S. L. (Eds.). (1994). *Handbook of psychotherapy and behavior change.* New York: John Wiley.

Bernstein, R. J. (1983). *Beyond objectivism and relativism: Science, hermeneutics, and praxis.* Philadelphia: University of Pennsylvania Press.

Beutler, L. E., & Clarkin, J. F. (1990). *Systematic treatment selection: Toward targeted therapeutic interventions.* New York: Brunner/Mazel.

Brentano, F. (1973). *Psychology from an empirical standpoint* (A. C. Rancurello, D. B. Terrell, & L. L. McAllister, Trans.). London: Routledge & Kegan Paul. (Original work published 1874)

Carr, D. (1986). *Time, narrative, and history.* Bloomington: Indiana University Press.

Curd, M., & Cover, J. A. (1998). *Philosophy of science: The central issues.* New York: Norton.

Faulconer, J. E., & Williams, R. N. (Eds.). (1990). *Reconsidering psychology: Perspectives from continental philosophy.* Pittsburgh, PA: Duquesne University Press.

Gholson, B., & Barker, P. (1985). Kuhn, Lakatos, and Laudan: Applications in the history of physics and psychology. *American Psychologist, 40*(7), 755-769.

Goldfried, M. R. (1980). Toward the delineation of therapeutic change principles. *American Psychologist, 35,* 991-999.

Held, B. S. (1995). *Back to reality: A critique of postmodern theory in psychotherapy.* New York: Norton.

Howard, G. S., Nance, D. W., & Meyers, P. (1986). *Adaptive counseling and therapy.* San Francisco: Jossey-Bass.

Jensen, J. D., Bergin, A. E., & Greaves, D. W. (1990). The meaning of eclecticism: New survey and analysis of components. *Professional Psychology: Research and Practice, 21*(2), 124-130.

Kuhn, T. S. (1970). *The structure of scientific revolutions* (2nd ed.). Chicago: University of Chicago Press.

Lazarus, A. A. (1995). Different types of eclecticism and integration: Let's be aware of the dangers. *Journal of Psychotherapy Integration, 5*(1), 27-39.

Lazarus, A. A., & Beutler, L. E. (1993). On technical eclecticism. *Journal of Counseling and Development, 71*(4), 381-385.

Lazarus, A. A., Beutler, L. E., & Norcross, J. C. (1992). The future of technical eclecticism. *Psychotherapy, 29*(1), 11-20.

Lazarus, A. A., & Messer, S. B. (1991). Does chaos prevail? An exchange on technical eclecticism and assimilative integration. *Journal of Psychotherapy Integration, 1*(2), 143-158.

Leahey, T. H. (1992). *A history of psychology: Main currents in psychological thought* (3rd ed.). Englewood Cliffs, NJ: Prentice Hall.

Merleau-Ponty, M. (1989). *The phenomenology of perception* (C. Smith, Trans.). London: Routledge. (Original work published 1962)

Norcross, J. C. (1986). Eclectic psychotherapy: An introduction and overview. In J. C. Norcross (Ed.), *Handbook of eclectic psychotherapy.* New York: Brunner/Mazel.

Norcross, J. C., & Newman, C. F. (1992). Psychotherapy integration: Setting the context. In J. C. Norcross & M. R. Goldfried (Eds.), *Handbook of psychotherapy integration* (pp. 3-45). New York: Basic Books.

Norcross, J. C., Prochaska, J. O., & Farber, J. A. (1993). Psychologists conducting psychotherapy: New findings and historical comparisons on the Psychotherapy Division membership. *Psychotherapy, 30,* 692-697.

Polkinghorne, D. E. (1988). *Narrative knowing and the human sciences.* Albany: State University of New York Press.

Poznanski, J. J., & McLennan, J. (1995). Conceptualizing and measuring counselors theoretical orientation. *Journal of Counseling Psychology, 42,* 411-422.

Prochaska, J. O., & DiClemente, C. C. (1986). The transtheoretical approach. In J. C. Norcross (Ed.), *Handbook of eclectic psychotherapy* (pp. 163-200). New York: Brunner/Mazel.

Slife, B. D. (1987). The perils of eclecticism as therapeutic orientation. *Theoretical and Philosophical Psychology, 7,* 94-103.

Slife, B. D., Reber, J. S., & Gantt, E. E. (2000). *Eclecticism and the philosophy of science.* Manuscript submitted for publication.

Slife, B. D., & Williams, R. N. (1995). *What's behind the research? Discovering hidden assumptions in the behavioral sciences.* Thousand Oaks, CA: Sage.

Thorne, F. C. (1973). Eclectic psychotherapy. In R. Corsini (Ed.), *Current psychotherapies.* Itasca, IL: F. E. Peacock.

Wachtel, P. L. (1977). *Psychoanalysis and behavior therapy.* New York: Basic Books.

Wachtel, P. L. (1987). *Action and insight.* New York: Guilford.

Yalom, I. D. (1980). *Existential psychotherapy.* New York: Basic Books.

Commentary

New Bottles, Old Wine?

Ted Packard
Kay Packard, PhD, MFT
University of Utah

Although we did not agree with all of the concepts presented by Slife and Reber, their chapter offers a theoretical and philosophical analysis of psychotherapy. As a profession, psychology has been so busy expanding practice opportunities and attempting to demonstrate efficacy that most of us have spent precious little time thinking carefully and systematically about the conceptual and philosophical underpinnings of our work. Slife and Reber have done us a favor by calling attention to the fact that our assumptions—be they systematic or seat-of-the-pants, eclectic or single theory, carefully delineated or automatic and unconscious—indeed influence our actions and clients' outcomes.

Our task is to respond from our vantage point as practitioners and to (a) highlight what we believe to be clinically relevant from the material presented, and (b) share our thoughts about enhancing the relevance of the ideas for practice.

Relevance for Clinical Practice

Slife and Reber emphasize the importance of responding to the "unique needs" of individual clients. This is an important and fundamental idea often lost in our current interest in developing empirically supported treatments that are cost-effective to administer. Gordon Allport likely would be especially pleased with this "idiographic" notion, as would a number of his mid-century humanistically oriented colleagues.

Slife and Reber correctly point out that theoretical integrationism and technical eclecticism ultimately are theoretical (or metatheoretical) statements that presume certain assumptions, biases, and methods no less than psychoanalytic approaches or any other single theory. Awareness of one's assumptions does indeed foster professional humility rather than the problematic arrogance pointed out forcefully by Slife and Reber.

Although the term "temporality" is new to us, we recognize the related concept of "context" as exceedingly important, as experienced and successful therapists will attest. Reinforcement *histories* and *prior* developmental experiences are useful in developing hypotheses about clients, but are never definitive in explaining the present or in predicting the future. Sensitive awareness of the here-and-now and flexible responsiveness to the moment-by-moment interaction are markers likely associated with unusually effective therapists.

We also liked Slife and Reber's emphasis on the fundamental importance of the *application* of theory, be it temporal or atemporal, as opposed to the assumptions and concepts that make up the theory itself. After all, it is what the therapist *does,* as opposed to her or his ideas, that influences the client to move in positive directions.

We could not agree more with the five qualities of temporal therapy described in the last section of the chapter. These are concepts known and highly valued by many successful therapists, and they are obvious candidates for inclusion in a consensus listing of "common clinical wisdom." In our own words, we summarize these five qualities as follows: (a) Never assume the client's problem from the initial diagnostic label or description. (b) Work first to develop a strong relationship, bond, or "alliance" with your client (a concept with massive support from the positivistic, empirical literature). (c) Focus on moment-to-moment client changes (a frequent admonition of contemporary experiential humanistic therapists). (d) Rather than trying to create or force change, recognize and channel ongoing and already occurring client change. (e) Never assume the role of expert; expect to sometimes be wrong and be willing to apologize sincerely. All of these are potent and useful concepts, be they derived from "temporal" theory or clinical experience.

Proposals for Improvement

Slife and Reber seem to imply that a temporal approach to psychotherapy would be atheoretical and neutral—no biases, no assumptions, and no preconceptions—leaving the therapist "free" to be with the client and to respond only to the present context. Such a position seems untenable, as even the most neutral conceptual model must of necessity involve assumptions about preferred methods and desirable end states. Thus, further elaboration by the authors of the theoretical underpinnings of their "temporal" approach would be most helpful. Is there a single temporal alternative, as implied by the authors, or are there many variants on this theme, as is the case with the atemporal approaches to theory that are described in the chapter? Further clarification is needed.

It seems neither credible nor fair to tar "all traditional theories of therapy" with the same atemporal brush, especially when the contrasting example is psychoanalysis, certainly one of the more focused and determinative approaches. There are a number of other contemporary atemporal approaches or theories of psychotherapy that appear to us to have considerably more in common with the temporal approach recommended by the authors than does traditional psychoanalysis; for example, general systems theories representing both biological and behavioral domains, including systemic family therapy with its emphasis on the importance of context. Other examples include social constructivist theories of psychotherapy, especially mainline feminist therapy, again with a strong emphasis on context, and traditional or contemporary experiential/humanistic approaches from Carl Rogers at mid-century to Leslie Greenberg and colleagues today, all emphasizing the centrality of the client and the necessity of the therapeutic relationship. Even recent attempts by behavioral scientists to apply concepts from chaos theory to social and behavioral phenomena seem to have something in common with the ideas of temporal theory.

In our view, the credibility of the argument advanced by Slife and Reber will be enhanced if they are more comprehensive in their review of contemporary atemporal theories of psychotherapies. Particularly in Slife and Reber's application, there seems much in common between the "temporal" approach they describe and contemporary models such as family systems therapy, feminist therapy, social constructivist approaches, and experiential/humanistic psychotherapies.

In closing, and to illustrate the point that new bottles may indeed be filled, at least partially, with old wine, we would like to review briefly an article by Gordon Allport that was published almost 40 years ago in *The Harvard Educational Review* (Allport, 1962). In the article, titled "Psychological Models for Guidance" (and psychotherapy), Allport shares his analysis of the three dominant theoretical approaches of the day: (a) humans perceived as reactive beings (behavioral and learning-based approaches), (b) humans perceived as reactive beings in-depth (psychoanalysis and its variants), and (c) humans perceived as beings-in-the-process of becoming (humanistic/experiential approaches). We submit there is more than a passing relationship between Allport's third model and some of the ideas presented by Slife and Reber. To illustrate this point, we conclude with some final thoughts from Allport:

> From the existential point of view the ideal counselor will strive to develop two attitudes in his client. Taken separately they seem antithetical; but fused into a world-view they provide strength for the future. One attitude is tentativeness of outlook. Since certainties are no longer certain, let all dogmas be fearlessly examined. . . . Taken by itself such tentativeness might well lead to ontological despair. Yet acceptance of the worst does not prevent us from making the best of the worst. Up to now psychologists have not dealt with the remarkable ability of human beings to blend a tentative outlook with firm commitment to chosen values. . . . Whenever the two attitudes coexist in a

life, we find important desirable by-products from the fusion. . . . Tentative-
ness and commitment are twin ideals for both counselor and client. To my
mind they lie at the heart and center of guidance, of teaching, and of living.
(pp. 19-20, 23)

Reference

Allport, G. (1962). Psychological models for guidance. *The Harvard Educational Review, 32,* 13-23.

Issue 11

Postmodernism

The Postmodern Turn

What It Means for Psychotherapy— and What It Doesn't

Barbara S. Held
Bowdoin College

Every therapy movement, indeed every movement, typically begins by rail-ing against the excesses or inadequacies of what preceded it. And the post-modern turn in psychotherapy is no exception. In its case, the excesses and in-adequacies of modernism itself are held up as the source of the evils, ills, and woes of the so-called postindustrial era. Of course, the postmodern movement, like all prior movements, professes itself to provide, if not *the* solution to the problems it defines, at least a better alternative.

In this chapter, I set forth an overview of the postmodern turn as it has manifested itself in psychotherapy. I give particular attention to what therapists who have taken the postmodern turn claim to be its revolutionary aspects, and I assess those claims critically in terms of their actual consequences for the-rapeutic theory and, more to the point of this volume, practice. In the course of my analysis, I hope to demonstrate that what the postmodern therapy movement means or intends for practice requires some, but by no means all, of the defining features of postmodern theory and philosophy itself. In fact, I shall argue that to achieve its goals for practice, that movement would be better off defying, or at least ignoring, postmodernism's defining prescription.

The Stage for the Postmodern Turn: Psychotherapy in Crisis

Those who find postmodernism appealing typically point an accusatory finger at the century-long dominance of a modern scientific approach to the study of human nature, including the nature of psychopathology and psychotherapy, characterizing that approach with various pejorative terms, including "positivist" "scientistic," "modernist," "objectivist," "empiricist," "rationalist," "reductionistic," "hegemonic," "oppressive," "dominant," "absolutist," and "totalizing" (e.g., Fishman, 1999; Freedman & Combs, 1996; Friedman, 1993; Kvale, 1992; McNamee & Gergen, 1992; Neimeyer & Mahoney, 1995; Omer & Alon, 1997; Rosen & Kuehlwein, 1996; White & Epston, 1990). But even some who criticize postmodernism nonetheless find in modern (social) science a source of pathology, as this statement about "the Modern Scientific Outlook" indicates:

> When the method of objectification is taken as the very definition of an epistemically mature stance toward life, trouble ensues. This view rather dogmatically absolutizes a certain detached, dispassionate, spectator view of knowing and relating to the world. Such abstraction and detachment may be necessary and appropriate for certain purposes, but in many situations, they will only hamper us or have harmful consequences. . . . A one-sided stress on the objectifying point of view may be an important source of some of the peculiar irrationalities and pathologies of modern life. (Richardson, Fowers, & Guignon, 1999, pp. 35-36)

Going beyond the problem of using modern science to study human behavior to its implications for psychotherapy, postmodernists have fastened on the need for complete ontological and epistemological overhaul if therapy is to be therapeutic instead of unhelpful or even harmful. One does not have to enlist in any postmodernist forces to notice that the discipline of psychotherapy is indeed "in crisis." In *Philosophy and Psychotherapy*, the philosopher Edward Erwin (1997) made this chilling observation:

> The overwhelming majority of the more than 400 psychotherapy procedures have not yet been shown to be more effective with real patients than a credible [italics added] placebo. . . . What cannot be true . . . given the great diversity of conflicting psychotherapeutic theories, is that psychotherapeutic expertise generally consists of theoretical knowledge about human behavior or the mind. (pp. 158-159)

Defining Features of the Postmodern Turn in Psychotherapy

Because of its many varieties and uses, postmodernism is difficult to capture in one defining description[1] (e.g., Best & Kellner, 1991; Fishman, 1999; Kvale, 1992; Rosenau, 1992).

I have previously summarized postmodernism's opposition to modernism by way of three commitments: (a) postmodernism rejects general, objective laws and truths in favor of local, unique, contextualized, or subjective "truths"; (b) postmodernism proclaims an indeterminacy or plurality of meaning in texts and events; and (c) postmodernism denies the legitimacy of any real and consistent ontological status or existence for the self, subject, or individual (Held, 1995, p. 10).

Although each of these three features is relevant to the postmodern turn in psychotherapy, the one feature that unites postmodernism in all its many incarnations is a nonskeptical adherence to the epistemological supposition that we cannot—either in science or in everyday life—attain knowledge of any objective, or knower-independent, reality. Instead, knowers make, construct, or constitute, *in the language of their local discursive or social contexts,* their own biased or subjective "realities." Thus "truth" (with scare quotes) is relative to each subjective knower (or each subjective group of knowers). Rather than bemoan their "negative philosophical judgment" about knowing (Pols, 1992, 1998), postmodernists celebrate this epistemological state of affairs as they reiterate over and over a discourse that proclaims with a unified voice the context dependence or knower dependence, the relativity or subjectivity, of all truth claims. Although that voice denies with particular vigor the claim that science can attain universal truths—it characterizes that claim as nothing less than the "absolutist" or "totalizing" discourse of modernity and its alleged positivism—the claim to *any* objective truth or reality is thoroughly rejected by postmodernism. This utterly general, utterly universal dismissal of truth claims of course constitutes the antirealist, constructivist or constructionist, or anti-objectivist[2] epistemology that is a defining feature of all forms of postmodernism, although the way I have characterized that dismissal here is particularly exemplary of the social-constructionist form of postmodernism that has so influenced psychology and psychotherapy.[3] The following quotations exemplify the promotion of some form of antirealist epistemology by therapists who have taken the postmodern turn[4]:

In *The Case for Pragmatic Psychology,* the psychologist Daniel Fishman (1999) gives these definitions of postmodernism:

> The changes in the '60s were associated with the emergence of an interrelated family of alternative visions called by such names as "postmodernism," "neopragmatism," "social constructionism," "deconstructionism," "cultural criticism," "hermeneutics," "interpretive theory," and "antifoundationalism." While there are very important differences among these frameworks, they all contrast themselves to modernism, assuming that reality is, to a large extent, "constructed" or "invented" by individuals and groups as a function of particular personal beliefs and historical, cultural, and social contexts. Thus "postmodernism" (the term I use to refer to these alternative views as a group) conceives of the nature of reality as relative, depending upon an observer's point of view. The postmodernist argues against the modernist's claim to achieve fundamental and objective knowledge about the world through the natural science method. (p. xxi)

A core idea in postmodernism is that we are always interpreting our experienced reality through a pair of conceptual glasses—glasses based on such factors as our present personal goals in this particular situation, our past experiences, our values and attitudes, our body of knowledge, the nature of language, present trends in contemporary culture, and so forth. It is never possible to take the glasses off altogether and view the world as it "really is." (p. 5)

The constructivist psychologist Robert Neimeyer (1993), in "An Appraisal of Constructivist Psychotherapies," argues,

Like the broader postmodern zeitgeist from which it derives, constructivist psychotherapy is founded on a conceptual critique of objectivist epistemology. In particular, it offers an alternative conception of psychotherapy as the quest for a more viable personal knowledge, in a world that lacks the fixed referents provided by a directly knowable external reality.[5] (p. 230)

The postmodern narrative therapists Jill Freedman and Gene Combs (1996), in *Narrative Therapy: The Social Construction of Preferred Realities*, explicitly offer a thoroughgoing antirealism and social constructionism:

1. Realities are socially constructed. 2. Realities are constituted through language. 3. Realities are organized and maintained through narrative. 4. There are no essential truths. (p. 22)

The "objectivity" of the modernist worldview, with its emphasis on facts, replicable procedures, and generally applicable rules, easily ignores the specific, localized meanings of individual people. . . . Postmodernists . . . choose to look at specific, contextualized details more often than grand generalizations, difference rather than similarity. (pp 21-22)

The postmodern narrative therapists Alan Parry and Robert Doan (1994), in *Story Re-Visions: Narrative Therapy in the Postmodern World*, write,

A delegitimized, postmodern world is a place without any single claim to a truth universally respected. (p. 10) In the demise of all grand narratives, we now live in a world in which personal narratives essentially stand alone as the means by which we pull together the text of our own lives. . . . Although this may all be frightening without the legitimating guidance of the grand narratives, it is also a liberating possibility. It frees us from the totalizing tyranny of the grand narratives. . . . A story told by a person in his/her own words . . . does not have to plead its legitimacy in any higher court of narrative appeal, because no narrative has any greater legitimacy than the person's own. . . . A story is a person's own story, and he/she is its poet. (pp. 25-27)

Defining Features of the Postmodern Turn in Psychotherapy: A Closer Look

If we look more closely at these representative quotations, nuances appear. For example, some postmodern therapists appear to endorse a more radical and some a less radical antirealism (see Held, 1995, 1998a). But an even closer look reveals something else, something decidedly less philosophical and, in my opinion, more important for the actual practice of therapy. That something else consists in the elevation of what is unique, personal, local, and idiosyncratic over the general (causal) laws of conventional systems of psychotherapy. For example, Fishman speaks of the importance of attention to "particular personal beliefs," the "observer's point of view," and "our present personal goals"; Neimeyer speaks of a "more viable personal knowledge"; Freedman and Combs speak of "specific, localized meanings of individual people"; and Parry and Doan speak of "personal narratives" and "a person's own story." Each of these theorists or therapists reflects the pervasive postmodern concern with getting at the particularities of each client's unique life experience, often in the liberatory attempt to overthrow the allegedly oppressive, pathology-inducing "dominant discourses" of science and society, including the discourse of so-called modern systems of psychotherapy. To use a popular metaphor, they seek to help people find their own "voice." As a psychotherapist, I myself am convinced of the importance of attending to each client's uniqueness or particularity in the actual doing of therapy; postmodernists are surely right that in many respects each of us is unique, a uniqueness that must be taken seriously in therapy if therapists are to be truly responsive to the struggles of their clients.

Still, there are questions. First, how unique or particular is each client? Does the uniqueness or particularity refer to each individual? Or to groups of individuals defined by the likes of historical, cultural, or discursive contexts, including the attitudes and values that prevail in those contexts? Even my small sample of quotations suggests there is some variation on this point (see Held, 1995, 1996a).

Another question, the one that is the focus of my present analysis, asks, If a *practical* concern among postmodern therapists consists in elevating the client's uniqueness or particularity above the theoretical generalities that have traditionally been used to guide practice, then why all the fuss about epistemology? Especially the fuss about the need for an antirealist or anti-objectivist epistemology? It is to this question that I now turn.

Why Postmodern Therapists Have Turned to an Antirealist, Anti-Objectivist, or Constructivist/Constructionist Epistemology

I have previously maintained that there may be as many reasons for the postmodern turn as there are therapists, that no single reason can fully capture the motivating force of all those who have taken this turn (Held, 1995, 1999c). But the question I return to again and again is why therapists are turning to postmodern theory and philosophy in their capacity *as* therapists. Why do some appear so compelled both by postmodernism's antirealist or anti-objectivist epistemology and its aversion to grand or general narratives, theories, and systems? What *practical* benefit can a thoroughgoing post-modernism afford therapists?

I have characterized the postmodern attempt to challenge the theoretical generalities of all systems of therapy as reflecting an antisystematic or anti-theoretical aspiration. Of course, this aspiration comes at a price: the lawfulness, replicability, or systematicity of therapeutic practice. To put the problem an-other way, how can therapists construct a *system* of therapy that preserves the unique particularity of clients? How can they construct a system of therapy that allows the practitioner to give clients' unique, contextualized meanings and ex-periences their due? Is it possible to have a theoretical system that guides prac-tice in some coherent or predictable way but does not impose a "dominant dis-course" in the form of theoretical generalities? As Fishman (1999) puts it, "The crucial point of my thesis of the need to reinvent psychology is that we need to incorporate diversity more systematically in our epistemological and resulting methodological models" (p. 26).

Before answering that last question, let us ask how an antirealist or anti-objectivist epistemology became the focal point of postmodern therapists—not just theorists, but practicing therapists. If I am correct that a primary *practical* goal is the individualization of their practice, the freeing of practice from the constraints of (allegedly irrelevant or misguided) theoretical generalities, then why all the attention to epistemology, especially an antirealist or anti-objectivist (i.e., postmodernist) epistemology? Even the quotation of Fishman just above illustrates this link between the systematic-antisystematic tension (the wish for a *systematic* diversity), on the one hand, and epistemology or methodology, on the other.

Let us begin with the obvious: Postmodern theory itself is founded on an in-sistent adherence to an antirealist, anti-objectivist, or constructivist/constructionist epistemology. Still we ask, How did some therapists decide that this type of epistemology would free practice from the constraints of the theoretical general-ities that once guided some of their own practices? To answer that question, let us follow a certain line of logic.

First we will attend to the primary method of postmodern narrative therapists, namely, helping clients to "restory," or "renarrate," the meaning of their life experiences. The discerning reader will immediately object that there is nothing inherently postmodernist about this process: So-called modernist psychotherapists have always done just that—although they have typically used terms such as "interpret," "understand," and "construe." But they have not typically adopted an antirealist epistemology—certainly not the thorough-going antirealism or anti-objectivism that now pervades the postmodern narra-tive therapy movement, that indeed defines the constructivism and social

constructionism that inform that movement. We must therefore consider another proposition: If the postmodernists are right that there is no (objective)
truth to be had by anyone (i.e., if antirealism were, paradoxically, true), then the
new therapeutic story, narrative, or interpretation could take any form—literally.
Therapists would in that case have more options for their restorying, renarrating,
or reinterpreting process. And they could use those options with a perfectly
clear conscience—that is, without the threat of therapist deceit or manipulativeness under which those who play fast and loose with the truth labor.

Why should this be so? Why should the rejection of objectivity protect
therapists against impending charges of manipulativeness? Because, if there
were a *knowable* objective reality, we could insist easily enough that the new therapeutic interpretations, understandings, or constructions should not violate
that reality, at least not the interpretations, understandings, or constructions of
therapists who put a premium on ethical practice. But if there *were* no objective
reality (an ontological condition that I have characterized as a more radical form
of antirealism) or if there were an objective reality but we could not *know* it as it
exists, independent of our knowing function (an epistemological condition that
I have characterized as a less radical form of antirealism), then reality could not
be expected to constrain the interpretive process. If all so-called "evidence"
were subjective or biased—a condition that would legitimate the common use in
postmodernist circles of scare quotes around the words "evidence," "facts,"
"objective," "reality," and "truth" to undermine even the possibility of objectivity—then therapists could more easily ignore "observations" that were inconve-
nient for, or incompatible with, their reinterpretive goals, since all "observations" would then have no (objective) truth status, no real weight.

Moreover, if there were no truth to be had (period!), there would be no
truth in any theory of human nature, including theories of human development,
psychopathology, or psychotherapy. Apropos of this, consider Fishman's (1999)
postmodernist claim: "From a postmodern perspective . . . it is not possible to
'discover' 'basic laws of human nature'; and the results of the [modern, positiv-
ist] enterprise are substantively irrelevant to the nonlaboratory world—because
of the contextual embeddedness of psychological knowledge" (p. 10). If the
postmodernists are right about this (and note the scare quotes in Fishman's
statement), there would be no need—especially no *moral* obligation—to impose
any general, predetermined theoretical assumptions about human nature on
clients to help them along. Indeed, such imposition could itself be immoral, by
constituting the necessarily arbitrary "dominant discourse"—those so-called
positivist proclamations—that are said to "marginalize" the "contextually embedded" (i.e., unique or particular) meanings that clients should be helped to
construct (but not discover) about their lives.

In short, if there were no (knowable) truth about human nature, all prior
concepts from psychology and psychotherapy could be dismissed, leaving the
therapist with nothing but the client's own unique life experiences[6] as the source
of content or meanings for the new therapeutic story or narrative—or so many
narrative therapists appear to suppose. No more Oedipal struggles, weak ego

defenses, cross-generational family coalitions, or faulty cognitions to get in the way and limit the range of possibility—of *unique* possibility. The therapeutic story, narrative, or interpretation of the client's difficulties could then be based on a bare *minimum* of predetermined general theoretical concepts, if indeed any crept in at all. In fact, the writings of many postmodern narrative therapists are liberally sprinkled with language that optimistically links the adoption of antirealism or anti-objectivism, on the one hand, and the promise of personal or individualistic (but not societal) liberation, on the other:

> The doors of therapeutic perception and possibility have been opened wide by the recognition that we are actively constructing our mental realities rather than simply uncovering or coping with an objective "truth." (Hoyt, 1996, p. l)

> Although this may all be frightening without the legitimating guidance of the grand narratives, it is also a liberating possibility. It frees us from the totalizing tyranny of the grand narratives. (Parry & Doan, 1994, p. 25)

> These are but a few examples of means by which people can be enabled to construct things from different viewpoints, thus liberating them from the oppression of limiting narrative beliefs and relieving the resulting pain. In this way those turning to us in times of trouble may come to transcend the restraints imposed by their erstwhile reliance on a determinate set of meanings and be freed from the struggle that ensues from imposing their beliefs on self and others. . . . For still others a stance toward meaning itself will evolve; one which betokens that tolerance of uncertainty, that freeing of experience which comes from acceptance of unbounded relativity of meaning. (Gergen & Kaye, 1992, p. 183)

What the Postmodern Turn Means: A Minimalist System of Therapy

The attempt to keep predetermined concepts to a bare minimum in practice suggests the use of a certain kind of theoretical system to guide practice. Elsewhere (Held, 1995, 1996a, 1998a) I have characterized the type of system postmodern therapists prefer as a "minimalist" or "incomplete" system of therapy. By this I mean that they try to eliminate two of the three most fundamental component parts of a generic model of therapy systems and to retain only one of those component parts. The three components, as I have conceived them, are (a) *predetermined descriptions* of problems, pain, or pathology—for example, depression, anxiety, relational problems; (b) *predetermined theories* about what causes problems, pain, or pathology—for example, a neurotransmitter defect, an early emotional trauma, irrational thoughts, a life story constricted by the dominant discourse; and (c) *predetermined theories cum methods* about how to alleviate problems, pain, or pathology—for example, challenging irrational beliefs or, if one is a postmodern therapist, challenging the so-called dominant or totalizing discourse.

We are now in a position to understand just how postmodern therapists attempt to individualize or liberate practice. They suppose they can accomplish this through the epistemological claim that all knowledge is biased, relative, or subjective—that is, tied to the particularities of knowers, including the particularities of the knower's context and all that that includes. But in actuality they pursue their goal by eliminating predetermined content—problem descriptions (Component 1) and their theorized causes (Component 2)—from the theoretical systems they construct and use. They seek to replace that generalized content with unique, context-dependent, client-determined meanings and goals, which of course can never be predetermined. But the real consequence of their activity is this: They have made the theoretical system of therapy they use less complete, or more minimal, in that it retains only Component 3, their predetermined, general method of problem resolution, namely, helping clients to restory or renarrate their (unique) life experiences. And so the practice "guided" by their minimalist theoretical system[7] must itself be less systematic, rule governed, constrained, and replicable; hence I call their aspirations antisystematic or antitheoretical. And I speak of "aspirations," because to the extent that postmodern therapists employ even a minimalist theoretical system to guide their efforts, there is still *something* systematic about their practice. Indeed, without some knowledge, some generalities, to guide practice, we would all be justified in asking what the practitioner's expertise consisted in (see Fishman, 1999; Held, 1995; Woolfolk, 1998).

What the Postmodern Turn Does Not Mean: The Use of an Antirealist, Anti-Objectivist, Constructivist or Constructionist Epistemology in Practice

To be sure, the struggle to individualize (and so to liberate) practice by means of an antirealist epistemological doctrine is problematic. Antirealism is at best irrelevant to the attainment of an individualized or nongeneralized practice, because, to the extent that such a practice is within our reach, it is more a function of the degree of minimalism of the theoretical system used to guide practice than a function of anyone's epistemological leanings. Put differently, we can interpret a minimalist system in either realist or antirealist terms and still have a more individualized practice, because that system in either case places fewer constraints on what must get attended to in practice. Conversely, we can interpret a nonminimalist system in either realist or antirealist terms and still have a less individualized practice, because that system in either case places more constraints on the content of therapy.

Moreover, postmodern therapists have not made their minimalist theoretical system—their general, predetermined method of restorying or renarrating—more open to an antirealist interpretation. Indeed, they do exactly the opposite: Postmodern therapists, in violation of their own professed antirealism, anti-objectivism, or constructivism/social constructionism, and even in violation of their own professed anti-"generalism," still make the universal claim that their therapeutic method helps all clients lead better lives—in reality! They make the practical claim that their narrative method is not only useful, it is truly or objectively useful. And they often go on to provide causal explanations of a conventionally objective or scientific sort to account for the effectiveness of their method. To be sure, then, the practical claim is itself a truth claim—a perfectly traditional ontological or causal claim[8]—that opposes the radical anti-realism or anti-objectivism of many postmodern therapists (see, e.g., Erwin, 1999a; Held, 1995, 1998b).

Whatever postmodern therapists consider the practical virtues of their epistemological doctrine to be, the fact of the matter is we can advocate strongly in favor of realism or objectivism and still hold tentatively any formulation—be it a scientific (theoretical) generality or an inference about a particular case— hold it, that is, with an openness to revision contingent on new evidence, including, in the case of therapy, the client's progress. Open-mindedness is not solely a postmodernist or antirealist virtue. Contrary to what many antirealists suppose, realism does not commit knowers to unwarranted claims to knowledge, or to dogmatic, authoritarian, absolutist, or static proclamations, or to leaving one's values at the door to the lab or the therapy consultation room, or to knowledge claims about all aspects of reality (Erwin, 1997, 1999a, p. 354, 1999b; Haack, 1996, 1998, 1999). Nor does the situatedness of the knower in the field to be known, including fields that are heavily value laden, preclude the successful striving for objectivity—by which I mean the striving for knowledge of how things *are:* If that striving were a fruitless fiction, there would indeed be no distinction between facts and values, between knower and known, as postmodernists like to proclaim. Realist knowing requires *both* a commitment to, a trust in, one's findings once there is sufficient evidence to warrant their assertion, *and* an openness to revision if further evidence calls for it. It does not require an inhuman or robotic knower: What one knows and how one feels about or evaluates the knowledge one has worked hard to attain, can, contrary to postmodernists, be distinguished from each other. Moreover, there is no automatic commitment to antirealism in the view, pervasive in postmodernist circles (and quite correct according to mounting cognitive psychology evidence), that knowers *actively* work to construct knowledge of reality rather than receiving it passively from the environment. I include in this cognitive activity the construction of theories to attain indirectly the many aspects of reality to which we have no direct rational awareness (Held, 1998b).

A realist or objectivist epistemology requires only that knowers can, in principle, attain some knowledge of, some approximation to, an extra-theoretical or independent reality; that knowers can have sufficient warrant for their assertions; and that they accept the limits of knowing (Erwin, 1999a; Haack, 1996, 1998, 1999; Pols, 1992, 1998). Scandalous stuff, this, in these postmodern days of perspectival "truth." But without the conviction that comes from hard-won evidence that gives warrant for our assertions, it would be difficult indeed to advocate our views—to truly take the responsibility for our views that postmodernists say they want to take.

More to the practical point, what therapist—postmodernist or otherwise—would want to argue that we should not strive to get the unique realities of our clients' lives as right as possible? After all, it is not inconceivable that those who hold the postmodernist notion that there is no objective truth to be had nonetheless practice in ways that are indistinguishable from those who hold the nonpostmodernist notion that working to approximate objective truth or reality is no waste of time (Held, 1998a, p. 269). Of course, whether postmodernist practice can be distinguished from nonpostmodernist practice is an empirical question (see Erwin, 1999a, pp. 363-364), as is the question of just what any particular client's difficulties and goals consist in.

I submit that therapists of all stripes must pay close attention to their clients. Moreover, if a therapist prefers to use a minimalist theoretical system, the kind postmodernist therapists profess, then the unique nuances of the client's life might dictate the content of therapy even more thoroughly, since there is little else to guide practice. Not surprising, in their writings postmodern therapists do indeed espouse giving keen attention to the unique particularities of their clients' lives (e.g., Hoyt, 1994; Neimeyer & Mahoney, 1995). But these therapists surely do not espouse giving keen attention for the purpose of getting an understanding of the client that bears no relationship to the client's true concerns: They seem just as concerned with knowing those concerns as do nonpostmodern therapists. That is to say, they seem to want a *realistic* picture of the client, a striving that means they operate in practice by virtue of a more realist or objectivist epistemology than they claim to use. After all, I doubt that they would argue that their prescription of keen observation gets them no closer to knowing what the nature of the client's experience of herself and the world really is than would nonkeen observation—no closer, that is, to having good warrant for their narrative constructions and reconstructions. If that were so, why bother to observe keenly? Or why bother to observe anything at all?

Yet that is exactly what their self-proclaimed adoption of antirealism or anti-objectivism implies. For it applies not only to the theoretical generalities postmodern therapists, in their antisystematic aspiration, wish to eliminate (except, of course, their own generalities) but also to all of life, including the lives of clients. No aspect of life is exempt from the sweeping antirealist, anti-objectivist, or constructivist/constructionist epistemology that many postmodern therapists vehemently propound. Of course, I maintain that these therapists do not *practice* antirealism when they strive to know what their clients think, feel, and do about their lives, an activity that can be distinguished from the value-laden activity of deciding what to *do* about those facts. Nor are there persuasive reasons to think that clients' personal meanings, views, or understandings must be given an antirealist interpretation simply because they are unique. This indeed constitutes the "negative philosophical judgment" about knowing that defines postmodernism, a judgment to which I now turn.

Solutions in Sight and the
Negative Philosophical Judgment

Fortunately, there is relief from the excesses of postmodernist epistemology in sight. This relief takes the form of attempts to solve the problem of the individualized or particularized nature of psychotherapy practice—of life or experience itself—without endorsing the extreme relativism of postmodernism. Here I briefly summarize three such cases, all of which favor a hermeneutic approach to psychology and psychotherapy by claiming that it is less distortive of the realities of lived experience, especially of the (self)interpretive nature of all human existence, than is the objectivist epistemology of the natural sciences that these authors wish to replace.

In *Re-Envisioning Psychology*, Richardson et al. (1999) challenge the excessive commitment to an individualistic or instrumental ethical ideal that they find in *both* modern and postmodern psychology and psychotherapy. They emphasize the trade-off between, on the one hand, the glorification of an individualistic autonomy in therapy, the (legitimate) striving for freedom from dogmatic generalities, and, on the other hand, the search for a basis of legitimate authority for individualistic ideals and goals, for obtaining meaningful commitments. The more autonomous we each become, the less foundation we have for our values; if we want to avoid the relativity or subjectivity of values to which both modernism and postmodernism fall prey, we must transcend our unique selves and goals, or so they argue persuasively.

Richardson et al.'s solution entails a hermeneutic approach to psychology and psychotherapy, which would infuse therapy with more communitarian or dialogical values by situating the individual knower in a web of cultural meanings, values, and background knowledge, all of which determine or constitute identity, affect, and behavior—the very stuff of psychology and psychotherapy. Rather than making practice more individualized or liberated by helping clients find their own subjective postmodern "voice" or "personal knowledge," they question the value of liberal individualism (and resulting instrumentalism) as an ethical foundation for both modern and postmodern practice. And although they do not directly concern themselves with the problem of particularizing practice as I have construed it, they do suggest, unlike both modern and postmodern therapeutic trends, that the content of therapy should incorporate a shared or dialogical search for answers to the fundamental moral question of how best to live our lives in the concrete (i.e., particular) situations (p. 263) in which we exist. But they take the problem of uniqueness seriously, by arguing that "each instance of [any] practice represents a unique interpretation . . . that in some measure redefines the practice" (p. 284). This of course constitutes the hermeneutic circle that for them calls into question the objectivist epistemology and natural scientific approach to therapy that is an object of their critique.

In *The Cure of Souls*, Woolfolk (1998) also criticizes the liberal individualism of modernity. But he expresses more direct concern with the problem of particularity and generality as I have construed it, by striving to infuse a scientific approach to psychotherapy, which provides necessary generalized knowledge, with the humanist's idiographic emphasis: "Humanists are correct in emphasizing the uniqueness of individual human beings and the difficulty of discovering scientific generalizations that usefully inform our understanding of individual persons" (p. 4). In addressing "The Idiographic Nature of Psychotherapy and Self-Understanding," he confronts the problem I have defined straightforwardly: "Psychotherapy is an application of this general [nomothetic] knowledge to a specific case that is always, in some respects, unique" (p. 92). Moreover, he links particularity to epistemology: "Some of the epistemic precariousness of psychotherapy . . . has to do with circumstances that are inevitable when what is known generally to be true is applied to particular cases, or when singular, person-specific knowledge is discovered and developed" (p. 91).

Woolfolk believes that scientific generalities are limited in their application to the human world, which must be understood by virtue of the particular contexts and values that give life its meanings and its malleability—both of which scientific laws and propositions and their technical application cannot incorporate (see Erwin, 1999b, in press, for analysis of the idiographic and subjectivity problems, respectively). Woolfolk disengages the postmodernist link between particularity and relativism by suggesting the use of humanistic critical interpretive or hermeneutic traditions—for example, the idiographic methods of history, law, and philosophy—to assess the truth of knowledge claims about the human world. And he combats the relativism of postmodernism's constructivist and constructionist epistemologies by claiming they have imported a distorted version of hermeneutics, one that eliminates truth and validity altogether in favor of "internal coherence, aesthetic appeal, or therapeutic efficacy" (p. 134). He relieves the words truth and validity of their postmodernist scare quotes, but he also qualifies, or at least changes, the definition of truth so as to relativize it to our context or horizon: "Understanding the actions of human beings involves uncovering truth, but truth that is constrained by a sociocultural horizon, truth that can be identified only from a particular vantage point" (p. 136).

In *The Case for Pragmatic Psychology*, Fishman (1999), like Woolfolk, tackles the problem of applying general knowledge to the unique particularities of individual cases. He too considers such biographically oriented traditions as case law and journalism as models for a less scientistic approach to therapy and wants to take what is best from both the data-based nomothetic ideal of modern positivist psychology and the contextually or interpretatively nuanced idiographic ideal of hermeneutic postmodern psychology to produce his own blend, which he calls a "case-based pragmatic psychology." But unlike Woolfolk, Fishman finds the human world so filled with unique complexities and contexts, so full of flux and change, that an unqualified postmodernist or constructionist epistemology—with all requisite scare quotes—is called for to understand it:

> Philosophical pragmatism is founded upon a social constructionist theory of knowledge. The world that exists independently of our minds is an unlimited complex of change and novelty, order and disorder. To understand and cope with the world, we take on different conceptual perspectives, as we might put on different pairs of glasses, with each providing us a different perspective on the world. The pragmatic "truth" of a particular perspective does not lie in its correspondence to "objective reality,"[9] since that reality is in constant flux. Rather, the pragmatic truth of a particular perspective lies in the usefulness of the perspective in helping us to cope and solve particular problems and achieve particular goals in today's world. (p. 130)

Fishman's solution to the generality-particularity problem is a science not of universal, decontextualized laws but of an ever-expanding database of specific cases that clinicians can match to target cases to guide them in dealing practically with the unique particularities that they inevitably encounter. Fishman seeks "guiding conceptions" or "conceptual guidelines" whose standard of warrant is limited to pragmatic utility. Thus he clearly realizes the limits of unique particularity in constructing a new *discipline* of psychology, which like any discipline necessitates generality: "The pragmatist agrees with the positivist about the value of generalizing, but also with the hermeneut about the need to retain context" (p. 291).

These three books offer new visions for psychology and psychotherapy, visions that wrestle with important assumptions, both ontological and epistemological, including the problem of getting from generality to particularity in any applied context. I applaud their incisive analyses and their unique visions for our field. But I do not find any of the reasons given for qualifying (if not dismissing) objectivity to be persuasive—not an ontology of "being in the world" or of flux and disorder, not the inherent value ladeness or subjectivity of therapeutic practice, not the problem of an individualistic or instrumental ethic, not the fact of human self interpretation, not the need to stay open to revision, and not even the problem of unique, contextualized particularity that I myself have explored. These authors have surely made observations that deserve nothing short of the descriptor "objective," because there is another way out of the problem of linking the particularized (or contextualized) and interpretive or (meaning-making) nature of our being with objective knowing, and that entails the courage to give individual knowers, in all their unique particularity, the agency that these authors appear to value: the agency to know what is the case, and so to be able to make a case.

Notes

1. Fishman (1999, pp. 5-9) differentiates four types of postmodernism—skeptical, critical, ontological, and pragmatic—each of which emphasizes one or more of the following six themes: foundationlessness, fragmentariness, constructivism, critical theory, ontological hermeneutics, and neopragmatism. He argues that "within psychology, it is mainly the skeptical and critical visions of postmodernism that have gained prominence," visions that reject the "hegemony of modernist, positivist psychology" (p. 7).

2. Throughout this chapter, I use these terms interchangeably to denote a postmodern or antirealist epistemology. At times I select some terms over others, depending on my intended emphasis.

3. See Held (1998b) for a discussion of the three most fundamental claims of social constructionism, and Held (1995, 1996a) for distinctions between the doctrines of social constructionism and constructivism.

4. See Held (1995, 1996b, 1998a, 1999a, 1999b) for additional quotations.

5. Note the repudiation of a "directly knowable external reality." This repudiation does not automatically reject a realist (or objectivist) epistemology, as the author appears to suppose, because realism does not require that all reality be known directly (i.e., without theoretical mediation) to be known with objectivity (see Held, 1995, 1998a; Pols, 1992).

6. Can meanings ever be truly unique, given their alleged constitution in cultural, historical, linguistic contexts? My question here pertains to the particularity or generality of that context: How broadly or narrowly should it be defined to interpret the meaning of anyone's discourse?

7. See Gergen (1998), who argues that the antirealist/antifoundational epistemological doctrine of social constructionism implies, by definition, a minimalist approach to theoretical content.

8. Antirealist philosophers of science sometimes support the making of such claims by denying that they are made in a traditional ontological spirit. They sometimes refer to the notion of "ontology of a language" to avoid the contradiction of making claims about how things are in the context of an antirealist or anti-objectivist epistemology. See Pols (1992, 1998) for elaboration.

9. See Haack (1996, 1997, 1998) for a challenge to this postmodernist or antirealist interpretation of pragmatism, especially on the part of the postmodern philosopher Richard Rorty.

References

Best, S., & Kellner, D. (1991). *Postmodern theory: Critical interrogations.* New York: Guilford.

Erwin, E. (1997). *Philosophy and psychotherapy.* London: Sage.

Erwin, E. (1999a). Constructivist epistemologies and therapies. *British Journal of Guidance and Counselling, 27,* 353-365.

Erwin, E. (1999b). *Is a science of psychotherapy possible? The subjectivity problem.* Manuscript submitted for publication.

Erwin, E. (in press). How valuable are psychotherapy experiments? The idiographic problem. *Journal of Clinical Psychology.*

Fishman, D. B. (1999). *The case for pragmatic psychology.* New York: New York University Press.

Freedman, J., & Combs, G. (1996). *Narrative therapy: The social construction of preferred realities.* New York: Norton.

Friedman, S. (Ed.). (1993). *The new language of change: Constructive collaboration in psychotherapy.* New York: Guilford.

Gergen, K. J. (1998). The place of material in a constructed world. *Family Process, 37,* 415-423.

Gergen, K. J., & Kaye, J. (1992). Beyond narrative in the negotiation of therapeutic meaning. In S. McNamee & K. J. Gergen (Eds.), *Therapy as social construction* (pp. 166-185). Newbury Park, CA: Sage.

Haack, S. (1996). Science as social?—Yes and no. In L. H. Nelson & J. Nelson (Eds.), *Feminism, science, and the philosophy of science* (pp. 79-93). Dordrecht, The Netherlands: Kluwer Academic Publishers.

Haack, S. (1997). "We pragmatists . . . .": Peirce and Rorty in conversation. *Partisan Review, 64,* 91-107.

Haack, S. (1998). *Manifesto of a passionate moderate: Unfashionable essays.* Chicago: University of Chicago Press.

Haack, S. (1999, July 9). Staying for an answer: The untidy process of groping for truth. *Times Literary Supplement,* pp. 12-14.

Held, B. S. (1995). *Back to reality: A critique of postmodern theory in psychotherapy.* New York: Norton.

Held, B. S. (1996a). Constructivism in psychotherapy: Truth and consequences. In P. R. Gross, N. Levitt, & M. W. Lewis (Eds.), *The flight from science and reason (Annals of the New York Academy of Sciences,* Vol. 775, pp. 198-206). New York: New York Academy of Sciences.

Held, B. S. (1996b). Solution-focused therapy and the postmodern: A critical analysis. In S. Miller, M. Hubble, & B. Duncan (Eds.), *The handbook of solution-focused brief therapy* (pp. 27-43). San Francisco: Jossey-Bass.

Held, B. S. (1998a). The antisystematic impact of postmodern philosophy. *Clinical Psychology: Science and Practice, 5,* 264-273.

Held, B. S. (1998b). The many truths of postmodernist discourse. *Journal of Theoretical and Philosophical Psychology, 18,* 193-217.

Held, B. S. (1999a). How brief therapy got postmodern, or, Where's the brief? In W. J. Matthews & J. H. Edgette (Eds.), *Current thinking and research in brief therapy* (Vol. 3, pp. 135-164). New York: Brunner/Mazel.

Held, B. S. (1999b). The question for postmodern therapists: To be or not to be theoretical. *Symposium, 3,* 5-26.

Held, B. S. (1999c). Reasons and reason: A reply to Morrison. *Symposium, 3,* 43-52.

Hoyt, M. F. (Ed.). (1994). *Constructive therapies.* New York: Guilford.

Hoyt, M. F. (1996). Introduction: Some stories are better than others. In M. F. Hoyt (Ed.), *Constructive therapies* (Vol. 2, pp. 1-32). New York: Guilford.

Kvale, S. (Ed). (1992). *Psychology and postmodernism.* London: Sage.

McNamee, S., & Gergen, K. J. (Eds.). (1992). *Therapy as social construction.* Newbury Park, CA: Sage.

Neimeyer, R. A. (1993). An appraisal of constructivist psychotherapies. *Journal of Consulting and Clinical Psychology, 61,* 221-234.

Neimeyer, R. A., & Mahoney, M. J. (Eds.). (1995). *Constructivism in psychotherapy.* Washington, DC: American Psychological Association.

Omer, H., & Alon, N. (1997). *Constructing therapeutic narratives.* Northvale, NJ: Jason Aronson.

Parry, A., & Doan, R. E. (1994). *Story re-visions: Narrative therapy in the postmodern world.* New York: Guilford.

Pols, E. (1992). *Radical realism: Direct knowing in science and philosophy.* Ithaca, NY: Cornell University Press.

Pols, E. (1998). *Mind regained.* Ithaca, NY: Cornell University Press.

Richardson, F. C., Fowers, B. J., & Guignon, C. B. (1999). *Re-envisioning psychology: Moral dimensions of theory and practice.* San Francisco: Jossey-Bass.

Rosen, H., & Kuehlwein, K. T. (Eds.). (1996). *Constructing realities: Meaning-making perspectives for psychotherapists.* San Francisco: Jossey-Bass.

Rosenau, P. M. (1992). *Post-modernism and the social sciences: Insights, inroads, and intrusions.* Princeton, NJ: Princeton University Press.

White, M., & Epston, D. (1990). *Narrative means to therapeutic ends.* New York: Norton.

Woolfolk, R. L. (1998). *The cure of souls: Science, values, and psychotherapy.* San Francisco: Jossey-Bass.

Commentary

The Dilemma of Realism and Antirealism: A Response to Held's Postmodern Turn

Amy Fisher Smith
Texas A&M University—Commerce

In her chapter, Barbara Held examines postmodernism and its implications for psychotherapy. From her perspective, postmodernism (especially in its social-constructionist forms) is characterized in part by its denial of "general, objective laws and truths in favor of local, unique, contextualized, or subjective 'truths.'" She views postmodernism's flat rejection of independent, objective truths as a reflection of its commitment to "antirealism," a form of "anti-objectivist" epistemology. Given the postmodernist commitment to antirealism, Held argues that at least two therapeutic implications follow.

First, because there are no "objective" truths of human nature and only multiple "subjective" truths, predetermined psychological theorizing or laws ought to be dismissed. This dismissal allows the therapist to focus on the subjective truths of the client, which are relative to each individual and unique client. Second, postmodernists attempt to keep pretheoretical and predetermined concepts to a minimum in practice to better comprehend the client's unique experiences and meanings.

Of course, the irony, from Held's view, is that postmodern therapists do not practice according to their formal antirealist epistemological theorizing. In their attempts to gain a clear or realistic view of their clients' particular subjectivities, Held contends, postmodern therapists betray an implicit reliance on more realist or objective epistemologies rather than the antirealism they theoretically espouse.

I certainly agree with Held that, as therapist, one needs access to the reality or truth of the client if one is to be successful in therapy. The therapist has to know what clients' personal values, beliefs, and experiences mean to them. Indeed, it is from this knowing that therapists exercise clinical judgment, rendering case conceptualizations and therapeutic interventions. Furthermore, as Held suggests, this knowing cannot be limited to knowledge of the client. Most therapists—even those of a constructivist postmodern bent—implicitly depend on general clinical knowledge in addition to knowledge of the client.

A practical question that arises in this discussion of knowledge and truth, however, is how we come to know what we know about clients. Certainly, as Held suggests, therapists come to know, or at least strive to know, something about clients. But does this striving for a "realistic picture" of the client constitute a knowledge of the client that is objective, absolute, and independent from the therapist? Held may be arguing for such an objectivist or realist epistemological possibility. Indeed, she asserts that the postmodernists are guilty of implementing such a possibility in their practice.

The possibility of achieving a realistic view of the client that approximates an objective knowledge independent of the therapist seems to have some practical difficulties. In my view, these practical difficulties hinge on the necessity for therapist values suspension that accompanies the realist's epistemological agenda. In other words, I see values suspension as a necessary, yet problematic, therapeutic strategy when realism is the philosophical grounds of therapy. For example, to achieve an "objective" view of clients, therapists must remove or suspend their biases, values, and beliefs. From the standpoint of realism, such values and beliefs can only cloud and obscure the supposed "reality" of clients. Hence therapists must attempt to adopt a neutral or transparent position by suspending their values to obtain the most objective, and therefore accurate, view of clients.

Even the postmodern therapists—who deny the possibility of achieving such "objective" knowledge—seem to implicitly endorse values suspension in the service of achieving a clearer view of the client. Of course, Held considers this search for a clearer "reality" evidence for the postmodernist reliance on realism. Indeed, in their efforts to minimize the role of psychological theory while maximizing clients' subjectivities, postmodern therapists seemingly endorse realist assumptions. That is, in practice, postmodern therapists may unwittingly attempt to adopt an "objective" view of their clients through therapist values suspension. As with therapists who endorse realism, then, antirealist postmodern therapists appear equally committed to values suspension as a means of understanding their clients' unique life experiences as objectively, and therefore as accurately, as possible.

Therapist values suspension actually serves dual purposes for the postmodern therapist. In addition to facilitating understanding and accurate knowledge of the client, suspending values supposedly helps protect clients' subjective realities from outside influences. For example, therapists must suspend their values lest they contaminate clients' subjective reality or truth. If the therapist's values are expressed in the therapy process, clients may be less likely to pursue their own subjective and unique truths, opting instead to follow the therapist's personal values.

For a postmodern or antirealist therapist who valorizes the subjective, this is tantamount to client indoctrination and manipulation. Recall that the new constructions or new narrative meanings that serve to help the client during therapy must emanate *from* the *client*—not from the therapist. Therefore therapists must hide or suspend their values during therapy to prevent such undue influence on the client. The upshot is that both the antirealist position and the realist position suggest the practical necessity for therapist values suspension— either in the service of privileging the client's subjectivity or for achieving an objective view.

The problem is that the suspension or potential removal of therapist values—a clinical strategy that both epistemological alternatives seem to implicate—has been challenged, both empirically and theoretically (Bergin, 1980; Beutler, 1979; Cushman, 1993; Jensen & Bergin, 1988: Jones, 1994; London, 1986; Richards & Bergin, 1997). Rather than being escapable or suspendable, therapist values are now thought to be unavoidable, and many researchers have addressed the inescapable sociopolitical impact of therapist values on clients (Beutler & Bergan, 1991; Kelly & Strupp, 1992).

Both the realist and antirealist positions may be problematic, then, from a practical standpoint, given the impossibility of suspending therapist values. From the stance of value inescapability, any view of the client is always and already an interpreted view. Therapists' views of clients are interpreted through the therapists' values, beliefs, and expectations. Therefore the possibility of achieving objective or realist knowledge of the client is hampered because the therapist, or knower, cannot be separated from what is known (i.e., the client). This inseparability between therapist and client also compromises the antirealist's attempts at protecting the client's subjectivity from outside influences (e.g., the therapist's values).

When knowing is discussed in the context of interpretation, it may appear that we have returned to notions of "subjective," "perspectival," and "relative" knowledge, espoused by the antirealist postmodernists. But emphasizing the inescapability of values and the primacy of interpretation does not necessarily lead us back to the assumptions of multiple subjective truths and relativism. Nonrelativistic and meaningful truths or knowledge can exist in value-laden interpretations (Richardson, Fowers, & Guignon, 1999). Indeed, this appears to be the case with psychotherapy. Therapists certainly hold truths and make truth claims in relation to their clients. These truth claims are founded on therapists' orienting values framework and ultimately guide treatment strategies and clinical interventions.

Of course, these truths and truth claims are not absolute and independent truths. When therapeutic truths are considered to be "objective" and static representations of an independent reality, clients potentially suffer detrimental effects. Clients suffer, because in the face of therapeutic "objective" truths, clients lose their possibility to be "other than" what the objective truth dictates. For example, I may come to know my clients through the knowledge and truth of the diagnostic categories of the *Diagnostic and Statistical Manual of Mental Disorders* (*DSM-IV*; American Psychiatric Association, 1994). If I treat the *DSM-IV* categories as an objective and independent truth, then clients can never exceed these categorical boundaries. In this case, the clients' diagnoses and the categories of mental illness are a greater or more significant reality than clients themselves. Clients become their diagnoses and the possibilities for change are limited.

As Held contends, therapists rely on a "realistic" knowledge of clients. In seeking such a "realistic" view, therapists gain knowledge of the client that facilitates client understanding and therapeutic direction. This knowledge cannot be the objective and independent knowledge asserted by a realist epistemology, however. Because therapists are unable to suspend or remove their values and beliefs, attaining an "objective" view of clients is problematic, if not impossible. Knowing the client, then, means interpreting the client through a preexisting set of grounding values that implicitly hold truth claims in relation to the client.

References

American Psychiatric Association. (1994). *Diagnostic and statistical manual of mental disorders* (4th ed.). Washington, DC: Author.

Bergin, A. E. (1980). Psychotherapy and religious values. *Journal of Consulting and Clinical Psychology, 48*(1), 95-105.

Beutler, L. E. (1979). Values, beliefs, religion and the persuasive influence of psychotherapy. *Psychotherapy: Theory, Research, and Practice, 16*(4), 432-440.

Beutler, L. E., & Bergan, J. (1991). Value change in counseling and psychotherapy: A search for scientific credibility. *Journal of Counseling Psychology, 38,* 16-24.

Cushman, P. (1993). Psychotherapy as moral discourse. *Journal of Theoretical and Philosophical Psychology, 13*(2), 103-113.

Jensen, J. P., & Bergin, A. E. (1988). Mental health values of professional therapists: A national Interdisciplinary survey. *Professional Psychology: Research and Practice, 19*(3), 290-297.

Jones, S. L. (1994). A constructive relationship for religion with the science and profession of psychology: Perhaps the boldest model yet. *American Psychologist, 49*(3), 184-199.

Kelly, T. A., & Strupp, H. H. (1992). Patient and therapist values in psychotherapy: Perceived changes, assimilation, similarity, and outcome. *Journal of Consulting and Clinical Psychology, 60*(1), 34-40.

London, P. (1986). *The modes and morals of psychotherapy* (2nd ed.). New York: Hemisphere.

Richards, P. S., & Bergin, A. E. (1997). *A spiritual strategy for counseling and psychotherapy.* Washington, DC: American Psychological Association Press.

Richardson F. C., Fowers, B. J., & Guignon, C. (1999). *Re-envisioning psychology: Moral dimensions of theory and practice.* San Francisco: Jossey-Bass.

Issue 12

Multiculturalism

Culture, Identity, and Loyalty

New Pathways for a Culturally Aware Psychotherapy

Blaine J. Fowers
University of Miami

Matters of culture have become a central preoccupation in our profession and in our society. Our collective deliberations and struggles about fashioning a reasonable approach to cultural differences is one of the defining conversations of our time. The social and intellectual movement commonly known as multiculturalism has galvanized a great deal of energy for rectifying the wrongs of racism and oppression and for increasing our acceptance of the value of diversity. It has called on us to deepen our recognition and appreciation of culture as a source of identity and meaning that should be respected and honored. In all of these respects, this movement speaks to the best in us and exhorts us to become better, more open, and more willing to embrace differentness. Multiculturalism has been necessary and beneficial, for there are many wrongs to be righted, there has been widespread prejudice and discrimination, and we have squandered untold social and intellectual resources out of sheer intolerance. There is no question but that the campaign for appreciating diversity has deeply affected our profession, just as it has influenced education, business, political activity, and society at large.

It is clear that multiculturalism is, at its core, a moral movement, one that is deeply concerned with what is right and wrong, better and worse, and that its persuasiveness is moral in origin. My colleagues and I have argued elsewhere that the power of this movement and its ability to influence psychology and mainstream society derives from its ability to appeal to the deeply held cultural values of the majority culture (Fowers & Richardson, 1996). This ability to evoke the values and ideals of Western civilization in support of honoring diversity does not mean that multiculturalism is solely a product of Western thought. This movement draws on many sources, but a significant part of its genius has been the way that it shows us in the West that the value of diversity is written into our heritage in spite of the frequent practice of intolerance.

Historically, our profession has been rather reluctantly prodded to recognize the importance of culture in human life. Strident appeals for respecting diversity have played an important role in establishing an intellectual and moral beachhead for recognizing the role of culture in psychology. Because the importance of cultural matters has now been largely accepted in the profession, however, we need to move beyond the militant cultural politics and the platitudes about respecting culture that have brought us this far. Ironically, in the drive to increase acceptance of cultural diversity, culture is often romanticized and mystified. Accepting cultural differences often seems to require that we refrain from questioning or engaging in a robust dialogue about cultural beliefs, practices, and customs. This sanctification of culture paralyzes us and impedes our ability to address important questions about culture in our professional work.

We need to develop practical frameworks that allow us to constructively engage cultural issues. The primary purpose of this chapter is to make culture more accessible and intelligible in the therapeutic setting by giving a more nuanced account of cultural attachments than we usually find in the literature. A secondary purpose is to indicate that culture is a primary theme in all of our professional work, whether we are working with people from a different cultural background or with people who share our background.

Culture and Identity

The question I want to address is not so much why we should respect other cultural ways of life, but what it is that we should respect. What is the tie that binds individuals to cultures so strongly? What is it about that bond that calls for respect and honor? The crux of valuing cultural differences seems to reside in two related beliefs: (a) that our cultural roots are an essential part of our identities, and (b) that everyone has the right to live in harmony with his or her cultural background. Appreciating the importance of culture means seeing that membership in a cultural group entails a particular kind of self-understanding, a more or less well defined view of one's place in the world, and a set of customs that outline the proper way to live. Thus we are acknowledging that cultural embeddedness is a powerful part of identity. I want to explore the nature of this profound bond between individuals and their cultural groups and what that means for addressing culture in psychotherapy.

I begin illustrating cultural attachments with the Rodriguez family. José and Yvette brought their 13-year-old son, Carlos, to our clinic recently for individual therapy. They were very unhappy with his behavior and wanted us to straighten him out. Being a family therapist by inclination and training, I instructed the student therapist who would work with them to have the whole family come to the first session. José was reluctant because he was busy and he felt that Yvette could explain the problem very well without him. Both parents were clear that the problem was with Carlos and their participation in therapy was not necessary. They reluctantly agreed to come, however.

In the first meeting, José and Yvette explained that Carlos had become very disobedient in the last year and a half. They were upset that he was spending time with the wrong kind of peers and they found his preference for rap music offensive. Their relationship with him was mired in a power struggle and the more they asserted their authority, the more defiant he became. In response to the latest parental ultimatum, Carlos had run away from home for a period of 2 weeks.

As his parents related this account of the difficulties they were having, Carlos sat slumped and sullen on the opposite side of the room. He was wearing enormously baggy jeans and a t-shirt with a belligerent rap group glaring out on the front. He responded to the therapist in monosyllables when she asked for his viewpoint. Even though he was nearly silent verbally, Carlos was shouting his opposition to his parents and to the therapy through his silence, his posture, and his clothing.

The Rodriguezes were fortunate that this scenario was not at all new to their therapist. She had seen several families with similar difficulties and she had lived this struggle with her own family as a first-generation Cuban American. She addressed immigration and acculturation issues early and found out that José and Yvette had emigrated from Colombia when Carlos was 2 years old. In the first session, she began to explore their immigration experience and to have them talk about the way they were raised in Colombia. José and Yvette were dumbfounded when Carlos first began to disobey them because they would never have considered being so disrespectful toward their parents. His defiance was a stinging humiliation to them because it so thoroughly repudiated their cultural understanding of how a family should operate.

Clearly, one of the central problems in this family was that it found itself in the front lines of a cultural conflict between the parents' more traditional Colombian values and the youth culture of the United States. The parents assumed that they would raise Carlos and their other children according to the norms they had learned in Colombia. When Carlos was small, that seemed to work out fine. As he entered adolescence, their plan for their family began to collapse. Carlos was walking the well-worn path of the adolescent rebel in American culture. He flew the flag of his demand for personal independence from every flagpole he could find. He had absorbed the central message of popular American culture that individual autonomy is an entitlement and is necessary to living a worthwhile life.

Recognizing the cultural dimension of this case was crucial to its successful resolution, but it poses some interesting questions as well. Why were José and Yvette so attached to their Colombian roots when they had intentionally left their country to come to the United States? How is it that Carlos had become so estranged from his Columbian roots? How does mainstream American culture exert such a strong influence on the young?

Identity

The extreme form of individualism in American culture, with its preoccupation with the separateness and independence of individuals, leads us to seriously underestimate the degree to which we become who we are because we live in our particular communities and nation. The philosopher Martin Heidegger (1962) provides a compelling account of the degree to which our identities are formed by our cultural environment. He reminds us that when we are born, we enter a social world that was complete before we arrived. It is richly endowed with meanings and commitments, many of which we inherit simply by being born into it. This life world surrounds us from our birth and forms the context in which our thoughts, feelings, and actions are made intelligible. A large part of becoming fully human is learning how to operate in and through the customs, values, and expectations of our families, our communities, and our cultural groups. This learning begins almost from the moment of birth and is very advanced before any of us has a chance to choose what we will learn and whether we want to accept this social world that is shaping us. We feel at home in our social world because we are woven into it.

Because we have to learn what it means to be human from our caretakers and the social world we inhabit, we find our initial possibilities for life in our surroundings. The shared understandings, customs, and practices of our cultural group are a kind of "cultural atmosphere" that we take in with every breath because it surrounds us continually. We are shaped by the meanings and aims of this life world without even noticing it, partly because these shared understandings are seldom stated explicitly. We absorb the meanings and aims of this life world from the ways in which our caretakers and teachers act and expect us to act. Because these shared understandings about life are assumed by everyone around us, we typically see them as self-evident. Just like the air we breath, we only notice the cultural customs that surround us when there is some disturbance, when someone does not do what we expect.

One of my favorite examples of how strongly culture shapes us is the ubiquity of time consciousness in modern civilization. It is remarkable how much we govern our activities and lives by the clock in mainstream American culture. Virtually everyone wears a watch, and we have clocks in almost every room. We make appointments, schedule our workdays, plan our meals, go to sleep, and wake up by the clock. We think of time as a limited and precious commodity, as if we only have so much time and time is money. When someone does not wear a watch or is late for a meeting, he or she risks being seen as irresponsible or inconsiderate. Even though some people take it more seriously than others, very few people actually disregard time. Arranging our activities according to this shared conception of time requires tremendous social coordination because it only works if virtually everyone participates. We take our time consciousness so much for granted that we even tend to forget that clocks have only been widely available for a little over 200 years. It is easy to find cultures where the awareness of the time of day or the date is considerably more fluid. The combination of the power of time consciousness and the way we take it for granted illustrates how profoundly our lives are shaped by our cultural understandings.

Our Social Selves

One of the defining narratives in our individualistic culture is to see ourselves as individuals pitted against a social world that constrains us and works against our attempts to realize our "genuine inner selves." Somewhat against the grain, Heidegger (1962) makes the intriguing suggestion that our membership in a social group is not a limitation or a burden. Instead, being a member of a social group actually enables us to become human in the first place. We can only obtain a real sense of substantial, meaningful identity through participating in a social group. Our belonging in a family, community, and culture gives us a way of life and a place in the world. Our cultural background provides us with a framework of meanings that gives us a grasp of things and shows us who we are and how we can act in that world. If we lacked this cultural background, we would not be free spirits or noble savages, but disoriented and impoverished, lacking any coherent direction in our lives. According to Heidegger, being an authentic person is not a matter of throwing off our cultural shells and freeing our inner nature, but of learning how to take up our heritage and to realize shared possibilities in a more coherent, focused, and creative way. After all, the idea that it is better to be a separate, independent individual is something that we learn through participation in our individualistically oriented culture. It is a shared ideal that is taught and reinforced in myriad ways. We do not share this ideal of individual freedom because we have all somehow magically arrived at it independently, but, ironically, because we have been taught individualism in our social group.

Obviously, we have choices in our lives, particularly as we mature and begin to reflect on our place in our social world and begin to recognize that it is possible to question meanings and practices that we usually take for granted. Exercising this freedom helps to give our lives a particular shape. The human ability to self-reflect and to reinterpret one's life creates the space for a self-constituting dialectic between individual freedom and cultural embeddedness. On the one hand, we inevitably draw our choices from the culturally given possibilities available to us. This means that we are always tied to our cultural upbringing and it makes our choices and actions understandable to others and compatible with our social world. On the other hand, we can reinterpret what we have inherited to create new prospects for living. In fact, every time we engage in a cultural practice, we are interpreting it, which makes the reinterpretation of culture almost continuous. As my colleagues and I have said elsewhere, "Our nature or being as humans is not just something we find (as in deterministic theories), nor is it something we just make (as in existential or constructionist views), instead, it is what we make of what we find" (Richardson, Fowers, & Guignon, 1999, p. 212).

Loyalty

From the foregoing, we can see that our identities are largely defined by our participation in a particular family, educational setting, occupation, cultural group, religious group, nation, and so forth. Fletcher (1993) discusses the connection between our identities and our social belonging in terms of loyalty. He highlights the deep attachment we feel toward the people and groups with whom we share a significant history. We tend to be partial or biased toward those with whom we live and who share important characteristics with us. Our loyalty to those with whom we have shared a significant past is due to the fact that our shared history helps to make us who we are. We are loyal to our families and our nation originally because our identities are inextricably tied to those attachments.

The dimensions of loyalty include a minimum condition in which we reject actions or ties that would constitute a betrayal and a maximum where we have a devoted or affirmative disposition toward the object of loyalty. For example, citizenship might entail no more than a minimal, passive loyalty that demands only that we do not join the enemy. In contrast, patriotism is a stronger form of loyalty, characterized by ardent affection and few limitations on commitment. For the patriot, the good of his or her country is his or her own good. Loyalty can become excessive when it is unlimited and blind. Unconditional adherence to any person, group, or ideal converts loyalty to idolatry (Fletcher, 1993).

It is important to recognize the limits of loyalty, because its prerational roots can leave us uncomfortable about potential excesses. This is particularly true with culture, where the dangers of intergroup conflict and tribalism are to be feared and avoided as much as intolerance and discrimination.

Loyalty is not a general or abstract experience. It arises only in the specific relationships we have with others or with our cultural group or nation. We are attached to particular people and to specific institutions, self-understandings, ideals, customs, and beliefs. These loyalties are always historical. We become committed to persons, groups, and ideals gradually, by sharing a significant history during which our identity is shaped or reshaped. The formation of individual identity occurs over time through ongoing engagement with someone or something. For example, our loyalty to our families grows out of years of upbringing, and our loyalty to our country develops through decades of instruction, ritual, and pageantry. Loyalty to culture, family, nation, and other formative groups is an acknowledgment of our debt to those groups for the identity and meaning that they have helped to make possible for us.

Because our loyalties are shaped by our personal histories, they are never completely fixed or static. Although loyalties are usually fairly stable, they are dynamic and subject to ebb and flow over time. Our loyalties may shift or even be reversed on the basis of important experiences or new interpretations of our relationships with others or as a result of resolving conflicting allegiances.

Being loyal is inherently exclusionary and discriminatory. We are born into a particular social world that is formative for our identities and most of us remain profoundly tied to this primary group. As Fletcher (1993) puts it, "By definition, these ties generate partialities in loyalties, loves and hates, dispositions to trust and distrust. In the realm of loyalty, inequality reigns: Outsiders cannot claim equal treatment with those who are the objects of loyal attachment" (p. 7). Our capacity for this kind of attachment is clearly limited. We cannot really commit ourselves to too many people or groups. In addition, the more objects of loyalty we have, the more loyalty conflicts we must face.

This means, of course, that loyalty has a built-in element of contingency. Each of us comes into our particular family, culture, and time through the inscrutable workings of historical chance, fate, or God's will. Understanding that our loyalties are initially beyond our choice can help us to be tolerant of others' loyalties, for we cannot truly say that our loyalties are the best or only ties available.

I want to emphasize that we express our loyalty to this social surround in every waking moment by our culturally informed ways of thinking, feeling, and acting. Wearing a watch and being aware of the time is an act of loyalty to our time-conscious culture. Striving to succeed as an individual may be more a matter of loyalty to our liberal individualistic culture than an expression of a putatively universal human self-interest.

We generally act on and embody our loyalties without thinking about it, because it simply seems natural and sensible to act in accordance with our social customs. Most of us, most of the time, are unaware of our loyalties, and although we can question prevailing social norms, we can not live without them. When we do question or criticize some aspect of our cultural life, we can only do so by relying on other background assumptions. We cannot step outside of culture altogether and attain some kind of God's eye point of view.

It is also important to recognize that the loyalties we experience toward our families, cultures, and nations are not merely psychological. We do experience loyalty psychologically, of course, but our loyalties run much, much deeper. Because we can only become fully human by living in social groups, we are ontologically tied to them. This means that our very being as a human is dependent on the modes of social involvement that our cultures provide. Our attachments to our families, cultures, and nations feel bone deep because they are. We owe much of our humanity to these groups, because without their guidance and structure we could not be fully human. Our participation in a cultural

life is not just a matter of giving ourselves a label and going along with a few rit-
uals and characteristic activities. Rather, the way that we live defines us as a
member of a particular group and identifies us in distinction to the other possibilities in our lives and to other groups. In this sense, our cultural background
actually helps to constitute who we are. It is not so much that we have an identity
as that we are our identity. When we act loyally, we are expressing an important
form of self-acceptance. "To love myself, I must respect and cherish those aspects of myself that are bound up with others. Thus, by the mere fact of my biog-
raphy I incur obligations toward others" (Fletcher, 1993, p. 16).

Perhaps the most important way that the concept of loyalty can help is by
rendering our attachment to culture more intelligible and accessible. Loyalty is a
concept that is readily grasped at an experiential level. Most of us know what it
means to be loyal, to stand by someone or something through thick and thin.
Loyalty is a kind of gut-level commitment, a deep attachment that is compelling
to us. We can, of course, elaborate on and explain the roots of our loyalties, but
explication is not necessary to loyalty. It operates with or without explanation; it
is part of our generally unreflective day-to-day activities.

Our experiential feel for loyalty makes it easier to comprehend the attachment to culture, particularly for those of us who are part of the majority culture. Cultural attachment can be quite opaque to us because we move among
like-minded others and our background assumptions and beliefs are shared by
most of the people with whom we are involved. Our cultural presuppositions
may only come into question when we interact with people from another cultural group, and then it is easy to pass the awkwardness off on "their strange
customs or ideas." All of us have experience with loyalty, however, in our families, our friendships, and our attachment to our country. It is easy to grasp in
terms of an experience we share, at some level, with everyone.

Loyalty and Constraint

As my colleagues and I have described elsewhere (Richardson et al., 1999),
Foucault (1980b) and other postmodernists also see our embeddedness in
culture as inescapable, but they describe these ties in far bleaker terms. Foucault
refers to the process of being socialized into a culture as "subjectification." He
sees subjectification as a matter neither of consent nor of coercion, but as the
mutual constraint involved in living in an ordered, but arbitrary, system of
"power/knowledge." From his perspective, knowledge is an outgrowth of a
particular set of power relations in a society rather than approximations of truth.
Knowledge is created to reflect and maintain power relations, and therefore
"truth" is simply an "effect" of the power relations that define a form of life.
What we might call "mental health" or "justice" are simply truth effects of the
power relations in a society. Foucault tells us that these systems of power/
knowledge are incessantly struggling for hegemony. Simply overthrowing
one regime will not enable us to be free, because the overthrow will be

accomplished in favor of another system of power relations. One set of power relations is in no way less dominating or better than another. They are only different configurations that appear and disappear down a historical path without destination or direction.

Foucault highlights the detailed social surveillance and control in our era as a key aspect of subjectification. This surveillance is, by the way, reflected in our peculiar modern obsession with the creation of a mentally healthy population. Foucault is incisive in his commentary on how modem penology, psychiatry, and other human sciences contribute to this surveillance and control. He argues that certain confessional or therapeutic practices help to bring individuals' self-understanding into harmony with the current social order (Foucault 1980b). For example, therapists induce clients to examine themselves until they find (or even fabricate) certain problems or tendencies. Therapists then persuade clients to take responsibility for suppressing or managing these difficulties to conform to current norms of health and productivity. Although we might not accept the whole of Foucault's position, we can see that it sheds light on how emotionally isolated modem individuals are trained to adapt to being cogs in the social and economic machinery and to criticize only themselves rather than the social order when this situation becomes problematic.

Generally, Foucault limits himself to uncovering the apparent origins of contemporary power relations and showing how their claims to truth arose from historical accidents and arbitrary machinations of power. Nevertheless, Foucault often expressed support for those who "resist" or "refuse" these operations to recover particular local knowledge or understanding. In the end, the best alternative that Foucault offers to complete subjugation is a kind of guerilla campaign against domination by ceaselessly creating and recreating ourselves "as a work of art" (Foucault, 1982). Subjectification ties the individual so tightly to his or her life world that independent thought and action are only accessible in the margins of his or her life.

Foucault's penetrating and bracing analysis of the ties that bind us to our social context are illuminating and helpful in certain respects, but he relies on several key presuppositions that undermine his perspective. At the risk of oversimplifying his analysis, I will only mention two crucial assumptions that serve my purposes here. Although Foucault recognizes the inescapable embeddedness of individuals in social life, he nevertheless seems to cherish the idea of individual freedom. His belief that individuals ought to be freer than they are shows up in his portrayal of our bonds to culture as oppressive and his suggestion that rebellion and struggle against this process are the only alternatives to total subjugation. If we are so completely subject to the social world, why is that a problem for Foucault? Why should we want to reduce our conformity if accommodations to power are so natural, fundamental, and total? His analysis provides no basis for valuing freedom or local knowledge above the more encompassing cultural order.

Another shortcoming of Foucault's perspective is in seeing the system of domination as monolithic. It is not, of course. There are always interminable debates and dissensions about how one should live within any set of "power relations." These legitimate and heartfelt disagreements are a crucial element of the real freedom we have as participants in culture, as we will see shortly. I see the hermeneutic reading of our participation in the traditions and social practices as better partly because this viewpoint makes it clear that cultures are always multivocal and characterized by ongoing debate about what it means to live well. Moreover, we are not simply helpless puppets of an overwhelming regime of power, because the cultural order exists only through our actions. Each individual act is an interpretation of the customs and practices of a form of life and these interpretations can and do lead to new formulations of the cultural order. (For a more detailed critique of Foucault's thought, see Taylor, 1985.)

Embeddedness and Freedom

Heidegger's formulation of our historical and cultural embeddedness helps us to set aside the myth of the radically disengaged individual who is independent of culture. Recognizing the shortcomings of Foucault's portrayal of the human condition suggests that we do not need to see ourselves as radically embedded subjects who are mere pawns of culture. Thus we appear to be profoundly shaped by our cultural context, but we also have significant latitude in how we enact our form of life. The concept of loyalty both captures the power and centrality of our social attachments and clarifies our freedom in the context of cultural embeddedness.

We have already examined our dependence on our social world for our identity. I want to turn now to exploring how the contours and conflicts of loyalty provide space for human freedom and discernment and for opening up some pathways for our professional work. Let us return to the Rodriguez family we met earlier. It is easy to see that José and Yvette have very strong loyalties to their cultural roots in Colombia. Their decision to emigrate to the United States was not a repudiation of their attachment to Colombian culture, nor did it mean that they wanted to become "American." They came to participate in the economic opportunities available here and for the relative safety in the United States from the violence rampant in their homeland. Without having worked it out explicitly, they fully expected to raise their family in America as they had been raised in Colombia.

Carlos did not, of course, have nearly as much loyalty to Colombian culture, because he came to Miami when he was 2 years old. His cultural loyalties were primarily developed in the United States. To be sure, he did receive a good deal of cultural training from his parents in their home and from his extended family in the United States and in Colombia. But these sources of enculturation were dwarfed by the incredible power of living in a media-saturated, Madison Avenue-fueled pop culture. Carlos absorbed the dominant messages of American culture through television, radio, movies, and their reverberations in his peer group. He was shaped by his experience in the United States and it is here that he is learning to be a participant in culture, so his loyalty is primarily informed by the prevailing values of personal autonomy, authenticity, and the primacy of the individual.

The Particularity of Loyalty. Loyalty can help us to better understand this family's cultural conflicts in two ways. First, loyalty is always directed toward someone or something. Loyalty is particular in character rather than universal. It arises only in the context of specific ongoing relationships to individuals, groups, entities, or ideals. Moreover, our loyalties to the particular individuals and groups with whom we have shared our lives are not total. There are specific aspects of each bond we have with others that define that relationship and us as participants in it. To violate these crucial elements of the relationship is to betray our loyalty. For example, sexual exclusivity is one of the defining elements of most marriages, and sexual involvement outside the marriage generally constitutes a profound betrayal of the marital relationship. Yet other important elements of a relationship may not be central to it, and loyalty does not require the same kind of devotion to those less central features of the relationship. To continue with our example, companionship is also important to most married couples, but few marriages require exclusivity in the area of companionship.

This specificity in our attachments makes it clear that it is too simplistic to say that we are loyal to a culture. Culture is always a rather uncertain target of loyalty. There is, of course, no delimited list of characteristics or commitments that can definitively capture any culture. This means that the shape of a culture is always subject to interpretation from a participant's particular viewpoint. No one will ever have the last word on what it means to be Cuban, Japanese, Mexican, or American.

Our cultural attachments are always related to the salient aspects of the social context in which we were formed. In the case of culture, we are more strongly tied to the particular facets of our culture that were emphasized in our socialization than we are to other elements. For example, as an American, I am very attached to the aspects of our culture that emphasize individual autonomy and initiative, personal authenticity and creativity, but I experience the consumerism and materialistic imperatives of American culture as repugnant. I find myself in a constant struggle with the myriad messages that exhort me to improve my life and my status by having a more expensive car, a bigger house, and so forth. These kinds of tensions exist in all cultures, and individuals must work out some kind of resolution to them by giving their allegiance to particular facets of culture rather than to some mythical, undifferentiated cultural whole. Such struggles grow out of membership in any culture, and we see these conflicts as much with mainstream Americans as with members of other cultural groups.

When we recognize that our attachment to culture is necessarily specific and partial rather than all-encompassing, we can see that differences between members of the same culture are to be expected as part of the multifaceted nature of culture. In fact, cultural traditions always contain a welter of voices that interpret the customs and practices of the group differently, and these alternative views are often in conflict. The ambiguity of culture is also temporal because all cultural traditions are also evolving over time.

The particularity of our loyalties helps us to appreciate the nuances of cultural attachment and thereby opens up valuable avenues for therapeutic work. Seeing cultural belonging in terms of loyalty presses us to look beyond merely saying that I am an Anglo-Saxon male or someone else is an African-American female. To truly understand our cultural loyalties, we must recognize which specific aspects of our identities are most salient for us. In the work with the Rodriguezes, the therapist explored the specific cultural allegiances the parents had toward Colombian ideals about the family. It turns out that José and Yvette felt that a high degree of closeness to and respect for parents was essential, but they did not demand absolute obedience from Carlos. This gave the therapist some room to work, because the polarization between the parents and their son had forced José and Yvette to take an uncharacteristically authoritarian stance as a last resort for extracting respect from Carlos.

As Carlos saw that his parents' position was softening, he was willing to acknowledge that he appreciated their involvement in his life. He felt lucky about their caring for him, especially when he saw how uninvolved some of his friends' parents were. At the same time, he expressed the characteristically American insistence on a good deal of autonomy, particularly in the face of his perception that they wanted to control his life. The language of respect was also very meaningful to him, but he wanted that to be a two-way street, with his parents showing respect for him and his growing capabilities in return for respecting them.

My supervisee cultivated these nascent areas of common ground by having each of them express what they wanted and by exploring why it was important to them. She pointed out commonalities and showed how much of what they wanted represented ways in which they were committed to the two cultures they were bridging as a family. One of the goals of therapy was to help the parents to better appreciate the aspects of American culture to which Carlos was attached and to help Carlos to better understand his Colombian heritage and how his parents were trying to live out that legacy.

The Rodriguezes were able to learn to understand the cultural divide on which they stood, and they developed some useful compromises that allowed them to remain true to both cultures while slavishly following neither. Carlos agreed to accept reasonable limitations on his activities, inform his parents about his whereabouts, and treat them with greater respect. José and Yvette learned that the clothing, music, and activities that they found objectionable were part of the normal accoutrements of youth culture rather than signs of their son's catastrophic decline into criminality and drug use. They agreed to grant him provisional freedom and respect, provided that he act in ways that merited the continuance of their trust.

The Multiplicity of Loyalty. The second way that loyalty can help us understand culture is that our loyalties are never so simple that they are directed to only one person or group. In the normal course of our lives, we are shaped by a variety of group memberships and ongoing relationships with others. All of us have multiple attachments to one or more cultures, the families that raised us, the families we have formed, our nations, our religions, our friends, our occupations or professions, and so forth. These various loyalties are not, of course, always compatible with each other. Tensions among these various loyalties are frequent, and harmonizing the competing obligations we have is a very important and often taxing part of our lives. Sometimes loyalty conflicts merely require us to modify our commitments and other times they threaten to fragment our lives. If, for example, one has a religious upbringing in the United States, one might have a more limited understanding of individual autonomy and self-interest, tempered perhaps by the concept of the fellowship of humans and warnings about the sins of greed and selfishness. Much of the time, we can harmonize these various loyalties without a great deal of difficulty. At other times, we find ourselves in a very painful conflict of loyalties. Conflicting allegiances can be an important aspect of the difficulties that clients present.

Although divided loyalties are often difficult and painful, they can provide a creative tension through which important problems can be resolved. The loyalty conflict within the Rodriguez family was actually helpful in working out their difficulties. Although José and Yvette were very committed to their Colombian way of life, some aspects of American culture also attracted them. Moreover, they were extremely devoted to their son and his well-being. Carlos, for his part, had been strongly influenced by his Colombian heritage and did not wish to jettison it entirely. He was similarly strongly attached to his parents. These tensions in their loyalties provided room for the therapist to work with them on coming together across the cultural divide they faced.

Questioning Loyalties

The concept of loyalty can also make other important contributions to our understanding of our cultural being. By terming adherence to cultural prescriptions as loyalty, we automatically honor those allegiances and indicate that we respect our own and others' cultural attachments. At the same time, a discussion of loyalties opens up a number of ways to question the nature of clients' commitment to their cultural background when that seems to be related to their difficulties. We might ask clients questions such as, "Does being a Cuban male mean that you have to do 'X' (where 'X' is a problematic action)?" "Is there another way to approach this problem that will not leave you feeling that you have betrayed your African-American heritage?" "Does being a member of mainstream American culture require you to place your individual interests above your obligations to others?"

The concept of loyalty also helps us to recognize that we can be insufficiently loyal to our cultural heritage or excessively loyal to it. Finding an appropriate balance between adherence to cultural norms and a critical distance from them can be a very important aspect of therapy.

One of the most significant ways that a deficiency of cultural loyalty manifests is in self-loathing. Many members of minority groups tragically internalize the prejudice and discrimination they face, and they come to see their cultural heritage through the eyes of its detractors. In such a situation, it is important for therapists to help their clients overcome this self-hatred and to develop a better appreciation of the positive aspects of their cultural legacy. Insofar as someone despises his or her cultural heritage, he or she will be disloyal to it and will thereby depreciate those aspects of self that are inextricably tied to that background. This suggests that human flourishing requires an honest and heartfelt affirmation of one's historical roots.

At the other extreme, some individuals develop a distorted or excessive loyalty to their cultural groups. When cultural allegiance becomes extreme, it can lead to xenophobia, prejudice, and an unwillingness to adapt cultural prescriptions to the contours of one's circumstances. A rigid adherence to cultural prescriptions can create significant difficulties when circumstances make the cultural norms problematic.

Alberto and Diana, a Cuban-American couple, found themselves struggling with the discontinuities of traditional gender roles and the gender politics of the United States. Alberto held very traditional views about being the head of the household and about Diana being responsible for the domestic chores of cooking, cleaning, childrearing, and being a sexually alluring lover. Diana was very unhappy with their allocation of household tasks and authority. Both partners have professional jobs and Diana has significant authority as the manager of a moderately sized retail store. Diana was particularly incensed by the discrepancy between the respect and deference she received at work and her feeling that she was a domestic servant at home. Alberto's traditional male pattern of spending time with his friends after work while Diana worked at home compounded her discontent. Although Diana did not see herself as a feminist, she had absorbed much of the feminist-inspired consciousness of gender inequity and was no longer willing to continue with their traditional gender roles. Alberto found her complaints groundless and was only willing to come to therapy because it was clear to him that his marriage was on the line.

As with the Rodriguezes, Alberto's attachment to his wife was paramount in working out their difficulties. His allegiance toward Diana was in conflict with the loyalty he felt toward his culture's prescriptions about gender roles. This kind of loyalty conflict is often crucial to therapeutic success. Our experience has been that when the marital attachment is not strong, there is little hope for resolving cultural and gender role tensions successfully. Because his wife was important to him, Alberto was willing to reconsider his staunch allegiance to traditional gender roles. This involved discussing the differences between gender-based expectations in Cuban culture and those in the United States. Therapy also focused on examining how he learned these roles in his family and how his sense of maleness was bound up with this division of labor. Alberto came to recognize that the cultural prescriptions he had inherited were only one way to arrange a marriage and that his strength as a man was not dependent on maintaining absolute authority in the home and a set of male privileges that had been identified as unjust by many people in this culture. This allowed him to reduce his loyalty to that particular aspect of his heritage. Because Diana wanted him to be more involved, she had to learn to include Alberto in raising their children, where she had previously excluded him as a "useless man."

In citing this example, I am not suggesting that egalitarian gender roles are unquestionably better than traditional roles. For many of us, the ethic of fairness and equality in marriage is very compelling. Yet we must recognize that this is, in part, an expression of our loyalty to American ideals about individual justice and equality. It is incumbent on all of us to understand that much of what we hold dear is an outgrowth of our embeddedness in a particular cultural and historical context rather than the endpoint of human evolution.

Culture and Loyalty in Therapy

The concept of loyalty can help us to gain a better grasp of the particularities and practicalities of culture in our professional work. I have argued that loyalty arises organically through the formative social world into which we are born. The guidance and orientation that our families and cultures provide in how to live help to constitute our identities. Because we are ontologically dependent on our cultural surround, we incur obligations of loyalty. Cultural influences continue to shape us throughout our lives, and the various currents we encounter are not necessarily compatible with each other. The particularity of our attachment to our cultural roots and the inevitable conflicts in our loyalties create considerable space for choice and discernment in our lives.

This attachment to culture is an unavoidable part of being human and the ambiguities, tensions, and conflicts of being a participant in culture are just as present among mainstream Americans as among members of minority groups. Matters of culture are important whether we are working with a member of another cultural group or someone who shares much of our own cultural background. In fact, as many chapter authors in this book have indicated, there are significant aspects of contemporary American culture that seem to be intricately related to many of the difficulties our clients face. Culture is not just about people from other groups; it is a powerful part of all of our identities. Exploring our clients' unquestioned adherence to problematic American cultural norms can help them to develop the critical distance necessary for thoughtful participation in contemporary society.

The concept of loyalty can helpfully inform therapeutic work in many ways. First, loyalty helps to make cultural attachments more easily intelligible to mainstream American therapists. It is a concept that has readily accessible experiential referents for us and allows us to reduce the mystification of culture.

Second, seeing cultural bonds in terms of loyalty can help us to honor these ties, particularly because we recognize the depth of cultural attachments in shaping individuals. At the same time, the concept of loyalty points to ways that we can raise questions about cultural prescriptions in a respectful manner. It is easy to recognize that even our most heartfelt loyalties can be misguided. Exploring ways to reinterpret our allegiances that bring them into greater harmony with other commitments or with our circumstances can be very beneficial to clients. The upshot is that there is always room for reinterpretation of the meaning of cultural membership. This allows for a range of choices within the ambit of loyal adherence to one's culture.

Third, a loyalty-based understanding clarifies that cultural bonds are partial and specific rather than monolithic and total. This helps us to better see the nuances of cultural allegiance, which opens up avenues of change that we would not recognize if we see attachment to culture in a more global and undifferentiated manner.

Fourth, this approach helps us see that loyalty conflicts are a natural part of human life and that these conflicts provide space for individual freedom and therapeutic action. Many of the situations our clients present to us are best seen as conflicts among their allegiances to individuals, groups, or ideals. Helping clients to find a way to realign their conflicting loyalties can aid them in living more integrated, focused lives.

Fifth, seeing cultural attachment in terms of loyalty makes it clear that people can be either insufficiently loyal or excessively loyal to their form of life. It is often difficult to know just how strongly one should devote oneself to cultural customs and prescriptions. It is all too easy to unreflectively align oneself with problematic cultural prescriptions that create significant difficulties in living. Conversely, in our excessively critical and fragmented society, individuals can become overly negative and detached from their cultural roots, contributing to self-hatred and anomie. Reflections on how to attain a secure and reasonable attachment to one's cultural legacy can be very important in therapeutic work.

Finally, I began this chapter by stressing the profoundly moral character of the multicultural movement. Any attempt to address the importance of culture without recognizing its deeply moral nature is bound to be sterile and misleading. Cultural norms, practices, and customs are the embodiment of a vision of the good, a collective attempt to bring certain ideals to life. As I outlined earlier, our commitments to a particular way of life are bone deep and our actions make a statement about what is good in life. When we participate in our way of life, we are not merely following a set of prescriptive rules because we were taught to do so. Rather, we enact our culture's norms because we believe that that is the right and proper way to live. The concept of loyalty is consistent with that moral thrust, because loyalty always involves attachment, indebtedness, and obligation. Moreover, in being loyal to our cultural heritage, we are attempting to live out our inherited cultural vision of what is good in life. It is impossible to live a moral life characterized by disloyalty. (Although it is possible, in the confusing realm of human affairs, to be disloyal to some of our commitments while we are serving others that we deem more important or central.)

The morality of loyalty differs in very important ways from the more familiar moralities of Kantian and utilitarian thought. The Kantian emphasis on abstract reason in the categorical imperative emphasizes that we should be impartial in our moral dealings by acting only in ways that we could will everyone to act. We should treat all others impartially as ends in themselves and never merely as means to our ends. In spite of the profound differences between Kantian and utilitarian ethics, they share a deep commitment to abstract reason and impartiality. The utilitarian holds that moral decisions should be based on dispassionate calculations that will indicate which actions lead to the most good for the largest number of people without regard for who those people are. These theories share a faith in abstract, impartial reason as the best basis for ethical decision making.

Loyalty, on the other hand, is all about partiality. It emphasizes our embeddedness in family, culture, and nation and that we are unavoidably partial to these groups. Our attachment to these groups and the way of life in which we have been socialized is deeper than abstract reason and more compelling than most calculations of consequences. These attachments are far more powerful in our actual, ground-level lives. Moreover, our loyalty to our cultural customs is not just a subjective preference, something that we can choose or let go of at will. The attachment to culture is a primary source of our individual identity, outlook, and desires. We can paraphrase Gadamer's famous aphorism about historical embeddedness to express this crucial feature of culture by saying that we do not own culture, culture owns us.

That is not to say that we should abandon abstract reason or regard for consequences. After all, faith in the beneficial nature of reason is a major aspect of modern Western culture and is an outgrowth of the development of the Western way of life. The value of reason is an important part of our culture to which we are also loyal. Therefore the practice of abstract reason is in fact one of our many loyalties rather than standing outside of our cultural embeddedness.

Combining the ability to recognize and honor all people's commitment to their way of life with the freedom to raise questions about how those cultural mores are enacted positions us favorably to help clients to reconsider and reinterpret problematic aspects of their lives. We must respect the bonds all of us have to our ways of life, and yet we cannot allow ourselves to become paralyzed by seeing cultural adherence as sacrosanct. Seeing the ties between individuals and cultures in terms of loyalty illuminates the vast space of questions that exist in all cultures. We can now see how the ambiguities of culture and loyalty conflicts leave a great deal of room for productive dialogue about what it means to be a good member of a given culture. This helps us to recognize that therapeutic work is centrally concerned with questions about the good life in our participation in a particular life world.

References

Fletcher, G. P. (1993). *Loyalty: An essay on the morality of relationships*. Oxford, UK: Oxford University Press.

Foucault, M. (1980a). *This history of sexuality: Vol. 1. An introduction* (R. Hurley, Trans.). New York: Vintage.

Foucault, M. (1980b). *Power/Knowledge: Selected interviews and other writings* (C. Gordon, Ed.). New York: Pantheon.

Foucault, M. (1982). On the geneology of ethics: An overview of work in progress. In H. Dreyfus & P. Rabinow, *Michel Foucault: Beyond structuralism and hermeneutics* (pp. 229-252). Chicago: University of Chicago Press.

Fowers, B. J., & Richardson, F. C. (1996). Why is multiculturalism good? *American Psychologist, 51,* 609-621.

Heidegger, M. (1962). *Being and time* (J. Macquarrie & E. Robinson, Trans.). New York: Harper & Row.

Richardson, F. C., Fowers, B. J., & Guignon, C. (1999). *Re-envisioning psychology: Moral dimensions of theory and practice*. San Francisco: Jossey-Bass.

Taylor, C. (1985). *Philosophy and the human sciences: Philosophical papers* (Vol. 2). Cambridge, UK: Cambridge University Press.

Commentary

Multiculturalism and Diversity: Response to Dr. Fowers

Agnes M. Plenk
The Children's Center, Salt Lake City, Utah

Multiculturalism and diversity, as Dr. Fowers indicates, is one of the most urgent problems in our profession at this time. Psychologists, like all mental health professionals, are at crossroads of viability. Some of our colleagues label psychology "a no longer viable professional resource" (Hall, 1997). Though I consider this a rather harsh statement, others in the field agree and insist that psychology needs to be proactive to maintain its position in the mental health field (Ponterotto, Casas, Suzuki, & Alexander, 1995; Sue, 1999). Dr. Fowers is quite optimistic that psychology has accepted the challenge of the multi-culturalists for change, but sees the struggle as a moral, not political, one, assuming that society as a whole and psychology in particular will recognize the importance of cultural differences and loyalty to one's family, group, and culture and permit all other groups the same privilege (Fowers and Richardson, 1996). This assumes, I think, a greater willingness on the part of many professionals to consider cultural diversity positively and give up the traditional preferred status and the power attached to it (Thomas & Febbraro, 1997) than is the case in reality. Are we maintaining the status quo "in accordance with our social customs" out of loyalty to our culture, but not permitting other culture groups the same? For the status quo to change we need major changes in our educational system. Acceptance and understanding of different cultures needs to happen much earlier than in graduate school, when we are expecting it from our students. With the arrival of the 21st century, the changes in racial composition of the population in the United States becomes even more evident (Cisz, 1998), as does the lack of proper representation of people of color in the student body and in university faculties. Outreach to minority students to enter the field of mental health services and the readiness of administrations of higher learning to employ qualified graduates is essential for the desired changes in diversity to occur (Sue, 1999). Changes in attitudes or in relinquishing power are more difficult for professionals who have received their training in the three traditional therapeutic modalities. Take, for example, awareness of time, which, as Dr. Fowers recognizes, as "an act of loyalty to our time-conscious culture" is not shared by many of our clients from different cultural groups. Being late for an appointment, even if it disturbs our plan for the day, is not always a sign of resistance to treatment, but might be loyalty to their culture. The general adherence to the 50-minute hour is certainly a hangover from the Eurocentric approaches to therapy and needs to be modified. Marathon sessions are often very helpful. Preoccupation with time and other culture-obsessive features are not in and of themselves good or bad, but must be considered in the framework of the client. Rogler (1999) mentions that clean clothes might be a reality issue for Native American adolescents if they have no running water and not deserving a diagnosis of obsessive-compulsive disorder. Errors proliferate when instruments are based on U.S. standards—for example, sleeping patterns differ greatly between different groups. Other difficulties arise when treatment methods are used based only on the client's psyche rather than exploring the cultural setting in which the client lives, as pointed out by Dr. Fowers's case examples.

Awareness of our own biases by developing our own individual sensitivity profile should be a required exercise, already demanded for a master's degree in social work in many states. We also need to recognize the profound differences in socioeconomic level between most therapists and their clients. This might lead to unrealistic expectations, resulting in therapeutic failures and withdrawal from treatment, and cause us often to be considered less helpful than the neighborhood barber or the pharmacist recommending herbal medications. Recommending bedtime routines to homeless families living in their cars comes to mind. It is essential to integrate traditional theories with increased cultural awareness. Entering into the client's world with "the lens of culture" (Ivey et al., 1993) or, as Sue (in Ivey et al., 1993) dramatically put it, "walking in another's moccasins," must be a primary consideration in counseling at this time. Most theories are rooted in European-American middle-class values with a style and technique not appropriate to different culture groups and the 21st century; we need not discard them, but we need to review them anew as culturally derived phenomena, leading possibly to a fourth therapeutic technique, multicultural counseling (MCT) (Ivey, 1993). Knowledge of differences in child rearing based on the parent's cultural belief system is essential in understanding family conflict (Harkness & Super, 1996), most pronounced in biracial or interethnic marriages but equally important for Europeans. All Europeans are not alike in expression of feelings, wishing to gain insight, or stressing autonomy in their children at an early age. We are discovering these differences with the influx of Eastern European immigrants and their identified children patients.

Marika, age 3, was referred to a day treatment center for emotionally disturbed preschoolers due to her aggressive behavior toward her younger sibling and her parents. Nobody in the family spoke English, and the family isolated itself from compatriots in the United States because of religious differences. Once in day treatment, the little girl made rapid progress in language acquisition and slowly was able to play with the others in the group. Her behavior toward her sibling improved, but her parents needed special outreach, including home visits, transportation for medical appointments, food and clothing deliveries, and even help finding newspapers in their native language. Tenacity of outreach finally reached the mother, who at one home visit showed us the family photo album, one of the few possessions they brought with them. Looking at pictures of their house, the church with the clock in the tower, the neighbor with his dog, released a flood of tears, but also was the beginning of a trusting relationship with the therapist. This led to conjoint sessions with both children and introduction of child-rearing ideas concerning autonomy, such as permitting Marika to play with neighbor children. Unfortunately, we were not able to reach the father, whose unhappiness converted to psychosomatic problems, his refusal to accept medical care ending in loss of his job. The mother, however, successfully entered the workforce and Marika went to kindergarten. We learned that openness and receptivity to new and untried ideas combined with looking beyond assumptions "plus naivete and respectful curiosity (should be considered) equal to knowledge and skill in the therapeutic process" (Dyche & Zayas, 1995, p. 399).

We each might have to give up some of our loyalties and our powers, just as the Europeans now are doing in forming the European Community. Theoreticians and practitioners will have to combine what has been useful in the past with present-day realities to create and practice a framework of mental health services helpful for the 21st century.

References

Cisz, J. (1998, August). *White privilege and the therapist's subjectivity.* Paper presented at the American Psychological Association Convention, San Francisco.

Dyche, L., & Zayas, M. (1995). The value of curiosity and naivete for the cross-cultural psychotherapist. *Family Process, 34,* 389-399.

Fowers, B., & Richardson, F. C. (1996). Why is multiculturalism good? *American Psychologist, 51,* 609-621.

Hall, C. J. (1997). Cultural malpractice: The growing obsolescence of psychology with the changing U.S. population. *American Psychologist, 52,* 642-650.

Harkness, S., & Super, C. (1996). *Parents' cultural belief systems.* New York: Guilford.

Ivey, A. E. (1995). Psychotherapy as liberation. In J. G. Ponterotto, J. M. Casas, L. A. Suzuki, & C. M. Alexander (Eds.), *Handbook of multicultural counseling.* Thousand Oaks, CA: Sage.

Ivey, A. E., Ivey, M. B., & Simek-Morgan, L., with contributions from Chatham, H. E., Pedersen, P. B., Rigazio-DiGilia, S. A., & Sue, D. W. (1993). *Counseling and psychotherapy: A multicultural perspective.* Boston: Allyn & Bacon.

Kevin, C., & Ponterotto, J. G. (1995). Racial identity development: Theory and research. In J. G. Ponterotto, J. M. Casas, L. A. Suzuki, & L. M. Alexander (Eds.), *Handbook of multicultural counseling.* Thousand Oaks, CA: Sage.

Ponterotto J. G., Casas, J. M., Suzuki, L. A., & Alexander, C. M. (Eds.). (1995). *Handbook of multicultural counseling.* Thousand Oaks, CA: Sage.

Rogler, L. H. (1999). Methodological sources of cultural insensitivity in mental health research. *American Psychologist, 54,* 424-443.

Sue, D. W., Andondo, P., & McDavis, R. J. (1992). Multicultural counseling competencies and standards. *Journal of Counseling and Development, 70,* 477-486.

Sue, D. W., & Sue, S. (1999). *Counseling the culturally different.* New York: John Wiley.

Thomas, T., & Febbraro, A. (1997). Norm, faculty and power in multiculturalism. *American Psychologist, 52,* 656-658.

Issue 13

Diagnosis

"Objectivity" in Diagnosis and Treatment

A Philosophical Analysis

Robert L. Woolfolk
Princeton University

There I was in my consulting room. I had just heard a woman's story. It was familiar, the stuff of therapy.

Lynn had been happily married, or so she had thought, to Steve, a successful and attentive man. They had been amicable friends and passionate lovers during the first half decade of marriage. Though always moody and mercurial, Steve seemed to affirm the value of their union with all his deeds and words.

Then came the children: two beloved daughters separated in age by a sensible 3 years. Steve seemed enthralled with parenthood, working reduced hours during the firstborn's initial year of life. After that things began to change. His moods swung on a longer arc. Eighteen months after the birth of their second child, he impetuously accepted a job in another state and was home only on weekends. This job lasted only a year. Steve returned to his former job, but not until after he and Lynn suffered through many acrimonious long-distance phone calls and tense weekends. There was compelling evidence that he had been involved in an extramarital affair, but he issued an unequivocal denial when confronted.

Lynn had interrupted a promising career in advertising out of a keenly felt moral imperative to be the primary caregiver to her children. She had recently resumed full-time work in her former field, but was feeling a mixture of resentment, despondence, guilt, and exhaustion. She related to me that she knew she needed challenging work outside the home to be fulfilled, but also believed she needed to change fields before returning to the workplace.

"These are my problems," Lynn said. As she spoke to me, my eyes drifted to the bookcase in my office. A copy of the *Diagnostic and Statistical Manual of Mental Disorders* (DSM-IV; American Psychiatric Association, 1994) sat on the third shelf, next to a book describing empirically supported treatments, which itself was adjacent to a recent survey of psychotropic drugs written for the non-medical practitioner.

Although I had spent little time with my client, it was already clear that those volumes were not going to be the first items I consulted in the treatment of this young woman. In fact, it occurred to me that they might be of no use at all. In this chapter, I examine some issues that help to explain why those manuals that currently are so pivotal in our field are so often of questionable relevance to the everyday exigencies of clinical practice.

In contemporary times, the mental health professions are dominated by perspectives that derive from both economic and ideological sources. The perspectives issue from various institutions: the multinational pharmaceutical industry; the managed care and health insurance industry; the clinical academic research industry; and various governmental agencies, including the National Institutes of Health. These institutions, supported broadly by most physicians and many other clinicians, have advanced the view that psychological treatment and assessment should be based on models derived from biomedicine. In such models, psychological problems are conceived as analogous to physical diseases and psychotherapy is conceptualized as a medical technology. Although these models purport to be objective and value free, this contemporary, "scientific," approach to mental health either uncritically presupposes certain values or brackets values in a fashion that trivializes, distorts, or ignores essential aspects of the distresses that bring people to therapy.

As we begin this new millennium, humanistic perspectives in the mental health professions have been all but washed away by the objectivist tide. Sadly, one of the most vigorous countertrends to scientism in psychotherapy is the relativistic, and ultimately nihilistic, set of views that derives from social constructionism. A Hobson's choice between objectivism and relativism awaits many newly credentialed professionals. But in a practical sense, at least with regard to assessment, the choice already is moot: Without a *DSM* diagnosis, treatment is not legitimate and not reimbursed. If present trends continue, we may see such rigid controls on treatment, with a highly differentiated set of current procedural terminology (CPT) codes, each keyed to a diagnosis.

Although I could rail against scientism in the field, I want to focus, at least initially, on what may appear, at first, as a rather startling assertion: The biomedical, objectivistic models favored by the mental health power structure are based on errors and confusions that are rather fundamental and obvious, once they are understood. These errors effectively serve to undermine the contemporary zeitgeist and reveal the disguised ideology that underlies it.

To provide some context for my analysis of the mistakes inherent in so-called value-free approaches to diagnosis and treatment, I begin by describing a contrast familiar in the philosophy of psychiatry, that between objectivism and normativism. Forgive me if I overdraw the distinction somewhat for purposes of illustration.

At the core of all objectivist positions is the naturalistic view that mental disorders involve a departure from the way in which the human organism was designed to function. Objectivists believe that psychopathology results from malfunctions of physical or psychological mechanisms and that these malfunctions can be characterized in terms that are value free. Objectivists assert that malfunctioning mechanisms can be discriminated from those that are functioning properly by a value-neutral empirical analysis Treatment, whether it be pharmacological or psychotherapeutic, is conceived as a technological intervention, the aim of which is the repair of the underlying dysfunction.

Normativists, on the other hand, hold that the conception of mental disorder is value laden and culturally embedded. They see pathology as relative to, and a reflection of, the values of a culture. Psychopathology is simply another form of social deviancy, or a kind of personal discomfort. Intervention is seen not as a value-neutral scientific technology, but as a process that interacts with personal and cultural values in complex ways.

Not surprising, normativists and objectivists differ notably in how they conceive the metamorphoses of such memorable psychopathologies of the past as drapetomania and masturbation. Presently, both camps regard the desires of slaves to escape captivity as appropriate and the satisfaction of sexual urges through self-stimulation as clinically benign. Normativists, believing that illness categories are essentially social constructions, tend to see such bygone "mental illnesses" as evidence for the cultural relativity of psychopathology and to view developments such as the depathologization of drapetomania as examples of moral, rather than scientific, progress. Objectivists, of course, do not deny that social forces determine the application of illness *labels*, as in the notorious case of Soviet psychiatrists diagnosing political dissidents with "sluggish schizophrenia" (Bloch & Reddaway, 1977). But objectivists attribute such retrospective psychiatric embarrassments to bad science and conceive of the attendant nosological revisions as resulting from empirical advances, for example, scientific progress demonstrating that there is no flawed psychological mechanism underlying the desire to escape slavery.

The conception of malfunction that is central to the objectivist position is intelligible only in relation to a conceptualization of proper or normal functioning, which is intelligible only in relation to the concept of a function. My approach in this chapter is to explore the crucial concepts of *function, proper function,* and *malfunction*. In the pages that follow, I attempt to analyze these concepts to explore the various ways that mental disorder is comprehended and to sharpen our understanding of how values figure in various concepts of mental illness. There are three principal ways in which the concept of function has been understood in the philosophical literature.

Etiological Function

An *etiological function* is defined in relation to its history of natural selection. The ascription of function is intended to explain the origin or maintenance of a trait or organ in a given population. Etiological functions are conceived as the effects of traits that enhanced fitness (the ability to survive and to reproduce) and therefore were favored by natural selection (Wright, 1976). When we describe the function of the heart as the circulation of blood, in an etiological sense we imply that hearts exist, in the first place, *because* they perform that function. The related concepts "proper function" of the heart or "normal" heart derive from the evolutionary story. Normal hearts do what they were selected for and the proper function of the heart is to perform the role for which it was designed by natural selection (Millikan, 1989). An organ is functioning properly in the etiological sense when it is performing the function that caused it to exist in its present form: "It is the, or a, proper function of an item (X) of an organism (O) to do what items of X's type did to contribute to the inclusive fitness of O's ancestors and caused the genotype, of which X is the phenotypic expression, to be selected by natural selection" (Neander, 1991, p. 174).

The definition of *malfunction* that follows from the etiological concept of function is, simply, the failure or deficiency of a organ in doing what caused it to become part of our equipment through natural selection. Etiological malfunctions are conceptually unproblematic, in that if we are Darwinians we can posit no mechanism other than natural selection that contributed to our species design. We assume that there is an objective, historically accurate answer to every question asked about human evolution. Most philosophers of biology assume that etiological functions and their related malfunctions can be determined objectively, at least in principle, by empirical evolutionary science. As a practical matter, however, determining the exact contribution of current traits to fitness in times past is, at best, an uncertain endeavor, given the rather primitive state of evolutionary science.

One effect of stipulating evolutionarily defined malfunction as a necessary condition for mental disorder is to restrict the range of phenomena to which the category applies. The etiological concept of malfunction underlies Wakefield's (1992) harmful dysfunction theory of mental disorder. In Wakefield's formulation, an etiological malfunction is a necessary (but not sufficient) condition for mental disorder. He avers, correctly, I believe, that many disorders recognized by Western psychiatry do not consist of malfunctions so defined. Wakefield has argued that limiting disorders to cases of malfunction not only keeps psychiatry more closely allied to the biological and cognitive sciences but also serves to protect us from such abuses as clitorectomizing masturbators and pathologizing slaves' aspirations to freedom.

The difficulties connected with applying etiological functions to psychiatric nosologies are numerous. What, for example, are we to make of that erstwhile mental illness, homosexuality, from an evolutionary perspective? Clearly reducing, on average, the procreative potential of any individual person with the trait, homosexuality looks like a good candidate for a mental illness from an evolutionary perspective. Homosexuality, however, could have enhanced the inclusive fitness of kinship groups, as do the sterile castes in naked mole rat and some insect populations. The trait may result from what biologists call "genetic drift," random variation that escapes natural selection. It is also possible that homosexuals may suffer from maladaptive sexual preferences, albeit caused by underlying genes that are linked pleiotropically with other fitness-enhancing traits. And last, it is still plausible, and certainly possible, that the trait may arise largely because of environmental influence. This last view is that of social learning theory—that sexual preferences are acquired through learning and conditioning, just as musical tastes are.

The parsimony produced by limiting psychopathology to cases of etiological malfunction is both theoretically and practically problematic. If we choose to define malfunction etiologically, many human capacities and proclivities and some mental disorders will lie outside the function-malfunction dimension. To possess an etiological function, a trait or capacity must have a history of selection, must have enhanced fitness, and must have been selected for. It also must have a function in the evolutionary sense to have the capacity to malfunction.

But some of our current psychological apparatus may have no function at all in the etiological sense. It is probable that some features of the mind are what Gould and Lewontin (1979) term "spandrels." Spandrels are features without initial adaptive value that arise as by-products of other correlated developments that are fitness enhancing and hence favored by natural selection. The mammalian navel, the white color of bones, and the human chin frequently are classified as spandrels. If there are numerous mental spandrels, as Gould (1997) has suggested, then we are replete with mental mechanisms that are indirect products of evolution, products have not been selected for and therefore possess no etiological function. Because spandrels have no etiological function, they cannot, in the etiological sense, malfunction.

Just as we can conceive of mental disorders that involve no malfunction because they never had any evolutionary function, we also can imagine that a mental disorder might result from a mechanism functioning exactly as evolution designed it (Murphy & Woolfolk, in press). The adaptive problems that caused the mind to evolve as it did are the ones we faced in long-vanished environments, of which our minds still bear the imprints. It is entirely likely that we have mental mechanisms ("modules") that evolved to meet challenges in those earlier environments. These modules may no longer be apt to bring about desirable behavior in our contemporary circumstances.

Mental disorders characterized by fear and avoidance may be cases in which internal mental mechanisms are functioning as designed. Identification and avoidance of dangerous situations is adaptive, and the "better safe than sorry" strategy is, relative to suffering false negatives, adaptively superior across the spectrum of species. Avoidant creatures from guppies (*Poecilia reticulate;* Dugatkin, 1992) to *Homo sapiens* live to procreate another day:

> Repeated false alarms may cost less than a single failure to respond when the danger is great. . . . Anxiety at the mere hint of danger is therefore common, even though it may appear needless to a casual observer. Because the costs of erring on the side of caution are usually less than those of risk taking, it is no wonder that anxiety disorders are frequent. (Marks & Nesse, 1994, p. 254)

The evolutionary account would have it that the proclivity to develop a conditioned avoidance of snakes, strangers, or heights is adaptive. Some evidence exists that humans and closely related species are "prepared" by natural selection to develop certain fears very rapidly (Mineka, Davidson, Cook, & Keir, 1984; Seligman, 1970). Thus it may be that at least some phobias do not represent the dysfunction of a mental mechanism, but rather its functioning as per design, albeit inconsistently with the current pattern of human interests.

Various other forms of psychopathology also may represent adaptive strategies that have been favored by natural selection. The social competition theory of depression (Price, Sloman, Gardner, Gilbert, & Rohde, 1994) hypothesizes that depression is an adaptive response to a fall in status or a loss in resource-holding power. The fitness-enhancing effects of a depression in such circumstances would include the conservation of energy, the reduction of costly behavior, the elicitation of aid from others, and the opportunity to develop new and potentially more effective tactics for gaining status. Individuals with Antisocial Personality Disorder and those with Histrionic Personality Disorder have been conceptualized as social "free riders," who seek to acquire group resources without adhering to the norms governing the acquisition of social status (Harpending & Sobus, 1987; Stevens & Price, 1996). Histrionics and sociopaths are conceived as nonreciprocators (cheaters) who employ disingenuous but successful strategies to gain resources and status. Finally, McGuire and Triosi (1998) argue that Attention-Deficit/Hyperactivity Disorder (ADHD) and its associated aggressiveness and high activity levels may lead to reproductive success in some environmental circumstances.

Thus behavior that qualifies for a *DSM* diagnosis could occur in the absence of any mechanism that is, in the etiological sense, malfunctioning. In one case, spandrels, there may be no adaptive function involved at all, hence, no malfunction. In the other case, mechanisms selected by evolution may, when functioning as designed, bring about patterns of behavior that for various reasons we would choose to classify as pathological.

Propensity Function

Many species, including our own, no longer occupy environments similar to those in which they evolved, resulting in mismatches between design and current environmental demands. Propensity functions take into account that a previously adaptive trait may no longer function to enhance fitness in its current environment, for example, the predatory equipment of domesticated animals that no longer hunt for food. Or traits that themselves originally conferred either no adaptive advantage or disadvantage subsequently could become fitness enhancing in a novel environment.

A propensity function (Bigelow & Pargetter, 1987) is defined in relation to its propensity to enhance fitness in any possible environment: historical, current, or future. When contrasted with the historical view of etiological functions, propensity functions are said to be "forward looking" in their import, in that they refer to probable future selective success rather than to a history of selection. Walsh (1996) has elaborated the propensity concept of function in the rubric of what he terms a "relational function." This view is that a function is the contribution that a trait makes to fitness, but that the contribution is always contextualized in an actual or potential environment and can be specified only relative to a given environment.

If our concept of malfunction is predicated on propensity functions rather than etiological functions, a somewhat different picture of malfunction emerges. The reason a heart malfunctions today is not because it fails to do what it was selected for, but because it performs in a fashion that diminishes our current capacities to survive and procreate. Because propensity functions are also environment-relative, unlike etiologically defined malfunctions, their malfunction can be a direct result of a mismatch between environment and evolutionary design, rather than a simple failure of a mechanism to function according to its design. Propensity functions allow us to state that our antediluvian limbic systems, albeit functional and salutary in earlier ages, now malfunction and produce pathologies, even though they operate as designed originally.

Because propensity functions involve the conferring of advantage relative to a specified environment, either actual or potential, categories predicated on propensity concepts are rather malleable. Almost any trait, in some environment, might enhance the chances of survival or procreation either of individuals or the kinship groups to which they belong. The trait would be subject to malfunctioning relative to its fitness-enhancing properties in that environment. For example, dark pigment would advantage individuals in tropical environments but not those who live close to the poles. In the tropics, albinism might be properly regarded as a genetic malfunction, but not so in locales where pigmentation conferred no advantage.

One consequence of employing propensity functions and the standards for proper functioning that derive from them is that to the degree that adherence to cultural values enhances fitness, proper functioning becomes intertwined with values. It is indeed likely that what would enhance fitness in current and future human environments is not independent of culture and its values. We can imagine a range of possibilities in this regard. For example, human aggressive proclivities, when they are high, might be regarded as functioning properly (in a propensity sense) in a warrior society. Pacific societies that abhor violence, however, may regard bellicose individuals as pathological.

What it takes to "get ahead" in different social networks is highly variable, frequently depending on norms and values. The propensity analysis of function introduces a degree of cultural and historical relativism into the determination of malfunction. Being labeled pathological may in itself influence survival chances and the ability to procreate; thus behavior might become pathological simply by being so labeled. Malfunctions predicated on propensity functions create the possibility of allowing back into psychiatric nosologies such infamous cases as drapetomania, simply on the assumption that attempting to escape slavery may have adversely affected slaves' chances of survival. Since propensity malfunctions imply lack of success in a given environment, they seem to resuscitate that old and much-maligned shibboleth, "adjustment to society."

Propensity functions have in common with historical functions that they make fitness (survival and procreation) the test. The fitness criterion is appropriate in the case of etiological functions since selection due to fitness caused the feature to be there in the first place. But how do we export the propensity model of malfunction to societies where people's chances to survive and procreate are not systematically biased by their psychological traits? The propensity perspective suggests that no psychopathology (none requiring malfunction as a necessary condition) would be present there. We, of course, easily can imagine a society where the brightest and the best (and the "healthiest") choose to not procreate or to procreate less than other groups. Birthrates in the United States and Europe already reflect this trend. Fitness seems an odd criterion to apply in these cases, but any alternative standard would surely derive from cultural values and related concepts of human flourishing.

Ahistorical Functions

An ahistorical function, sometimes referred to as a "Cummins" function, (Cummins, 1975), after the philosopher who proposed it, makes no reference to the history or origin of the trait or organ involved. Functions simply describe the causal relations among systems and their component parts, such that "the function of a part of a system is its causal contribution to some specified activity of the system" (Walsh & Ariew, 1996, p. 493). In this kind of framework, it is the function of heart to pump blood, not because of its history of natural selection, but because the heart is a component of a larger system, the circulatory system, in which it plays a vital causal role.

Cummins functions are termed "interest relative," meaning that the function of a component is always relative to a given analysis of a system that comprises the component. The designation of the system may be the result of an arbitrary explanatory interest. Many different systems can be posited that concurrently contain the component. The Cummins function of the heart is to pump blood, but only in the context of explaining human physiology. Alternatively, if we wish to give an account of an electrocardiogram (EKG), we can describe an electrophysiological system wherein it can turn out to be the case that the function of the heart is to produce the electrical signals that result in EKG tracings. The heart can also function as a lethal target, one that is penetrated by bullets or arrows and thereafter exudes blood, if our explanation is of assassination.

The Cummins function refers solely to cause and effect in a containing system specified by an analytic inquiry. No background context of inquiry is privileged over any other, as is the case with the privileging of an evolutionary account by historical functional analysis. Cummins functions potentially can provide great latitude with regard to the designation of function and malfunction. For example, a kidney malfunctions when it fails to remove water from the blood, but its failure in a Cummins sense has to do with a preestablished systemic goal, that is, maintaining salutary blood hydration. Its malfunction is *only* relative to its causal role in effecting a specified outcome in a system.

But many different kinds of outcomes are associated with living systems. Such systems subsist and procreate, but they also become diseased and die. And if our interest is in the explanation of the processes of disease and death, we may construct functional analyses that illustrate the contributions of our organs to such baneful outcomes. In this kind of endeavor, various containing systems with interacting components can be described. In such analyses, we can speak properly, in the Cummins sense, of the coronary arteries functioning to accumulate plaque; the lungs, to host pneumococci; and cancer cells, to interfere with cellular nutrition.

Because the causal contribution of a component of a system is relative to an explanatory interest and to a context of inquiry, virtually any effect of any organ can be classified as a Cummins function. This situation has led some writers to claim that the concepts proper function and malfunction do not apply to Cummins functions. Other writers have stated that the malfunction of a Cummins function is intelligible only in relation to goals provided by background theories. Wachbroit (1994) states that malfunction presupposes a concept of "biological normality," (as distinct from mere statistical or normality in relation to social norms). This is the conception of biological normality presumably employed in the notions of a normal heart, a normal response, and a normal environment. Thus, in the case of Cummins functions, we require background assumptions concerning biological or psychological normality or desirability to impute malfunction to a component in a system. These assumptions likely will emanate from the practical arena of clinical medicine or from the culture at large.

Cummins functions are employed, unproblematically, in medicine and the biological sciences to describe cause-and-effect relationships involving organisms. In these fields, there is universal acceptance of the proposition that a heart that cannot pump blood is a malfunctioning heart and is therefore pathological. The consensus on such judgments of malfunction does not depend on an evolutionary account of why hearts exist, but rather unanimity of opinion on the question of what hearts are for.

Conclusions and Implications

So what can we conclude from the preceding discussion?

1. There is a normative element in psychodiagnosis that remains despite various efforts to define psychopathology in terms of biological or psychological malfunction. Even when the big guns of evolutionary biology and cognitive science are trained on the mental health professions, they cannot blast away the inherent and irreducible evaluative dimensions of the field.

2. The assumptions underlying scientistic approaches in psychiatry and clinical psychology clearly have been dealt a severe blow, but the implications of my analysis extend beyond the mental health professions. With a little work, it can be shown that the preceding analysis I have given of malfunction applies with equal validity to somatic pathology. Thus all forms of human malady and all forms of treatment are deeply embedded in human values. Psychotherapy and somatic medicine are not qualitatively distinct in the sense that Thomas Szasz believed, one being an objective scientific technology and the other a form of practical moral discourse.

The value judgments underlying somatic medicine are simply less obvious and frequently less controversial than those that undergird psychotherapy. A full discussion of this topic would require more space than I have here. But both medical diagnoses and their related Cummins functions appear to be value free to the extent that there is agreement on the proper characterization of a system, even though this characterization may have nothing to do with our species design. We all want our hearts to circulate the blood, even if they have not been "designed to do so." We would like our arteries to be unobstructed and therefore "healthy" at age 55, although this end was surely not an objective of natural selection. What we wish to explain and why those explananda are important to us, the relation of knowledge and human interests, seem crucial here in making the functional analyses of somatic medicine appear to be evaluatively neutral. The "proper functioning," or "normality," of the body is uncontroversial only to the extent that there is consensus on what constitutes health and infirmity. Human beings universally disvalue death, discomfort, and incapacity. Therefore, to the extent that somatic structures and processes are relatively invariant and reliably related to universally desired health outcomes, Cummins functional systems can be constructed in a common background of explanatory and valuational interests, therefore seeming to be universal and objective.

The medicalization of everyday life appeals to some because it appears to remove many human problems from the uncertain, arbitrary, and contentious realm of values and places them in the epistemologically secure, definitive, and value-free realm of science. These days, in the mental health professions, a biological explanation trumps a psychological or sociological one. But if we understand that no psychiatric nosology or classification of physical diseases is a natural-kind grouping, that the *DSM* is not like the periodic table of elements, then medicalization emerges as a kind of cultural exchange of one vocabulary of values for another. Medicalization is simply one among many features of modernity wherein we put our trust in the scientist (and the harder his or her science, the better) and despair of a consensus of valuation arrived at on any basis other than the discourse of expertise.

Slaying the dragon of objectivism, whether it be in somatic medicine or psychiatry, is simply one step that leads to a more holistic, complex, humanistic, interpretive view of all the health care professions. These practices emerge as rich mixtures of science, technology, and what the sociologists term "directive structure." In them, theory, technique, and norms are intermingled and blurred. Health itself is understood not as a thing definable apart from culture and human interests, as, for example, mass or velocity might be, but rather as a dimension of human flourishing. This holistic view construes health care as a multifaceted institutional vehicle that structures and influences our negotiation of the life world.

Psychotherapy, in particular, has a vantage point from which we derive constant cogent reminders that human flourishing is more than the correspondence of our biology with some objective, scientific standard of functioning (Woolfolk, 1998). Psychotherapy provides the testimony that serves to correct the most alarming feature of the biomedical colossus—its materialism. To give just one example, we are buffeted these days by biological psychiatrists, pharmaceutical advertising, and various spokespersons (ranging from Tipper Gore to Colin Powell) with messages that depression (often called the "common cold" of psychiatry) is nothing more than a metabolic illness, a simple biochemical imbalance that is easily corrected with the proper medication. Such accounts assume that one's culture, sociological position, interpersonal relations, or worldview are at most marginally relevant correlates of an autonomous and intrapersonal disease process, largely genetically based. Depression is constructed as a nomothetic biological phenomenon that transcends its human context. We psychotherapists (along with medical anthropologists and depressed patients) are in a position to know that it just isn't so. Our vantage point enables us to view human suffering from angles that the psychiatric power structure cannot stretch to see, encumbered as it is by hubris and arrogance. We must keep the faith and continue to provide the humanistic correctives that seem so rarely generated by the scientific establishment.

References

American Psychiatric Association. (1994). *Diagnostic and statistical manual of mental disorders* (4th ed.). Washington, DC: Author.
Bigelow, J., & Pargetter, R. (1987). Functions. *Journal of Philosophy, 84*, 181-196.

Bloch, S., & Reddaway, P. (1977). *Psychiatric terror*. New York: Basic Books.

Cummins, R. (1975). Functional analysis. *Journal of Philosophy, 72,* 741-765.

Dugatkin, L. (1992). Tendency to inspect predators predicts mortality risk in the guppy (Poecilia reticulata). *Behavioral Ecology, 3,* 124-127.

Gould, S. (1997). The exaptive excellence of spandrels as a term and prototype. *Proceedings of the National Academy of Sciences of the United States of America, 94,* 10750-10755.

Gould, S., & Lewontin, R. (1979). The spandrels of San Marco and the Panglossian paradigm: A critique of the adaptationist programme. *Proceedings of the Royal Society, London, 205,* 581-598.

Harpending, H., & Sobus, J. (1987). Sociopathy as an adaptation. *Ethology and Sociobiology, 8,* 63S-72S.

Marks, I., & Nesse, R. (1994). Fear and fitness: An evolutionary analysis of anxiety disorders. *Ethology and Sociobiology, 15,* 247-261.

McGuire, M., & Triosi, A. (1998). *Darwinian psychiatry*. New York: Oxford University Press.

Millikan, R. (1989). In defense of proper functions. *Philosophy of Science, 56,* 288-302.

Mineka, S., Davidson, M., Cook, M., & Keir, R. (1984). Observational conditioning of snake fear in rhesus monkeys. *Journal of Abnormal Psychology, 93,* 355-372.

Murphy, D., & Woolfolk, R. (in press). The harmful dysfunction analysis of mental disorder. *Philosophy, Psychiatry, and Psychology*.

Neander, K. (1991). Functions as selected effects: The conceptual analyst's defense. *Philosophy of Science, 58,* 168-184.

Price, J., Sloman, L., Gardner, R., Gilbert, P., & Rohde, P. (1994). The social competition hypothesis of depression. *British Journal of Psychiatry, 164,* 309-315.

Seligman, M. (1970). On the generality of the laws of learning. *Psychological Review, 77,* 406-418.

Stevens, A., & Price, J. (1996). *Evolutionary psychiatry*. New York: Routledge.

Wachbroit, R. (1994). Normality as a biological concept. *Philosophy of Science, 61,* 579-591.

Wakefield, J. (1992). The concept of mental disorder: On the boundary between biological and social values. *American Psychologist, 47,* 373-388.

Walsh, D. (1996). Fitness and function. *British Journal for the Philosophy of Science, 47,* 553-574.

Walsh, D., & Ariew, A. (1996). A taxonomy of functions. *Canadian Journal of Philosophy, 26,* 493-514.

Woolfolk, R. (1998). *The cure of souls: Science, values, and psychotherapy*. San Francisco: Jossey-Bass.

Wright, L. (1976). *Teleological explanations: An etiological analysis of goals and functions*. Berkeley: University of California Press.

Commentary

"Objectivity" in Diagnosis and Treatment: A Philosophical Analysis

Daniel K. Judd
Brigham Young University

Several years ago, an individual was referred to me for therapy who had been an unsuccessful applicant for a position with a local police department. During our first session, he explained to me that when he had inquired as to why he did not get the job and what he could do to increase the likelihood of being hired in the future, he was told by his prospective employer that they had some concerns about his mental stability. When he asked them to be specific about their concerns, they eventually told him that his psychological profile indicated that he did not have sufficient "ego strength" to be a good police officer. They suggested he seek professional help and discouraged him from applying a second time.

Further inquiry revealed that as a part of the screening process my client had been given several diagnostic measures, including the Minnesota Multiphasic Personality Inventory (MMPI). When I obtained the evaluator's report, it stated that my client had "abnormal thought processes," and low ego strength. The report also mentioned the possibility of my client being "schizophrenic."

Although I wanted to be open to the concerns of the evaluator, in my interactions with my client I could not find any evidence of what might be construed as mental confusion or low ego strength. The only confusion I could find was my client's sincere concern over his newly discovered low ego strength and possible identity as a schizophrenic.

On closer examination as to why he scored the way he did on various scales of the MMPI, I discovered that although some of his scales were mildly elevated, his "abnormal" scores were more an indication of his guilelessness and culture than reliable measures of mental illness. For example, when I asked him to explain to me why he answered yes to the question, "I see things or animals or people around me that others do not see" (Hathaway & McKinley, 1951), he described for me one of his unique skills as a deer hunter. With a hint of pride (ego strength), he told me of his ability to see the deer before others were able to do so. Thus he was able to see animals that others could not see—hardly an indication of "abnormal thinking," let alone schizophrenia. Of special concern to me were this young man's answers in the affirmative to such questions as, "Everything is turning out just like the prophets in the Bible said it would," "I have had some very unusual religious experiences," "Christ performed miracles such as changing water into wine," and "I pray several times every week." Answering yes to these questions counted against his score on the ego strength scale (see Judd, 1987). We quickly learned that the MMPI was not friendly to skilled deer hunters or believers in things religious, and if you were both you were really in trouble.

My client was able to eventually secure employment in the profession of his choice, but what a sad commentary on the use and abuse of psychological objectification through testing and labeling. The human resource people at the police force where my client first applied had been taught to rely on and give credence to MMPI scores in the very same way they interpreted the drug screen analysis. If the applicants tested positive for marijuana on a drug screen or one of the various scales on their MMPI profile was not in a specific range, they were automatically disqualified.

Dr. Woolfolk's chapter is an important statement concerning the dangers of "the medicalization of everyday life." In our ambitions to be *real* doctors practicing *real* science, we can be in danger of losing our own souls, as well as losing the possibility of helping to cure the souls of those with whom we work.

As you can surmise from my introductory example and comment, I am in agreement with Dr. Woolfolk's critique of the assumption of "objectivity" in psychotherapy. Although I offer a couple of suggestions for making Dr. Woolfolk's message more accessible to the therapeutic community, for the most part you will find my comments to be a "second witness" to what he has shared with us.

Although Dr. Woolfolk's warnings of scientistic objectivism are well argued and presented, his chapter also mentions the opposite problem—relativism. I personally judge openness and a willingness not to buy into the dogmatic approaches of traditional therapy as virtues, but I have also been around long enough to know that any virtue pressed to an extreme becomes a vice. Dr. Woolfolk correctly states that "a Hobson's choice between objectivism and relativism awaits many newly credentialed professionals."

The Christian apologist C. S. Lewis (1960) warned us that error is usually found in "pairs—pairs of opposites," and we are drawn into one because of our serious dislike for the other (p. 160). Dr. Woolfolk's descriptions of the dangers of objectivism and relativism are first rate, but perhaps his chapter would benefit (especially for clinicians) from a more detailed explanation and relevant examples of what he proposes as an alternative. Just how does a nonscientistic psychotherapy differ from one that is relativistic?

I remember well as a graduate student attempting to make an argument for the legitimacy of a clinical study eventually titled, "Agentive Theory as Therapy: An Outcome Study" (Judd, 1987). One of the professors examining my prospectus was concerned that my proposal included a qualitative analysis of the clients' experience in therapy. His concern was that my qualitative analysis was not going to be rigorous, but simply an undisciplined conversation—in Irvin Yalom's (1980) description, an excuse for "wooly" therapists to "do their thing" (p. 5). We were able to convince him otherwise, but his point was an important one. We must be very good at what we do and not use any license that we have fought for as an excuse for incompetence, both in our own practices and, perhaps especially, with the young students we train. Even though we might not look to the *DSM-IV* in the same way others do, we must be diligent in seeking to understand and assist the people who embody the descriptions contained therein.

In addition to identifying and understanding the dangers of the self-serving motives of the pharmaceutical, health insurance, academic, and research industries (which Dr. Woolfolk does well), I also believe we must take an honest look at ourselves. We must ask ourselves the question why we as individuals have bought into as much of the medicalization of psychotherapy as we have. Are there other reasons to be addressed beyond the traditional ones we discuss in this volume? Why is it that we are insulted or perhaps embarrassed if someone points out the fact that we have an EdD instead of a PhD or that we are psychologists and not psychiatrists? Perhaps we need to ask ourselves if we have too much of that labeled "ego strength" I mentioned earlier.

The part of Dr. Woolfolk's chapter that I was happy to see in the beginning but seemed to disappear all to quickly was his case study of Lynn and Steve. I realize I am stating the obvious, but perhaps in addition to asking members of the therapeutic community to take more seriously the theoretical underpinnings of what they are doing, those of us in the theoretical community need to make our philosophical work more clinically relevant. "That's not my place," you say? Balderdash; let us pay the extra price and do it anyway.

A second part of Dr. Woolfolk's case study I want to comment on is his inclusion of Lynn's "moral imperative":

> Lynn had interrupted a promising career in advertizing out of a keenly felt moral imperative to be the primary caregiver to her children. She had recently resumed full-time work in her former field, but was feeling a mixture of resentment, despondence, guilt, and exhaustion. She related to me that she knew she needed challenging work outside the home to be fulfilled, but believed she needed to change fields.

As I briefly mentioned earlier, Dr. Woolfolk deals eloquently with the limitations of the traditional scientistic perspective and mentions the dangers of the relativistic but does not give the attention I was looking for to the moral domain.

What about Lynn's "keenly felt moral imperative"? Is Lynn alone in knowing what is right? Can she have confidence in her "keenly felt moral imperative"? What is our role as therapists? All of us have had it imposed on us that we are not to impose our moral values on others, so what do we do with the question of morality? If we encourage Lynn to decide for herself, is that not relativism?

References

Hathaway, S. R., & McKinley, J. C. (1951). *Minnesota Multiphasic Personality Inventory: Manual.* New York: Psychological Corporation.

Judd, D. K. (1987). Religious affiliation and mental health. *Association of Mormon Counselors and Psychotherapists, 12*(2), 71-87.

Lewis, C. S. (1960). *Mere christianity.* New York: Macmillan.

Yalom, I. D. (1980). *Existential psychotherapy.* New York: Basic Books.

Issue 14

Feminism

Bringing Feminist Issues to Therapy

Jeanne Marecek
Swarthmore College

Second-wave feminism grew out of the civil rights movement and the youth culture of the 1960s. The women in what was then called the women's liberation movement fought for equal rights and an end to the outright discrimination that pervaded American society. Since then, women from diverse backgrounds, generations, and nations have taken up the cause of women's emancipation and devised forms of feminism to fit their needs and circumstances. Today, there is no single, agreed-on way to be a feminist, but a profusion of feminisms.

Feminist therapy was forged in the crucible of the women's liberation movement at the end of the 1960s. Protests against the mental health establishment had been commonplace in the progressive movements of the 1960s. Activists challenged the broad powers of the mental health establishment to deny patients' civil rights. They accused practitioners of stifling nonconformity, and the practitioners in turn diagnosed such protest behaviors as disturbed. The early women's movement objected strenuously to the feminine psychology promulgated in psychoanalytic theory, then the reigning paradigm in psychiatry. Psychoanalytic constructs included the double orgasm theory, penis envy, and women's "inner space" (Buhle, 1998). Feminists also objected to the insistence on marriage and motherhood as criteria of female maturity and fulfillment, arguing that this stigmatized single women and lesbians, as well as many women of color. In *Women and Madness* (1972), a text that was highly influential in its day, Phyllis Chesler spelled out what she saw as the double bind for women. Traditional femininity was extolled as the ideal of mental health for women at the same time that such diagnostic categories as hysterical personality and dependent personality disorder rendered femininity a disorder. Chesler's claim seemed to be supported by the studies of Broverman and her colleagues (Broverman, Broverman, Clarkson, Rosenkrantz, & Vogel, 1970), which suggested that therapists' criteria for positive mental health matched their description of the ideal man, whereas their image of "a typical mental patient" resembled that of the ideal woman.

At first, feminists positioned themselves outside the mental health system and spoke against it. Almost immediately, however, feminists in the mental health professions put forth the idea of feminist therapy as a means of changing the system from within. The initial descriptions of feminist therapy emphasized consciousness raising (CR), a technique borrowed from the small-group practice of the women's liberation movement (Brodsky, 1973; Kirsh, 1974). In its original form, CR had been modeled after the "rap" groups of the Black Power movement and the "speak bitterness" sessions of Mao's revolutionary army. CR was conceived as a tool for women to analyze the sociopolitical structures of gender through their personal experiences. It was intended to create solidarity among women and incite them to collective action for societal change. When therapists appropriated CR, however, the focus became personal; goals of political mobilization and societal transformation were put aside. Many feminists who were not therapists deplored this appropriation of CR, viewing it as co-optation (see, e.g., Hanisch, 1971). As we will see, debates about the relation of therapy to politics thread through the history of feminist therapy to the present moment. What happens when psychotherapy, a technology of individual change, is yoked to a politics of societal transformation? Can therapy be a political act? Or is therapy antithetical to political change? Should a goal of feminist therapy be to incite clients to collective political action? Indeed, an issue of the journal *Women and Therapy* (Volume 21, No. 2, 1998) was devoted entirely to this question.

In the ensuing decades, feminist ideas, critiques, and values have been interpellated into many systems of therapy (see Enns, 1997, for a review). Feminists have recast theories of clinical disorders, focusing particularly on problems of high prevalence among women. Feminist therapists have devised interventions for disorders such as eating problems (Bloom, Gitter, Gutwill, Kogel, & Zaphiropoulos, 1994), sexual difficulties (Barbach, 1975; Hall, 1998), depression (Jack, 1999), childhood sexual abuse (Courtois, 1996; Herman, 1992), and relationship violence (Goldner, 1999). Moreover, concepts and ideas of feminism have been extended to work with men and boys, as well as couples and families. Deborah Luepnitz (1988), for example, describes feminist-informed family therapy with a young man from the inner city and his family. *Men's Ways of Being*, edited by Christopher McLean, Maggie Carey, and Cheryl White (1996), presents several accounts of innovative feminist practice by male therapists concerned with such gender-related problems as bullying by boys, violence against intimate partners, and gay relationships.

Making a Difference: Feminism in Therapy

What practical implications does a feminist stance have for psychotherapy? The practice of feminist therapy has far outstripped both theory development and research. The voluminous literature bubbles over with ideas, often argued with eloquence and strong conviction. But it is a literature that points in many different directions at the same time. This is hardly surprising, as for the most part the authors are practitioners operating outside the academy, as are their intended readers. Theoretical rigor, internal consistency, and empirical verification are not their priorities. Moreover, the literature encompasses so many feminisms and so many psychotherapies that the task of synthesizing them all is impossible. I have chosen to trade comprehensiveness for coherence, limiting myself to a single slice of feminist therapy. Another writer, with a different angle of vision, might capture a wholly different slice. This is, as most readers will agree, both a strength and a weakness of feminist therapy.

I set my sights on feminist family therapy, a field galvanized by publication of the book *Women in Families: A Framework for Family Therapy* (McGoldrick, Anderson, & Walsh, 1989). I choose feminist family therapy for many reasons. Feminism received a warmer reception and a more serious hearing from family therapists than from other sectors of the mental health professions. Moreover, although feminist family therapy has developed at a fast pace, many feminist family therapists have been self-conscious about their theoretical commitments. They are conversant with narrative theory, postmodern thought, and social constructionism, as well as with academic feminist theory. Although I am not a family therapist, I share their theoretical commitments and interests. Moreover, I share with feminist family therapists a substantive interest in the micropolitics of gender in personal relations.

I describe four concepts that have been identified by consensus groups of experts as core to feminist therapy (Hill & Ballou, 1998; Parker, 1998; Wyche & Rice, 1997). I discuss efforts to put these concepts into practice. But this is not intended as a canonical list of feminist practices. Feminism represents a general philosophy that stands outside any particular system of therapy; the application of that philosophy that takes shape in one mode of therapy might impede the therapeutic work in another. A caveat: Many of the values, practices, and concerns that I describe below are not unique to feminism. Much of what follows will probably lead some readers to think, "But that's just good therapy," or, "I always do that." One prominent feminist therapist counters such reactions by saying, "Well, then, I guess you're a feminist, but you just haven't realized it." Although some might applaud her inclusive gesture, I take issue with her line of reasoning. What defines therapy as feminist is not a congeries of actions, but rather the philosophical framework that organizes and informs those actions. An unwitting feminist is an oxymoron.

Putting the Person in Context

For feminists, gender—necessarily in concert with ethnicity, race, class, sexuality, and other markers of hierarchy—is a central feature of social life and social hierarchy. Feminists bring to therapy a focus on the gender system—the institutions, social practices, language, and normative beliefs that govern relations between men and women and that establish and normalize the power differences between them. Feminist therapists view clients' difficulties and strengths in relation to the gender system. This angle of vision goes beyond cataloguing symptoms and syndromes to a consideration of behavior in context. It sometimes dislodges conventional meanings of clients' behavior and may even overturn conventional judgments about what is healthy or unhealthy. For example, rather than assume that a wife's chronic anger is a problem to be corrected, a feminist might ask whether it is a healthy response to an unfair or corrosive situation. A feminist might question whether characterizations (including self-characterizations) such as bitch, nagging, irritable, and premenstrual syndrome (PMS) are serving as means of controlling a woman rather than straightforward descriptors of behavior.

Many truisms in psychotherapy are not scientific facts but normative beliefs about groups of people (men and women, whites and blacks, middle-class people and poor people, straights and gays); these beliefs often reaffirm and justify social inequalities. Feminists have been concerned to challenge clinical constructs that smack of these normative beliefs and that have served to keep women (and other groups) in a one-down position. For example, autonomy has long been considered an attribute of positive mental health, but is autonomy good—or even possible—for women? The ideal of autonomy is modeled on the experiences of high-status men, who commandeer the invisible work of women to create the illusion of self-sufficiency (Hare-Mustin & Marecek, 1986). Men's autonomy is propped up by the efforts of their wives, who supply domestic needs and raise children, and their secretaries, who manage day-to-day demands at work. Harriet Lerner (1983) has challenged the claim that women are the excessively dependent sex. She noted that women are called on to serve others' needs but cannot ask others to take care of their needs in return. Most women, Lerner noted, "are far more expert in worrying about the needs of others than in identifying and assertively claiming their own needs" (p. 698). Instead of being too dependent, Lerner claims, women are not dependent enough.

Cultural assumptions about gender and sexuality permeate scientific knowledge of sex, shaping the questions that have been asked, the methods used to answer them, and the interpretations made. Leonore Tiefer (1994) has documented the assumptions that underlie the human sexual response cycle (HSRC), a metaphor popularized by Masters and Johnson in the 1960s and now the prevailing account of human sexuality. The significance of the HSRC can hardly be overestimated: It is taught in human sexuality courses and enshrined in medical school textbooks. Moreover, the nosology of sexual dysfunctions in the *Diagnostic and Statistical Manual of Mental Disorders* (DSM; American Psychiatric Association, 1994) draws its language and its ideas from the HSRC. Tiefer criticizes the HSRC (which she calls a "universal machine without a motor") for its exclusive genital focus: its definition of sexuality as the performances of fragmented body parts, its biological reductionism, its emphasis on speed and efficiency as indicators of sexual competence. The HSRC privileges heterosexual intercourse and orgasm; it trivializes (e.g., as "foreplay") or ignores many erotic experiences that women value and prefer. Furthermore, Tiefer raises the larger question of whether sexual performance should be equated with "health" or "mental health" at all.

Women's eating problems are the culture-bound syndrome par excellence in contemporary American society. Feminist theorists have examined the gender-laden motifs and themes invoked by food, eating, diets, self-indulgence, self-denial, body size, and fat (Bloom et al., 1994). Becky Thompson (1995) extended this work to women who do not fit the profile of the typical client with an eating disorder—women of color, lesbian women, and women from impoverished backgrounds. The women Thompson interviewed experienced their eating practices as means of coping with emotional strain; bingeing and dieting offered comfort, distraction, and a way to "numb out." Most traced their eating problems to times of severe emotional crisis; these included adolescent struggles over coming out as a lesbian, childhood experiences of sexual abuse, and financial desperation. Thompson's work challenges explanations for women's eating problems that rely solely on the "culture of thinness." It also serves as a reminder that gender is always intertwined with other dimensions of social hierarchy.

Mother blaming has deep roots in both popular culture and the psychotherapy professions, roots amply fertilized by many theories of human development (Caplan, 1989; Luepnitz, 1988). Recognizing and challenging mother blaming has been important to feminist therapists. In an early Delphi study of feminist family therapists, one of the two feminist principles on which consensus was reached was "Stop blaming mothers." As Virginia Goldner puts it,

> Non-feminist work, by not reading the relationship through the lens of gender, buries gender and along with that [therapists] bury inequality. And when that happens, given the nature of power, they hold women responsible for unhappinesses that are really the result of injustice. Women are blamed for their own victimization and they're blamed for children not turning out better. (in Parker, 1998, p. 19)

Can a feminist analysis that situates mothering in its social and cultural context help counter mother blaming? Consider a familiar scenario:

> A mother and her 15-year-old daughter are at loggerheads over the daughter's clothing, makeup, curfew, and companions. The mother forbids her daughter to associate with certain boys, to drive around in boys' cars, and to hang out in shopping malls. Worried that her daughter is (or is soon to be) engaging in sex, she furtively checks through her daughter's dresser drawers, purse, and diary.

Some therapists might declare this mother intrusive, overcontrolling, or enmeshed in her daughter's life. When seen in relation to white middle-class culture, however, the mother's behavior takes on different meanings. Although mother-daughter antagonism is often regarded as a normal part of adolescent development, it does not occur in much of the world. Even in the United States, it is not the norm in all social groups. Moreover, white middle-class culture has ambivalent reactions to adolescent sexuality. Adolescents are saturated with sexual imagery in music, videos, and commercial appeals, yet they are urged to postpone sexual involvement. Ideologies of romantic love and sexual desire are contradictory and in flux. Such cultural discourses as "raging hormones" and "male sex drive" accord male sexual pleasure the status of a biological need. To get sex, boys tell lies, ply girls with alcohol and drugs, threaten blackmail, and even use a degree of physical coercion; such behaviors are regarded as ordinary and reasonable, at least in adolescent peer culture if not in broader segments of the culture. Yet girls are the designated gatekeepers for sex, even though they often have little negotiating power in sexual situations. In this context, a mother's concern for her teenage daughter seems neither malign nor pathological. Rather than questioning what intrapsychic issues motivate that concern, a therapist might instead explore ways in which a concerned mother might help her daughter strike a balance between pleasure and safety, identify her needs (for both pleasure and self-protection), and develop skills to negotiate sexual situations.

Diversity in Context. Gender is not the only axis of social hierarchy. To be a woman means to be subordinate, but all women are not subordinate in the same way and not all forms of subordination are necessarily experienced as such. The meanings of gender are different for women of different ethnic backgrounds, economic circumstances, and sexual orientations. When therapists work across ethnicity or sexuality or class lines, most often it is the client who comes from the minority background. In such situations, therapists who wish to avoid stereotyping may be tempted to treat the client "just like everyone else." Such a strategy erases crucial aspects of clients' experience and identity. It also forecloses discussions of the ways in which racism, ethnic prejudice, heterosexism, and homophobia affect clients' experiences and contribute to their difficulties (Raja, 1998).

Many psychological theories unwittingly presume that the values and experiences of the Anglo-American middle class are universal. Ideas of optimal well-being, maturity, and appropriate developmental milestones are culture bound and class bound, and shaped and reshaped with the passage of time. The ideal of autonomy, alluded to earlier, is not only gendered, but also likely to be unattainable for individuals in less affluent situations. In many South Asian and East Asian cultures, for example, individuation and separation from one's family of origin are not developmental imperatives for young adults. White therapists working with African-American women may dismiss the significance of church membership as a source of community and coping in hard times, as well as a venue for leadership. Cultural differences play directly into diagnosis and treatment recommendations. In many non-Anglo cultures, the idioms of psychological distress are likely to be somatic rather psychological (Comas-Dias, 1987; Kleinman, 1984). Moreover, some therapeutic interventions may be misconstrued by or unacceptable to members of certain cultural groups. Somasunderam (1998) points out, for example, that many South Asian women are reluctant to disclose and discuss sexual matters, including sexual assaults, even in a medical or therapeutic context.

Cultural sensitivity is not cultural relativism; it does not demand that we abandon moral and ethical judgments. Radhika Coomaraswamy, a Sri Lankan human rights activist, points out that so-called indigenous cultural values too often have been invoked to protect male prerogatives and legitimate men's domination over women. For example, wife beating and the denial of women's rights to education or health care may be justified as part of "Islamic culture" or "Asian family values." In any social group, cultural setting, or religious group, however, belief systems are not monolithic. There are always individuals and groups who dissent from the dominant point of view and find certain practices objectionable.

In sum, features of the social context shape clients' experiences, including the difficulties that brought them to treatment, their options for change, and the resources available to them. Gender is central to the way social life is organized, but it does not have a single form or meaning across all social groups. A feminist analysis of the social context and the gender system gives special attention to power, the topic we turn to next.

Bringing Power to the Foreground

Feminism brings to therapy an unabashed commitment to justice and fairness. Feminist family therapists hold that power disparities underlie many problems that bring couples to treatment (Parker, 1998). In heterosexual relationships, power disparities include the lopsided distribution of household and family responsibilities, the implicit privileging of men's points of view, and the primacy of men's needs and interests. Unequal economic resources contribute to the unequal distribution of power: The person with less money—usually the woman—accommodates more. Feminists in family therapy have insisted that family life is embedded in the larger society, not a haven apart from it. Family difficulties need to be understood in relation to gendered features of society, such as women's diminished earning power, the gendered division of family labor and wage labor, the simultaneous idealization and blaming of mothers, and the stigma faced by single women and lesbians. Unless therapy takes into account men's and women's disparate material and social resources, it will perpetuate unfair outcomes.

Feminist family therapists have devised ways of working to redistribute power in couples. Some therapists use the initial fact-finding phase of therapy to investigate who does and does not hold power in what situations and how each partner exercises the power he or she has. They may ask partners to ponder how their decision making reflects and reinstates the power imbalance between them. They may give couples the homework assignment of observing the operation of power in mundane aspects of family life: Who controls the money?

Who does particular household tasks? Does one partner's paid work take priority over his or her family responsibilities? Who takes up the slack? Who takes time off from work when children are sick? What consequences do the current gender arrangements have for each partner? What are the pluses and minuses of the gender-linked patterns the couple currently engages in? How are those patterns tied to the issues that brought the couple into therapy?

Feminist therapists working in the framework of narrative therapy or social construction focus attention on language practices that perpetuate gendered power imbalances by naturalizing them or disguising them as something else. Hanne Haavind (1984), a Norwegian family therapist, has described femininity as subordination that appears to be something else, and masculinity as domination that appears reasonable, benevolent, and not striven for. For instance, the requirement that women devote themselves to the care of others is often redescribed as their female nature and glorified as positive feminine virtue; a husband's power over his wife may be characterized as the exercise of God-given authority or the result of natural male superiority.

Feminist therapists working in a narrative framework may insert new language practices in place of ones that perpetuate and naturalize power imbalances. Consider a therapeutic encounter in which Michael White worked with a middle-aged married couple (analyzed by Kogan & Gale, 1997). Tom and Jane both identified Jane's nagging and her controlling behavior as problems that they would like to address in therapy. "Nagging" is not just a neutral description of a behavior, but a value-laden interpretation. In this instance, it labels Jane's attempts to influence Tom (in other words, to assert power in the relationship) as excessive, domineering, and unpleasant. Moreover, labeling these interactions as "nagging" implies that Jane is solely responsible for them. As White proceeds to ask the couple for more details about the patterns they would like to change, he alters the description of Jane's behavior. Instead of "nagging" and "controlling," he refers to Jane as "taking too much responsibility in the relationship." This shift in terminology casts Jane's actions in a new, more positive light, as well as opening the question of Tom's contribution. It invites different ways for the couple to think about themselves and about how they might create more positive interactions.

Brian Jory and Debra Anderson (1999) describe a therapeutic approach for working with abusive men. They challenge the obfuscating language that men use to describe controlling, manipulative, condescending, or paternalistic behavior toward their wives or partners. For example, a man involved in a secret extramarital affair might say, "The reason I haven't told [my wife] the truth is for her own good. She couldn't handle it." Jory and Anderson challenge that account by asking the man what other motives he might have for lying. Are the effects of such behavior actually "good" for his partner? These therapists declare openly that relationships based on mutuality and reciprocity work better and are more emotionally satisfying for both partners. They make explicit reference to values of justice, fairness, morality, and gender equality. Note that the therapists' values (not explicitly labeled as feminist, but grounded on principles of gender equality and mutual respect) are not only announced to clients but also actively promoted as part of the treatment.

Violence Against Women. A pundit once remarked that there is no incest taboo, just a taboo on talking about it. Bringing intimate violence and sexual coercion out of the closet and into public conversation has been the hallmark accomplishment of second-wave feminism. Women took the risk to break the deep cultural silence on gender-linked violence by stepping forward to admit they had been victims of incest, wife beating, or rape. Feminists coined new terms—"date rape," "sexual harassment," "childhood sexual abuse," and "wife beating"—to replace euphemisms like rough sex, just a joke, fooling around, or working out a yes. These terms enunciated the problem of violence against women in direct, unambiguous ways. Feminists insisted that intimate violence against women was an outgrowth of culturewide gender arrangements, not a matter of isolated personal pathology.

Even today, many victims of gender-linked violence are silenced by shame, fear of blame, confusion over what is acceptable male sexual behavior, loyalty to their victimizers, or fear of reprisals. It is not uncommon for clients in therapy to "confess" experiences of assault, rape, molestation, or abuse that occurred decades earlier. These are not "recovered" memories but rather occurrences that the client has chosen to keep secret. With an awareness of the prevalence of violent and coercive behavior in intimate settings, many feminist therapists include direct questions about such experiences when they are taking a history.

Research on violence against women has laid bare the many ways in which it diminishes women's lives and possibilities. The corrosive effects of victimization have been well documented. Secondary victimization at the hands of insensitive police officers, emergency room personnel, or mental health workers can compound these effects. In circumstances where violence against women is so common and perpetrators so seldom held accountable, all women live under the threat of violence and limit their lives accordingly (Gordon & Riger, 1991). As therapists have worked with victims, victimizers, and victimization, they have come face to face with new complexities. Not all victims suffer lasting effects of what they have endured, and many reject the identity of a victim. Moreover, some victimizers have been victims and vice versa. Recent feminist work has countered the tendency to reduce the issues and actors to categories ("victim," "perp," "trauma") that caricature women as sexually innocent and without agency and men as demonic savages (Haaken, 1998; Lamb, 1999). Some have analyzed the confused and contradictory cultural messages to victims and perpetrators about blame, responsibility, forgiveness, and accountability (Lamb, 1996). Furthermore, although gender-based violence and sexual abuse need to be taken seriously, some feminists worry that these concerns will eclipse other gendered power imbalances.

Collaboration and Shared Power in Therapy

Feminists have recast the relationship between therapist and client to emphasize collaboration and mutual responsibility. The commitment to sharing the
power in therapy has a number of different roots. Egalitarianism and sharing
power have been features of second-wave American feminism from its start.
Moreover, early feminist therapists argued that hierarchical therapy relationships replicated the patterns of subordination that women clients were struggling to overturn in their lives outside therapy (Chesler, 1972). They saw that a
therapy relationship with a woman who was a feminist could afford an opportunity for the client to experience a more powerful stance.

The notion of feminist therapy as an "egalitarian" relationship soon gave
way to the recognition that psychotherapy could not, by definition, be a relationship between equals. Rich and nuanced conversations have ensued among feminist therapists about how client-therapist relationships could be collaborative
and for what reasons. Sharing power has remained a key goal. A collaborative
stance gives clients more power to determine the direction and pace of therapy.
It is respectful of clients' competence and knowledge about themselves. At the
same time, it helps to demystify therapy and the therapist's expertise. Moreover,
by assuming a collaborative stance, therapists carve out space for clients to
disagree with them, to raise questions and challenges, to express discomfort,
and to get angry.

Feminist therapists have experimented with a variety of practices to
share power in therapy. The most widely used and frequently discussed is
self-disclosure by the therapist. Clients typically disclose much that is embar-
rassing, shameful, and painful. In conventional approaches to therapy, therapists disclose next to nothing. Self-disclosures by a therapist can put the relationship on a more equal footing. Perhaps the most common disclosure is that
the therapist has struggled with issues akin to those the client faces. In addition
to dispelling tendencies to hold the therapist in awe, such disclosures can also
serve to instill hope of recovery. Other types of disclosures may be intended to
show clients that their therapists are ordinary and fallible human beings. Moreover, when therapists work with clients from cultural or class backgrounds different from their own, self-disclosures can bring out cultural differences and
conflicting values, so that they can be examined and worked through. Although
feminists are strong advocates of self-disclosure in therapy, they have also
recognized that self-disclosures must be appropriate. Questions of what, when,
how, and why to disclose have been discussed at length, with both ethical and
theoretical considerations brought to bear (cf. Ballou, 1995; Wyche & Rice, 1997).

More generally, many feminist therapists—though not all—prefer a stance
that is relatively informal and that stresses mutuality. Many connect their feminism to challenging the usual boundaries of the therapeutic relationship. Consider some examples (from interviews with feminist therapists; see Marecek &
Kravetz, 1998):

A therapist loans jewelry to a client to wear while attending the wedding of the client's estranged son. The therapist's goal is "to remind her of the new person she has become in therapy."

A therapist accepts an invitation from a client to accompany her to an art exhibition at the end of their session.

A therapist mentions to her client that she was too busy to have lunch that day and accepts a banana from her.

A therapist declines an invitation from her therapy group to "go partying" to celebrate one member's birthday. When the party group's limousine arrives at her door unexpectedly, she accepts a piece of birthday cake.

Each of these anecdotes was recounted by a particular therapist as an exemplar of her feminist practice; not all feminist therapists would agree that each was appropriate and therapeutic.

Other practices intended to empower clients in the therapy relationship have been suggested. Some therapists encourage potential clients to interview a number of therapists before choosing one to work with. Some negotiate written contracts with clients to set goals and to clarify mutual responsibilities. Others have clients review (or coauthor) case notes or collaborate in selecting a diagnosis to be recorded for insurance purposes. An important question that has not been examined yet is how these and other power-sharing practices affect clients. Do clients receive therapists' gestures of power sharing and collaboration in the spirit in which they are offered?

Discussions of empowering clients in feminist therapy often conceptualize power as a unified entity that rests (or does not rest) with an individual. This idea, though appealing in its simplicity, is neither the only way to conceive of power nor, in my view, the best. There are many kinds of power and they do not operate in unidirectional ways, whether in a therapy session or in real life. Power operates diffusely through webs of relationships and language practices. Although in many circumstances, women exert less power than men do, both men and women are enmeshed in multiple systems of power; although in some ways clients exert less power in therapy than their therapists do, both are enmeshed in systems of power.

Consider a situation in which a family is referred for treatment because one of the children is having problems in school. The mother is a ready participant, but the father is reluctant and skeptical and makes an appearance only occasionally. When the father attends a session, the therapist engages in what Deborah Luepnitz (1988) labels "father coddling." The therapist lavishes a disproportionate amount of attention on the father, working overtime to support and encourage him, congratulating him for his contributions, even stroking his ego. The father has moved to the center of the therapy, but not by exercising power directly or deliberately here. Paradoxically, it is his lack of active engagement that gives him undue influence.

In feminist narrative therapy, concepts of decentering and subjugated discourses have proven useful in reorganizing the power relations in the therapy encounter. Often it is therapists themselves who are placed in the central position while their clients take up the position of passive objects of scrutiny and judgment. In such cases, therapists may deliberately privilege other points of view, turning questions back to the questioner and avoiding interpretations, advice, or instruction. By asking "expansion questions," therapists encourage clients to amplify, revise, and reinterpret their stories of their experiences. In working with couples and families, therapists make it a priority to bring forward the stories and experiences of members who are usually marginalized or ignored.

Therapy Is Not Value Free

Therapy, as Rachel Hare-Mustin (1998) has written, "is a cultural activity of modern EuroAmerican society, a social practice that reproduces . . . gender, class, race and ethnicity systems" of the societies in which it is practiced (p. 47). Therapy, for the most part, is grounded in a cultural ideology that extols the individual, that defines freedom as the lack of social constraint, and that holds the examined life to be better than the unexamined one and reason superior to emotion. Mental health is defined strictly as a matter of personal satisfaction and individual advancement, not the common good or community solidarity.

History is replete with examples of diagnostic categories and treatment practices that reproduced gender, racial, and class systems of the times. For example, for nearly a hundred years, women and girls who experienced "excessive sexual desire" might be diagnosed as nymphomaniacs; in some cases, the prescribed treatment was clitoridectomy. Neurasthenia, a diagnosis given to many prominent women at the beginning of the 20th century, was treated with prolonged periods of enforced bed rest, solitude, and a complete interdiction on reading and writing. Drapetomania was a purported psychiatric condition that impelled slaves to run away from their masters. Our own times have spawned a jumble of diagnostic labels, some authorized by the *DSM*, some intended for inclusion, and others that circulate through popular culture and in and out of therapists' vernacular—PMS, sex addiction, paraphilic rapism, self-defeating personality disorder, borderline personality, battered woman syndrome, codependency, abortion trauma syndrome, Internet addiction, male delusional dominating disorder.

This burgeoning list indicates the rhetorical force of medicalized language as well as the politics and values of the larger culture. Such diagnostic categories simultaneously draw on and create idioms of distress. These in turn influence and reflect the way that members of the culture understand and experience suffering.

A feminist stance guides how therapists understand psychological problems and how they work in therapy. Yet feminists are not unique in bringing a value commitment to therapy; it is only that feminists make their values overt.

All therapy engages values and ethical commitments. Therapy that supports the values of the status quo may seem value free, but it is not. Such "value-free" therapy may covertly support male privilege; endorse heterosexuality; promote middle-class patterns of behavior as models of mental health; and perhaps condone sexist, homophobic, and racist attitudes and actions. Feminist therapists are sometimes criticized for being guided by politics rather than therapeutic principles. The feminist response is that politics and therapy are not mutually exclusive and cannot be disentangled.

An Open-Ended Conclusion

Feminist therapy joins a movement for social transformation to a technology for improving or repairing the individual. Although some early feminists argued that feminist therapy was an impossibility, it has flourished for over 30 years. Nonetheless, many practitioners recognize inherent contradictions. Laura Brown (1992), a prominent practitioner and theorist, sees that she must "voice her doubts to those she teaches, trains and writes for" and remind her audiences of "the fact that the first feminist responses to psychotherapy were to identify its destructive and controlling influences on women" (p. 240). Robin Sesan and Melanie Katzman (1998) describe their feminist therapy as "a compromise" borne of "essential tensions" between feminist theory and therapy practice (p. 83). Moreover, a feminist commitment to empowering clients and demystifying therapy does not square easily with the stance of authoritative expertise that medical professionalism customarily entails.

A recent position paper published by a working group of feminist therapists celebrated the coming of age of feminist therapy with the subtitle, "From Dialogue to Tenets" (Wyche & Rice, 1997). Leaving aside the question of whether such a move has actually taken place, I would not celebrate it. I prefer to approach feminist therapy—indeed, all therapy—in the spirit of what Foucault termed "problematization," a spirit that always leaves the door open for original, unconventional, and radical reformulations. Feminist therapy, like all therapy, is an unfinished project, and I hope it will always remain so. Like an amoeba, it has continually reshaped itself in response to the ebb and flow of culture over the past 30 years (Marecek, 1999). As the gender politics of the culture continue to shift, we can be sure that new clients, new problems, new ways of working, and indeed new feminisms will emerge.

References

American Psychiatric Association. (1994). *Diagnostic and statistical manual of mental disorders* (4th ed.). Washington, DC: Author.

Ballou, M. (1995). Naming the issue. In E. Rave & C. Larson (Eds.), *Feminist ethics casebook.* New York: Guilford.

Barbach, L. (1975). *For yourself.* New York: Anchor Books.

Bloom, C., Gitter, A., Gutwill, S., Kogel, L., & Zaphiropoulos, L. (1994). *Eating problems: A feminist psychoanalytic treatment model.* New York: Basic Books.

Brodsky, A. M. (1973). The consciousness-raising group as a model of therapy for women. *Psychotherapy: Theory, Research, and Practice, 10,* 24-29.

Broverman, I. K., Broverman, D. M., Clarkson, F. E., Rosenkrantz, P. S., & Vogel, S. R. (1970). Sex-role stereotypes and clinical judgments of mental health. *Journal of Consulting and Clinical Psychology, 34*(1), 1-7.

Brown, L. S. (1992). While waiting for the revolution. *Feminism and Psychology, 2*(2), 237-253.

Buhle, M. J. (1998). *Feminism and its discontents.* Cambridge, MA: Harvard University Press.

Caplan, P. J. (1989). *Don't blame mother.* New York: Harper & Row.

Chesler, P. (1972). *Women and madness.* New York: Doubleday.

Comas-Dias, L. (1987). Feminist therapy with mainland Puerto Rican women. *Psychology of Women Quarterly, 11,* 461-474.

Courtois, C. A. (1996). *Healing the incest wound: Adult survivors in therapy.* Binghampton, NY: Norton.

Enns, C. Z. (1997). *Feminist theories and feminist psychotherapies.* Binghampton, NY: Haworth.

Goldner, V. (1999). Morality and multiplicity: Perspectives on the treatment of violence in intimate life. *Journal of Marital and Family Therapy, 25,* 325-336.

Gordon, M. T., & Riger, S. (1991). *The female fear.* Chicago: University of Illinois Press.

Haaken, J. (1998). *Pillar of salt.* New Brunswick, NJ: Rutgers University Press.

Haavind, H. (1984). Love and power in marriage. In H. Holter (Ed.), *Patriarchy in a welfare state* (pp. 136-167). Oslo, Norway: Universitets Forlaget.

Hall, M. (1998). *The lesbian love companion.* San Francisco: HarperSanFrancisco.

Hanisch, C. (1971). The personal is political. In J. Agel (Ed.), *The radical therapist.* New York: Ballantine.

Hare-Mustin, R. T. (1998). Challenging traditional discourses in psychotherapy: Making space for alternatives. *Journal of Feminist Family Therapy, 10*(3), 39-56.

Hare-Mustin, R. T., & Marecek, J. (1986). Autonomy and gender: Some questions for therapists. *Psychotherapy, 23*(2), 205-212.

Herman, J. (1992). *Trauma and recovery.* New York: Basic Books.

Hill, M., & Ballou, M. (1998). Making therapy feminist: A practice survey. *Women and Therapy, 21,* 1-16.

Jack, D. C. (1999). Ways of listening to depressed women in qualitative research: Interview techniques and analysis. *Canadian Psychology, 40*(2), 91-101.

Jory, B., & Anderson, D. (1999). Intimate justice: Part 2. Fostering mutuality, reciprocity, and accommodation in therapy for psychological abuse. *Journal of Marital and Family Therapy, 25*(3), 349-364.

Kirsh, B. (1974). Consciousness-raising groups as therapy for women. In V. Franks & V. Burtle (Eds.), *Women and therapy: New psychotherapies for a changing society* (pp. 326-354). New York: Brunner/Mazel.

Kleinman, A. (1984). *The illness narratives.* New York: Basic Books.

Kogan, S., & Gale, J. (1997, August). *Decentering therapy: A conversation analysis of Michael White's narrative therapy.* Paper presented at the meeting of the American Psychological Association, Chicago.

Lamb, S. (1996). *The trouble with blame: Victims, perpetrators, and responsibility.* Cambridge, MA: Harvard University Press.

Lamb, S. (Ed.). (1999). *New versions of victims: Feminists struggle with the concept.* New York: New York University Press.

Lerner, H. G. (1983). Female dependency in context: Some theoretical and technical considerations. *American Journal of Orthopsychiatry, 53*(4), 697-705.

Luepnitz, D. A. (1988). *The family interpreted.* New York: Basic Books.

Marecek, J. (1999, June). *Feminist identities in the '90s: Necessity is the mother of (re)invention.* Paper presented at the Seventh International Interdisciplinary Congress on Women, Tromsø, Norway.

Marecek, J., & Kravetz, D. (1998). Power and agency in feminist therapy. In I. B. Seu & M. C. Heenan (Eds.), *Feminism and psychotherapy: Reflections on contemporary theories and practices* (pp. 13-29). London: Sage.

McGoldrick, M., Anderson, C. M., & Walsh, F. (Eds.). (1989). *Women in families: A framework for family therapy.* New York: Norton.

McLean, C., Carey, M., & White, C. (1996). *Men's ways of being.* Boulder, CO: Westview.

Parker, L. (1998). The unequal bargain: Power issues in couples therapy. *Feminist Family Therapy, 10*(3), 17-37.

Raja, S. (1998). Culturally sensitive therapy for women of color. *Women and Therapy, 21*(4), 67-84.

Sesan, R., & Katzman, M. (1998). Empowerment and the eating-disordered client. In I. B. Seu & M. C. Heenan (Eds.), *Feminism and psychotherapy: Reflections on contemporary theories and practices* (pp. 78-95). London: Sage.

Somasunderam, D. (1998). *Scarred minds.* Colombo, Sri Lanka: Vijitha Yapa.

Thompson, B. W. (1995). *A hunger so wide and deep.* Minneapolis: University of Minnesota Press.

Tiefer, L. (1994). *Sex is not a natural act and other essays.* Boulder, CO: Westview.

Wyche, K., & Rice, J. (1997). Feminist therapy: From dialogue to tenets. In J. Worell & N. Johnson, (Eds.), *Shaping the future of feminist psychology* (pp. 57-71). Washington, DC: American Psychological Association.

Commentary

Bringing Feminist Issues to Therapy

Marybeth Raynes, LCSW, MFT

Jeanne Marecek's chapter identifies several key components of feminist therapy along with its contribution to other models of psychotherapy in a clear, accessible manner. A particular strength is the map she provides to blind spots about gender in mainstream therapies. And as she indicates, therapy is political; social change must occur beyond therapy in order for the lives of women, men, and children to improve.

In this discussion of feminist therapy, it seems ironic for Dr. Marecek and myself to speak in a sequential assertion-and-rebuttal manner. Let me resist that unfeminist process in two ways; first, by recognizing how different her chapter and my response would be if we presented them collaboratively, engaging in a simultaneous, integrated dialogue. As we discovered when talking face to face, we see each other's view more completely and find more points of similarity and engaged discourse in a dialogue than when reading each other's writings separately. Second, by revealing my own context, I join in a practice strongly advocated by feminist therapists. I am a white, middle-aged therapist in private practice who works with a balance of women and men as individuals, couples, and families. In my work, I have found it important to integrate many models of therapy and I am additionally informed by other fields of thought, such as family systems theory and practice, cognitive-behavioral strategies, biological and medical models, as well as developmental and transpersonal psychology.

Despite the many strengths of her chapter and our overlapping views, there are some weaknesses. First, the polemic tone in some sections may discourage the collaboration that she invites between feminist and mainstream writers and therapists, who increasingly value multiple perspectives in a connective discourse. Second, she oversimplifies feminism. Indeed, there are many "feminisms" and feminist therapies, which include a continuum of liberal, cultural, radical, and socialist views (Enns, 1992). Also, she seems generally to discount men as people in her work and assumes that masculine structures are the primary source of women's problems. Third, although she correctly emphasizes the need for changes in social roles and the larger culture, she ignores the critical roles of intrapsychic and behavioral development needed for both individual and societal change (Wade, 1996). Fourth, she weakens some of her assertions by the blanket denigration of self-help publications, women's empowerment, dissociative disorders, and Attention-Deficit/Hyperactivity Disorder (ADHD); inclusion of an inaccurate *DSM-IV* diagnosis, self-defeating personality disorder; and omission of women's violence. Fifth, the practical focus is limited and deserves to be enlarged. Assuming our writings form a complementary picture, I would like to build on her descriptions of strategies and techniques.

What is feminist therapy? It is a relational model that holds that an authentic relationship between client and therapist is the primary vehicle for change. All strategies and techniques, whatever their origin, may be used if placed in a framework of feminist analysis and values. Additionally, these methods must be practiced in a manner fair and equal to both genders (Enns, 1992) and actively include peoples of every race, class, creed, ethnicity, culture, affectional or sexual orientation, and disability or special need.

Despite the wide diversity among practitioners, there are at least five core components of feminist therapy. The following abbreviated list of techniques in each area is an introduction to the general framework of feminist psychotherapy.

A. Equality

1. Engage in egalitarian practices to balance the unequal roles in the therapeutic relationship. Collaborate on diagnosis and therapy contracts, negotiate fees, offer information about clients' rights, encourage a consumer attitude towards therapy, and notify your clients that they have control of the agenda of therapy as long as it meshes with ethical practices (Lerman & Porter, 1990).

2. Discuss the power dynamics of therapy (Brown, 1994) and demystify the therapist as the authority by admitting mistakes and acknowledging that clients' ideas are as useful as the therapist's views. Focusing on the interpersonal dynamics of power is also important, such as exploring clients' capacities to influence others skillfully, as well as attending to clients' attempts to control relationships without regard to the impact of what they do on others (McLeod, 1994).

3. Monitor your own needs for power and money (Greenspan, 1995).

B. Empathy, Mutuality, and Collaboration

1. Clarify that women's and men's sense of self occurs in relationship with others, and that mature autonomy is a skillful balance between the two (Miller, 1991).

2. Accept all emotions, including anger (McLellan, 1995). Include your emotions in the therapeutic process while maintaining primary focus on the client (Enns, 1992).

3. Express caring, trust, and nurturing within ethical limits. Model self-nurturing.

4. Collaborate on creating safe processes in the therapy relationship, rather than a holding a rigid focus on boundaries to create safety (Greenspan, 1995).

5. Listen with receptivity to the whole person (McLellan, 1995). Minimize instructive, directive, and interpretive stances. Ask questions to encourage a new narrative (Gottlieb & Gottlieb, 1996).

C. Gender and Social Context

1. Acknowledge that clients know their own gender and cultural context as no others. Explore how the connections between their intrapsychic selves and others are always embedded in the social and political context of childhood, current life, gender, class, race, etc. (Walters, Papp, & Silverstein, 1988).

2. State the limits of your particular perspective, thereby revealing where you may or may not be helpful. As appropriate, refer to a therapist who can mirror clients' reality with direct experience (McLeod, 1994).

3. Normalize your clients' concerns and explain how negative labels and limited access to social justice arise directly from the context in which they live (Enns, 1992).

4. Continue therapist training through study, therapy, supervision, and peer consultation.

D. Social Change

1. Participate in social change actions in your social and professional contexts (Brown, 1994; Lerman & Porter, 1990).

2. Explore with clients the connections between social change, individual growth, and relationship development. Discuss, as appropriate, their interests in social change actions in their various social and political groups.

3. Use bibliotherapy and provide research information according to clients' interest.

E. Feminist Ethics

1. Follow the "Feminist Code of Ethics" (Lerman & Porter, 1990), follow the ethical code of therapist profession, and seek reconciliation of perceived differences. Inquire consistently into your own biases, limits, and possible discriminatory practices.

2. Support your clients' moral codes and ethical principles (Weiner, 1999).

3. Discuss possible overlapping relationships that may legitimately occur out of therapy. Use proactive measures such as exploring possible hazards, negotiating boundaries, processing all meetings in therapy, and consulting with other therapists about concerns (Adelman & Barred, 1990).

Now and in the future, feminist therapy will continue to be "a voice for the least powerful and most oppressed . . . [and] to continually challenge mainstream theories and practices to be more inclusive of human diversity" (Brown & Brodsky, 1992, p. 57). Importantly, feminist therapists are now using this lens on themselves by challenging complacency or uniformity in feminist thought and practice (Enns, 1992); looking for other voices of diversity (such as those of men, children, and families [Gross, 1999]); and seeking to integrate with other fields of other psychotherapies such as family systems, psychoanalytic approaches, and cognitive-behavioral models. We need these reflective, synthesizing processes of discourse for our clients, ourselves, psychotherapy, and all of humankind.

References

Adelman, J., & Barred, S. (1990). Overlapping relationships: The importance of the feminist ethical perspective. In L. Lerman & N. Porter (Eds.), *Feminist ethics in psychotherapy* (pp. 87-91). New York: Springer.

Brown, L. (1994). *Subversive dialogues: Theory in feminist therapy.* New York: Basic Books.

Brown, L., & Brodsky, A. (1992). Future of feminist therapy. *Psychotherapy, 29*(1), 51-57.

Enns, C. (1992). Toward integrating feminist psychotherapy and feminist philosophy. *Professional Psychology: Research and Practice, 23*(6), 453-466.

Enns, C. (1997). *Feminist theories and feminist psychotherapies, origins, themes, and variations.* New York: Harrington Press

Gottlieb, D., & Gottlieb, C. (1996). The narrative/collaborative process in couples therapy: A postmodern perspective. In M. Hill & E. Rothblum (Eds.), *Couples therapy: Feminist perspectives* (pp. 37-48). Binghampton, NY: Haworth.

Greenspan, M. (1995). Out of bounds. *Common Boundary, 13*(4), 51-58.

Gross, E. (1999). *Using feminist theories for work with families.* Salt Lake City, UT: University of Utah, Summer Institute for Human Services, Graduate School of Social Work.

Lerman, H., & Porter, N. (Eds.). (1990). Feminist code of ethics. In *Feminist ethics in psychotherapy* (pp. 37-40). New York: Springer.

McLellan, B. (1995). *Beyond psychodepression: A feminist alternative therapy.* Melbourne, Australia: Spinifex.

McLeod, E. (1994). *Women's experience of feminist therapy and counseling.* Philadelphia: Open University Press.

Miller, J. (1991). The development of women's sense of self. In J. Jordan, A. Kaplan, J. Miller, I. Stiver, & J. Surrey (Eds.), *Women's growth in connection* (pp. 11-26). New York: Guilford.

Wade, J. (1996). *Chances of mind: A holonomic theory of the development of consciousness.* New York: State University of New York Press.

Walters, M., Carter, B., Papp, P., & Silverstein, O. (1988). *Toward a feminist perspective in family therapy—The invisible web: Gender patterns in family relationships.* New York: Guilford.

Weiner, K. (1999). Morality and responsibility: Necessary components of feminist therapy. In E. Kaschak & M. Hill (Eds.), *Beyond the rule book: Moral issues and dilemmas in the practice of psychotherapy* (pp. 105-116). Binghamton, NY: Haworth.

Conclusion: The Values of Psychotherapy

Daniel N. Robinson
Georgetown & Brigham Young Universities

The excellent discussion in this volume has been clear and cogent and certainly could not benefit from any summary I might presume to offer. The chapters stand on their own. I found them informative, if only because my own contact with issues in clinical psychology has been limited. Accordingly, I will confine my remarks to what I would hope might be of some interest to those likely to read this volume, and this alone must incline me toward a number of quite general observations. It is my hope that specialists will find something worth abstracting from these generalities in ways that will be of benefit to other professionals.

The truism according to which psychology is a "hybrid" discipline is nowhere more obvious than in the practices and perspectives that define clinical practice. Here we find not ambiguous values, but well-defined values that just happen to be in conflict. At the most general level, the conflict is between what for the sake of brevity I will call humanistic and scientific values. The former ground all considerations of caring, "therapy," empathy—all considerations that enter into the sincere desire to understand a life other than one's own and to bring something of value to it. As the textbooks insist, though usually without much by way of critical reflection, the core value of science is something called "objectivity," which is what is supposed to be left over when we have stripped our efforts of every trace of empathy, caring, hopefulness, altruism, and kindred sentiments.

At a somewhat more specific level, this very conflict then generates kindred conflicts in choosing the right model of explanation. Science, at least since the time of Hume, has confined its aspirations to the identification of efficient causal modalities. To explain an event on this account (made famous for psychologists by Carl Hempel) is to subsume it under a general law. Wherever we find reliable regularities, we are able to predict, and wherever we are able to predict we have more or less "explained" the event in question. For example, if 88% of those judged to be free of treatable mental disorders see an ambiguous pattern as a butterfly, we must be on the way toward a reassuring Hempelian explanation. It is notable at this point that such a conception of science renders the explanation of *singular events* problematic, the very events that are now at the center of the most advanced thinking in the most advanced science. That is, it is not clear what a Hempelian explanation of the big bang would look like. I mention this by way of drawing attention to the fact that the tension between so-called idiographic and so-called nomothetic explanations is not confined to psychology.

When we set out to explain, or in other words to understand, just what it is that has *this* patient or client incapable of entering into satisfying relationships, however, we begin to search for factors that lack the properties of efficient causes. Indeed, we generally abandon the causal model of explanation and undertake instead a search for what are sometimes called "reasons explanations." Both common sense and broad experience in the world reassure thoughtful adults, even those with doctoral degrees, that Smith's inability to form and maintain friendships of worth is not likely to be covered by the deductive-nomological model of explanation. If it were, then Smith's problem would be a species of mechanical or chemical malfunction calling for the services of specialists in biochemistry and even neurosurgery. No, we understand that to explain Smith's problem is more akin to explaining Napoleon's failure at Waterloo than to explaining the descent of balls perched at the apex of an inclined plane.

To the extent that humanistic and scientific values are not isomorphic, and to the extent that one consequence of this is a distinctive difference in what counts as "explanation" in the value domain of each, there would seem to be little room for a credible rapprochement or pax philosophica. And this makes me wonder why so much visible passion seems to be expended by those who criticize the clinicians for their "unscientific" labors and by those clinicians who defend themselves by producing arid statistical summaries of outcomes that describe not a patient, but only a collection of data.

This very matter of idiographic and nomothetic modes of inquiry and explanation was well understood, if in different terms, by Aristotle, who actually came before Allport. As Aristotle calmly notes in his *Physics,* there are two different explanations of, for example, "anger," available to us depending on whether we are interested in a physical or philosophical understanding. Radical changes in the temperature of the blood may be common to all instances of anger, whereas the belief that one has been wrongly slighted by another may be unique to this person's anger.

But there is much confusion surrounding this distinction. It has been suggested that attention to idiographic approaches carries with it what some have called the "danger of N=1." Now, just what is this alleged danger? Probably the most scientifically grounded branch of all of experimental psychology is the field of psychophysics, where N=1 is entirely serviceable. Physics itself would not have got very far had physicists believed that the best approach to science is to roll many balls down inclined planes, compute averages and standard deviations, and then offer values of *p* as the best predictor of just what might happen next. It is surely suggestive, even if not portentous, that none of the developed sciences has ever found much use for "analysis of variance." There are exceptions, I am sure; I think some work in x ray diffraction might have benefited from such an analysis. But the truer mark of developed science is *measurement,* which is different from estimates of probability or reassurances as to how "confident" we are allowed to be.

On the matter of balls and inclined planes, if a study is conducted properly and in a framework that already includes a developed theory, *one ball will do!* This has long been understood in research fields as different as clinical medicine and classical mechanics. Once one has a developed theory of physiological function, the laws of physiology will be evident in every single specimen and, by the same token, the violation of said laws will instantly qualify the deviant as "ill." I often illustrate this point with the example of an epidemiologist summoned to a village to determine whether there has been an outbreak of disease. Imagine the following report being turned in:

> I've examined all 1,000 residents and am pleased to say that 997 of them have temperatures of 104 degrees, with only three falling to 98.6. I think we can contain the disorder by isolating these three.

To make the case all too briefly, whether or not a discipline or science has or will have general laws with which to explain instances cannot be settled in advance on the basis of sample size. Typically it is the daring and integrative theory that dictates just the sort of findings that will tell for or against it. Absent a developed and defensible theoretical framework, the enterprise collapses into a vapid and tedious ritual of fact gathering.

What would seem to be needed, then, is a defensible theory of what seems on the record to be the nature of human nature itself, as this expresses itself under the most favorable conditions. Presumably conditions are favorable when human beings are spared an early death, debilitating or incapacitating diseases, political regimes that preclude the development of powers of moral and civic judgment, and modes of instruction or indoctrination that foreclose whole realms of thought and inquiry. We are, of course, a wonderfully adaptable species, in large measure because we are especially good at getting the physical world to adapt to our own needs and desires. Lacking feathers, we invent aerodynamics. Lacking flawless memories, we invent books and libraries. Lacking herculean strength, we invent devices that increase our mechanical advantage.

Owing to this very versatility, these very powers of invention, there seems to be neither a ceiling nor a fence circumscribing our possibilities, and this insensibly gives rise to the notion that no generality regarding our best interests is defensible. That is, we confuse virtually limitless potentiality with the very different notion of unlimited options for the good life, as if the power to make a mountain of chocolate constituted an argument against self-restraint. But the record of history is not silent on these subjects. Every recorded age turns up persons worthy of profound respect and attempts at emulation, as well as lives that must have been horrors to those living them. The text here is not filled with numbers; it is filled with judgments, and like it or not the former cannot be substituted for the latter.

Not only is the history of our brief epoch on earth fairly well documented, but we even have a number of sages who have tested the record for its larger implications. My own candidate for the most systematic and discerning of these teachers is Aristotle, but the choices here are many and the conclusions are not radically different among those who have undertaken a systematic study. Most seem convinced that there is a difference between a merely scripted life and one that is authentically lived. Aristotle notes the difference between the hand of a statue of a physician and that of a physician; the former is a hand in name only, for it does not engage in the activity that constitutes the healing arts. So too with any feigned form of activity.

It is widely assumed by those we have reason to listen to that a life is authentic to the extent that its most defining features are chosen rather than imposed, where the choice itself is valid as a choice. It is a choice among well-understood alternatives. This is not to say that elements of stress or even social pressure are absent; only that such elements *incline but do not determine,* for if they are determinative, then the action is in fact a *reaction* and it is not authentically the actor's own. We see then that the notion of "autonomy" is really quite empty unless we have good reason to believe that those who are "law unto themselves" are not traipsing about sleepwalking or in the thrall of controlling addictions or stupefied by a chronic ignorance of what life could be like. If autonomy is a value—nothing less than a "therapeutic" value—then it too is to flourish and not merely exist. We might guess it would be small comfort to Goya's "Giant" to learn he was "autonomous."

If choices are to be potentiating rather than paralyzing, a form of moral order is presupposed. Just in case we have convinced ourselves that there is no way of establishing the moral worthiness of one set of choices over another, it is not at all clear just what "psychotherapy" is treating. After all, who says contentment is to be preferred to misery, or clarity to confusion, or decency to self-degradation? Therapists claiming to be "morally neutral" or to be guided by that will-o'-the-wisp "value neutrality" are engaged in a form of self-deception no less injurious for being ridiculous.

Does all this constitute a rehearsal of the conflict between scientific and humanistic values? Does it not call for the abandonment of "objectivity"? I should like to consider this notion of "objectivity," for the manner in which it is understood is, in my view, at the bottom of many confusions.

In her recent Josiah Berlin lectures at Oxford, Lorraine Daston has closely examined the history of the concept of objectivity and has shown it to be a variegated one. A single illustration will, I think, be eye-opening for some. When diligent botanists of the 17th century committed themselves to drawing to the most exacting standards a given specimen, they judged their efforts to be only preliminary. Once a single specimen was accurately depicted, it became necessary to present the "truth" of the thing, which then called for skilled artists to locate the specimen in a painted garden, which is to say, in the true and real context in which such specimens are found. Note, then, the difference between the "objective" rendering of the specimen and the scientific presentation of the thing as it is actually found. Let us be clear, then, that accuracy is no guarantor of truth—a point Wolfgang Köhler (1938) made so trenchantly in *The Place of Value in a World of Facts.*

There is still another reservation to be recorded on this matter of objectivity. When one claims to be "objective" in research or inquiries of one or another sort, what quality or state or attribute is the reference of the term? I believe the most defensible answer to the question is that objectivity is a *moral* term. It refers finally to a disciplined disposition in the matter of evidence and argument. It refers to the suspension of purely personal desires or motives and their replacement by an utterly depersonalized attitude. Were we morally neutral up and down the line, one of the first casualties would be objectivity itself, for even if our neutrality did not lead to out-and-out fraud it would surely disregard mere, if not gross, exaggeration and concealment.

Finally, I would hope to fortify the humanistic resources and perspectives in psychotherapy by reminding clinicians of the central part they have taken in keeping the discipline of psychology alive and defined. It is always the clinic that puts simplistic and confident theory on notice. It is the unpredicted successes and failures taking place in the real world that both demand and test assistance coming from the scientific quarter. It is then one of the "values" of psychotherapy to settle for a vexing reality if the only alternative is a consoling fiction. I would hope, in their pursuit of reliable measures and methods, their attention to developments in the basic sciences, their attachment to what is perhaps the less refined thinking in science itself, that psychotherapists would not lose their allegiance to the core values of psychotherapy, values that are, and must be at bottom, moral, civic, humanistic, and realistic. There are baser values!

Reference

Kohler, W. (1938). *The place of value in a world of facts.* New York: Liveright.

Name Index

Allport, Gordon, 235-236, 237
Anderson, C. M., 307
Anderson, D., 312
Antonovsky, A., 149
Aristotle, 63, 326
Arkowitz, H., 213
Arnkoff, D. B., 213
Austad, C. S., 130, 132, 133

Bacon, F., 182
Bakhtin, M., 158, 159, 160, 161
Bandura, A., 199, 205, 208
Barlow, D. H., 205
Barrett, D., 175
Bateson, Gregory, 189-190
Bellah, R., 152, 153, 154
Benjamin, L. S., 93-95
Berger, Peter, 149-150
Bergin, A. E., 213
Beutler, L. E., 216, 218
Bigelow, J., 293
Bilynsky, N. S., 132-133
Black, M. J., 123
Bohm, D., 63
Boring, E. G., 171
Bork, Robert H., 201
Brentano, Franz, 221, 222
Brewer, W. F., 199
Brodsky, A. M., 306
Broverman, D. M., 305
Broverman, I. K., 305

Brown, L. S., 317
Bryant, R. A., 173
Buhle, M. J., 305

Cameron, Norman, 196, 199
Carey, M., 306
Carr, D., 231
Caruso, R. C., 182
Chesler, Phyllis, 305, 315
Cisz, J., 281
Clarkson, F. E., 305
Coles, R., 151
Comas-Dias, L., 310
Combs, Gene, 244, 245
Craske, M. G., 205
Cummings, N. A., 133, 137
Cummins, R., 294-295
Cushman, P., 150-151, 161-162
Daston, Lorraine, 329
Dawes, R. M., 135
Dennett, D., 57
DiClemente, C. C., 213, 215
Dilthey, W., 30
Doan, Robert, 244, 248
Doherty, William, 161
Dupre, J., 55

Einstein, A., 81
Emerson, C., 158
Engel, G., 70

Subject Index

About the Editors
and Contributors

Sally H. Barlow is Professor in the Clinical Psychology Graduate Program at Brigham Young University in Provo, Utah, where her duties include individual and group supervision, psychodynamic psychotherapy, and diversity issues. She has been teaching and researching in the area of psychotherapy for the past two decades. She has presented at national and international conferences on such topics as group psychotherapy, violence and aggression, and spirituality. She holds diplomas from the American Board of Professional Psychology in both clinical and group psychology.

Lorna Smith Benjamin, PhD, for many years was Professor of Psychiatry, University of Wisconsin–Madison. There, in addition to teaching psychopathology and psychotherapy to psychiatry residents, she had a large clinical practice. Now in the Department of Psychology at the University of Utah, she is using her Structural Analysis of Social Behavior (SASB) for research in object relations. She is the author of *Interpersonal Diagnosis and Treatment of Personality Disorders.*

Lynne A. Bennion has a PhD in clinical psychology from Purdue University. She is an Associate Clinical Professor at the Brigham Young University Counseling and Career Center, where she provides psychotherapy to BYU students, supervises predoctoral psychology interns and other trainees, and teaches university courses. Her areas of professional interest include mood disorders, eating disorders, posttraumatic stress disorder, and supervision.

Allen E. Bergin is Professor Emeritus at Brigham Young University in the Department of Psychology in Provo, Utah. Winner of numerous national and international awards, he is most noted for his pioneering work in psychotherapy reasearch and spiritual interventions.

Marian S. Bergin is a licensed clinical social worker in private practice in American Fork, Utah. Using a cognitive-psychodynamic approach, she treats a varied clientele while specializing in personality disordered clients. She has been an adjunct faculty member in psychology at Brigham Young University, supervising clinical psychology graduate students in psychotherapy practica. She has also worked as an acute care psychiatric unit therapist and an emergency room crisis worker in a large general hospital in Provo, Utah. Additionally, in the hospital she was program director of Adult Psychiatry, program director of the Depression Center, and clinical coordinator of the Eating Disorders unit. She has written, published, and lectured on a variety of mental health subjects.

Constance T. Fischer is Professor of Psychology, and Director of the Psychology Clinic at Duquesne University. She also conducts a part-time practice of clinical psychology (psychotherapy, consultation, psychological assessment). She has authored *Individualizing Psychological Assessment* and coedited Volume 2 of *Duquesne Studies in Phenomenological Psychology* (with A. Giorgi and E. Murray) and *Client Participation in Human Services: The Prometheus Principle* (with S. Brodsky) and is editing *Qualitative Research Methods for Psychology: Case Demonstrations*. She is a consulting editor for *The Journal of Humanistic Psychology, The Humanistic Psychologist,* and *Methods: A Journal for Human Science.* Current pursuits include promoting use of qualitative research and of collaborative psychological assessment practices and conducting her own research on the phenomenon of becoming angry.

Blaine J. Fowers is Associate Professor of Counseling Psychology at the University of Miami. He received his PhD from the University of Texas at Austin in 1987. He is an approved supervisor in the American Association for Marital and Family Therapists and a licensed psychologist. His primary scholarly commitment is to developing a better understanding of the moral and ethical dimension of psychology, both in research and practice. His empirical work is devoted to clarifying the role of cultural values in marriage and the family and he is currently investigating the prevalence of cultural values in research on marriage. He is the author of *Beyond the Myth of Marital Happiness* (2000) and a coauthor of *Re-Envisioning Psychology* (1999). He has published numerous articles on culture and psychology, including "Why Is Multiculturalism Good?" published in *American Psychologist.* He has also published widely on the philosophy of social science and the pervasive individualism in our research and therapy.

James M. Harper, PhD, is Professor of Marriage and Family Therapy and Director of the School of Family Life at Brigham Young University. A licensed psychologist and marriage and family therapist, he has a private clinical practice and supervises other therapists. He is an approved Supervisor and Fellow with the American Association for Marriage and Family Therapy.

Barbara S. Held, PhD, is the Barry N. Wish Professor of Psychology and Social Studies at Bowdoin College in Brunswick, Maine. She is the author of many scholarly articles, among them "Constructivism in Psychotherapy: Truth and Consequences," in *The Flight from Science and Reason* (edited by Paul R. Gross, Norman Levitt, and Martin W. Lewis), *Annals of the New York Academy of Sciences* (Volume 775, 1996). She is also the author of *Back to Reality: A Critique of Postmodern Theory in Psychotherapy* (1995), in which she provides theoretical and philosophical analysis of the postmodern/linguistic turn in psychotherapy. A licensed clinical psychologist, she has practiced psychotherapy for many years in Maine.

Lisa Tsoi Hoshmand, PhD, is Professor and Division Director of the Division of Counseling and Psychology at Lesley University in Cambridge, Massachusetts. She is the author and editor of three books, including *Creativity and Moral Vision in Psychology: Narratives on Identity and Commitment in a Postmodern Age* (1998). A clinical psychologist and counselor educator, she has written on topics related to professional education, research praxis, critical inquiry, and cultural and moral perspectives in psychology and adult development. She has served one term as the associate editor of the *Journal of Theoretical and Philosophical Psychology* and as a member of the editorial board of the *Journal of Counseling Psychology, The Counseling Psychologist, Journal of Community Psychology,* and *Journal of Constructivist Psychology.* She was previously Professor of Counseling at the California State University, Fullerton, and Professor and Director of Clinical Training at the American School of Professional Psychology, Hawaii campus.

Lynn D. Johnson received his PhD from the University of Utah in counseling psychology. He has worked in mental health centers and in private practice, and in 1984 formed The Brief Therapy Center of Utah, located in Salt Lake City. From 1986 to 1995, he was a consultant to Aetna Insurance in helping the company develop its managed care programs. His interests are in improving therapy processes and outcomes. He and his wife raise four children in their spare time.

Daniel K. Judd is Associate Professor of Ancient Scripture at Brigham Young University in Provo, Utah. He holds a PhD in counseling psychology and an MS in family studies. In addition to his teaching; administrative duties; and counseling practice with individuals, couples, and families, he has specialized in both quantitative and qualitative research concerning the relationship of mental health and religion. His most recent publication is "Religion, Mental Health, and the Latter-day Saints." He is presently engaged in a major research project looking at the relationship between marriage and religion.

Jeanne Marecek is Professor of Psychology and a member of the Women's Studies Program at Swarthmore College in Pennsylvania, where she teaches courses on clinical psychology, women and gender, qualitative research, and feminist theory. She earned her PhD from Yale University, with specialties in clinical and social psychology. She is coauthor, with Rachel Hare-Mustin, of *Making a Difference: Psychology and the Construction of Gender* (1990). She has written numerous chapters and journal articles on gender, qualitative inquiry, and clinical psychology. Her present research focuses on feminist therapists and uses discursive approaches to study the varied identities, therapeutic stances, and meanings of feminism that they embrace. She has also worked in Sri Lanka for over a decade. Her research there focuses on suicide, a social problem that has recently reached epidemic proportions. Her research concerns the circumstances, meanings, and consequences of suicidal acts in rural contexts, as well as the development of intervention programs. She serves on the board of directors of the Women's Therapy Center in Philadelphia and on the Executive Committee of the American Institute for Sri Lankan Studies. She is also Vice Patron of Nest, a rural psychosocial outreach program in Sri Lanka.

Stanley B. Messer is Professor and Chairperson in the Department of Clinical Psychology at the Graduate School of Applied and Professional Psychology at Rutgers University at New Brunswick, New Jersey. He received a BSc in honors psychology from McGill University and MA and PhD degrees in clinical psychology from Harvard University, and completed a psychotherapy fellowship program at Hillside Hospital in Glen Oaks, New York. He is coauthor of *Models of Brief Psychodynamic Therapy: A Comparative Approach* (with C. S. Warren, 1995), associate editor of *History of Psychotherapy: A Century of Change* (with D. K. Freedheim et al., 1992), coeditor of *Essential Psychotherapies: Theory and Practice* (with A. S. Gurman, 1995), *Hermeneutics and Psychological Theory* (with R. L. Woolfolk and L. A. Sass, 1988), and *Psychoanalytic Therapy and Behavior Therapy: Is Integration Possible?* (with H. Arkowitz, 1984), among other works. He has written extensively on topics such as psychotherapy integration, brief psychotherapy, and case formulation in relation to psychotherapy, and he has conducted empirical research on the process of psychotherapy. He was an associate editor of *American Psychologist* and is on the editorial board of several other journals. He maintains a clinical practice in Highland Park, New Jersey.

Louis A. Moench, MD, practices general and forensic psychiatry in Salt Lake City, Utah, where in this "decade of the brain" he still talks and listens to patients in a large, multispecialty medical clinic. A medical graduate and now clinical Professor of Psychiatry at the University of Utah, he completed his psychiatry residency at the University of Pennsylvania, learning psychotherapy from Aaron Beck (cognitive), Lester Luborsky (psychodynamic), Paul Brady (behavioral), and Sal Menuchin (structural), all under more or less the same roof. He is an examiner of candidates for the American Board of Psychiatry and Neurology and is active in the governance of the American Psychiatric Association, serving on the Assembly Executive Committee and the committees producing the *Diagnostic and Statistical Manual of Mental Disorders* (DSM), the APA Practice Guidelines, and the guidelines for electroconvulsive therapy, as well as the committee operating the Practice Research Network.

Stevan Lars Nielsen is Associate Clinical Professor at the Brigham Young University (BYU) Counseling and Career Center in Provo, Utah, where his duties include assessment and treatment of college students and teaching as an adjunct professor with BYU's Department of Psychology. He also maintains a private practice, which includes therapy, assessment, and consulting. He earned his doctorate in clinical psychology from the University of Washington in 1984. He served as a psychologist in the United States Army for seven years, where he provided psychological services in diverse settings (tents in German forests, hospitals in Frankfurt, Germany, and San Francisco) and with diverse clients (soldiers, retired soldiers, and their families). His research interests include studying the effectiveness of psychological services actually provided in real world settings. (The parameters of everyday practice probably bear scant resemblance to the worlds where psychological treatments and assessments are studied). His most recent publications deal with assessment and treatment of religious clients, including a forthcoming book written with W. Brad Johnson and Albert Ellis on treatment of religious clients with Rational Emotive Behavior Therapy.

Judy Norman, DSW, LCSW, is Associate Professor, School of Social Work, at Brigham Young University in Provo, Utah. She maintains clinical affiliation with LDS Hospital, Psych Resources, Salt Lake City, Utah. She primarily teaches graduate clinical courses and clinically supervises small groups of graduate students. She is a longtime board member, including past Vice President, of the National Association of Social Workers/Utah chapter. Her research interests include mood disorders in adults and children, women and mental health, and multicultural as well as socioeconomic framework for assessment and intervention.

Kay Packard is Clinical Associate Professor in the Department of Educational Psychology at the University of Utah. She has an MSW from the University of Utah and a PhD in Marriage and Family Therapy from Brigham Young University. She is a licensed clinical social worker and has worked in various agency settings, as an independent practitioner, and most recently as a staff member at the University of Utah Counseling Center. She is the coauthor of *Multidimensional Psychotherapy.*

Ted Packard is Professor in the Department of Educational Psychology and a former Director of the Counseling Center at the University of Utah. He has worked with clients and supervised students for over 30 years. His PhD is in counseling psychology from the University of Minnesota. He writes regularly on topics associated with both the statutory and voluntary regulation of professional psychology and is President of the American Board of Professional Psychology during 2000-2001.

Agnes M. Plenk is Adjunct Professor in the Department of Educational Psychology at the University of Utah and in the Department of Clinical Psychology at Brigham Young University in Provo, Utah. She was born in Hungry and received her early professional education at the University of Vienna. She continued her training at Northwestern University, receiving a BS and an MA and working toward a PhD in clinical psychology and a minor in anthropology. She worked at the Chicago Psychoanalytic Institute and the Institute for Juvenile Research before completing her PhD at the University of Utah in the department of Educational Psychology. She is the founder of The Children's Center, a day treatment center for preschool children with behavioral problems, and was its chief psychologist and executive director until 1986. Currently, she supervises interns and residents at The Children's Center and acts as consultant to a genetic research project. She is a child advocate and active in mental health organizations and a licensed psychologist (former president of the Utah Psychological Association, [UPA]), a member of the UPA and the American Psychological Association, and a Fellow of the American Orthopsychiatric Association. She is the originator of "The Plenk Storytelling Test" and the author of *Helping Young Children at Risk—A Psycho-Educational Approach*, as well as a number of papers in her field.

Donald E. Polkinghorne is Professor in the Division of Counseling Psychology at the University of Southern California, where he holds the Attallah Chair in Humanistic Psychology. He is a fellow in the American Psychological Association's Division of Counseling Psychology and a fellow and past president in the Division of Theoretical and Philosophical Psychology. His educational background includes an undergraduate degree in religious studies from Washington University in St. Louis, Missouri, and graduate degrees from Yale University, Hartford Seminary Foundation, and the Union Graduate Institute. His PhD is in psychology.

His scholarly publications have focused on the epistemological foundations of qualitative research and the implications of Continental philosophy for psychological theory and research. His publications include four books: *An Existential-Phenomenological Approach to Education, Methodology for the Human Science, Narrative Knowing and the Human Sciences*, and *Human Science and Praxis*. In addition to his scholarly work, Polkinghorne is a licensed psychotherapist. He received his clinical training at the Norwich, Connecticut and the Waterbury, Vermont state hospitals. He maintains a part-time psychotherapy practice and serves as an oral examiner for the California Psychology Licensing Board.

Marybeth Raynes is a marriage and family therapist and clinical social social worker who maintains a private psychotherapy practice in Salt Lake City, Utah.

She is a clinical member of the American Association of Marriage and Family Therapists as well as a clinical diplomate, National Association of Social Workers. She holds an MS in Marriage and Family Relationships and an MSW. Over the course of her career, she has taught clinical social work courses as well as relationship development and dynamics courses at the university level and has published numerous articles and chapters in books, addressing mental health topics, women's issues, and spirituality. She is the coeditor of *Peculiar People: Mormons and Same-Sex Attraction*. She also speaks regularly to public and professional groups on these topics and has been actively involved in women's groups and feminist issues for 30 years.

Jeffrey S. Reber is Assistant Professor of Psychology at State University of West Georgia. He recently received his PhD in psychology from Brigham Young University and he has published papers regarding theoretical and philosophical implications of eclectic psychotherapy, the nature and importance of truth in psychotherapy, and the possibility and meaning of altruism. He has also produced work concerning the assumptions and implications of evolutionary psychology and women's experience with and perceptions of sexual harassment.

Frank C. Richardson is Professor of Educational Psychology at the University of Texas at Austin. His empirical research has focused on cognitive-behavioral approaches to the treatment of anxiety and stress. His writing includes a number of articles that have appeared in *American Psychologist* and other leading journals, as well as chapters in several books, examining the cultural and moral value underpinnings of modern psychology and psychotherapy. He is coauthor of *Stress, Sanity, and Survival* (with Robert Woolfolk) and of *Re-Envisioning Psychology* (with Blaine Fowers and Charles Guignon). He has practiced individual therapy, marital therapy, and group therapy part-time for many years. Currently, his scholarly interests center on the philosophy of social science, topics in philosophical psychology, and topics in religion and psychology.

Daniel N. Robinson is Distinguished Research Professor and Professor of Psychology at Georgetown University in Washington, D. C., and Faculty Fellow at Oxford University. He is past president of the Division 24 and Division 26 of the American Psychological Association.

Joseph F. Rychlak is Professor Emeritus at Loyola University of Chicago. In addition to teaching for over 40 years at five different universities, he has distinguished himself as a psychotherapist, author, theorist, and researcher. He is a Fellow of both the American Psychological Association and the American Psychological Society and served twice as President of the APA Division of Theoretical and Philosophical Psychology. He is known as a rigorous humanist who submits his nonmechanistic theoretical claims to traditional scientific tests.

Brent D. Slife is currently Professor in the Department of Psychology at Brigham Young University in Provo, Utah, where he holds a joint appointment on the clinical and theoretical faculties. A previous Director of Clinical Training at Baylor University, he continues to manage a private practice in family and group psychotherapy. He was recently the President of the APA Division for Theoretical and Philosophical Psychology. He has over 100 published articles on the theoretical underpinnings of psychotherapy. His recent books include *Time and Psychological Explanation, What's Behind the Research: Discovering Hidden Assumptions in the Behavioral Sciences, Taking Sides: Clashing Views on Controversial Psychological Issues,* and *Managing Values in Psychotherapy.*

Amy Fisher Smith is Assistant Professor in the Department of Psychology and Special Education at Texas A&M University–Commerce. After formal training in clinical psychology, she completed a clinical internship at the South Texas Veterans Health Care System in San Antonio. Currently, she contributes to the training of both doctoral and master's level counseling and school psychology students. Her research interests include the relationship between psychotherapy, ethics, and the role of therapist values. Her most recent publications focus on the theory and practical implications of values in practice.

Diane L. Spangler received her PhD in clinical psychology from the University of Oregon. She received a National Research Service Award from the National Institute of Mental Health for her doctoral research and went on to a research fellowship in the Department of Psychiatry at the Stanford School of Medicine, where she investigated cognitive-behavioral theory and therapy. She has published a number of articles and book chapters on the theory, practice, and mechanisms of action of cognitive-behavioral therapy and has received awards from the American Psychological Association, National Institute of Mental Health, International Association of Cognitive Psychotherapy, and the Association for the Advancement of Behavior Therapy for this work. Currently, she is a member of the psychology faculty at Brigham Young University and maintains a private practice specializing in the treatment of mood, anxiety, and eating disorders.

Hendrika Vande Kemp is Professor of Psychology at Fuller Theological Seminary, where she teaches clinical courses on family psychology, family therapy, dreams in psychotherapy, interpersonal assessment and psychotherapy, and physical disabilities. She completed her clinical training at the University of Massachusetts in Amherst (PhD, 1977) and Topeka State Hospital. She has published clinically focused articles in *Family Therapy, Family Process, Journal of Marital and Family Therapy, The Psychotherapy Patient, Teaching of Psychology,* and *Journal of Psychology and Christianity.* She is the editor of *Family Therapy: Christian Perspectives* (1991). As a historical and theoretical psychologist, she has authored many book chapters and published articles in encyclopedias, dictionaries, and journals such as *Journal of the History of the Behavioral Sciences, Journal of Psychology and Theology, American Psychologist, International Journal for the Psychology of Religion,* and

Journal of Individual Psychology. She is the author of *Psychology and Theology 1672-1965: A Historical and Annotated Bibliography* (1984).

Richard N. Williams is Professor of Psychology at Brigham Young University in Provo, Utah. His interests include the conceptual foundations of psychological theories and the relationship between traditional and postmodern perspectives. He is coauthor of *What's Behind the Research: Discovering Hidden Assumptions in the Behavioral Sciences* (with Brent D. Slife) and has published in the area of human agency and the ethical foundations of human being.

Robert L. Woolfolk is currently Visiting Professor of Psychology at Princeton University. He has contributed to both the empirical psychology and the philosophical literatures. His most recent book is *The Cure of Souls.*

Timothy J. Zeddies, PhD, is an Associate Clinical Psychologist, Camino Real Community Mental Health and Mental Retardation Center. He is on the editorial board of *Psychoanalytic Psychology;* is Chair of the Film Studies Group; is on the Education and Training Committee, both for the San Antonio Society for Psychoanalytic Studies; and is outgoing National Cochair of the Graduate Student Committee for the Division of Psychoanalysis (39) of the American-Psychological Association. He has published numerous articles related to comparative psychoanalysis, unconscious mental processes, clinical training, and the ethical and moral aims of psychoanalytic treatment. His forthcoming book, coauthored with Frank C. Richardson, is titled *Analytic Authority and the Good Life in Relational Psychoanalysis.*

Lightning Source UK Ltd.
Milton Keynes UK
UKOW020855090413

208924UK00002B/46/A